Also by G. Scott Thomas

History

Presidential Election Record Book 2020
Counting the Votes
A New World to Be Won
Advice From the Presidents
The United States of Suburbia
The Pursuit of the White House

Demographics

Dreamtowns
Micropolitan America
The Rating Guide to Life in America's Fifty States
Where to Make Money
The Rating Guide to Life in America's Small Cities

Sports

Baseball's Best (and Worst) 2023 Yearbook
Cooperstown at the Crossroads
A Brand New Ballgame
The Best (and Worst) of Baseball's Modern Era
Leveling the Field

PRESIDENTIAL ELECTION HANDBOOK
1789-2024

PRESIDENTIAL ELECTION HANDBOOK
1789-2024

G. Scott Thomas

NIAWANDA BOOKS

Presidential Election Handbook 1789-2024

Copyright © 2023 by G. Scott Thomas

Niawanda Books
949 Delaware Road
Buffalo, NY 14223
www.niawandabooks.com

Printed in the United States of America

First Edition
10 9 8 7 6 5 4 3 2 1

Contents

PRESIDENTIAL ELECTION HANDBOOK
1789-2024

1. Preview: 2024

ABRAHAM LINCOLN WAS A MASTER politician—one of the greatest in American history—yet he demonstrated no particular aptitude for election forecasting.

Lincoln enjoyed a pair of key advantages over his Democratic challenger, George McClellan, in the 1864 presidential campaign. The Republican president possessed the power of incumbency, and he benefited from an electorate that had been reshaped in his favor. Eleven Southern states, all of which had opposed Lincoln in 1860, were now waging war against the North. The 1864 election was confined to 25 loyal states, including 18 that had supported Lincoln in 1860 and three others that had been admitted to the Union since his initial win.

These circumstances seemed to portend victory for the president, yet he gloomily disagreed. "This morning, as for some days past," Lincoln wrote in August 1864, "it seems exceedingly probable that the administration will not be reelected." His prediction, excessively negative though it proved to be, was echoed by other savvy political observers. John Fremont, the 1856 Republican nominee, declared Lincoln to be "politically, militarily, and financially a failure" who would undoubtedly lose to McClellan. Horace Greeley, the renowned editor of the *New York Tribune*, agreed. "Mr. Lincoln is already beaten," Greeley wrote. "He cannot be elected."

The absurdity of these forecasts became evident when the incumbent rolled to an easy win in November. Lincoln overwhelmed McClellan by margins of 212 to 21 in electoral votes and more than 10 percentage points in popular votes. The president had remained pessimistic all the way to Election Day—"about this thing I am very far from being certain"—yet the massive scope of his victory was undeniable.

The lesson, perhaps, is that no candidate, especially one as habitually melancholic as Lincoln, should dare to forecast an election in which he is personally involved. But what about Fremont and Greeley? They were knowledgeable about American politics and safely distant from the campaign, yet their predictions were as erroneous as Lincoln's.

A modern social scientist might suggest that the problem was a lack of data. Public-opinion polls weren't part of 1864's political infrastructure; reliable surveys wouldn't materialize until another three generations had passed. A forecaster in Lincoln's era didn't have the luxury of consulting reams of computer printouts before formulating a prediction. He simply had to rely on his instincts, misguided through they sometimes might be.

But, to be fair, it must also be admitted that polls haven't always been reliable as predictive tools. Their flaws first became evident in 1936, when a highly publicized survey by the *Literary Digest* concluded that Republican Alfred Landon would easily unseat the Democratic incumbent, Franklin Roosevelt. It was a wildly inaccurate forecast. FDR buried Landon in the Electoral College, 523-8, the greatest landslide in any presidential contest since 1820.

Public-opinion experts eventually judged the magazine's methodology to be faulty. The *Digest* had surveyed more than 2 million respondents—an impressively large number—yet its pool was heavily skewed toward wealthy individuals who were more likely to vote for Republican candidates. The resulting controversy destroyed the *Digest*'s reputation and contributed to the publication's demise in 1938.

An emerging breed of pollsters stepped into the breach, pledging to conduct their surveys with scientific precision. The most prominent of these newcomers, George Gallup, employed modern polling techniques to correctly predict Roosevelt's 1936 victory. Gallup and his counterparts became known for accuracy and trustworthiness as the years rolled by. Their reputations were firmly established by 1948, when all of the major polls predicted that Republican Thomas Dewey would easily defeat the Democratic president, Harry Truman.

Truman was one of the few dissenters. "I wonder how far Moses would have gone if he had taken a poll in Egypt," the president snapped. But the mainstream press accepted the survey results as gospel. *Newsweek* interviewed 50 political reporters during the fall campaign, finding them in unanimous agreement that Dewey was destined to win the presidency. The same belief motivated the *Chicago Tribune* to publish a morning-after headline that had no basis in fact: DEWEY DEFEATS TRUMAN.

The voters, of course, decided otherwise. They gave Truman a resounding victory by margins of 114 electoral votes and 2.1 million popular votes. Gallup and his fellow pollsters wallowed in embarrassment. "I don't want to seem malicious," said Wilfred Funk, who had been editor of the late *Literary Digest.* "But I can't help but get a good chuckle out of this."

Survey-research firms tightened their procedures and regained the public's confidence in coming decades, though they continued to miss the mark on occasion. A single election-eve poll incorrectly envisioned Richard Nixon as the presidential winner in 1960, and another mistakenly said the same of Hubert Humphrey in 1968. Several October polls predicted a tight race between incumbent Jimmy Carter and challenger Ronald Reagan in 1980, though Reagan actually breezed to a lopsided victory.

And then there was 2016. A wide array of pollsters and other prognosticators insisted that Democrat Hillary Clinton was certain to win the presidency. Sam Wang, a Princeton University professor acclaimed for the accuracy of his election forecasts, was so convinced of Clinton's inevitability that he pledged to eat an insect if Donald Trump received as many as 240 electoral votes, a total that still would have left the Republican nominee 30 votes short of victory. Wang ate a cricket on CNN after Trump defeated Clinton in the Electoral College, 304-227.

These examples prove conclusively that predicting an election is—and always has been—more of an art than a science. The likelihood of error remains sizable, despite the ever-increasing volumes of data available to forecasters.

It is especially foolish to issue a prediction well in advance of an election. The errors cited above—ranging from Lincoln's time to the present day—all occurred within three months of the voters' final decision. If the time span is lengthened beyond that frame, the probability of an incorrect forecast becomes substantially larger.

Consider a randomly selected group of three consecutive presidential contests between 1972 and 1980. Polling data and conventional wisdom would have inspired the following predictions a year prior to each Election Day:

■ Edmund Muskie was a cinch to secure the Democratic nomination in 1972 and run a close race with the Republican incumbent, Richard Nixon.

■ Hubert Humphrey was the odds-on favorite to be named the Democratic nominee in 1976. (Support for a political unknown from Georgia, Jimmy Carter, remained below 5 percent in the final Gallup Poll of 1975.)

■ Edward Kennedy was almost certain to snatch the Democratic nomination from Carter in 1980, and then become the frontrunner to reach the White House.

Each of these forecasts seemed safe and logical 12 months in advance of the relevant election. Each proved to be totally incorrect.

The Trends

LESSON LEARNED. THIS INITIAL CHAPTER offers a preview of the 2024 presidential election, a contest that still seemed a distant prospect at the time of publication, 13 months prior to Election Day. The following text examines 24 trends that almost certainly will manifest themselves during the long race ahead, trends that will strongly influence the final results on November 5, 2024.

As for the name of the eventual winner? Well, you won't find any guesses here.

1. The gerontocracy will remain firmly in charge.

Dwight Eisenhower marked his final birthday as president of the United States with a large, yet informal party. He stepped onto the White House lawn at midday on October 14, 1960, to accept congratulations from 6,000 friends and admirers, who serenaded him with a chorus of "Happy Birthday to You." The sunny autumn day was the 70th anniversary of Eisenhower's birth; he was the first president to reach that milestone while still in office.

Americans were accustomed to thinking of their country as young and vibrant, a belief confirmed by the nation's median age in 1960—the midpoint for all citizens—of just 29.5 years. The race to succeed Eisenhower as president, then in its final stages, featured two vigorous contestants, John Kennedy (who had turned 43 in May) and Richard Nixon (47 in January). It seemed incongruous that the current leader of this youth-oriented nation was a man who had been eligible for Social Security for five years.

Perceptions would change in the decades ahead, as the electorate grew considerably older. America's median age shot up to 38.6 years by 2020, its highest level ever, and the year's presidential nominees greatly exceeded that figure. Incumbent Donald Trump's age, as of Election Day, was 74.38 when carried to two decimal places. The opponent who defeated him, Joseph Biden, became the oldest person to win a presidential election at

77.95. The Dwight Eisenhower who was wrapping up his second term in 1960 would have seemed relatively young in their company.

Trump and Biden weren't unusual in their advanced ages. Eight contenders in the 2020 race have been classified by this book as qualified candidates, indicating that they mounted serious campaigns. Six of the eight had passed their 70th birthdays prior to 2020. The group's average age of 69.50 was the steepest for any group of qualified candidates in history.

Here are the eight elections with the highest average ages:

1. 2020 (8 candidates)................................69.50
2. 1848 (8 candidates)................................64.13
2. 2016 (15 candidates)..............................64.13
4. 1808 (3 candidates)................................63.19
5. 1928 (10 candidates)..............................62.11
6. 2008 (10 candidates)..............................61.54
7. 1828 (2 candidates)................................61.47
8. 2012 (8 candidates)................................61.22

You'll note that every election since 2008 is included on this list, and the early signs point to 2024's eventual inclusion. Yes, much could change in the months ahead, but it's a fact that Biden and Trump established themselves as early frontrunners for their parties' upcoming nominations. Their respective ages on Election Day will be 81.95 and 78.38.

2. Politicians born in the 1950s are facing a shutout.

Pundits commonly believed that baby boomers—persons who were born during the incredibly fertile period between 1946 and 1964—would dominate American politics in the early portion of the 21st century.

That prediction especially held true for the 40.5 million Americans born in the heart of the boom, the years from 1950 through 1959. The nation's annual birth total reached 4 million for the first time in 1954 and peaked at 4.3 million three years later. The massive cohort of Fifties Babies was expected to produce several future presidents.

But that forecast has not come to fruition. Nobody born during the 1950-1959 span has been elected to the White House or, for that matter, has even received a major-party nomination for president. That makes the 1950s the only decade between the 1730s and the 1960s to suffer such a shutout.

The graph on the following page shows the birth decades for the 117 major-party nominees in America's 59 presidential campaigns. If a candidate was nominated twice or more, each nomination is counted separately here:

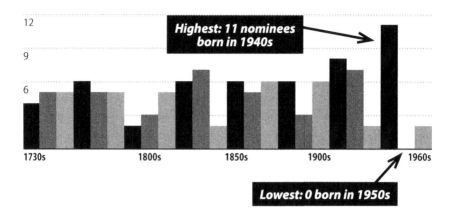

The window of opportunity is shrinking for politicians who were born in the 1950s. The youngest among them will turn 65 in 2024 and 69 when the subsequent election is held. If voters decide to pivot to a younger president—as they did in replacing Eisenhower with Kennedy—the window will shut completely.

It's difficult to explain why the Fifties Babies have failed to fulfill their political promise, but a hint is offered by the graph above. Candidates born in the 1940s have been hogging the stage, winning 11 nominations (three more than any other decade), a number that will increase if Biden and/ or Trump receive their parties' nods in 2024. Opportunities for younger contenders have been few and far between.

3. History suggests that a youth movement is (eventually) coming.

It isn't uncommon for Americans to choose a relatively young candidate as the replacement for a considerably older commander-in-chief. There have been seven instances when voters elected a new president at least 10 years younger than the winner of the previous contest:

■ Andrew Jackson was eight months past his 65th birthday when he was reelected in 1832. His vice president, Martin Van Buren, became the subsequent presidential victor in 1836, shortly before he turned 54.

■ William Henry Harrison won the 1840 election at the advanced age of 67.73, this at a time when the nation's median age was merely 17.8. Harrison died only 31 days after assuming the presidency, giving voters a reason to question their collective decision. They turned to 49-year-old James Polk in 1844.

■ Zachary Taylor, like Harrison an older military hero, was just shy of 64 when he was elected president in 1848. He, again like Harrison, died in office, inspiring voters to bounce back to a younger contender. Franklin Pierce won in November 1852, the same month in which he turned 48.

■ The electorate continued its yo-yo cycle in 1856, replacing Pierce with 65-year-old James Buchanan, who would voluntarily (and happily) leave the White House in March 1861, a month prior to his 70th birthday. Buchanan was replaced by Abraham Lincoln, who was 51.72 years old when elected in 1860.

■ We've already discussed the shift that occurred a century after the Buchanan-Lincoln transition. Dwight Eisenhower was succeeded by 1960's victor, John Kennedy, the youngest candidate (43.43 years) ever elected president.

■ Consecutive campaigns in the 1980s yielded three winners of advanced age: Ronald Reagan in 1980 (69.73 years old) and 1984 (73.73), then George H.W. Bush in 1988 (64.39). Voters shifted to Bill Clinton in November 1992, less than three months after he turned 46.

■ George W. Bush was by no means an old man when his second term concluded in January 2009. He left the White House midway between his 62nd and 63rd birthdays. But his successor, Barack Obama, was only 47.24 when elected in 2008.

Obama, of course, was eventually replaced by Donald Trump and then Joseph Biden, two of the three oldest presidents America has ever had. It seems likely that the cycle of history will eventually assert itself, spinning young candidates back into favor. Perhaps not in 2024, but relatively soon.

4. The West will continue to be shut out of the White House.

The West finally entered the political mainstream in the 1960s.

It's true that a pair of Californians had received three presidential nominations, all bestowed by the Republican Party, over the previous century or so—John Fremont in 1856 and Herbert Hoover in 1928 and 1932—with Hoover even serving four years as president. But it was in the 1960s that the region truly began to assert its growing political and demographic power. Richard Nixon of California and Barry Goldwater of Arizona emerged as successive Republican nominees in 1960 and 1964, the first instance of two Westerners achieving such a high honor in back-to-back presidential races.

Both of those campaigns fell short of the White House, though Nixon did bounce back to win reelection to the presidency as a Californian in 1972. (He had secured his first term in 1968 as a New York resident.) Ronald Reagan, a former California governor, followed up with two national victories in the 1980s, confirming the West's role as a major player in presidential politics.

Or so it seemed. The other three regions enjoyed victories in the subsequent nine elections—especially the South—but the West was shut out. Here are the winners (and their home states and regions) since Reagan:

1988 — George H.W. Bush, Texas (South)
1992 — Bill Clinton, Arkansas (South)
1996 — Bill Clinton, Arkansas (South)
2000 — George W. Bush, Texas (South)
2004 — George W. Bush, Texas (South)
2008 — Barack Obama, Illinois (Midwest)
2012 — Barack Obama, Illinois (Midwest)
2016 — Donald Trump, New York (East)
2020 — Joseph Biden, Delaware (East)

It's true that these things run in cycles. The South failed to elect a single new president between Zachary Taylor (1848) and Jimmy Carter (1976), largely because of hard feelings and stereotypes that lingered on both sides for a century after the Civil War, magnified by the stubborn refusal of most white Southerners to acknowledge the constitutional rights of blacks. (Lyndon Johnson of Texas did win the 1964 election, but he had already been elevated to the presidency upon John Kennedy's assassination.) Time and a degree of racial progress paved the way for five straight Southern victories from 1988 to 2004.

The Midwest and East had suffered their own droughts until recently, the former going without a victorious candidate since Harry Truman in 1948, the latter since Kennedy in 1960 (or more accurately, Richard Nixon in 1968, during his brief New York residency). But they have combined to win every election since 2008.

The West finds itself at a disadvantage in 2024, given that the early presidential frontrunners hail from the East (Biden) and South (Trump, now a Florida resident). But the region is simply too large to ignore—its residents collectively cast more than 37 million votes in 2020—and too powerful to be kept off the board much longer. Look for new presidential contenders to emerge from California and other Western states by 2028 or 2032 at the latest.

5. Most primary elections in 2024 will be meaningless.

If you wished to devise a lengthy, confusing, largely worthless system to choose presidential nominees, you would be hard-pressed to invent anything worse than the current arrangement.

Here's how it operated in recent decades: Candidates in both parties concentrated their time and money on Iowa, which kicked off the season with the first presidential caucuses, and New Hampshire, which followed with the first presidential primary. It was axiomatic that a contender had to perform well in both states or risk the imminent cessation of his campaign. Most of the later primaries were of lesser or no importance.

The concept defied logic. Iowa and New Hampshire are small, largely rural states that are unrepresentative of the nation as a whole. They collectively had 4.6 million residents in 2020, just 1.4 percent of the national total, and their minority populations were exceptionally small. No corporation would base a national marketing campaign solely on consumer surveys conducted in Iowa and New Hampshire, yet the major parties had been doing something equally mindless since the 1970s.

The ground rules changed slightly in 2020. The Iowa caucuses were so badly mismanaged that their results were rendered meaningless. Joseph Biden, the early favorite for the Democratic nomination, then bombed out in New Hampshire, finishing fifth in a crowded field with only 8.4 percent of the vote.

But Biden's campaign treasury remained just large enough to bankroll a final stand. The battleground was South Carolina, another relatively small state without a major urban center. The former vice president scored a resounding victory in that primary—running up a margin of nearly 29 percentage points over runner-up Bernie Sanders—and the crowded pool of Democratic contenders drained almost immediately.

Biden was one of six major candidates in the Democratic field when South Carolinians voted on the last Saturday in February. Two of his challengers, Pete Buttigieg and Amy Klobuchar, respectively finished fourth and sixth. They suspended their campaigns within 48 hours. Two others, Michael Bloomberg and Elizabeth Warren, gave up after doing poorly on Super Tuesday, a series of primaries three days after South Carolina. Sanders was the only Democratic contender who chose to keep pushing against Biden.

The race for 2020's Democratic nomination, for all intents and purposes, reached its conclusion by March 7, despite the fact that 30 states had not yet conducted their primary elections. Biden was crowned as the party's de facto nominee less than a week after South Carolina, even though the national convention remained more than five months in the future.

The political schedule has been altered for 2024, deemphasizing Iowa and pushing South Carolina into a position of greater importance, but the process will remain the same. A handful of early primaries will determine which candidates receive media coverage and a steady flow of donations—and which are relegated to obscurity and elimination. Each party's nominee will emerge at a remarkably early date.

Roughly 20 million Democrats engaged in the senseless act of casting primary ballots in the weeks and months after Biden's triumph in the first days of March. Sixteen primary elections were staged later than June 1, three months after all Democrats learned the name of their nominee. You can expect the late primaries to be similarly meaningless this time around.

6. Donald Trump will set all-time records for primary elections.

Trump was widely considered to be the early frontrunner for his third consecutive Republican presidential nomination in 2024. He is almost certain to win several upcoming primaries, even if the party eventually chooses somebody else to carry its standard in the fall campaign.

Trump is close to breaking two all-time records for primary elections. The first is the number of victories in individual state primaries by a candidate in either major party, Republican or Democratic. Here are the current top five:

1. George H.W. Bush 78
2. Donald Trump 72
3. Bill Clinton 65
3. Ronald Reagan 65
5. George W. Bush 63

The second record within Trump's grasp is the total number of votes received in all primary elections for either major party. These are the five leaders in the present rankings:

1. Hillary Clinton 34,833,999
2. Donald Trump 31,971,040
3. Barack Obama 25,838,376
4. Bernie Sanders 22,781,804
5. Ronald Reagan 20,649,375

If Trump wins seven primaries and 2.9 million votes in 2024, he will vault into first place on both lists. It's difficult to imagine him falling short, given that he notched 39 victories and drew 18.2 million votes in the 2020 Republican primaries.

7. Both conventions will be meaningless.

There was a time—decades and decades ago—when party conventions truly called the shots. Democratic and Republican delegates streamed into host cities every four years to nominate presidential and vice-presidential candidates for the fall campaign.

The process could be messy, time-consuming, and irrational. H.L. Mencken, the famed journalist, covered every major-party gathering between 1904 and 1948. "There is something about a national convention that makes it as fascinating as a revival or a hanging," he said happily. "It is vulgar, it is ugly, it is stupid, it is tedious, it is hard upon both the higher cerebral centers and the gluteus maximus, and yet it is somehow charming."

A few conventions exceeded vulgarity and ugliness by descending into pure chaos. The 1860 Democratic convention was one such gathering. Delegates failed to agree on a nominee after 57 ballots that year and simply went home. The party's Northern and Southern wings eventually chose separate tickets.

The 1924 Democratic convention went nearly twice as long, 103 ballots, which remains the all-time record. The roll was called over and over again for nine straight days. The nomination was finally bestowed upon John Davis, a former ambassador to Great Britain, though it came at the price of a fatally divided party. Davis deflected any congratulations offered by friends and allies. "Thanks," he said solemnly. "But you know what it's worth." He was buried by Calvin Coolidge in a November landslide.

Primary elections eclipsed conventions shortly after television arrived on the scene. The last multi-ballot convention—probably the last that anybody will ever see—occurred in 1952, when the Democrats required three roll calls to nominate Adlai Stevenson. Subsequent candidates found it easier to reach primary voters directly by TV, thereby short-circuiting the party machinery. "If it ever goes into a back room," John Kennedy said in 1960, "my name will never emerge." So he went the primary route, sweeping every state election he entered, essentially forcing the Democratic convention to grant him the nomination. Future presidential hopefuls would follow his template.

The balance tipped heavily toward primaries between 1960 and 1980. Party conventions, which had been indispensable components of the political process in earlier decades, degenerated into aimless spectacles staged for TV audiences, extended telecasts of partisan speeches and promotional videos. A reporter asked the Democratic national chairman in 1996, Don Fowler, why his party even bothered to hold a summer convention when its nominee had essentially been picked in the spring. "We'll continue to have it," Fowler said with a smile, "as long as you keep covering it."

Two more meaningless conventions are slated for 2024—the Republicans in Milwaukee in mid-July, the Democrats in Chicago a month later. Nothing of importance will happen at either one.

8. Joseph Biden could become the fifth candidate to be named to at least four major-party tickets.

The Founding Fathers disdained partisanship. A party system, said George Washington, "agitates the community with ill-founded jealousies and false alarms." Thomas Jefferson agreed. "If I could not go to heaven but with a party," he famously said, "I would not go at all."

This high-minded rhetoric served as camouflage—a smoke screen, if you will—for the strong political passions that swirled throughout the republic's early years. Separate alliances grew up around Washington and Jefferson, eventually coalescing under the respective labels of Federalists and Democratic-Republicans. Neither of these parties ever held a formal convention—the first such gathering wouldn't occur until the campaign of 1832—yet they did manage to achieve informal agreement on their national tickets.

This book goes back in time to assign credit for pre-convention nominations. John Adams, for example, is classified here as the Federalist nominee for vice president in 1789 and 1792 (winning both times) and the party's choice for president in 1796 and 1800 (winning the first, losing to Jefferson in the second). That makes him the first candidate to appear on four major-party tickets.

Three politicians matched Adams's achievement after conventions were instituted. Two—Franklin Roosevelt and Richard Nixon—actually went him one better with appearances on five tickets. Below is the short list of recipients of at least four major-party nominations for president (PRES) and vice president (VPRES). Party abbreviations and relevant years are included:

John Adams (PRES: F-1796, 1800; VPRES: F-1789, 1792)
Franklin Roosevelt (PRES: D-1932, 1936, 1940, 1944; VPRES: D-1920)
Richard Nixon (PRES: R-1960, 1968, 1972; VPRES: R-1952, 1956)
George H.W. Bush (PRES: R-1988, 1992; VPRES: R-1980, 1984)

Joseph Biden is poised to join this select group. He broke through on the national level in 2008, when Barack Obama tapped him as the Democratic vice-presidential nominee. He was reelected in 2012, then advanced to the presidency in 2020. If Biden again receives his party's presidential nod in 2024, he will become the fifth candidate in U.S. history to appear on four major-party tickets.

9. The nation appears to be on track for its first presidential rematch in 68 years.

No surprise here. Biden defeated Donald Trump in 2020's general election, and both men subsequently emerged as early favorites for the 2024 nominations of their respective parties. If the oddsmakers prove to be correct, the two will square off for a second time.

There have been six prior instances of major-party nominees facing each other on two occasions, always in consecutive elections:

> 1796 and 1800
> > John Adams and Thomas Jefferson with one win apiece
> 1824 and 1828
> > John Quincy Adams and Andrew Jackson with one win apiece
> 1836 and 1840
> > Martin Van Buren and William Henry Harrison with one win apiece
> 1888 and 1892
> > Benjamin Harrison and Grover Cleveland with one win apiece
> 1896 and 1900
> > William McKinley with two wins over William Jennings Bryan
> 1952 and 1956
> > Dwight Eisenhower with two wins over Adlai Stevenson

Each of the first four rematches, as you can see, was won by the candidate who had lost the initial contest, a trend that bodes well for Trump. But the final two repeats—the only such occurrences in the past 130 years—featured victors who increased their margins the second time, a good sign for Biden. (McKinley received 271 electoral votes in 1896, then 292 in 1900. Eisenhower climbed from 442 in 1952 to 457 in 1956.)

But the bad news for all Americans is that rematches tend to be unusually vitriolic. Three examples make the point:

■ The campaign of 1800 was the most vituperative in the nation's early years. The Federalists alleged that Jefferson planned to assemble a radical, atheistic administration. The Democratic-Republicans accused John Adams of laying the groundwork for a New World monarchy.

■ Jackson believed that victory had been snatched from him in 1824 by John Quincy Adams, who was elected by the House of Representatives after both contenders failed to reach a majority in the Electoral College. Adams solicited the support of a third candidate, Henry Clay, then made Clay his secretary of state. "So you see," Jackson roared, "the Judas of the West (Clay) has closed the contract and will receive the 30 pieces of silver." His violent anger fueled his successful 1828 campaign.

■ The Van Buren-Harrison replay in 1840 evolved into one of the nastiest races in history. The Democrats accused Harrison of being a mindless time-server whose only desires were a government pension and a barrel of hard cider. They called him "General Mum," implying that his positions on the issues of the day were unknown. The Whigs blasted Van Buren as a heartless plutocrat who lived in isolation in an expensively renovated White House. "Van, Van is a used-up man," they chanted.

Hard feelings surfaced in the other three rematches, too, a pattern that will undoubtedly hold true if Trump and Biden face off in 2024.

10. Everything isn't as cut and dried as it seems.

Most pundits in 2023 spoke as if a Trump-Biden rematch the following year were a virtual certainty. History suggests that a bit of caution would be in order.

The 2024 campaign may well bring us the seventh presidential rerun, though it might also end with one or both frontrunners falling to the wayside prior to the Republican and Democratic conventions.

The past 15 campaigns have featured more than a dozen contenders who emerged as favorites for party nominations a year in advance, yet plummeted to earth soon thereafter. There isn't enough space here to analyze their declines, but you certainly remember some of their names. Each of these politicians—some of whom eventually decided not to run— ranked first in his or her party in public-opinion polls a year or so before the listed election:

> Republicans — Nelson Rockefeller (1964), George Romney (1968), Ronald Reagan (1976), Rudy Giuliani (2008), Jeb Bush and Scott Walker (2016)
>
> Democrats — Edmund Muskie (1972), Edward Kennedy (1976), Gary Hart (1988), Mario Cuomo (1992), Joseph Lieberman and Howard Dean (2004), Hillary Clinton (2008)

Trump and Biden are special cases, of course, one a former president, the other the current occupant of the Oval Office. But their exalted positions don't grant them immunity.

Harry Truman was vague about a reelection campaign in 1952, the same stance taken by Lyndon Johnson in 1968. Yet both competed in March's New Hampshire primary, where they struggled. Truman lost to Estes Kefauver, a folksy Tennessee senator whose symbol was a coonskin cap. Johnson defeated a senator who campaigned against the Vietnam War, Eugene McCarthy of Minnesota, albeit by an uncomfortably small margin. Both presidents announced their political retirements by the end of the month.

11. The presumptive nominees look weak on paper.

Biden and Trump enter 2024 with similar baggage. Both are elderly, both are relatively unpopular, and both have been nationally prominent for decades, straining the patience of an attention-deficit electorate that prefers the new over the old.

Their inadequacies are documented by the **potential index (PI)**, a statistic unique to this book. PI reflects a candidate's likelihood of electoral success, based on nine personal and political characteristics. (Flip to page 51 for a full explanation.)

Trump's potential index for 2024 is 7.2 on a 10-point scale, while Biden's is 6.2. Those scores, which are remarkably small for a former or current president, are depressed by the advanced ages of both men. The average PI for Trump and Biden—6.7—is lower than the corresponding averages for major-party nominees in nearly two-thirds of all previous elections (38 of 59).

Prior or current service in the Oval Office inflates a candidate's PI, which is why the scores for Trump and Biden—weak though they may be—are higher for 2024 than for earlier years. Their past indexes were so much lower, in fact, that they can be found on the following list of the five worst PIs for general-election winners. (W, by the way, stands for Whig among the parenthetical party abbreviations.)

1. Donald Trump (R-2016) 3.1
2. Herbert Hoover (R-1928) 4.0
3. Zachary Taylor (W-1848) 4.1
4. Joseph Biden (D-2020) 4.3
5. James Buchanan (D-1856) 5.1

This list suggests a correlation between a candidate's lack of political potential and his subsequent performance in the White House. Trump, Hoover, Taylor, and Buchanan all rank among the 10 worst presidents in American history, according to a 2022 survey of 141 presidential scholars by Siena College. The jury is still out on Biden, though his popularity scores in public-opinion polls have been consistently low.

Recent presidents who sought second terms boasted potential indexes at the high end of the scale. Here's the roll over the past four decades: Ronald Reagan (1984, PI 8.1), George H.W. Bush (1992, PI 8.2), Bill Clinton (1996, PI 8.5), George W. Bush (2004, PI 9.3), and Barack Obama (2012, PI 8.3). Trump and Biden are the only outliers, the only candidates with presidential experience who fall below 8.0. Their relative lack of potential is cause for concern.

12. Polarization has reached a 90-year peak, and it seems to be getting worse.

There's no need to write at length about the absence of bipartisan cooperation in Washington or the lack of political civility across the land. We're all aware that polarization has reached absurdly high levels.

It's possible to chart its growth with a stat known as **average state deviation**, which measures state-by-state variations in support for major-party nominees. A low ASD suggests that voting patterns are fairly consistent across the nation, while a high score indicates that percentages are wildly erratic between one state and another. The latter is a telltale sign of polarization.

ASD is calculated by comparing an individual's national popular-vote percentage (PV%) to his PV% in each state, and then averaging those differences. Joseph Biden, for example, drew 51.31 percent of all U.S. votes in 2020. His percentage in New York (60.87 percent) was 9.56 points above his national level, while his share in North Dakota (31.78 percent) was 19.53 points below. If we average the absolute values of his deviations in New York, North Dakota, and the other 49 states (including D.C.), we arrive at a figure of 9.73 points. That was the typical gap between Biden's national support and his performance in any given state.

Donald Trump's average deviation, as you would expect, was nearly identical at 9.71 points. The ASD for any election is the midpoint between the average deviations for both major-party nominees—in 2020's case, 9.72.

Polarization began its steady creep after the victory of Democrat Bill Clinton in 1992, the election of a Republican Congress in 1994, and the subsequent deterioration of the relationship between the executive and legislative branches. ASD had slipped to 5.01 points in 1992, its lowest level since 1960, a sign that political sentiments were roughly similar across the country. But the polarizing trend has been gaining strength ever since, as the following graph shows:

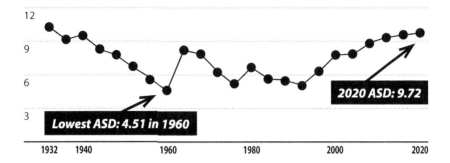

There's no reason to expect this trend to change in 2024, especially given the anticipated pairing of candidates. But it's important not to get carried away. Yes, 2020's ASD of 9.72 points was the highest since 10.20 in the desperate Depression year of 1932, when tensions ran high between Franklin Roosevelt and Herbert Hoover.

But things have been worse—much worse. ASD soared as high as 20.30 points in 1860, a surefire indicator of severe political stress. The Civil War broke out just five months after that contentious election.

13. We could draw closer to a record for political instability.

Americans elected a Democratic president in 2012, a Republican in 2016, and a Democrat in 2020. This back-and-forth action is typical, isn't it?

Well, no. There have been only four instances of different parties consecutively winning three or more presidential elections. Those cases are listed below, with abbreviations of winners' affiliations in parentheses:

1. 1836-1852 (D-W-D-W-D) 5
1. 1880-1896 (R-D-R-D-R) 5
3. 1972-1980 (R-D-R) 3
3. 2012-2020 (D-R-D) 3

It's more common for the party in power to retain its lease on the White House than to be evicted. Incumbent parties have won 34 of the 58 elections that followed George Washington's initial victory, a success rate of 59 percent.

But if Donald Trump or any other Republican wins in 2024, America will find itself in the midst of a rare run of instability, the first party alternation extending at least four elections since the 19th century.

That would still leave us considerably short of a second record in this category. The eight elections between 1832 and 1860 were won by eight different individuals. (The years of their wins are shown here in parentheses.) Three of those presidents retired after their terms: Andrew Jackson (1832), James Polk (1844), and James Buchanan (1856). Two died in office: William Henry Harrison (1840) and Zachary Taylor (1848). Two lost reelection bids: Martin Van Buren (1836) and Franklin Pierce (1852). The streak was finally broken when Abraham Lincoln (1860) won a second term in 1864.

Ten other streaks—including the current one—have yielded at least three different presidents in consecutive elections. Here's the rundown, with the first and last winner in each case listed in parentheses:

1. 1832-1860 (Andrew Jackson-Abraham Lincoln) 8
2. 1872-1896 (Ulysses Grant-William McKinley)..7
3. 1916-1932 (Woodrow Wilson-Franklin Roosevelt)......................................5
4. 1900-1912 (William McKinley-Woodrow Wilson)..............................4
4. 1956-1968 (Dwight Eisenhower-Richard Nixon)................................4
6. 1792-1800 (George Washington-Thomas Jefferson) 3
6. 1820-1828 (James Monroe-Andrew Jackson)................................3
6. 1944-1952 (Franklin Roosevelt-Dwight Eisenhower)....................3
6. 1972-1980 (Richard Nixon-Ronald Reagan).................................3
6. 1984-1992 (Ronald Reagan-Bill Clinton) 3
6. 2012-2020 (Barack Obama-Joseph Biden) 3

If the Republicans are victorious in 2024, the streak of different winners would reach four: Barack Obama (2012), Donald Trump (2016), Joseph Biden (2020), Someone New (2024). That would still be only halfway toward the all-time record, which couldn't be tied until 2040.

14. Joseph Biden must build his base to retain the White House.

The assumption here is that Biden will be renominated by the Democratic Party in 2024, even though polls indicate a significant percentage of Democrats would prefer to shift to a younger candidate.

Biden's popular-vote margin in 2020 was impressively large. He defeated Trump by more than seven million votes. But he survived a tougher fight in the Electoral College, drawing 306 votes there, only 36 more than the 270 required for victory.

Democratic nominees have won 22 of the 59 presidential elections. Nearly two-thirds of those successful Democrats—14 of 22—drew more than 60 percent of the available electoral votes. Biden was among the eight who failed to reach that threshold:

1. Woodrow Wilson (D-1916) 52.17%
2. Grover Cleveland (D-1884)..............54.61%
3. Jimmy Carter (D-1976)......................55.20%
4. John Kennedy (D-1960)....................56.43%
5. Joseph Biden (D-2020) 56.88%

6. Harry Truman (D-1948)......................57.06%
7. Martin Van Buren (D-1836)..............57.82%
8. James Buchanan (D-1856)...............58.78%

None of these seven Democrats (excluding Biden) was reelected four years later. Kennedy, of course, was favored to win a second term prior to his assassination, but the others were not so well positioned politically. Cleveland, Carter, and Van Buren ran again and were defeated. (Cleveland would return to the White House four years after his 1888 loss.) Wilson wanted to seek a third term, but was incapacitated by a stroke. Truman and Buchanan both had grown to be highly unpopular and wisely decided to retire.

Biden faces an uphill battle to avoid the fate of these Democratic predecessors. His approval ratings, as measured by the Gallup Poll, dropped below 50 percent in August 2021 and reached their nadir at 37 percent in April 2023 before rebounding slightly. He will need to push that score higher—build his base, as the politicians say—if he is to avoid the fate suffered by Carter, the last Democratic president defeated for reelection.

15. Donald Trump must battle history to regain the White House.

The assumption here is that Trump will be renominated by the Republican Party in 2024, even though polls indicate a significant percentage of Republicans would prefer to shift to a different candidate.

Trump's problem is that Americans tend to dismiss, overlook, or even ignore ex-presidents after they leave the main stage. Successful comebacks are exceedingly rare. Only five former presidents mounted serious campaigns to regain the White House, and four failed miserably:

■ An economic depression derailed Martin Van Buren's reelection campaign in 1840. The Whigs caustically dubbed him "Martin Van Ruin," and voters gleefully tossed him out. But conditions improved by 1844, and the Whigs fell into disarray. Van Buren emerged to fill the void, though he had a problem. The Democratic Party required a two-thirds supermajority to win its nomination. Van Buren drew almost 55 percent on the convention's first ballot—sufficient for victory under the 21st century's rules—but never got close to the then-necessary two-thirds. James Polk went on to win the nomination and the presidency, while Van Buren fumed about "the opposition and persecution to which I have been exposed."

■ Van Buren tried again in 1848, running under the banner of an anti-slavery party, the Free Soil Party. He didn't carry a single state, though he did pull roughly 10 percent of all popular votes.

■ The second ex-president to stage a comeback was Millard Fillmore, who had served as Zachary Taylor's vice president and had been elevated to the White House upon Taylor's death in 1850. Fillmore lost the Whig nomination to Winfield Scott in 1852, briefly went into retirement, and reappeared in 1856 as the standard-bearer for the anti-immigration American Party, which formed a coalition with the few Whigs still on the scene. (Most had drifted into the new Republican Party.) Fillmore carried Maryland, but failed to break through anywhere else.

■ Ulysses Grant won successive elections in 1868 and 1872, and it was assumed that his political career was over. The Civil War hero left the White House in March 1877, and he and his wife departed on a two-year world tour. Grant's presidential appetite reawakened while he circled the globe, and he jumped into the Republican race in 1880. He received 304 votes on the first ballot—just 75 short of the threshold for the nomination—but the convention deadlocked. The Republicans finally turned to James Garfield on the 36th ballot.

■ Grover Cleveland is the lone success story for ex-presidents. He, like Donald Trump, won his national electoral debut, failed in his first try for a second term, but remained prominent in his party (Democratic, in Cleveland's case) because of a lack of plausible opponents. Cleveland easily won his third straight nomination in 1892, then ousted Benjamin Harrison, the Republican who had defeated him in the general election four years earlier.

■ Theodore Roosevelt dug himself into a hole after winning the election of 1904. "Under no circumstances," he announced, "will I be a candidate for or accept another nomination." He fulfilled his pledge in March 1909, leaving the White House at the politically young age of 50, even though he had come to regret his decision. It was inevitable that he would return to the fray, which he did in 1912. Roosevelt challenged his presidential successor, William Howard Taft, for the Republican nomination, but Taft controlled the party machinery and held him off.

Roosevelt's case is especially relevant to 2024 because of his response to his convention defeat. He trooped his Republican delegates to a nearby hall in Chicago, where he pledged to run a third-party campaign in the fall. "We stand at Armageddon," he shouted, "and we battle for the Lord!" Roosevelt's Progressive Party carried six states, and he finished second to Democrat Woodrow Wilson in the Electoral College. Taft was a distant third.

It's easy to envision Trump reacting in a similar manner—minus the high-flying rhetoric—if the Republican convention were to rebuff him in 2024. Roosevelt shattered the Republican Party, guaranteeing a Democratic victory, and a third-party run by Trump would almost certainly have the same impact.

16. Trump must rectify the widespread slippage he suffered in 2020.

Trump not only must surmount the historical forces aligned against him, as noted above, but he also needs to win back millions of votes that he lost during his second campaign.

The latter might seem to be a strange assertion, given that Trump set a Republican record in 2020 by drawing more than 74.2 million popular votes, exceeding his 2016 total by roughly 11.2 million.

But it's important to remember that voter turnout increased massively between the two elections—from a total of 136.67 million voters in 2016 to 158.43 million in 2020.

The Democrats were the main beneficiaries of this upsurge in public involvement. Joseph Biden received 81.28 million popular votes, a gain of 23.4 percent from Hillary Clinton's count of 65.85 million four years previously. Trump's total, on the other hand, grew by only 17.8 percent from 62.98 million in the earlier election to 74.22 million in the latter.

Here's another way to look at it: The Democrats picked up 15.43 million popular votes in 2020, while Trump added only 11.24 million. That's the gap that he must somehow close in 2024.

It won't be easy. Trump's two-party share—his split of only those votes cast for the Democratic and Republican tickets (leaving out all minor-party candidates)—wasn't particularly impressive in 2016, 48.89 percent. (Don't forget that Trump trailed Clinton in popular votes.) But his two-party figure was even worse in 2020, 47.73 percent.

His decline was especially significant because it was widespread. Trump's two-party shares dropped in all but seven states. His sharpest downturn occurred in a reliably Democratic state, Colorado, where his split fell by 4.26 percentage points between 2016 and 2020. Second on the list, however, was a state that is just as solidly in the Republican camp, Nebraska, where Trump slipped by 3.77 points.

The table on the next page shows the 11 states where Trump's two-party shares declined by at least three percentage points:

1. Colorado ....-4.26
2. Nebraska ....-3.77
3. Delaware ....-3.63
4. Kansas ....-3.62
5. New Hampshire ....-3.55
6. Wyoming ....-3.23
7. Alaska ....-3.13
8. Vermont ....-3.11
9. Maine ....-3.07
10. Connecticut ....-3.05
11. Maryland ....-3.01

Trump was harshly critical of fellow Republican Mitt Romney's 2012 campaign against Barack Obama, charging that Romney was "one of the dumbest and worst candidates in the history of Republican politics." He insisted that Romney "lost an election that should have easily been won."

It's interesting, in that light, to note that Trump's 2020 two-party percentages were worse than the corresponding 2012 figures for Romney in nearly half of the states, 23 in all. The biggest disparity occurred in the state that Romney represents as a senator, Utah, where the 2012 Republican nominee finished 13.93 points ahead of Trump's 2020 share.

17. Reapportionment will give Republicans a small boost.

Seats in the House of Representatives are reapportioned every 10 years, reflecting the results of the latest federal census. Those changes flow through to the Electoral College, since each state's number of electors is the sum of its two senators and its House members.

The 2020 census will have its first impact on presidential politics in 2024, and the reshuffling of electoral votes will slightly favor the Republicans, potentially handing them three additional votes. It's a logical outcome, given that the Republican Party fares especially well in Sunbelt states that are among the nation's growth leaders.

This trend has been evident for decades. Joseph Biden won 26 states (including the District of Columbia) in 2020, earning 306 votes in the Electoral College. Listed below are other years when new Democratic presidents were elected (plus the upcoming election). If a candidate had carried the same 26 states, these are the electoral votes he or she would have received:

1976 314
1992 310
2008 309
2020 306
2024 303

Five of the states that Biden carried in 2020 subsequently lost electoral votes due to reapportionment (California, Illinois, Michigan, New York, and Pennsylvania), while two of his states added votes (Colorado and Oregon). That's a net Electoral College loss of three votes for the Democrats in 2024.

The long-term decline in the party's base, as shown in the previous table, has been 11 electoral votes over the previous half-century. It's not a major drop, though it could flip the balance in an especially close race. Two elections during the past 200 years were decided by tighter margins—1876 by a single electoral vote and 2000 by five.

18. Both parties enter the 2024 campaign with significant pockets of strength.

Forty-one states have been carried by the same party in every presidential election since 2008—21 states by Democratic nominees, 20 by Republican candidates.

Most of these streaks can be traced beyond the past four campaigns, many to the previous century. The District of Columbia has stuck with the Democrats in all 15 races since joining the electoral mix in 1964, the longest current run of single-party loyalty. Nine states have gone with the Republicans in each of the 14 presidential contests since 1968: Alaska, Idaho, Kansas, Nebraska, North Dakota, Oklahoma, South Dakota, Utah, and Wyoming.

Only 10 states have been carried by nominees of both parties since 2008. Most, as you would expect, are highly competitive battlegrounds, though three defy that characterization. Indiana gave strong support to Republican candidates in the past three elections, and Iowa and Ohio enthusiastically climbed on board for Donald Trump's two campaigns. It seems reasonable to add these three Midwestern states to the Republican column, giving us this breakdown of dependable states:

Democratic..... 21 states, 232 electoral votes
Republican...... 23 states, 189 electoral votes

Joseph Biden—or any other Democratic nominee—will benefit from a head start in 2024, since the party's pool of reliable electoral votes is just 38 short of the total required for victory. But the Republicans aren't far behind with a sum of 189, itself just 81 shy of the magic number of 270.

19. Only seven states will truly be in play in 2024.

The upcoming campaign might have a surprise or two in store. Perhaps the race will become unexpectedly competitive in a few states that have leaned decisively toward the Democrats or Republicans in recent years. Only time will tell.

But we can be sure of this: Only seven states meet a pair of stipulations that stamp them as true battlegrounds:

■ They were carried by nominees of both parties in the four presidential elections from 2008 through 2020.

■ Their winners in 2016 and 2020 drew less than 53 percent of the votes cast for the Democratic and Republican nominees, also known as two-party votes.

The Democrats and Republicans will be concentrating their firepower on these seven states, swamping their citizens with thousands of television commercials, millions of campaign flyers, and a cacophony of political rhetoric. Each state is listed below with its 2024 Electoral College allocation, the year it began its current streak of one-party support, and the candidates who won the state in 2016 and 2020 (each followed in parentheses by his two-party share):

Arizona
Electoral votes: 11. Start of current streak: 2020 (Democratic). Winner in 2016: Trump (51.89%). Winner in 2020: Biden (50.16%).
Florida
Electoral votes: 30. Start of current streak: 2016 (Republican). Winner in 2016: Trump (50.62%). Winner in 2020: Trump (51.70%).
Georgia
Electoral votes: 16. Start of current streak: 2020 (Democratic). Winner in 2016: Trump (52.66%). Winner in 2020: Biden (50.12%).
Michigan
Electoral votes: 15. Start of current streak: 2020 (Democratic). Winner in 2016: Trump (50.12%). Winner in 2020: Biden (51.41%).
North Carolina
Electoral votes: 16. Start of current streak: 2012 (Republican). Winner in 2016: Trump (51.90%). Winner in 2020: Trump (50.68%).
Pennsylvania
Electoral votes: 19. Start of current streak: 2020 (Democratic). Winner in 2016: Trump (50.38%). Winner in 2020: Biden (50.59%).
Wisconsin
Electoral votes: 10. Start of current streak: 2020 (Democratic). Winner in 2016: Trump (50.41%). Winner in 2020: Biden (50.32%).

The Democrats seemingly face the easier task. If their nominee can hold tight to his aforementioned base of 232 electoral votes, he would need to pull just 38 from the battleground states to clinch a national victory. Wins in Michigan, Pennsylvania, and Wisconsin—states that Biden carried in 2020—would be sufficient in 2024, as would several other combinations.

The Republicans would require an extra 81 electoral votes to augment their base of 189 and regain the White House. Victories in Florida, North Carolina, Georgia, and Pennsylvania would yield precisely that number. Trump carried the first two states in that group in 2020, while losing the final two by exceedingly narrow margins. But don't forget that he won all four in 2016—and indeed, he swept all seven battleground states that year.

20. Third parties may emerge in 2024, though the odds will be against them.

Americans love third parties in theory, but not in practice.

The Gallup Poll has posed the same question several times during the past two decades: "In your view, do the Republican and Democratic parties do an adequate job of representing the American people, or do they do such a poor job that a third major party is needed?"

The results have been remarkably steady across the span of time. Fifty-eight percent of respondents expressed desire for a third party in 2007, virtually matching the 2022 reading of 56 percent. Average support for a third party has been 55 percent in all Gallup Polls since 2003.

So why is America still in the grasp of a two-party system?

Democrats and Republicans have framed the nation's political structure to perpetuate their control and exclude outsiders. They have entrenched their own primary elections as pathways to power, spurning independent candidates. They have enacted statewide restrictions to keep minor parties off of ballots. And they have structured campaign-finance laws to bar (or, at best, delay) the flow of funds to candidates outside the two-party sphere.

And there's another problem: If a third-party candidate somehow defies the odds and attains political prominence—usually because of preexisting fame or fortune—most voters tend to ignore them.

Candidates on third-party lines have drawn more than two percent of all popular votes—*a measly two percent!*—only six times in the past 60 years:

1. Ross Perot (Independent-1992) 18.91%
2. George Wallace (American Independent-1968) 13.53%
3. Ross Perot (Reform-1996) 8.40%
4. John Anderson (National Unity-1980) 6.61%
5. Gary Johnson (Libertarian-2016) 3.29%
6. Ralph Nader (Green-2000) 2.74%

Perot had already achieved fame as a somewhat eccentric billionaire when he launched his independent campaign in 1992. Voters were in a foul mood—angered by an economic recession and a federal tax hike—and they briefly latched onto Perot as an appealing alternative. He vaulted ahead of the major-party nominees, George H.W. Bush and Bill Clinton, in public-opinion polls five months prior to 1992's general election, peaking at 36 percent. But roughly half of his new supporters eventually jumped off the bandwagon. Perot fell below 19 percent in popular votes and did not win a single vote in the Electoral College.

The trajectory was similar for the other third-party candidates listed above. They typically scored well in polls conducted during the summer and early fall, then suffered serious declines by November. Many Americans, it seems, appreciate the concept of an alternative to the Democrats and Republicans, yet worry about its impact. They fret that any vote cast for a third-party candidate will simply be wasted.

That concern is probably the biggest impediment to a pair of third-party campaigns widely discussed—though not confirmed—for 2024. One would be a moderate ticket fashioned by an advocacy organization, No Labels, possibly with Joe Manchin, a Democratic senator from West Virginia, as its presidential standard-bearer. The other would feature a conservative anti-Trump candidate, Liz Cheney, a former Republican congresswoman from Wyoming.

Both of these potential campaigns, if they come to fruition, would be greeted happily by America's jaded electorate. But history suggests that the enthusiasm would eventually wane—and that most voters would dutifully troop back to the Democratic and Republican tickets by November.

21. Voter turnout is almost certain to fall.

Americans voted in record numbers in the most recent presidential election. Roughly 158.4 million people cast ballots in 2020, a massive increase of more than 21.7 million votes (or 15.9 percent) from the previous high of almost 136.7 million, which had been established four years earlier.

This enormous jump was easy to explain. "There is no doubt in my mind that Donald Trump is the reason we saw record turnout in 2020. Whether you love him or hate him, he drives passion and drives people to vote," said Michael McDonald, a University of Florida professor and political analyst. Emotions ran high as voters on both sides streamed to the polls: Republicans to defend Trump, Democrats to unseat him.

Millions of these participants returned to voting booths in 2020 after remaining on the sidelines in previous elections. The turnout rate—the share of the voting-age population that actually cast ballots—consequently soared from 54.8 percent in 2016 to 62.0 percent in 2020. The latter figure was the highest in 60 years, dating back to the competitive race between John Kennedy and Richard Nixon in 1960:

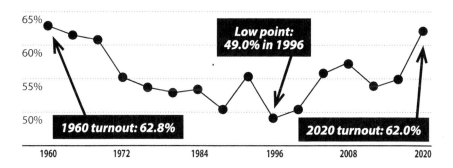

The upswing in political involvement in 2020 was rightly hailed as a promising sign. "We know that voting is habit-forming, so once someone has cast a ballot, they tend to be more likely to do so in the future," said Jacob Neiheisel, a political-science professor at the University at Buffalo.

Yet there are two reasons to be dubious about the long-term direction of the participation arrow:

■ Turnout rates fluctuated within a narrow eight-point band during the 12 presidential elections that preceded 2020—bottoming out at 49.0 percent in 1996, peaking at 57.1 percent in 2008. The median rate for that entire period (1972-2016) was just 53.7 percent. It remains to be seen if 2020's jump to 62.0 percent was a true breakthrough or merely an aberration.

■ A rerun of 2020's presidential race may not inspire as much excitement as the original. Sixty percent of the voters polled by NBC in April 2023, including a third of the Republicans, said they did not want Trump to run again in 2024. And 70 percent of the respondents, including half of the Democrats, said the same about Biden. *Axios*, a political newsletter, summed up this attitude as "Trump-Biden fatigue."

A similar sense of exhaustion was evident in all three presidential rematches since the Civil War, with turnout rates dropping each time:

Benjamin Harrison-Grover Cleveland 79.3% (1888), 74.7% (1892)
William McKinley-William Jennings Bryan 79.3% (1896), 73.2% (1900)
Dwight Eisenhower-Adlai Stevenson 61.6% (1952), 59.3% (1956)

Most of these candidates were admittedly quite dull and incapable of inspiring widespread excitement. The sole exception was Bryan, a charismatic orator who stampeded the 1896 Democratic convention with his famous "Cross of Gold" speech and remained a party favorite despite his loss to McKinley in 1896.

But even Bryan began to pall on the voters as his second campaign drew toward its close in 1900. He tried to rouse his lethargic audiences, declaring that he remained steadfastly devoted to the principles he had enunciated four years earlier. "I stand just where I stood," he shouted. That was too much for the *New York Press*, which spoke for a weary nation. "Sit down, Mr. Bryan," said a *Press* editorial. "You must be awfully tired, too."

The same sentiment is currently evident across the land. It is easy to imagine the turnout rate declining from 2020's peak if Trump and Biden grace the ballot again.

22. Another close general election is more likely than not.

Forty-two presidential elections have been conducted since the Republican Party arrived on the scene in 1856. That means there have been 42 head-to-head matchups between Democratic and Republican nominees.

I divided that lengthy span into six groups of equal size—covering seven consecutive elections apiece—from the earliest contests between the two parties (1856-1880) to the most recent (1996-2020), aiming to gauge the level of competition between the Democrats and Republicans in each period.

I used two different measures, both based on two-party splits. My first step was simply to count the races that were extremely close, defined as elections in which the winner received no more than 52 percent of the votes cast for the Democratic and Republican nominees (thereby excluding minor-party candidates). Fewer than a third of all contests—13 of 42—were so tightly fought, and more of them occurred in the most recent period (1996-2020) than any other:

1856-1880	2 of 7
1884-1908	3 of 7
1912-1936	1 of 7
1940-1964	1 of 7
1968-1992	2 of 7
1996-2020	4 of 7

My second move was to compare average margins of victory in the different periods. Here's an explanation, using 2008 as an example. These were the popular-vote percentages that year: Barack Obama (Democrat) 52.93 percent, John McCain (Republican) 45.65 percent, others 1.42 percent. I excluded the latter group, yielding two-party shares of 53.69

percent for Obama and 46.31 percent for McCain. That translated to a margin of 7.38 percentage points.

I did the same math for the other 41 races, then averaged the two-party margins for all seven groups. The results confirmed the previous table's findings. Tight races have indeed occurred with the greatest frequency in our own times, with a typical gap of just 4.37 points between Democratic and Republican nominees during the 1996-2020 span. Here are the average two-party margins (in percentage points):

1856-1880	7.85
1884-1908	6.53
1912-1936	21.58
1940-1964	10.15
1968-1992	10.02
1996-2020	4.37

It's clear that we're living in an unusually competitive era, a trend confirmed by this fact: No Democratic or Republican nominee has drawn more than 53.0 percent of a year's popular votes (including those cast for minor-party candidates) since George H.W. Bush in 1988. Winners of the eight subsequent elections (1992-2020) all fell below that threshold, the longest such streak in history. And four of those victors didn't receive even a majority of popular votes: Bill Clinton (1992 and 1996), George W. Bush (2000), and Donald Trump (2016).

A similar pattern can be found in the Electoral College, where every winner since 1992 has drawn fewer than 75 percent of the available electoral votes. Their performances contrast sharply with the generally uncompetitive races in the previous seven decades. Thirteen of that period's 18 elections (1920-1988) featured winners who exceeded 75 percent in the Electoral College. Five actually topped 90 percent: Franklin Roosevelt (1936), Lyndon Johnson (1964), Richard Nixon (1972), and Ronald Reagan (1980 and 1984).

But that was then, and this is now. I noted a few pages ago that both parties enter the 2024 campaign with significant (and reliable) bases of support. The stage is set for another nail-biting campaign, continuing the trend that began in the 1990s. It shows no signs of abating.

23. There won't be any significant election fraud.

Let's get real. The election of 2020 might have been the cleanest in American history. It certainly was audited, recounted, and litigated more heavily than any of its 58 predecessors. Yet none of those probes found any definitive evidence of fraud.

A sizable percentage of Republican voters continue to ignore the overwhelming evidence, insisting that the previous election was plagued with irregularities. But many of the party's leaders have conceded the truth:

■ A Republican-funded audit in Arizona's largest county—initiated to prove that Donald Trump had been shortchanged—actually found that Joseph Biden's 2020 margin was slightly larger than originally reported. "Truth is truth, and numbers are numbers," conceded the Republican president of Arizona's State Senate.

■ Republican legislators in Michigan spent months investigating their state's election machinery, believing that it had been weaponized against Trump. They finally issued a 55-page report that admitted Biden had carried the state. "This committee found no evidence of widespread or systematic fraud in Michigan's prosecution of the 2020 election," it said.

■ Eight prominent conservatives—all dedicated Republicans—reviewed the myriad allegations of fraud made by their party's standard-bearer. They rejected every single accusation. "We conclude that Donald Trump and his supporters had their day in court and failed to produce substantive evidence to make their case," they said in a joint report in mid-2022.

There is only one logical conclusion: Trump's claims were angry (and unsupported) rants by a candidate who was unwilling to admit defeat. The probes that he demanded had only one effect. They proved that the 2020 election had been conducted cleanly and above board. There's no reason to believe that 2024 will be any different.

That's not to say that a national election—in 2020 or any other year—has ever been flawlessly conducted. There will always be registered voters who cast ballots in the wrong precincts, unregistered citizens who somehow finagle their way into voting booths, and election supervisors who make mathematical errors (inadvertently or otherwise).

But significant and widespread fraud—duplicity great enough to alter the outcome of an election—has rarely been alleged with any plausibility, certainly not in 2020. Two notable exceptions, however, did occur in 1876 and 1960.

Nobody will ever know which candidate truly won in 1876. Multiple sets of returns were submitted by three Southern states and Oregon. Congress eventually established a 15-member commission to sift through the charges and countercharges. A majority of the panel's members were Republicans, and they unsurprisingly decided to award all 20 disputed electoral votes to Rutherford Hayes, their party's nominee. Hayes consequently carried the Electoral College by a single vote (185-184) over Democrat Samuel Tilden.

John Kennedy's chances of victory in 1960 pivoted on Illinois and Texas, which had 51 electoral votes between them. He carried both by narrow margins, though evidence suggested that his totals had been padded by the states' Democratic machines. A Chicago precinct that contained fewer than 50 registrants nonetheless counted 79 votes for Kennedy, one among dozens of similar instances reported in Illinois's major city. Democrat-controlled election boards in Texas allegedly invalidated thousands of ballots cast for Republican nominee Richard Nixon.

Tilden and Nixon opted not to pursue legal challenges. Each understood how difficult it would be to overturn the certified results of an election, and each knew that the impact of a challenge might be catastrophic for the nation in general and his own future in specific. Tilden exited with a joke. "I think I can retire to private life," he said, "with the consciousness that I shall receive from posterity the credit of having been elected to the highest position in the gift of the people without any of the cares and responsibilities of the office." Nixon saw no benefit in a legal battle that he might easily lose. "Charges of 'sore loser' would follow me through history," he later explained, "and remove any possibility of a further political career."

Their strategic retreats served both men well. Tilden emerged as the frontrunner for the Democratic nomination in 1880, though he ultimately decided not to pursue it. His health had deteriorated since 1876 and would remain unstable until his death in 1886. Nixon, of course, resurfaced to win the presidency in 1968.

If Donald Trump had shown similar grace in 2020, he would have avoided most of his subsequent legal problems. It's easy to imagine that he would have been better positioned to take advantage of Joseph Biden's political weakness in 2024.

24. The Electoral College will overstate the margin of victory in 2024.

This prediction is a slam dunk. The Electoral College always makes an election appear to be more decisive than it actually was.

Consider the most recent example. Joseph Biden won a narrow majority of popular votes in 2020. Biden was supported by 81.28 million voters (51.31 percent), compared to Donald Trump's 74.22 million (46.85 percent). Biden's margin of 4.46 percentage points was undeniable, yet not overwhelming.

But the gap was considerably wider in the Electoral College, which Biden carried 306 to 232. Biden received 56.88 percent of all electoral votes, while Trump took the remaining 43.12 percent. That gave Biden a comfortable margin in the Electoral College of 13.76 points, more than triple his advantage in popular votes.

Precisely 50 elections have been conducted since voting by citizens became widespread in 1824. The same trend has occurred in all 50, with each victorious candidate drawing a higher percentage of electoral votes than popular votes, a natural consequence of the winner-take-all structure of the Electoral College. If a presidential hopeful carries a state by a narrow margin—even as small as a single popular vote—he receives all of its electoral votes.

Distortion is inevitable under such a system, often making a divided electorate appear to be cohesive. James Garfield squeaked past Winfield Hancock in 1880 by 0.09 percentage points, the smallest popular-vote margin in history. Yet the Electoral College had no doubts: Garfield 214, Hancock 155. The election of 1960 was the second-closest in popular-vote percentage, with John Kennedy and Richard Nixon separated by 0.17 points. But Kennedy easily carried the electoral-vote tally, 303 to 219.

The same process can transform a decisive win into a landslide of legendary proportions. That occurred twice for Ronald Reagan, who barely eked out a popular-vote majority in 1980's three-way race (50.75 percent), then fared considerably better in 1984 (58.77 percent). Both victories were comfortable, though neither was extraordinary. But the Electoral College misleadingly elevated Reagan to superhuman status as he topped 90 percent both times, successively burying Jimmy Carter (489-49) and Walter Mondale (525-13).

The electoral-vote system has many obvious shortcomings, but its distortion of the popular will is one of the worst. It implies that the winner enjoys a greater mandate than he has actually been given, and it suggests that the loser has been repudiated more soundly than is truly the case.

25. Something strange will happen.

Wait a second. Didn't this chapter promise to examine *24* likely trends? Consider this a bonus.

If anything is certain about the 2024 campaign—or any political campaign—it's that something completely unanticipated will occur. It's well and good to review historical trends, as we've done throughout the previous pages, but it's also wise to remember the disclaimer that appears at the bottom of investment advertisements: "Past performance is no guarantee of future results."

Let's be honest. Political crystal balls—even those that belong to esteemed pundits—are notoriously cloudy.

Who, for example, might have predicted in 1992 that the son of the incumbent president and the wife of his challenger would themselves receive major-party nominations in the future? Or who could have imagined in early 2008 that an obscure senator, a black man in a race-conscious country, would be the president-elect by year's end? Or who would have foreseen that the respective winners of the 2016 and 2020 elections would be the host of a reality TV show and a senator whose two previous presidential campaigns had ended quickly and badly?

The best rule for watching the 2024 election is a very simple one: Expect the unexpected.

The Rest of this Book

So much for the campaign that lies ahead. The rest of this book is concerned with the full string of presidential races from the dawn of independence up to modern times, all 59 elections between 1789 and 2020.

This initial future-oriented chapter is followed by four others that delve into the past by collecting and analyzing election returns in different ways:

■ **Chapter 2: Elections** — This section offers a series of statistical breakdowns for each campaign, summarizing the results of primary elections, party conventions, and general elections. Each candidate's performance is translated into his or her campaign score, which is unique to this volume.

■ **Chapter 3: Candidates** — A total of 308 men and women have been certified as 1789-2020 presidential candidates, based on qualification levels established by this book. Their career stats are collected here.

■ **Chapter 4: States** — Results of all elections since 1900 are gathered on a state-by-state basis in this chapter, along with basic statewide statistics and lists of home-state presidential candidates.

■ **Chapter 5: Records** — The final chapter is organized like a sports record book. It contains 173 lists of extreme accomplishments in presidential politics.

It's time for us to dive back into the past. Our first order of business—the initial topic in Chapter 2—is a 13-page explanation of the terms and statistics that are found throughout this book.

2. Elections

MANY OF THE FOUNDING FATHERS were surprisingly unenthusiastic about democracy. George Mason, a wealthy Virginia plantation owner and land baron, typified their disdain for the political instincts of the common man. "It would be [as] unnatural to refer the choice of a proper character for chief magistrate to the people," Mason scoffed, "as it would to refer a trial of colors to a blind man."

The Founders designed a safeguard to prevent the nation's farmers and laborers from participating in the election of the president of the United States. The Constitution established the Electoral College, a small assembly of political and financial elites. Each of its members would cast two votes. The candidate receiving the most support would become president, and the runner-up would be vice president. The middle and working classes would have no say whatsoever.

The Electoral College worked to perfection when it debuted in 1789. All 69 electors voted for George Washington. John Adams, the new vice president, finished a distant second with 34 electoral votes. No other contender received more than nine.

But the double-ballot system was inherently flawed, as became clear in 1800. The Democratic-Republican Party's nominees for president and vice president, Thomas Jefferson and Aaron Burr, received 73 electoral votes apiece, leaving it to the House of Representatives to break the tie, as stipulated by the Constitution. Lawmakers slogged through 36 roll calls before Jefferson emerged as the winner. The new president urged Congress to enact the 12th Amendment prior to the election of 1804, henceforth requiring members of the Electoral College to cast separate votes for president and vice president.

The amendment streamlined the Founders' political scheme without altering its underlying principle. The elites, acting through the Electoral

College, retained total control of the presidential selection process. The common people were still barred from participation.

This monopoly, of course, was destined to be challenged. The everyday Americans who were helping to build the new country inevitably demanded a voice in how it was run. A few states gradually allowed white men to vote for members of the Electoral College or for presidential candidates directly, a concession that would have horrified Mason and his associates. Isolated states and counties began distributing ballots in the early years of the 19th century, though it wasn't until 1824 that meaningful national popular-vote totals could be tabulated.

A second innovation followed in less than a decade. The Anti-Masonic Party, a fringe organization motivated by a rabid hatred of Freemasonry, decided to hold a national convention to choose its 1832 presidential nominee. The outcome should have raised doubts about the value of such gatherings. The Anti-Masons nominated William Wirt, a former Mason who fondly remembered his lodge as "a social and charitable club." Yet the major parties were impressed. They had previously relied on congressional caucuses and informal networks of state leaders to anoint their presidential candidates. They now decided to convene national meetings of their own.

The first conventions of the Democratic and National Republican parties were harmonious. The Democrats unanimously nominated Andrew Jackson for a second term in 1832, and 167 of 168 National Republican delegates endorsed Henry Clay. But subsequent conventions were often drenched in acrimony or indecision. The Whigs, for example, required 53 ballots to select a nominee in 1852, the same year the Democrats called the roll 49 times.

The convention remained the sole vehicle for nominating presidential candidates into the 20th century. That began to change with the advent of the primary election in 1912. Primaries were relatively insignificant at first—serving as simple barometers of public opinion—but they gained importance over time. No candidate can be nominated these days without running successfully in the primaries, especially the initial midwinter contests. The summer conventions merely rubber-stamp the decisions made by primary voters months before. There hasn't been a multi-ballot convention since 1952, and it's unlikely we will ever see another.

America's first nine presidential elections were remarkably simple affairs that focused solely on the Electoral College. The gradual introduction of additional layers—popular votes (1824), conventions (1832), and primaries (1912)—greatly lengthened the national political calendar and consequently increased the volume of statistics that were generated.

Qualification Levels

REGISTERING AS AN OFFICIAL CANDIDATE for president is remarkably easy. Visit the Federal Election Commission's website, download FEC Form 2, answer the eight questions, and send the completed document to Washington. That's all there is to it.

A total of 1,198 people filed the necessary paperwork in 2020, ranging alphabetically from Max Abramson and Matthew Abraugh to Darren Zook and Jeffrey Zorn. Their names are undoubtedly unfamiliar to you. That's because fewer than two dozen of the nearly 1,200 registrants mounted full-scale campaigns in 2020. Most of the others submitted their names on a lark or under the spell of a delusion.

It's essential to separate the serious contenders from the mass of carefree spirits, publicity seekers, minor-party fanatics, and occasional lunatics who clog the list of presidential candidates. This book stipulates five requirements—known as **qualification levels**—that address this need. If a candidate reaches any of these benchmarks in a given year, he or she is defined as a qualified candidate:

■ **Receive at least 3.95 percent of all votes cast in a party's primary elections,** with an added requirement that the candidate be listed on the ballots of at least two states. The latter provision eliminates so-called favorite-son candidates who run only in their home states, a fairly common occurrence prior to 1968.

■ **Receive at least 3.95 percent of all votes cast on the first ballot or last ballot (if there is more than one) at a major-party convention.** A candidate doesn't need to reach both of these thresholds. Either one suffices.

■ **Receive at least 1.95 percent of all popular votes** cast nationwide in a general election.

■ **Receive one or more electoral votes.**

■ The final level applies only to candidates in the modern period from 1960 to the present day: **Receive at least 3.95 percent of the votes cast within a given party in either the Iowa caucuses or the New Hampshire primary.** This rule acknowledges the inflated importance acquired by those two states in the nomination process.

A presidential hopeful needs to reach just one of these levels in a given year to be designated as a **qualified candidate**, thereby warranting inclusion in this book. Anybody who falls short of all five levels is labeled as nonqualified and is essentially ignored. (You might be curious, by the way, about the precision in a few of the rules above. Why 1.95 or 3.95 percent? Because they round to 2 or 4 percent, that's all.)

Parties and Nominees

A TOTAL OF 308 MEN and women have achieved official status in the 59 presidential elections since 1789, mounting 467 qualified candidacies in all. (Henry Clay and James Blaine share the record by qualifying in five elections apiece.) Most of these contenders belonged to the seven major parties recognized by this book, which are abbreviated this way:

D: Democratic (1832-present)
DR: Democratic-Republican (1789-1828)
F: Federalist (1789-1816)
NR: National Republican (1828-1832)
R: Republican (1856-present)
SD: Southern Democratic (1860)
W: Whig (1836-1852)

The only major party that might surprise you is the Southern Democratic Party, which split off from the main Democratic organization in 1860, surely the most contentious year in American political history. (Yes, even worse than 2020.) The two factional nominees—Democrat Stephen Douglas and Southern Democrat John Breckinridge—essentially battled to a draw. Douglas received more popular votes, Breckinridge more electoral votes. They went head to head in 29 states, with Breckinridge receiving more support in 15, Douglas in 14. It seems fair to treat both as major-party candidates.

It also should be explained why this book dates the Democratic-Republicans and Federalists back to 1789. No official parties contested that first campaign, but opposing factions were already bickering, and much to George Washington's great displeasure, they quickly blossomed into full-blown parties. "How unfortunate and how much it is to be regretted," Washington complained. But this split was a fact of political life from the very start. Its existence has been acknowledged by the insertion of the eventual political affiliations of 1789's qualified candidates.

The American political system has maintained a remarkable symmetry since those early skirmishes between the Federalists and Democratic-Republicans. The Federalists faded away after 1816, replaced in turn by National Republicans, Whigs, and Republicans. The Democratic-Republicans morphed into Democrats by 1832. This evolutionary process guaranteed that two major parties were (almost always) in the field at any given time, prepared to do battle.

This book recognizes 117 major-party nominees in the 59 presidential elections, an average of 1.98 per year. Nominations have been matters of official record since the first convention was held in 1832, but a bit of subjectivity is needed to designate nominees for selected contests between 1789 and 1828 (and a couple that came later):

■ George Washington is considered to be the only major-party nominee in 1789 and 1792. Plenty of other candidates received electoral votes in those two elections—primarily for vice president under the double-ballot system—but Washington was the dominant figure.

■ John Adams (Federalist) and Thomas Jefferson (Democratic-Republican) are listed as nominees in the remaining two double-ballot elections, 1796 and 1800. Jefferson tied with his running mate, Aaron Burr, in the Electoral College in 1800, but he clearly was his party's choice for president.

■ James Monroe faced no competition in 1820, the last election to feature only one major-party nominee.

■ The election of 1824 was a real mess. The Democratic-Republican congressional caucus formally nominated William Crawford, tapping him as the party's designated candidate. But it proved to be a hollow honor. Three-quarters of its members boycotted the caucus, opting to support other contenders. Andrew Jackson and John Quincy Adams emerged as the top candidates, and hence are considered by this book to be 1824's major-party nominees. Crawford suffered a stroke, which paralyzed and nearly blinded him. He played no major role in the fall campaign.

■ The Whigs chose a confusing strategy in 1836. They decided not to hold a convention, but rather to run a team of regional candidates for president. Two of those Whig standard-bearers—William Henry Harrison and Hugh White—received enough support to be considered official nominees.

■ We've already discussed the special case of 1860, the last election with more than two major-party nominations.

There are plenty of minor parties, too. You'll encounter 21 minor parties in the charts throughout this book. You'll even find a few cases where a single candidate is tied to a major party and minor party in the same election. If the two parties are linked by a hyphen, the candidate ran on both tickets at the same time. If they're separated by a slash, the candidate began in one party and switched in midstream to the second.

Here are the minor-party abbreviations:

AI: American Independent
AM: Anti-Masonic
AW: American-Whig
CU: Constitutional Union
FL: Farmer-Labor
FS: Free Soil
GBK: Greenback
GRN: Green
I: Independent
LIB: Libertarian
LR: Liberal Republican
LTY: Liberty
NU: National Unity
P: Progressive
POP: Populist
PRO: Prohibition
REF: Reform
SOC: Socialist
SRD: States' Rights Democratic
TC: Taxpayers and Constitution
U: Union

This is as good a place as any, I think, to insert an apology to anybody offended by the frequent use of masculine pronouns throughout this book. All of America's presidents—and almost all of the presidential candidates meeting the qualification standards—have been men. The use of "he" instead of "he or she" is meant to be simpler, not discriminatory.

So much for the basics. Let's move on to a discussion of concepts of a more advanced nature.

Political Analytics

THIS BOOK FEATURES FOUR ORIGINAL statistics—you might categorize them as "political analytics"—that were unveiled in my 2015 book, *Counting the Votes*. I explained each formula in great detail at the time, so I'm going to be relatively succinct here. If you'd like to examine the step-by-step process for generating any of these stats, I recommend that you refer to the earlier book.

Potential Index

The dictionary defines potential as "a quality that something has that can be developed to make it better" or "an ability that someone has that can be developed to help that person become successful." The key phrase in both of those definitions—"can be developed"—makes it clear that potential, by itself, is no guarantee of victory. If a candidate doesn't aspire to success, doesn't work with sufficient vigor, and doesn't benefit from an occasional fortuitous break, his or her potential is unlikely to be fulfilled.

American history is replete with politicians who appeared formidable on paper, yet were unable to fashion a rendezvous with destiny. They failed to develop their qualities and abilities, they picked the wrong times to launch campaigns, or they were simply and unavoidably unlucky.

I have calculated a **potential index (PI)** for each candidate, quantifying his or her possibility of success in a given election, based on an analysis of personal and political characteristics.

It's impossible to measure spirit, intensity, and other intangibles, of course, but the PI formula does capture nine important factors that help shape a candidate's potential:

$$PI = Siz + Reg + Age + Job + Maj + Sta + Fed - Min - Rep$$

History tells us that the odds of reaching the White House are better for a resident of a large state such as California or New York than a person who hails from tiny Wyoming or Alaska, better for a candidate in his 50s than somebody in his 30s or 70s (notwithstanding the recent victories by senior citizens), and better for a prominent senator or governor than a person who holds a more obscure position such as congressman or Cabinet member.

These principles drive the PI formula, which takes into account the size of a candidate's home state (*Siz*); the region in which that state is located (*Reg*); his age (*Age*); his current position (*Job*) in politics or business; and his previous experience on a major-party national ticket (*Maj*), in a state-wide political office (*Sta*), or in a federal post with a high profile (*Fed*). The formula deducts points from anybody who is a minor-party candidate (*Min*) or is a repeat contender with at least two previous presidential campaigns under his belt (*Rep*).

The points allocated to these nine factors are delineated in my 2015 book. What matters here is that the final result is expressed on a 10-point scale, rounded to a single decimal place. The higher the score, the stronger a candidate's potential.

There is a direct correlation between a candidate's PI and his or her likelihood of success. The odds of ultimate victory are three times better for somebody with an index of 8.0 to 10.0 than for a competitor in the range of 6.0 to 7.9. Only four candidates have been elected president despite potential indexes below 5.0: Zachary Taylor (1848), Herbert Hoover (1928), Donald Trump (2016), and Joseph Biden (2020).

Campaign Score

The overall performance of each qualified candidate—we're no longer dealing with potential, but with actual outcomes—is quantified in his **campaign score (CS)**. It's calculated on a 100-point scale and is rounded to two decimal places.

A candidate's CS is based on votes received in primary elections, conventions, and general elections, with bonuses for securing a major-party nomination and winning in November. Variations of the formula are applied to different eras, reflecting changes in political conditions. Candidates in the nation's earliest years, for example, did not run in primaries, advance to conventions, or receive popular votes. The formula takes these disparities into account.

The six versions of the CS formula are described at considerable length in *Counting the Votes*. All of them, regardless of era, have the same basic structure:

$$CS = Qua + Nom + Gen + Min + Win$$

Anybody who reaches one or more of the five qualification levels (*Qua*) is awarded 10 points. A major-party nominee (*Nom*) gets another 40 points, while each unsuccessful candidate for a nomination receives a lesser amount, based on his results in the primaries and at the convention. Anybody who draws support in the general election (*Gen*) receives a share of a 50-point pool, according to his percentages of electoral and popular votes. An independent or minor-party candidate (*Min*) is eligible for an allocation of as many as 30 points. And each general-election winner (*Win*) is awarded a bonus that equals one-tenth of his or her *Gen* score.

If you wish to know more, I refer you again to *Counting the Votes*. The key fact here is that CS is a remarkably good indicator of a candidate's success (or lack of same) in a given year. General-election winners typically land between 75 and 100 points, ranging from landslide victors in the 90s to nail-biters in the upper 70s. Major-party nominees who lose general elections are grouped from the 50s to the middle 70s. They're followed by significant minor-party candidates and strong (but ultimately unsuccessful) contenders for major-party nominations, who can be found in the 30s and 40s. The remaining qualified candidates—those who have little, if any, impact—are lumped between 10 and 29 on the CS spectrum.

Campaign scores are plotted on a standardized scale, facilitating direct comparisons of results from different elections. We can therefore say with justification that the most successful candidates of all time were George Washington (identical scores of 96.18 in 1789 and 1792), James Monroe (CS 96.04 in 1820), Franklin Roosevelt (CS 95.88 in 1936), Richard Nixon (CS 95.25 in 1972), and Ronald Reagan (CS 95.13 in 1984).

Return on Potential

Return on potential (ROP) determines whether a candidate fulfilled his or her promise in a given election. The underlying principle is the same as the one followed by portfolio managers when they calculate whether they're receiving a suitable return on their investments. It's a simple comparison of performance to potential.

The formula in this case is CS divided by PI. The result is multiplied by 10 and rounded to the nearest whole number.

If a candidate's ROP exceeds 100, he has done better than could have been expected. A two-digit score, on the other hand, is a sign that he has failed to meet his potential.

Donald Trump, for example, entered the 2016 race with a low potential index of 3.1, an appropriate figure for a 70-year-old political neophyte. But he stunned the experts by winning the Electoral College, an accomplishment reflected in his impressively high ROP of 254.

The 2020 campaign was a different matter. Trump's PI soared to 7.5, befitting his status as an incumbent president. Yet he lost the election by a sizable margin, a reversal reflected in his slightly subpar ROP of 96.

Equalized Statistics

It's meaningless to compare vote totals from different elections, especially those that were widely separated in time.

Ulysses Grant won the presidency in 1868 with slightly more than three million votes, while Joseph Biden secured his 2020 victory with an all-time record of 81.28 million. A mismatch in Biden's favor, don't you think? Not at all. Biden's total was 27 times larger, it's true, but his share of the popular vote (51.31 percent) was actually 1.35 percentage points smaller than Grant's (52.66 percent).

The reason for the vast disparity between the raw numbers for Grant and Biden is obvious. The American electorate is perpetually expanding. Only 5.7 million votes were cast in 1868, dwarfed by 2020's total of slightly more than 158.4 million.

The process of equalization eliminates time as a factor, paving the way for fair and sensible comparisons of results from different elections. It also allows us to contrast the career totals for different candidates.

There are five sets of equalized statistics, each denoted by the addition of a terminal X to a statistical abbreviation:

- **Equalized electoral votes (EVX)**
- **Equalized popular votes (PVX)**
- **Equalized first-ballot convention votes (ConFBX)**
- **Equalized last-ballot convention votes (ConLBX)**
- **Equalized primary votes (PriVX)**

All five formulas have the same simple structure, with a standard base being multiplied by a candidate's vote percentage. The respective bases are 538 votes for the Electoral College, 100 million popular votes for a general election, 1,000 votes for a party's convention, and 10 million votes for its primaries.

Let's glance back at Grant and Biden to see the process in action. Grant's share of 1868's general-election PV total, when carried to six decimal places, was 52.663724 percent. If multiply that figure by the base of 100 million votes, Grant ends up with 52,663,724 equalized popular votes. That's clearly superior to Biden's 2020 PVX of 51,305,744.

Equalization puts candidates from all eras on an equal footing. If a contender drew 40 percent of a year's electoral votes, he is consistently credited with an EVX of 215, no matter if he ran in 1808 (when only 175 electoral votes were actually cast) or 2020 (when the real total was 538).

An additional benefit is the ability to easily (and safely) add equalized statistics from different years. Franklin Roosevelt consequently emerges as the giant of presidential politics—the field's Babe Ruth, if you will—with his career EVX of 1,901 and his lifetime PVX of 226 million. Every other candidate in U.S. history is at least 40 percent behind the first total and 30 percent short of the second.

Election Breakdowns

THIS CHAPTER OFFERS A STATISTICAL breakdown of each of the 59 presidential elections between 1789 and 2020. They are, of course, displayed in chronological order.

The box scores for the early elections are fairly sparse, reflecting the electorate's limited participation and the correspondingly small yield of statistics. The political process—and its numerical output—grew more complicated through the years, expanding the entries in this book.

Here's what you'll find:

Basics

Election number: A simple count from the first presidential election (1789) to the 59th (2020).

Winner: The candidate who won the election, with his party affiliation in parentheses.

Incumbent: The sitting president (and his party) as of election day.

U.S. population: The official U.S. Census Bureau population for any year ending in zero, or an estimate by the author (through 1896) or the Census Bureau (since 1904) for any other year. The estimate for 1864 encompasses all of the United States, even those states that were in revolt.

States: The number of states that cast votes in the Electoral College. (The District of Columbia is counted as a state.)

Electoral votes: The number of electoral votes cast. (If one or more electors did not vote, the listed figure will not equal the total membership of the Electoral College.) The number indicated for each double-ballot election (1789-1800) is the number of electors, not the number of electoral votes cast.

Popular votes: The number of popular votes cast.

Voter turnout: The percentage of persons of voting age who participated in the election, as reported by the American Presidency Project at the University of California at Santa Barbara.

Top Candidates

This graph depicts the campaign scores for the year's three top-rated candidates. The winner's bar is black; the others are gray.

Field

Candidate: Any candidate who posted a campaign score of 10.00 or higher is listed, followed by his party abbreviation.

PI: Potential index.

Age: The candidate's age as of November 1 of the given year, rounded to two decimal places.

State: The state in which the candidate maintained a voting address.

Position: The position for which the candidate was best known, usually his current or most recent position.

N: Major-party nominees are designated by an X.

W: The general-election winner is designated by an X.

CS: Campaign score. Candidates are ranked from highest to lowest CS.

General Election

Candidate: This table includes any candidate in the field who received support in the general election. Candidates are ranked by EV, then PV.

EV: Electoral votes.

EV%: The percentage of all electoral votes cast. Percentages for each double-ballot election (1789-1800) are based on the number of electors.

SC: States carried. (If two or more candidates tied for the electoral-vote lead in a given state, each is credited with a state carried.)

PV: Popular votes.

PV%: The percentage of all popular votes cast.

Electoral Votes

Everybody who received electoral votes in a given year is included in this table. A candidate's national total is shown in parentheses after his or her surname, followed by a state-by-state breakdown of those votes.

Popular Votes

State: An alphabetical listing of states that cast popular votes.

Total PV: The total number of popular votes cast in each state.

Candidates: Columns for candidates are arrayed from left to right in order of their national totals of popular votes.

Nomination

Candidate: This table includes any candidate in the field who received convention and/or primary votes for a given party's nomination. Candidates are ranked in order of ConLB, then ConFB, then PriV.

ConFB: Votes received on the first ballot at a convention. Fractional totals have been rounded to the nearest whole number.

FB%: The percentage of all votes cast on the first ballot.

ConLB: Votes received on the last ballot at a multi-ballot convention. (The number of the last ballot is indicated in brackets.) Fractional votes have been rounded to the nearest whole number.

LB%: The percentage of all votes cast on the last ballot.

PriW: The number of primary elections won by a candidate.

PriV: The votes received in a party's primary elections.

PriV%: The percentage of all votes cast in a party's primary elections. Percentages may seem to be unusually low for many contenders prior to 1968. That's because of the prevalence of favorite-son candidates in those years. A favorite son—usually a governor or senator—ran only in his home state to maintain control of the state's convention delegation. Many of them drew significant numbers of primary votes. But favorite sons, by definition, failed to meet this book's qualification requirement that a candidate be listed on the primary ballots of at least two states. Hence they are not included in this table.

Equalized Statistics

Candidate: Any candidate who posted a campaign score of 10.00 or higher is listed here. Candidates are ranked in order of CS, though the score itself is not included in this table.

EVX: Equalized electoral votes, based on a national total of 538. Flip back three pages in this book for an explanation of the concept of equalization, which applies to all columns in this table.

PVX: Equalized popular votes, based on a national total of 100 million.

ConFBX: Equalized votes on the first ballot at a convention, based on a national total of 1,000.

ConLBX: Equalized votes on the last ballot at a multi-ballot convention, again out of a total of 1,000.

PriVX: Equalized votes received in a party's primary elections, based on a national total of 10 million.

Election of 1789

Basics — 1789

Election number — 1
Winner — George Washington (F)
Incumbent — none
U.S. population — 3,812,757
States — 10
Electoral votes — 69
Popular votes — n.a.
Voter turnout — n.a.

Top Candidates — 1789

George Washington (CS 96.18)

John Adams (CS 64.00)

John Jay (CS 51.15)

Field — 1789

Candidate	PI	Age	State	Position	N	W	CS
George Washington (F)	5.6	57.69	Va.	Former general	X	X	96.18
John Adams (F)	4.4	54.01	Mass.	Former ambassador	—	—	64.00
John Jay (F)	4.1	43.89	N.Y.	Cabinet member	—	—	51.15
Robert Harrison (F)	2.3	44.00	Md.	State judge	—	—	45.73
John Rutledge (F)	4.5	50.12	S.C.	Former governor	—	—	45.73
John Hancock (F)	4.3	52.77	Mass.	Governor	—	—	35.97
George Clinton (DR)	2.6	50.27	N.Y.	Governor	—	—	31.09
Samuel Huntington (F)	4.7	58.33	Conn.	Governor	—	—	26.29
John Milton (F)	3.1	49.00	Ga.	State official	—	—	26.29
James Armstrong (F)	4.0	61.00	Ga.	State official	—	—	21.42
Benjamin Lincoln (F)	4.8	56.77	Mass.	Former general	—	—	21.42
Edward Telfair (DR)	4.8	54.00	Ga.	Former governor	—	—	21.42

General Election — 1789

Candidate	EV	EV%	SC	PV	PV%
Washington	69	100.00%	10	—	—
Adams	34	49.28%	2	—	—
Jay	9	13.04%	1	—	—
Harrison	6	8.70%	1	—	—
Rutledge	6	8.70%	0	—	—
Hancock	4	5.80%	0	—	—
Clinton	3	4.35%	0	—	—

Candidate	EV	EV%	SC	PV	PV%
Huntington	2	2.90%	0	—	—
Milton	2	2.90%	0	—	—
Armstrong	1	1.45%	0	—	—
Lincoln	1	1.45%	0	—	—
Telfair	1	1.45%	0	—	—

Electoral Votes — 1789

Washington (69) — Connecticut (7), Delaware (3), Georgia (5), Maryland (6), Massachusetts (10), New Hampshire (5), New Jersey (6), Pennsylvania (10), South Carolina (7), Virginia (10)

Adams (34) — Connecticut (5), Massachusetts (10), New Hampshire (5), New Jersey (1), Pennsylvania (8), Virginia (5)

Jay (9) — Delaware (3), New Jersey (5), Virginia (1)

Harrison (6) — Maryland (6)

Rutledge (6) — South Carolina (6)

Hancock (4) — Pennsylvania (2), South Carolina (1), Virginia (1)

Clinton (3) — Virginia (3)

Huntington (2) — Connecticut (2)

Milton (2) — Georgia (2)

Armstrong (1) — Georgia (1)

Lincoln (1) — Georgia (1)

Telfair (1) — Georgia (1)

Equalized Statistics — 1789

Candidate	EVX	PVX	ConFBX	ConLBX	PriVX
Washington	538	—	—	—	—
Adams	265	—	—	—	—
Jay	70	—	—	—	—
Harrison	47	—	—	—	—
Rutledge	47	—	—	—	—
Hancock	31	—	—	—	—
Clinton	23	—	—	—	—
Huntington	16	—	—	—	—
Milton	16	—	—	—	—
Armstrong	8	—	—	—	—
Lincoln	8	—	—	—	—
Telfair	8	—	—	—	—

Election of 1792

Basics — 1792

Election number — 2
Winner — George Washington (F)
Incumbent — George Washington (F)
U.S. population — 4,172,906
States — 15
Electoral votes — 132
Popular votes — n.a.
Voter turnout — n.a.

Top Candidates — 1792

George Washington (CS 96.18)

John Adams (CS 67.23)

George Clinton (CS 59.98)

Field — 1792

Candidate	PI	Age	State	Position	N	W	CS
George Washington (F)	9.7	60.69	Va.	President	X	X	96.18
John Adams (F)	6.4	57.01	Mass.	Vice president	—	—	67.23
George Clinton (DR)	3.2	53.27	N.Y.	Governor	—	—	59.98
Thomas Jefferson (DR)	6.7	49.55	Va.	Cabinet member	—	—	26.68
Aaron Burr (DR)	4.7	36.73	N.Y.	Senator	—	—	19.07

General Election — 1792

Candidate	EV	EV%	SC	PV	PV%
Washington	132	100.00%	15	—	—
Adams	77	58.33%	8	—	—
Clinton	50	37.88%	4	—	—
Jefferson	4	3.03%	1	—	—
Burr	1	0.76%	0	—	—

Electoral Votes — 1792

Washington (132) — Connecticut (9), Delaware (3), Georgia (4), Kentucky (4), Maryland (8), Massachusetts (16), New Hampshire (6), New Jersey (7), New York (12), North Carolina (12), Pennsylvania (15), Rhode Island (4), South Carolina (8), Vermont (3), Virginia (21)

Adams (77) — Connecticut (9), Delaware (3), Maryland (8), Massachusetts (16), New Hampshire (6), New Jersey (7), Pennsylvania (14), Rhode Island (4), South Carolina (7), Vermont (3)

Clinton (50) — Georgia (4), New York (12), North Carolina (12), Pennsylvania (1), Virginia (21)

Jefferson (4) — Kentucky (4)

Burr (1) — South Carolina (1)

Equalized Statistics — 1792

Candidate	EVX	PVX	ConFBX	ConLBX	PriVX
Washington	538	—	—	—	—
Adams	314	—	—	—	—
Clinton	204	—	—	—	—
Jefferson	16	—	—	—	—
Burr	4	—	—	—	—

Election of 1796

Basics — 1796

Election number — 3
Winner — John Adams (F)
Incumbent — George Washington (F)
U.S. population — 4,706,570
States — 16
Electoral votes — 138
Popular votes — n.a.
Voter turnout — n.a.

Top Candidates — 1796

John Adams (CS 77.27)

Thomas Jefferson (CS 74.00)

Thomas Pinckney (CS 61.70)

Field — 1796

Candidate	PI	Age	State	Position	N	W	CS
John Adams (F)	5.7	61.01	Mass.	Vice president	X	X	77.27
Thomas Jefferson (DR)	6.9	53.55	Va.	Former Cabinet member	X	—	74.00
Thomas Pinckney (F)	4.1	46.02	S.C.	Ambassador	—	—	61.70
Aaron Burr (DR)	4.7	40.73	N.Y.	Senator	—	—	54.24
Samuel Adams (DR)	3.7	74.10	Mass.	Governor	—	—	50.36
Oliver Ellsworth (F)	4.8	51.51	Conn.	Supreme Court justice	—	—	43.29
George Clinton (DR)	3.0	57.27	N.Y.	Former governor	—	—	33.54
John Jay (F)	5.1	50.89	N.Y.	Governor	—	—	28.66
James Iredell (F)	3.6	45.07	N.C.	Supreme Court justice	—	—	23.85
John Henry (DR)	4.7	46.00	Md.	Senator	—	—	21.42
Samuel Johnston (F)	6.5	62.88	N.C.	Former senator	—	—	21.42
George Washington (F)	9.1	64.69	Va.	President	—	—	21.42
Charles C. Pinckney (F)	3.9	50.68	S.C.	Ambassador	—	—	18.98

General Election — 1796

Candidate	EV	EV%	SC	PV	PV%
J. Adams	71	51.45%	9	—	—
Jefferson	68	49.28%	7	—	—
T. Pinckney	59	42.75%	5	—	—
Burr	30	21.74%	2	—	—
S. Adams	15	10.87%	0	—	—
Ellsworth	11	7.97%	2	—	—

Candidate	EV	EV%	SC	PV	PV%
Clinton	7	5.07%	1	—	—
Jay	5	3.62%	0	—	—
Iredell	3	2.17%	0	—	—
Henry	2	1.45%	0	—	—
Johnston	2	1.45%	0	—	—
Washington	2	1.45%	0	—	—
C. Pinckney	1	0.73%	0	—	—

Electoral Votes — 1796

J. Adams (71) — Connecticut (9), Delaware (3), Maryland (7), Massachusetts (16), New Hampshire (6), New Jersey (7), New York (12), North Carolina (1), Pennsylvania (1), Rhode Island (4), Vermont (4), Virginia (1)

Jefferson (68) — Georgia (4), Kentucky (4), Maryland (4), North Carolina (11), Pennsylvania (14), South Carolina (8), Tennessee (3), Virginia (20)

T. Pinckney (59) — Connecticut (4), Delaware (3), Maryland (4), Massachusetts (13), New Jersey (7), New York (12), North Carolina (1), Pennsylvania (2), South Carolina (8), Vermont (4), Virginia (1)

Burr (30) — Kentucky (4), Maryland (3), North Carolina (6), Pennsylvania (13), Tennessee (3), Virginia (1)

S. Adams (15) — Virginia (15)

Ellsworth (11) — Massachusetts (1), New Hampshire (6), Rhode Island (4)

Clinton (7) — Georgia (4), Virginia (3)

Jay (5) — Connecticut (5)

Iredell (3) — North Carolina (3)

Henry (2) — Maryland (2)

Johnston (2) — Massachusetts (2)

Washington (2) — North Carolina (1), Virginia (1)

C. Pinckney (1) — North Carolina (1)

Equalized Statistics — 1796

Candidate	EVX	PVX	ConFBX	ConLBX	PriVX
J. Adams	277	—	—	—	—
Jefferson	265	—	—	—	—
T. Pinckney	230	—	—	—	—
Burr	117	—	—	—	—
S. Adams	58	—	—	—	—
Ellsworth	43	—	—	—	—
Clinton	27	—	—	—	—
Jay	19	—	—	—	—
Iredell	12	—	—	—	—
Henry	8	—	—	—	—
Johnston	8	—	—	—	—
Washington	8	—	—	—	—
C. Pinckney	4	—	—	—	—

Election of 1800

Basics — 1800

Election number — 4
Winner — Thomas Jefferson (DR)
Incumbent — John Adams (F)
U.S. population — 5,308,483
States — 16
Electoral votes — 138
Popular votes — n.a.
Voter turnout — n.a.

Top Candidates — 1800

Thomas Jefferson (CS 77.84)

John Adams (CS 73.21)

Aaron Burr (CS 65.31)

Field — 1800

Candidate	PI	Age	State	Position	N	W	CS
Thomas Jefferson (DR)	7.6	57.55	Va.	Vice president	X	X	77.84
John Adams (F)	7.2	65.01	Mass.	President	X	—	73.21
Aaron Burr (DR)	4.9	44.73	N.Y.	Former senator	—	—	65.31
Charles C. Pinckney (F)	4.4	54.68	S.C.	Former ambassador	—	—	63.01
John Jay (F)	3.3	54.89	N.Y.	Governor	—	—	18.98

General Election — 1800

Candidate	EV	EV%	SC	PV	PV%
Jefferson	73	52.90%	9	—	—
Burr	73	52.90%	9	—	—
Adams	65	47.10%	8	—	—
Pinckney	64	46.38%	7	—	—
Jay	1	0.73%	0	—	—

NOTE: Jefferson was elected president by the House of Representatives on the 36th ballot. The final vote was 10 states for Jefferson, 4 states for Burr, 2 states abstaining.

Electoral Votes — 1800

Jefferson (73) — Georgia (4), Kentucky (4), Maryland (5), New York (12), North Carolina (8), Pennsylvania (8), South Carolina (8), Tennessee (3), Virginia (21)

Burr (73) — Georgia (4), Kentucky (4), Maryland (5), New York (12), North Carolina (8), Pennsylvania (8), South Carolina (8), Tennessee (3), Virginia (21)

Adams (65) — Connecticut (9), Delaware (3), Maryland (5), Massachusetts (16), New Hampshire (6), New Jersey (7), North Carolina (4), Pennsylvania (7), Rhode Island (4), Vermont (4)

Pinckney (64) — Connecticut (9), Delaware (3), Maryland (5), Massachusetts (16), New Hampshire (6), New Jersey (7), North Carolina (4), Pennsylvania (7), Rhode Island (3), Vermont (4)

Jay (1) — Rhode Island (1)

Equalized Statistics — 1800

Candidate	EVX	PVX	ConFBX	ConLBX	PriVX
Jefferson	285	—	—	—	—
Adams	253	—	—	—	—
Burr	285	—	—	—	—
Pinckney	250	—	—	—	—
Jay	4	—	—	—	—

Election of 1804

Basics — 1804

Election number — 5
Winner — Thomas Jefferson (DR)
Incumbent — Thomas Jefferson (DR)
U.S. population — 6,010,004
States — 17
Electoral votes — 176
Popular votes — n.a.
Voter turnout — n.a.

Top Candidates — 1804

Thomas Jefferson (CS 93.05)

Charles Cotesworth Pinckney (CS 59.38)

Field — 1804

Candidate	PI	Age	State	Position	N	W	CS
Thomas Jefferson (DR)	9.2	61.55	Va.	President	X	X	93.05
Charles C. Pinckney (F)	5.1	58.68	S.C.	Former ambassador	X	—	59.38

General Election — 1804

Candidate	EV	EV%	SC	PV	PV%
Jefferson	162	92.05%	15	—	—
Pinckney	14	7.96%	2	—	—

Electoral Votes — 1804

Jefferson (162) — Georgia (6), Kentucky (8), Maryland (9), Massachusetts (19), New Hampshire (7), New Jersey (8), New York (19), North Carolina (14), Ohio (3), Pennsylvania (20), Rhode Island (4), South Carolina (10), Tennessee (5), Vermont (6), Virginia (24)
Pinckney (14) — Connecticut (9), Delaware (3), Maryland (2)

Equalized Statistics — 1804

Candidate	EVX	PVX	ConFBX	ConLBX	PriVX
Jefferson	495	—	—	—	—
Pinckney	43	—	—	—	—

Election of 1808

Basics — 1808

Election number — 6
Winner — James Madison (DR)
Incumbent — Thomas Jefferson (DR)
U.S. population — 6,804,233
States — 17
Electoral votes — 175
Popular votes — n.a.
Voter turnout — n.a.

Top Candidates — 1808

James Madison (CS 84.36)

Charles Cotesworth Pinckney (CS 66.03)

George Clinton (CS 28.01)

Field — 1808

Candidate	PI	Age	State	Position	N	W	CS
James Madison (DR)	6.8	57.63	Va.	Cabinet member	X	X	84.36
Charles C. Pinckney (F)	3.9	62.68	S.C.	Former nominee	X	—	66.03
George Clinton (DR)	4.0	69.27	N.Y.	Vice president	—	—	28.01

General Election — 1808

Candidate	EV	EV%	SC	PV	PV%
Madison	122	69.71%	12	—	—
Pinckney	47	26.86%	5	—	—
Clinton	6	3.43%	0	—	—

Electoral Votes — 1808

Madison (122) — Georgia (6), Kentucky (7), Maryland (9), New Jersey (8), New York (13), North Carolina (11), Ohio (3), Pennsylvania (20), South Carolina (10), Tennessee (5), Vermont (6), Virginia (24)

Pinckney (47) — Connecticut (9), Delaware (3), Maryland (2), Massachusetts (19), New Hampshire (7), North Carolina (3), Rhode Island (4)

Clinton (6) — New York (6)

Equalized Statistics — 1808

Candidate	EVX	PVX	ConFBX	ConLBX	PriVX
Madison	375	—	—	—	—
Pinckney	144	—	—	—	—
Clinton	18	—	—	—	—

Election of 1812

Basics — 1812

Election number — 7
Winner — James Madison (DR)
Incumbent — James Madison (DR)
U.S. population — 7,666,314
States — 18
Electoral votes — 217
Popular votes — n.a.
Voter turnout — n.a.

Top Candidates — 1812

James Madison (CS 80.17)

DeWitt Clinton (CS 71.10)

Field — 1812

Candidate	PI	Age	State	Position	N	W	CS
James Madison (DR)	8.7	61.63	Va.	President	X	X	80.17
DeWitt Clinton (F-DR)	3.7	43.67	N.Y.	Mayor	X	—	71.10

General Election — 1812

Candidate	EV	EV%	SC	PV	PV%
Madison	128	58.99%	11	—	—
Clinton	89	41.01%	7	—	—

Electoral Votes — 1812

Madison (128) — Georgia (8), Kentucky (12), Louisiana (3), Maryland (6), North Carolina (15), Ohio (7), Pennsylvania (25), South Carolina (11), Tennessee (8), Vermont (8), Virginia (25)

Clinton (89) — Connecticut (9), Delaware (4), Maryland (5), Massachusetts (22), New Hampshire (8), New Jersey (8), New York (29), Rhode Island (4)

Equalized Statistics — 1812

Candidate	EVX	PVX	ConFBX	ConLBX	PriVX
Madison	317	—	—	—	—
Clinton	221	—	—	—	—

Election of 1816

Basics — 1816

Election number — 8
Winner — James Monroe (DR)
Incumbent — James Madison (DR)
U.S. population — 8,596,011
States — 19
Electoral votes — 217
Popular votes — n.a.
Voter turnout — n.a.

Top Candidates — 1816

James Monroe (CS 90.10)

Rufus King (CS 62.07)

Field — 1816

Candidate	PI	Age	State	Position	N	W	CS
James Monroe (DR)	7.3	58.51	Va.	Cabinet member	X	X	90.10
Rufus King (F)	7.1	61.61	N.Y.	Senator	X	—	62.07

General Election — 1816

Candidate	EV	EV%	SC	PV	PV%
Monroe	183	84.33%	16	—	—
King	34	15.67%	3	—	—

Electoral Votes — 1816

Monroe (183) — Georgia (8), Indiana (3), Kentucky (12), Louisiana (3), Maryland (8), New Hampshire (8), New Jersey (8), New York (29), North Carolina (15), Ohio (8), Pennsylvania (25), Rhode Island (4), South Carolina (11), Tennessee (8), Vermont (8), Virginia (25)
King (34) — Connecticut (9), Delaware (3), Massachusetts (22)

Equalized Statistics — 1816

Candidate	EVX	PVX	ConFBX	ConLBX	PriVX
Monroe	454	—	—	—	—
King	84	—	—	—	—

Election of 1820

Basics — 1820

Election number — 9
Winner — James Monroe (DR)
Incumbent — James Monroe (DR)
U.S. population — 9,638,453
States — 24
Electoral votes — 232
Popular votes — n.a.
Voter turnout — n.a.

Top Candidates — 1820

James Monroe (CS 96.04)

John Quincy Adams (CS 17.96)

Field — 1820

Candidate	PI	Age	State	Position	N	W	CS
James Monroe (DR)	8.7	62.51	Va.	President	X	X	96.04
John Quincy Adams (DR)	5.0	53.31	Mass.	Cabinet member	—	—	17.96

General Election — 1820

Candidate	EV	EV%	SC	PV	PV%
Monroe	231	99.57%	24	—	—
Adams	1	0.43%	0	—	—

Electoral Votes — 1820

Monroe (231) — Alabama (3), Connecticut (9), Delaware (4), Georgia (8), Illinois (3), Indiana (3), Kentucky (12), Louisiana (3), Maine (9), Maryland (11), Massachusetts (15), Mississippi (2), Missouri (3), New Hampshire (7), New Jersey (8), New York (29), North Carolina (15), Ohio (8), Pennsylvania (24), Rhode Island (4), South Carolina (11), Tennessee (7), Vermont (8), Virginia (25)
Adams (1) — New Hampshire (1)

Equalized Statistics — 1820

Candidate	EVX	PVX	ConFBX	ConLBX	PriVX
Monroe	536	—	—	—	—
Adams	2	—	—	—	—

Election of 1824

Basics — 1824

Election number — 10
Winner — John Quincy Adams (DR)
Incumbent — James Monroe (DR)
U.S. population — 10,818,874
States — 24
Electoral votes — 261
Popular votes — 365,833
Voter turnout — 26.9%

Top Candidates — 1824

Andrew Jackson (CS 69.65)

John Quincy Adams (CS 67.41)

William Crawford (CS 46.97)

Field — 1824

Candidate	PI	Age	State	Position	N	W	CS
Andrew Jackson (DR)	5.9	57.63	Tenn.	Senator	X	—	69.65
John Quincy Adams (DR)	5.6	57.31	Mass.	Cabinet member	X	X	67.41
William Crawford (DR)	5.4	52.69	Ga.	Cabinet member	—	—	46.97
Henry Clay (DR)	3.7	47.55	Ky.	Representative	—	—	46.84

General Election — 1824

Candidate	EV	EV%	SC	PV	PV%
Jackson	99	37.93%	11	151,271	41.35%
Adams	84	32.18%	7	113,122	30.92%
Crawford	41	15.71%	3	40,856	11.17%
Clay	37	14.18%	3	47,531	12.99%

NOTE: Adams was elected president by the House of Representatives on the first ballot. The final vote was 13 states for Adams, 7 states for Jackson, 4 states for Crawford.

Electoral Votes — 1824

Jackson (99) — Alabama (5), Illinois (2), Indiana (5), Louisiana (3), Maryland (7), Mississippi (3), New Jersey (8), New York (1), North Carolina (15), Pennsylvania (28), South Carolina (11), Tennessee (11)

Adams (84) — Connecticut (8), Delaware (1), Illinois (1), Louisiana (2), Maine (9), Maryland (3), Massachusetts (15), New Hampshire (8), New York (26), Rhode Island (4), Vermont (7)

Crawford (41) — Delaware (2), Georgia (9), Maryland (1), New York (5), Virginia (24)

Clay (37) — Kentucky (14), Missouri (3), New York (4), Ohio (16)

Popular Votes — 1824

State	Total PV	Jackson	Adams	Clay	Crawford	Other
Alabama	13,603	9,429	2,422	96	1,656	—
Connecticut	10,647	—	7,494	—	1,965	1,188
Delaware	—	—	—	—	—	—
Georgia	—	—	—	—	—	—
Illinois	4,671	1,272	1,516	1,036	847	—
Indiana	15,838	7,444	3,071	5,316	—	7
Kentucky	23,338	6,356	—	16,982	—	—
Louisiana	—	—	—	—	—	—
Maine	12,625	—	10,289	—	2,336	—
Maryland	33,214	14,523	14,632	695	3,364	—
Massachusetts	42,056	—	30,687	—	—	11,369
Mississippi	4,894	3,121	1,654	—	119	—
Missouri	3,432	1,166	159	2,042	32	33
New Hampshire	10,032	—	9,389	—	643	—
New Jersey	19,837	10,332	8,309	—	1,196	—
New York	—	—	—	—	—	—
North Carolina	36,109	20,231	—	—	15,622	256
Ohio	50,024	18,489	12,280	19,255	—	—
Pennsylvania	47,073	35,736	5,441	1,690	4,206	—
Rhode Island	2,344	—	2,144	—	—	200
South Carolina	—	—	—	—	—	—
Tennessee	20,725	20,197	216	—	312	—
Vermont	—	—	—	—	—	—
Virginia	15,371	2,975	3,419	419	8,558	—
Total	365,833	151,271	113,122	47,531	40,856	13,053

Equalized Statistics — 1824

Candidate	EVX	PVX	ConFBX	ConLBX	PriVX
Jackson	204	41,349,742	—	—	—
Adams	173	30,921,759	—	—	—
Crawford	85	11,167,937	—	—	—
Clay	76	12,992,540	—	—	—

Election of 1828

Basics — 1828

Election number — 11
Winner — Andrew Jackson (DR)
Incumbent — John Quincy Adams (NR)
U.S. population — 12,143,862
States — 24
Electoral votes — 261
Popular votes — 1,148,018
Voter turnout — 57.6%

Top Candidates — 1828

Andrew Jackson (CS 84.82)

John Quincy Adams (CS 68.27)

Field — 1828

Candidate	PI	Age	State	Position	N	W	CS
Andrew Jackson (DR)	6.9	61.63	Tenn.	Former senator	X	X	84.82
John Quincy Adams (NR)	7.7	61.31	Mass.	President	X	—	68.27

General Election — 1828

Candidate	EV	EV%	SC	PV	PV%
Jackson	178	68.20%	15	642,553	55.97%
Adams	83	31.80%	9	500,897	43.63%

Electoral Votes — 1828

Jackson (178) — Alabama (5), Georgia (9), Illinois (3), Indiana (5), Kentucky (14), Louisiana (5), Maine (1), Maryland (5), Mississippi (3), Missouri (3), New York (20), North Carolina (15), Ohio (16), Pennsylvania (28), South Carolina (11), Tennessee (11), Virginia (24)

Adams (83) — Connecticut (8), Delaware (3), Maine (8), Maryland (6), Massachusetts (15), New Hampshire (8), New Jersey (8), New York (16), Rhode Island (4), Vermont (7)

Popular Votes — 1828

State	Total PV	Jackson	Adams	Other
Alabama	18,618	16,736	1,878	4
Connecticut	19,378	4,448	13,829	1,101
Delaware	—	—	—	—
Georgia	20,004	19,362	642	—
Illinois	14,222	9,560	4,662	—
Indiana	39,210	22,201	17,009	—
Kentucky	70,776	39,308	31,468	—
Louisiana	8,687	4,605	4,082	—
Maine	34,789	13,927	20,773	89
Maryland	45,796	22,782	23,014	—
Massachusetts	39,074	6,012	29,836	3,226
Mississippi	8,344	6,763	1,581	—
Missouri	11,654	8,232	3,422	—
New Hampshire	44,035	20,212	23,823	—
New Jersey	45,570	21,809	23,753	8
New York	270,975	139,412	131,563	—
North Carolina	51,747	37,814	13,918	15
Ohio	131,049	67,596	63,453	—
Pennsylvania	152,220	101,457	50,763	—
Rhode Island	3,580	820	2,755	5
South Carolina	—	—	—	—
Tennessee	46,533	44,293	2,240	—
Vermont	32,833	8,350	24,363	120
Virginia	38,924	26,854	12,070	—
Total	1,148,018	642,553	500,897	4,568

Equalized Statistics — 1828

Candidate	EVX	PVX	ConFBX	ConLBX	PriVX
Jackson	367	55,970,638	—	—	—
Adams	171	43,631,459	—	—	—

Election of 1832

Basics — 1832

Election number — 12
Winner — Andrew Jackson (D)
Incumbent — Andrew Jackson (D)
U.S. population — 13,614,424
States — 24
Electoral votes — 286
Popular votes — 1,293,973
Voter turnout — 55.4%

Top Candidates — 1832

Andrew Jackson (CS 87.20)

Henry Clay (CS 62.61)

William Wirt (CS 35.63)

Field — 1832

Candidate	PI	Age	State	Position	N	W	CS
Andrew Jackson (D)	7.8	65.63	Tenn.	President	X	X	87.20
Henry Clay (NR)	6.4	55.55	Ky.	Senator	X	—	62.61
William Wirt (AM)	3.9	59.98	Md.	Former Cabinet member	—	—	35.63
John Floyd (D)	4.2	49.52	Va.	Governor	—	—	22.71

General Election — 1832

Candidate	EV	EV%	SC	PV	PV%
Jackson	219	76.57%	16	701,780	54.24%
Clay	49	17.13%	6	484,205	37.42%
Floyd	11	3.85%	1	0	0.00%
Wirt	7	2.45%	1	100,715	7.78%

Electoral Votes — 1832

Jackson (219) — Alabama (7), Georgia (11), Illinois (5), Indiana (9), Louisiana (5), Maine (10), Maryland (3), Mississippi (4), Missouri (4), New Hampshire (7), New Jersey (8), New York (42), North Carolina (15), Ohio (21), Pennsylvania (30), Tennessee (15), Virginia (23)
Clay (49) — Connecticut (8), Delaware (3), Kentucky (15), Maryland (5), Massachusetts (14), Rhode Island (4)
Floyd (11) — South Carolina (11)
Wirt (7) — Vermont (7)

Popular Votes — 1832

State	Total PV	Jackson	Clay	Wirt	Other
Alabama	14,291	14,286	5	—	—
Connecticut	32,833	11,269	18,155	3,409	—
Delaware	8,386	4,110	4,276	—	—
Georgia	20,750	20,750	—	—	—
Illinois	21,481	14,609	6,745	97	30
Indiana	57,152	31,652	25,473	27	—
Kentucky	79,741	36,292	43,449	—	—
Louisiana	6,337	3,908	2,429	—	—
Maine	62,153	33,978	27,331	844	—
Maryland	38,316	19,156	19,160	—	—
Massachusetts	67,619	13,933	31,963	14,692	7,031
Mississippi	5,750	5,750	—	—	—
Missouri	5,192	5,192	—	—	—
New Hampshire	43,793	24,855	18,938	—	—
New Jersey	47,760	23,826	23,466	468	—
New York	323,393	168,497	154,896	—	—
North Carolina	29,799	25,261	4,538	—	—
Ohio	158,350	81,246	76,566	538	—
Pennsylvania	157,679	90,973	—	66,706	—
Rhode Island	5,747	2,051	2,871	819	6
South Carolina	—	—	—	—	—
Tennessee	29,425	28,078	1,347	—	—
Vermont	32,344	7,865	11,161	13,112	206
Virginia	45,682	34,243	11,436	3	—
Total	1,293,973	701,780	484,205	100,715	7,273

Democratic Nomination — 1832

Candidate	ConFB	FB%	ConLB	LB%	PriW	PriV	PriV%
Jackson	283	100.00%	—	—	—	—	—

National Republican Nomination — 1832

Candidate	ConFB	FB%	ConLB	LB%	PriW	PriV	PriV%
Clay	167	99.41%	—	—	—	—	—

Equalized Statistics — 1832

Candidate	EVX	PVX	ConFBX	ConLBX	PriVX
Jackson	412	54,234,516	1,000	—	—
Clay	92	37,420,023	994	—	—
Wirt	13	7,783,393	—	—	—
Floyd	21	0	—	—	—

Election of 1836

Basics — 1836

Election number — 13
Winner — Martin Van Buren (D)
Incumbent — Andrew Jackson (D)
U.S. population — 15,244,368
States — 26
Electoral votes — 294
Popular votes — 1,503,534
Voter turnout — 57.8%

Top Candidates — 1836

Martin Van Buren (CS 80.26)

William Henry Harrison (CS 64.80)

Hugh White (CS 54.62)

Field — 1836

Candidate	PI	Age	State	Position	N	W	CS
Martin Van Buren (D)	6.8	53.91	N.Y.	Vice president	X	X	80.26
William Henry Harrison (W)	4.9	63.73	Ohio	Former senator	X	—	64.80
Hugh White (W)	6.3	63.01	Tenn.	Senator	X	—	54.62
Daniel Webster (W)	5.0	54.79	Mass.	Senator	—	—	26.29
Willie Person Mangum (W)	5.4	44.48	N.C.	Senator	—	—	22.34

General Election — 1836

Candidate	EV	EV%	SC	PV	PV%
Van Buren	170	57.82%	15	764,176	50.83%
Harrison	73	24.83%	7	550,816	36.64%
White	26	8.84%	2	146,107	9.72%
Webster	14	4.76%	1	41,201	2.74%
Mangum	11	3.74%	1	0	0.00%

Electoral Votes — 1836

Van Buren (170) — Alabama (7), Arkansas (3), Connecticut (8), Illinois (5), Louisiana (5), Maine (10), Michigan (3), Mississippi (4), Missouri (4), New Hampshire (7), New York (42), North Carolina (15), Pennsylvania (30), Rhode Island (4), Virginia (23)
Harrison (73) — Delaware (3), Indiana (9), Kentucky (15), Maryland (10), New Jersey (8), Ohio (21), Vermont (7)

White (26) — Georgia (11), Tennessee (15)
Webster (14) — Massachusetts (14)
Mangum (11) — South Carolina (11)

Popular Votes — 1836

State	Total PV	Van Buren	Harrison	White	Webster	Other
Alabama	37,296	20,638	—	16,658	—	—
Arkansas	3,714	2,380	—	1,334	—	—
Connecticut	38,093	19,294	18,799	—	—	—
Delaware	8,895	4,154	4,736	—	—	5
Georgia	47,259	22,778	—	24,481	—	—
Illinois	33,589	18,369	15,220	—	—	—
Indiana	74,423	33,084	41,339	—	—	—
Kentucky	70,090	33,229	36,861	—	—	—
Louisiana	7,425	3,842	—	3,583	—	—
Maine	38,740	22,825	14,803	—	—	1,112
Maryland	48,119	22,267	25,852	—	—	—
Massachusetts	74,732	33,486	—	—	41,201	45
Michigan	12,052	6,507	5,545	—	—	—
Mississippi	20,079	10,297	—	9,782	—	—
Missouri	18,332	10,995	—	7,337	—	—
New Hampshire	24,925	18,697	6,228	—	—	—
New Jersey	51,729	25,592	26,137	—	—	—
New York	305,343	166,795	138,548	—	—	—
North Carolina	50,153	26,631	—	23,521	—	1
Ohio	202,931	97,122	105,809	—	—	—
Pennsylvania	178,701	91,466	87,235	—	—	—
Rhode Island	5,673	2,962	2,710	—	—	1
South Carolina	—	—	—	—	—	—
Tennessee	62,197	26,170	—	36,027	—	—
Vermont	35,099	14,040	20,994	—	—	65
Virginia	53,945	30,556	—	23,384	—	5
Total	1,503,534	764,176	550,816	146,107	41,201	1,234

Democratic Nomination — 1836

Candidate	ConFB	FB%	ConLB	LB%	PriW	PriV	PriV%
Van Buren	265	100.00%	—	—	—	—	—

Whig Nomination — 1836

(No convention)

Equalized Statistics — 1836

Candidate	EVX	PVX	ConFBX	ConLBX	PriVX
Van Buren	311	50,825,322	1,000	—	—
Harrison	134	36,634,755	—	—	—
White	48	9,717,572	—	—	—
Webster	26	2,740,277	—	—	—
Mangum	20	0	—	—	—

Election of 1840

Basics — 1840

Election number — 14
Winner — William Henry Harrison (W)
Incumbent — Martin Van Buren (D)
U.S. population — 17,069,453
States — 26
Electoral votes — 294
Popular votes — 2,411,808
Voter turnout — 80.2%

Top Candidates — 1840

William Henry Harrison (CS 87.90)

Martin Van Buren (CS 65.49)

Henry Clay (CS 42.42)

Field — 1840

Candidate	PI	Age	State	Position	N	W	CS
William Henry Harrison (W)	8.7	67.73	Ohio	Former senator	X	X	87.90
Martin Van Buren (D)	9.1	57.91	N.Y.	President	X	—	65.49
Henry Clay (W)	6.7	63.55	Ky.	Former nominee	—	—	42.42
Winfield Scott (W)	5.8	54.39	N.J.	General	—	—	27.88

General Election — 1840

Candidate	EV	EV%	SC	PV	PV%
Harrison	234	79.59%	19	1,275,390	52.88%
Van Buren	60	20.41%	7	1,128,854	46.81%

Electoral Votes — 1840

Harrison (234) — Connecticut (8), Delaware (3), Georgia (11), Indiana (9), Kentucky (15), Louisiana (5), Maine (10), Maryland (10), Massachusetts (14), Michigan (3), Mississippi (4), New Jersey (8), New York (42), North Carolina (15), Ohio (21), Pennsylvania (30), Rhode Island (4), Tennessee (15), Vermont (7)
Van Buren (60) — Alabama (7), Arkansas (3), Illinois (5), Missouri (4), New Hampshire (7), South Carolina (11), Virginia (23)

Popular Votes — 1840

State	Total PV	Harrison	Van Buren	Other
Alabama	62,511	28,515	33,996	—
Arkansas	11,839	5,160	6,679	—
Connecticut	56,879	31,598	25,281	—
Delaware	10,852	5,967	4,872	13
Georgia	72,322	40,339	31,983	—
Illinois	93,175	45,574	47,441	160
Indiana	117,605	65,280	51,696	629
Kentucky	91,104	58,488	32,616	—
Louisiana	18,912	11,296	7,616	—
Maine	92,802	46,612	46,190	—
Maryland	62,280	33,528	28,752	—
Massachusetts	126,825	72,852	52,355	1,618
Michigan	44,029	22,933	21,096	—
Mississippi	36,525	19,515	17,010	—
Missouri	52,923	22,954	29,969	—
New Hampshire	59,956	26,310	32,774	872
New Jersey	64,454	33,351	31,034	69
New York	441,543	226,001	212,733	2,809
North Carolina	80,735	46,567	34,168	—
Ohio	272,890	148,043	123,944	903
Pennsylvania	287,695	144,023	143,672	—
Rhode Island	8,631	5,213	3,263	155
South Carolina	—	—	—	—
Tennessee	108,145	60,194	47,951	—
Vermont	50,782	32,440	18,006	336
Virginia	86,394	42,637	43,757	—
Total	2,411,808	1,275,390	1,128,854	7,564

Democratic Nomination — 1840

Candidate	ConFB	FB%	ConLB	LB%	PriW	PriV	PriV%
Van Buren	244	100.00%	—	—	—	—	—

Whig Nomination — 1840

Candidate	ConFB	FB%	ConLB[5]	LB%	PriW	PriV	PriV%
Harrison	91	35.83%	148	58.27%	—	—	—
Clay	103	40.55%	90	35.43%	—	—	—
Scott	57	22.44%	16	6.30%	—	—	—

Equalized Statistics — 1840

Candidate	EVX	PVX	ConFBX	ConLBX	PriVX
Harrison	428	52,881,075	358	583	—
Van Buren	110	46,805,301	1,000	—	—
Clay	—	—	406	354	—
Scott	—	—	224	63	—

Election of 1844

Basics — 1844

Election number — 15
Winner — James Polk (D)
Incumbent — John Tyler (I)
U.S. population — 19,295,947
States — 26
Electoral votes — 275
Popular votes — 2,703,659
Voter turnout — 78.9%

Top Candidates — 1844

James Polk (CS 81.33)

Henry Clay (CS 71.05)

Martin Van Buren (CS 50.00)

Field — 1844

Candidate	PI	Age	State	Position	N	W	CS
James Polk (D)	6.7	49.00	Tenn.	Former governor	X	X	81.33
Henry Clay (W)	5.6	67.55	Ky.	Former nominee	X	—	71.05
Martin Van Buren (D)	8.7	61.91	N.Y.	Former president	—	—	50.00
Lewis Cass (D)	5.1	62.06	Mich.	Former Cabinet member	—	—	34.91
James Birney (LTY)	2.6	52.74	Mich.	Movement leader	—	—	17.35
Richard Johnson (D)	5.6	64.04	Ky.	Former vice president	—	—	17.19

General Election — 1844

Candidate	EV	EV%	SC	PV	PV%
Polk	170	61.82%	15	1,339,494	49.54%
Clay	105	38.18%	11	1,300,004	48.08%
Birney	0	0.00%	0	62,103	2.30%

Electoral Votes — 1844

Polk (170) — Alabama (9), Arkansas (3), Georgia (10), Illinois (9), Indiana (12), Louisiana (6), Maine (9), Michigan (5), Mississippi (6), Missouri (7), New Hampshire (6), New York (36), Pennsylvania (26), South Carolina (9), Virginia (17)
Clay (105) — Connecticut (6), Delaware (3), Kentucky (12), Maryland (8), Massachusetts (12), New Jersey (7), North Carolina (11), Ohio (23), Rhode Island (4), Tennessee (13), Vermont (6)

Popular Votes — 1844

State	Total PV	Polk	Clay	Birney	Other
Alabama	63,403	37,401	26,002	—	—
Arkansas	15,150	9,546	5,604	—	—
Connecticut	64,616	29,841	32,832	1,943	—
Delaware	12,247	5,970	6,271	—	6
Georgia	86,247	44,147	42,100	—	—
Illinois	109,057	58,795	45,854	3,469	939
Indiana	140,157	70,183	67,866	2,108	—
Kentucky	113,237	51,988	61,249	—	—
Louisiana	26,865	13,782	13,083	—	—
Maine	84,933	45,719	34,378	4,836	—
Maryland	68,690	32,706	35,984	—	—
Massachusetts	132,037	53,039	67,062	10,830	1,106
Michigan	55,560	27,737	24,185	3,638	—
Mississippi	45,004	25,846	19,158	—	—
Missouri	72,522	41,322	31,200	—	—
New Hampshire	49,187	27,160	17,866	4,161	—
New Jersey	75,944	37,495	38,318	131	—
New York	485,882	237,588	232,482	15,812	—
North Carolina	82,521	39,287	43,232	—	2
Ohio	312,300	149,127	155,091	8,082	—
Pennsylvania	331,645	167,311	161,195	3,139	—
Rhode Island	12,194	4,867	7,322	—	5
South Carolina	—	—	—	—	—
Tennessee	119,957	59,917	60,040	—	—
Vermont	48,765	18,041	26,770	3,954	—
Virginia	95,539	50,679	44,860	—	—
Total	2,703,659	1,339,494	1,300,004	62,103	2,058

Democratic Nomination — 1844

Candidate	ConFB	FB%	ConLB[9]	LB%	PriW	PriV	PriV%
Polk	0	0.00%	231	86.84%	—	—	—
Cass	83	31.20%	29	10.90%	—	—	—
Van Buren	146	54.89%	0	0.00%	—	—	—
Johnson	24	9.02%	0	0.00%	—	—	—

Whig Nomination — 1844

Candidate	ConFB	FB%	ConLB	LB%	PriW	PriV	PriV%
Clay	275	100.00%	—	—	—	—	—

Equalized Statistics — 1844

Candidate	EVX	PVX	ConFBX	ConLBX	PriVX
Polk	333	49,543,748	0	868	—
Clay	205	48,083,135	1,000	—	—
Van Buren	—	—	549	0	—
Cass	—	—	312	109	—
Birney	0	2,296,998	—	—	—
Johnson	—	—	90	0	—

Election of 1848

Basics — 1848

Election number — 16
Winner — Zachary Taylor (W)
Incumbent — James Polk (D)
U.S. population — 21,812,860
States — 30
Electoral votes — 290
Popular votes — 2,879,184
Voter turnout — 72.7%

Top Candidates — 1848

Zachary Taylor (CS 78.93)

Lewis Cass (CS 71.66)

Martin Van Buren (CS 42.02)

Field — 1848

Candidate	PI	Age	State	Position	N	W	CS
Zachary Taylor (W)	4.1	63.94	La.	General	X	X	78.93
Lewis Cass (D)	6.9	66.06	Mich.	Senator	X	—	71.66
Martin Van Buren (FS)	7.1	65.91	N.Y.	Former president	—	—	42.02
Henry Clay (W)	5.1	71.55	Ky.	Former nominee	—	—	37.63
Winfield Scott (W)	5.0	62.39	N.J.	General	—	—	27.96
James Buchanan (D)	8.2	57.52	Pa.	Cabinet member	—	—	25.17
Levi Woodbury (D)	7.0	58.86	N.H.	Supreme Court justice	—	—	24.61
Daniel Webster (W)	7.0	66.79	Mass.	Senator	—	—	16.31

General Election — 1848

Candidate	EV	EV%	SC	PV	PV%
Taylor	163	56.21%	15	1,361,393	47.28%
Cass	127	43.79%	15	1,223,460	42.49%
Van Buren	0	0.00%	0	291,501	10.12%
Clay	0	0.00%	0	89	0.00%

Electoral Votes — 1848

Taylor (163) — Connecticut (6), Delaware (3), Florida (3), Georgia (10), Kentucky (12), Louisiana (6), Maryland (8), Massachusetts (12), New Jersey (7), New York (36), North Carolina (11), Pennsylvania (26), Rhode Island (4), Tennessee (13), Vermont (6)

Cass (127) — Alabama (9), Arkansas (3), Illinois (9), Indiana (12), Iowa (4), Maine (9), Michigan (5), Mississippi (6), Missouri (7), New Hampshire (6), Ohio (23), South Carolina (9), Texas (4), Virginia (17), Wisconsin (4)

Popular Votes — 1848

State	Total PV	Taylor	Cass	Van Buren	Other
Alabama	61,659	30,482	31,173	—	4
Arkansas	16,888	7,587	9,301	—	—
Connecticut	62,398	30,318	27,051	5,005	24
Delaware	12,432	6,440	5,910	82	—
Florida	7,203	4,120	3,083	—	—
Georgia	92,317	47,532	44,785	—	—
Illinois	124,596	52,853	55,952	15,702	89
Indiana	152,394	69,668	74,695	8,031	—
Iowa	22,271	9,930	11,238	1,103	—
Kentucky	116,865	67,145	49,720	—	—
Louisiana	33,866	18,487	15,379	—	—
Maine	87,625	35,273	40,195	12,157	—
Maryland	72,359	37,702	34,528	129	—
Massachusetts	134,748	61,072	35,281	38,333	62
Michigan	65,082	23,947	30,742	10,393	—
Mississippi	52,456	25,911	26,545	—	—
Missouri	72,748	32,671	40,077	—	—
New Hampshire	50,104	14,781	27,763	7,560	—
New Jersey	77,745	40,015	36,901	829	—
New York	455,944	218,583	114,319	120,497	2,545
North Carolina	79,826	44,054	35,772	—	—
Ohio	328,987	138,656	154,782	35,523	26
Pennsylvania	369,092	185,730	172,186	11,176	—
Rhode Island	11,049	6,705	3,613	726	5
South Carolina	—	—	—	—	—
Tennessee	122,463	64,321	58,142	—	—
Texas	17,000	5,281	11,644	—	75
Vermont	47,897	23,117	10,943	13,837	—
Virginia	92,004	45,265	46,739	—	—
Wisconsin	39,166	13,747	15,001	10,418	—
Total	2,879,184	1,361,393	1,223,460	291,501	2,830

Democratic Nomination — 1848

Candidate	ConFB	FB%	ConLB[4]	LB%	PriW	PriV	PriV%
Cass	125	43.10%	179	61.72%	—	—	—
Woodbury	53	18.28%	38	13.10%	—	—	—
Buchanan	55	18.97%	33	11.38%	—	—	—

Whig Nomination — 1848

Candidate	ConFB	FB%	ConLB[4]	LB%	PriW	PriV	PriV%
Taylor	111	39.64%	171	61.07%	—	—	—
Scott	43	15.36%	63	22.50%	—	—	—
Clay	97	34.64%	32	11.43%	—	—	—
Webster	22	7.86%	14	5.00%	—	—	—

Equalized Statistics — 1848

Candidate	EVX	PVX	ConFBX	ConLBX	PriVX
Taylor	302	47,283,987	396	611	—
Cass	236	42,493,290	431	617	—
Van Buren	0	10,124,431	—	—	—
Clay	0	3,091	346	114	—
Scott	—	—	154	225	—
Buchanan	—	—	190	114	—
Woodbury	—	—	183	131	—
Webster	—	—	79	50	—

Election of 1852

Basics — 1852

Election number — 17
Winner — Franklin Pierce (D)
Incumbent — Millard Fillmore (W)
U.S. population — 24,647,585
States — 31
Electoral votes — 296
Popular votes — 3,161,830
Voter turnout — 69.6%

Top Candidates — 1852

Franklin Pierce (CS 89.52)

Winfield Scott (CS 63.01)

Millard Fillmore (CS 45.85)

Field — 1852

Candidate	PI	Age	State	Position	N	W	CS
Franklin Pierce (D)	7.0	47.94	N.H.	Former senator	X	X	89.52
Winfield Scott (W)	4.2	66.39	N.J.	General	X	—	63.01
Millard Fillmore (W)	9.1	52.82	N.Y.	President	—	—	45.85
Lewis Cass (D)	6.9	70.06	Mich.	Senator	—	—	42.18
James Buchanan (D)	7.9	61.52	Pa.	Former Cabinet member	—	—	35.79
John Hale (FS)	5.4	46.59	N.H.	Senator	—	—	25.71
Daniel Webster (W)	6.0	70.79	Mass.	Cabinet member	—	—	18.52
William Marcy (D)	5.9	65.89	N.Y.	Former Cabinet member	—	—	17.50
Stephen Douglas (D)	6.9	39.52	Ill.	Senator	—	—	15.51
Joseph Lane (D)	3.1	50.88	Ore.	Territorial delegate	—	—	13.59

General Election — 1852

Candidate	EV	EV%	SC	PV	PV%
Pierce	254	85.81%	27	1,607,510	50.84%
Scott	42	14.19%	4	1,386,942	43.87%
Hale	0	0.00%	0	155,210	4.91%
Webster	0	0.00%	0	6,994	0.22%

Electoral Votes — 1852

Pierce (254) — Alabama (9), Arkansas (4), California (4), Connecticut (6), Delaware (3), Florida (3), Georgia (10), Illinois (11), Indiana (13), Iowa (4), Louisiana (6), Maine (8), Maryland (8), Michigan (6), Mississippi (7), Missouri (9), New Hampshire (5), New Jersey (7), New York (35), North Carolina (10), Ohio (23), Pennsylvania (27), Rhode Island (4), South Carolina (8), Texas (4), Virginia (15), Wisconsin (5)

Scott (42) — Kentucky (12), Massachusetts (13), Tennessee (12), Vermont (5)

Popular Votes — 1852

State	Total PV	Pierce	Scott	Hale	Other
Alabama	44,147	26,881	15,061	—	2,205
Arkansas	19,577	12,173	7,404	—	—
California	76,810	40,721	35,972	61	56
Connecticut	66,781	33,249	30,359	3,161	12
Delaware	12,673	6,318	6,293	62	—
Florida	7,193	4,318	2,875	—	—
Georgia	62,626	40,516	16,660	—	5,450
Illinois	154,974	80,378	64,733	9,863	—
Indiana	183,176	95,340	80,907	6,929	—
Iowa	35,364	17,763	15,856	1,606	139
Kentucky	111,643	53,949	57,428	266	—
Louisiana	35,902	18,647	17,255	—	—
Maine	82,182	41,609	32,543	8,030	—
Maryland	75,120	40,022	35,077	21	—
Massachusetts	127,103	44,569	52,683	28,023	1,828
Michigan	82,939	41,842	33,860	7,237	—
Mississippi	44,454	26,896	17,558	—	—
Missouri	68,801	38,817	29,984	—	—
New Hampshire	50,535	28,503	15,486	6,546	—
New Jersey	83,926	44,301	38,551	336	738
New York	522,294	262,083	234,882	25,329	—
North Carolina	78,891	39,788	39,043	—	60
Ohio	352,903	169,193	152,577	31,133	—
Pennsylvania	387,920	198,568	179,182	8,500	1,670
Rhode Island	17,005	8,735	7,626	644	—
South Carolina	—	—	—	—	—
Tennessee	115,486	56,900	58,586	—	—
Texas	20,223	14,857	5,356	—	10
Vermont	43,838	13,044	22,173	8,621	—
Virginia	132,604	73,872	58,732	—	—
Wisconsin	64,740	33,658	22,240	8,842	—
Total	3,161,830	1,607,510	1,386,942	155,210	12,168

Democratic Nomination — 1852

Candidate	ConFB	FB%	ConLB[49]	LB%	PriW	PriV	PriV%
Pierce	0	0.00%	279	96.88%	—	—	—
Cass	116	40.28%	2	0.69%	—	—	—
Douglas	20	6.94%	2	0.69%	—	—	—
Buchanan	93	32.29%	0	0.00%	—	—	—
Marcy	27	9.38%	0	0.00%	—	—	—
Lane	13	4.51%	0	0.00%	—	—	—

Whig Nomination — 1852

Candidate	ConFB	FB%	ConLB[53]	LB%	PriW	PriV	PriV%
Scott	131	44.26%	159	53.72%	—	—	—
Fillmore	133	44.93%	112	37.84%	—	—	—
Webster	29	9.80%	21	7.10%	—	—	—

Equalized Statistics — 1852

Candidate	EVX	PVX	ConFBX	ConLBX	PriVX
Pierce	462	50,841,127	0	969	—
Scott	76	43,865,167	443	537	—
Fillmore	—	—	449	378	—
Cass	—	—	403	7	—
Buchanan	—	—	323	0	—
Hale	0	4,908,866	—	—	—
Webster	0	221,201	98	71	—
Marcy	—	—	94	0	—
Douglas	—	—	69	7	—
Lane	—	—	45	0	—

Election of 1856

Basics — 1856

Election number — 18
Winner — James Buchanan (D)
Incumbent — Franklin Pierce (D)
U.S. population — 27,838,856
States — 31
Electoral votes — 296
Popular votes — 4,054,647
Voter turnout — 78.9%

Top Candidates — 1856

James Buchanan (CS 79.35)

John Fremont (CS 68.16)

Millard Fillmore (CS 45.15)

Field — 1856

Candidate	PI	Age	State	Position	N	W	CS
James Buchanan (D)	5.1	65.52	Pa.	Former Cabinet member	X	X	79.35
John Fremont (R)	5.3	43.78	Calif.	Former senator	X	—	68.16
Millard Fillmore (AW)	7.4	56.82	N.Y.	Former president	—	—	45.15
Franklin Pierce (D)	8.1	51.94	N.H.	President	—	—	43.05
Stephen Douglas (D)	7.1	43.52	Ill.	Senator	—	—	18.86
John McLean (R)	4.2	71.64	Ohio	Supreme Court justice	—	—	15.19

General Election — 1856

Candidate	EV	EV%	SC	PV	PV%
Buchanan	174	58.78%	19	1,836,072	45.28%
Fremont	114	38.51%	11	1,342,345	33.11%
Fillmore	8	2.70%	1	873,053	21.53%

Electoral Votes — 1856

Buchanan (174) — Alabama (9), Arkansas (4), California (4), Delaware (3), Florida (3), Georgia (10), Illinois (11), Indiana (13), Kentucky (12), Louisiana (6), Mississippi (7), Missouri (9), New Jersey (7), North Carolina (10), Pennsylvania (27), South Carolina (8), Tennessee (12), Texas (4), Virginia (15)

Fremont (114) — Connecticut (6), Iowa (4), Maine (8), Massachusetts (13), Michigan (6), New Hampshire (5), New York (35), Ohio (23), Rhode Island (4), Vermont (5), Wisconsin (5)

Fillmore (8) — Maryland (8)

Popular Votes — 1856

State	Total PV	Buchanan	Fremont	Fillmore	Other
Alabama	75,291	46,739	—	28,552	—
Arkansas	32,642	21,910	—	10,732	—
California	110,255	53,342	20,704	36,195	14
Connecticut	80,360	35,028	42,717	2,615	—
Delaware	14,598	8,004	310	6,275	9
Florida	11,191	6,358	—	4,833	—
Georgia	99,020	56,581	—	42,439	—
Illinois	239,334	105,528	96,275	37,531	—
Indiana	235,401	118,670	94,375	22,356	—
Iowa	92,310	37,568	45,073	9,669	—
Kentucky	142,058	74,642	—	67,416	—
Louisiana	42,873	22,164	—	20,709	—
Maine	109,689	39,140	67,279	3,270	—
Maryland	86,860	39,123	285	47,452	—
Massachusetts	170,048	39,244	108,172	19,626	3,006
Michigan	125,558	52,136	71,762	1,660	—
Mississippi	59,647	35,456	—	24,191	—
Missouri	106,486	57,964	—	48,522	—
New Hampshire	69,774	31,891	37,473	410	—
New Jersey	99,396	46,943	28,338	24,115	—
New York	596,486	195,878	276,004	124,604	—
North Carolina	84,963	48,243	—	36,720	—
Ohio	386,640	170,874	187,497	28,121	148
Pennsylvania	460,937	230,772	147,963	82,202	—
Rhode Island	19,822	6,680	11,467	1,675	—
South Carolina	—	—	—	—	—
Tennessee	133,582	69,704	—	63,878	—
Texas	48,005	31,995	—	16,010	—
Vermont	50,675	10,569	39,561	545	—
Virginia	150,233	90,083	—	60,150	—
Wisconsin	120,513	52,843	67,090	580	—
Total	4,054,647	1,836,072	1,342,345	873,053	3,177

Democratic Nomination — 1856

Candidate	ConFB	FB%	ConLB[17]	LB%	PriW	PriV	PriV%
Buchanan	136	45.78%	296	100.00%	—	—	—
Pierce	123	41.39%	0	0.00%	—	—	—
Douglas	33	11.15%	0	0.00%	—	—	—

Republican Nomination — 1856

Candidate	ConFB	FB%	ConLB	LB%	PriW	PriV	PriV%
Fremont	520	91.71%	—	—	—	—	—
McLean	37	6.53%	—	—	—	—	—

Equalized Statistics — 1856

Candidate	EVX	PVX	ConFBX	ConLBX	PriVX
Buchanan	316	45,283,153	458	1,000	—
Fremont	207	33,106,335	917	—	—
Fillmore	15	21,532,158	—	—	—
Pierce	—	—	414	0	—
Douglas	—	—	111	0	—
McLean	—	—	65	—	—

Election of 1860

Basics — 1860

Election number — 19
Winner — Abraham Lincoln (R)
Incumbent — James Buchanan (D)
U.S. population — 31,443,321
States — 33
Electoral votes — 303
Popular votes — 4,685,561
Voter turnout — 81.2%

Top Candidates — 1860

Abraham Lincoln (CS 78.38)

John Breckinridge (CS 60.76)

Stephen Douglas (CS 57.06)

Field — 1860

Candidate	PI	Age	State	Position	N	W	CS
Abraham Lincoln (R)	6.2	51.72	Ill.	Former representative	X	X	78.38
John Breckinridge (D/SD)	4.7	39.79	Ky.	Vice president	X	—	60.76
Stephen Douglas (D)	7.0	47.52	Ill.	Senator	X	—	57.06
John Bell (CU)	4.6	64.70	Tenn.	Former senator	—	—	46.37
William Seward (R)	8.2	59.46	N.Y.	Senator	—	—	39.70
Robert Hunter (D)	7.0	51.53	Va.	Senator	—	—	21.10
James Guthrie (D)	3.9	67.91	Ky.	Former Cabinet member	—	—	19.34
Simon Cameron (R)	7.8	61.65	Pa.	Senator	—	—	18.62
Salmon Chase (R)	8.7	52.80	Ohio	Former governor	—	—	18.38
Edward Bates (R)	5.2	67.16	Mo.	Former representative	—	—	18.22
Andrew Johnson (D)	6.9	51.84	Tenn.	Senator	—	—	13.19

General Election — 1860

Candidate	EV	EV%	SC	PV	PV%
Lincoln	180	59.41%	18	1,865,908	39.82%
Breckinridge	72	23.76%	11	848,019	18.10%
Bell	39	12.87%	3	590,901	12.61%
Douglas	12	3.96%	1	1,380,202	29.46%

Electoral Votes — 1860

Lincoln (180) — California (4), Connecticut (6), Illinois (11), Indiana (13), Iowa (4), Maine (8), Massachusetts (13), Michigan (6), Minnesota (4), New Hampshire (5), New Jersey (4), New York (35), Ohio (23), Oregon (3), Pennsylvania (27), Rhode Island (4), Vermont (5), Wisconsin (5)

Breckinridge (72) — Alabama (9), Arkansas (4), Delaware (3), Florida (3), Georgia (10), Louisiana (6), Maryland (8), Mississippi (7), North Carolina (10), South Carolina (8), Texas (4)

Bell (39) — Kentucky (12), Tennessee (12), Virginia (15)

Douglas (12) — Missouri (9), New Jersey (3)

Popular Votes — 1860

State	Total PV	Lincoln	Douglas	Breckinridge	Bell	Other
Alabama	90,122	—	13,618	48,669	27,835	—
Arkansas	54,152	—	5,357	28,732	20,063	—
California	119,827	38,733	37,999	33,969	9,111	15
Connecticut	74,819	43,488	15,431	14,372	1,528	—
Delaware	16,115	3,822	1,066	7,339	3,888	—
Florida	13,301	—	223	8,277	4,801	—
Georgia	106,717	—	11,581	52,176	42,960	—
Illinois	339,666	172,171	160,215	2,331	4,914	35
Indiana	272,143	139,033	115,509	12,295	5,306	—
Iowa	128,739	70,302	55,639	1,035	1,763	—
Kentucky	146,216	1,364	25,651	53,143	66,058	—
Louisiana	50,510	—	7,625	22,681	20,204	—
Maine	100,918	62,811	29,693	6,368	2,046	—
Maryland	92,502	2,294	5,966	42,482	41,760	—
Massachusetts	169,876	106,684	34,370	6,163	22,331	328
Michigan	154,758	88,481	65,057	805	415	—
Minnesota	34,804	22,069	11,920	748	50	17
Mississippi	69,095	—	3,282	40,768	25,045	—
Missouri	165,563	17,028	58,801	31,362	58,372	—
New Hampshire	65,943	37,519	25,887	2,125	412	—
New Jersey	121,215	58,346	62,869	—	—	—
New York	675,156	362,646	312,510	—	—	—
North Carolina	96,712	—	2,737	48,846	45,129	—
Ohio	442,866	231,709	187,421	11,406	12,194	136
Oregon	14,758	5,329	4,136	5,075	218	—
Pennsylvania	476,442	268,030	16,765	178,871	12,776	—
Rhode Island	19,951	12,244	7,707	—	—	—
South Carolina	—	—	—	—	—	—
Tennessee	146,106	—	11,281	65,097	69,728	—
Texas	62,855	—	18	47,454	15,383	—
Vermont	44,644	33,808	8,649	218	1,969	—
Virginia	166,891	1,887	16,198	74,325	74,481	—
Wisconsin	152,179	86,110	65,021	887	161	—
Total	4,685,561	1,865,908	1,380,202	848,019	590,901	531

Democratic Nomination — 1860

Candidate	ConFB	FB%	ConLB[59]	LB%	PriW	PriV	PriV%
Douglas	146	48.02%	191	62.87%	—	—	—
Breckinridge	0	0.00%	8	2.48%	—	—	—
Guthrie	36	11.72%	6	1.82%	—	—	—
Hunter	42	13.86%	0	0.00%	—	—	—
Johnson	12	3.96%	0	0.00%	—	—	—

Republican Nomination — 1860

Candidate	ConFB	FB%	ConLB[3]	LB%	PriW	PriV	PriV%
Lincoln	102	21.89%	340	72.96%	—	—	—
Seward	174	37.23%	122	26.07%	—	—	—
Chase	49	10.52%	2	0.43%	—	—	—
Cameron	51	10.84%	0	0.00%	—	—	—
Bates	48	10.30%	0	0.00%	—	—	—

Equalized Statistics — 1860

Candidate	EVX	PVX	ConFBX	ConLBX	PriVX
Lincoln	320	39,822,510	219	730	—
Breckinridge	128	18,098,559	0	25	—
Douglas	21	29,456,494	480	629	—
Bell	69	12,611,105	—	—	—
Seward	—	—	372	261	—
Hunter	—	—	139	0	—
Guthrie	—	—	117	18	—
Cameron	—	—	108	0	—
Chase	—	—	105	4	—
Bates	—	—	103	0	—
Johnson	—	—	40	0	—

Election of 1864

Basics — 1864

Election number — 20
Winner — Abraham Lincoln (R)
Incumbent — Abraham Lincoln (R)
U.S. population — 34,558,173
States — 25
Electoral votes — 233
Popular votes — 4,030,986
Voter turnout — 73.8%

Top Candidates — 1864

Abraham Lincoln (CS 92.17)

George McClellan (CS 61.66)

Thomas Seymour (CS 23.41)

Field — 1864

Candidate	PI	Age	State	Position	N	W	CS
Abraham Lincoln (R)	8.9	55.72	Ill.	President	X	X	92.17
George McClellan (D)	4.7	37.91	N.J.	General	X	—	61.66
Thomas Seymour (D)	6.8	57.09	Conn.	Former governor	—	—	23.41
Horatio Seymour (D)	8.0	54.42	N.Y.	Governor	—	—	14.23
Ulysses Grant (R)	5.6	42.51	Ill.	General	—	—	13.35

General Election — 1864

Candidate	EV	EV%	SC	PV	PV%
Lincoln	212	90.99%	22	2,220,845	55.09%
McClellan	21	9.01%	3	1,809,449	44.89%

Electoral Votes — 1864

Lincoln (212) — California (5), Connecticut (6), Illinois (16), Indiana (13), Iowa (8), Kansas (3), Maine (7), Maryland (7), Massachusetts (12), Michigan (8), Minnesota (4), Missouri (11), Nevada (2), New Hampshire (5), New York (33), Ohio (21), Oregon (3), Pennsylvania (26), Rhode Island (4), Vermont (5), West Virginia (5), Wisconsin (8)
McClellan (21) — Delaware (3), Kentucky (11), New Jersey (7)

Popular Votes — 1864

State	Total PV	Lincoln	McClellan	Other
California	105,890	62,053	43,837	—
Connecticut	86,958	44,673	42,285	—
Delaware	16,922	8,155	8,767	—
Illinois	348,236	189,512	158,724	—
Indiana	280,117	149,887	130,230	—
Iowa	138,025	88,500	49,525	—
Kansas	21,580	17,089	3,836	655
Kentucky	92,088	27,787	64,301	—
Maine	115,099	68,104	46,995	—
Maryland	72,892	40,153	32,739	—
Massachusetts	175,493	126,742	48,745	6
Michigan	160,023	88,551	71,472	—
Minnesota	42,433	25,031	17,376	26
Missouri	104,346	72,750	31,596	—
Nevada	16,420	9,826	6,594	—
New Hampshire	69,630	36,596	33,034	—
New Jersey	128,747	60,723	68,024	—
New York	730,721	368,735	361,986	—
Ohio	471,283	265,674	205,609	—
Oregon	18,350	9,888	8,457	5
Pennsylvania	572,707	296,391	276,316	—
Rhode Island	23,067	14,349	8,718	—
Vermont	55,740	42,419	13,321	—
West Virginia	34,877	23,799	11,078	—
Wisconsin	149,342	83,458	65,884	—
Total	4,030,986	2,220,845	1,809,449	692

Democratic Nomination — 1864

Candidate	ConFB	FB%	ConLB	LB%	PriW	PriV	PriV%
McClellan	174	76.99%	—	—	—	—	—
T. Seymour	38	16.81%	—	—	—	—	—
H. Seymour	12	5.31%	—	—	—	—	—

Republican Nomination — 1864

Candidate	ConFB	FB%	ConLB	LB%	PriW	PriV	PriV%
Lincoln	494	95.18%	—	—	—	—	—
Grant	22	4.24%	—	—	—	—	—

Equalized Statistics — 1864

Candidate	EVX	PVX	ConFBX	ConLBX	PriVX
Lincoln	490	55,094,337	952	—	—
McClellan	48	44,888,496	770	—	—
T. Seymour	—	—	168	—	—
H. Seymour	—	—	53	—	—
Grant	—	—	42	—	—

Election of 1868

Basics — 1868

Election number — 21
Winner — Ulysses Grant (R)
Incumbent — Andrew Johnson (D)
U.S. population — 37,981,591
States — 34
Electoral votes — 294
Popular votes — 5,722,440
Voter turnout — 78.1%

Top Candidates — 1868

Ulysses Grant (CS 85.63)

Horatio Seymour (CS 67.61)

George Pendleton (CS 36.43)

Field — 1868

Candidate	PI	Age	State	Position	N	W	CS
Ulysses Grant (R)	6.3	46.51	Ill.	General	X	X	85.63
Horatio Seymour (D)	7.5	58.42	N.Y.	Former governor	X	—	67.61
George Pendleton (D)	6.7	43.29	Ohio	Former representative	—	—	36.43
Andrew Johnson (D)	7.4	59.84	Tenn.	President	—	—	26.37
Sanford Church (D)	5.0	53.54	N.Y.	Former state official	—	—	18.54
Winfield Hancock (D)	6.0	44.71	Pa.	General	—	—	18.46
Asa Packer (D)	6.0	62.84	Pa.	Former representative	—	—	16.55
James English (D)	7.0	56.64	Conn.	Governor	—	—	13.99
James Doolittle (D)	7.9	53.83	Wis.	Senator	—	—	13.27
Joel Parker (D)	6.7	51.94	N.J.	Former governor	—	—	13.27

General Election — 1868

Candidate	EV	EV%	SC	PV	PV%
Grant	214	72.79%	26	3,013,650	52.66%
Seymour	80	27.21%	8	2,708,744	47.34%

Electoral Votes — 1868

Grant (214) — Alabama (8), Arkansas (5), California (5), Connecticut (6), Florida (3), Illinois (16), Indiana (13), Iowa (8), Kansas (3), Maine (7), Massachusetts (12), Michigan (8), Minnesota (4), Missouri (11), Nebraska (3), Nevada (3), New Hampshire (5), North Carolina (9), Ohio (21), Pennsylvania (26), Rhode Island (4), South Carolina (6), Tennessee (10), Vermont (5), West Virginia (5), Wisconsin (8)

Seymour (80) — Delaware (3), Georgia (9), Kentucky (11), Louisiana (7), Maryland (7), New Jersey (7), New York (33), Oregon (3)

Popular Votes — 1868

State	Total PV	Grant	Seymour	Other
Alabama	149,594	76,667	72,921	6
Arkansas	41,190	22,112	19,078	—
California	108,656	54,588	54,068	—
Connecticut	98,570	50,789	47,781	—
Delaware	18,571	7,614	10,957	—
Florida	—	—	—	—
Georgia	159,816	57,109	102,707	—
Illinois	449,420	250,304	199,116	—
Indiana	343,528	176,548	166,980	—
Iowa	194,439	120,399	74,040	—
Kansas	43,630	30,027	13,600	3
Kentucky	155,455	39,566	115,889	—
Louisiana	113,488	33,263	80,225	—
Maine	112,962	70,502	42,460	—
Maryland	92,795	30,438	62,357	—
Massachusetts	195,508	136,379	59,103	26
Michigan	225,632	128,563	97,069	—
Minnesota	71,620	43,545	28,075	—
Missouri	152,488	86,860	65,628	—
Nebraska	15,291	9,772	5,519	—
Nevada	11,689	6,474	5,215	—
New Hampshire	68,304	37,718	30,575	11
New Jersey	163,133	80,132	83,001	—
New York	849,771	419,888	429,883	—
North Carolina	181,498	96,939	84,559	—
Ohio	518,665	280,159	238,506	—
Oregon	22,086	10,961	11,125	—
Pennsylvania	655,662	342,280	313,382	—
Rhode Island	19,511	13,017	6,494	—
South Carolina	107,538	62,301	45,237	—
Tennessee	82,757	56,628	26,129	—
Vermont	56,224	44,173	12,051	—
West Virginia	49,321	29,015	20,306	—
Wisconsin	193,628	108,920	84,708	—
Total	5,722,440	3,013,650	2,708,744	46

Democratic Nomination — 1868

Candidate	ConFB	FB%	ConLB[22]	LB%	PriW	PriV	PriV%
Seymour	0	0.00%	317	100.00%	—	—	—
Pendleton	105	33.12%	0	0.00%	—	—	—
Johnson	65	20.51%	0	0.00%	—	—	—
Church	34	10.73%	0	0.00%	—	—	—
Hancock	34	10.57%	0	0.00%	—	—	—
Packer	26	8.20%	0	0.00%	—	—	—
English	16	5.05%	0	0.00%	—	—	—
Doolittle	13	4.10%	0	0.00%	—	—	—
Parker	13	4.10%	0	0.00%	—	—	—

Republican Nomination — 1868

Candidate	ConFB	FB%	ConLB	LB%	PriW	PriV	PriV%
Grant	650	100.00%	—	—	—	—	—

Equalized Statistics — 1868

Candidate	EVX	PVX	ConFBX	ConLBX	PriVX
Grant	392	52,663,724	1,000	—	—
Seymour	146	47,335,472	0	1,000	—
Pendleton	—	—	331	0	—
Johnson	—	—	205	0	—
Church	—	—	107	0	—
Hancock	—	—	106	0	—
Packer	—	—	82	0	—
English	—	—	50	0	—
Doolittle	—	—	41	0	—
Parker	—	—	41	0	—

Election of 1872

Basics — 1872

Election number — 22
Winner — Ulysses Grant (R)
Incumbent — Ulysses Grant (R)
U.S. population — 41,705,136
States — 35
Electoral votes — 349
Popular votes — 6,470,674
Voter turnout — 71.3%

Top Candidates — 1872

Ulysses Grant (CS 89.28)

Horace Greeley (CS 58.76)

Thomas Hendricks (CS 43.62)

Field — 1872

Candidate	PI	Age	State	Position	N	W	CS
Ulysses Grant (R)	9.0	50.51	Ill.	President	X	X	89.28
Horace Greeley (D-LR)	4.8	61.74	N.Y.	Journalist	X	—	58.76
Thomas Hendricks (D)	8.2	53.15	Ind.	Former senator	—	—	43.62
Gratz Brown (D-LR)	7.8	46.43	Mo.	Governor	—	—	27.03
Charles Jenkins (D)	5.1	67.82	Ga.	Former governor	—	—	11.89
David Davis (D)	5.1	57.65	Ill.	Supreme Court justice	—	—	10.97

General Election — 1872

Candidate	EV	EV%	SC	PV	PV%
Grant	286	81.95%	29	3,598,468	55.61%
Hendricks	42	12.03%	4	0	0.00%
Brown	18	5.16%	2	0	0.00%
Jenkins	2	0.57%	0	0	0.00%
Davis	1	0.29%	0	0	0.00%
Greeley	—	—	—	2,835,315	43.82%

NOTE: Greeley died on November 29, 1872, which was after the general election, but before the tabulation of electoral votes. His electors scattered their votes among four candidates.

Electoral Votes — 1872

Grant (286) — Alabama (10), California (6), Connecticut (6), Delaware (3), Florida (4), Illinois (21), Indiana (15), Iowa (11), Kansas (5), Maine (7), Massachusetts (13), Michigan (11), Minnesota (5), Mississippi (8), Nebraska (3), Nevada (3), New Hampshire (5), New Jersey (9), New York (35), North Carolina (10), Ohio (22), Oregon (3), Pennsylvania (29), Rhode Island (4), South Carolina (7), Vermont (5), Virginia (11), West Virginia (5), Wisconsin (10)

Hendricks (42) — Kentucky (8), Maryland (8), Missouri (6), Tennessee (12), Texas (8)

Brown (18) — Georgia (6), Kentucky (4), Missouri (8)

Jenkins (2) — Georgia (2)

Davis (1) — Missouri (1)

Popular Votes — 1872

State	Total PV	Grant	Greeley	Other
Alabama	169,716	90,272	79,444	—
Arkansas	79,300	41,373	37,927	—
California	95,785	54,007	40,717	1,061
Connecticut	95,992	50,307	45,685	—
Delaware	21,822	11,129	10,205	488
Florida	33,190	17,763	15,427	—
Georgia	138,906	62,550	76,356	—
Illinois	429,971	241,936	184,884	3,151
Indiana	349,779	186,147	163,632	—
Iowa	216,365	131,566	71,189	13,610
Kansas	100,512	66,805	32,970	737
Kentucky	191,552	88,970	100,208	2,374
Louisiana	128,692	71,663	57,029	—
Maine	90,523	61,426	29,097	—
Maryland	134,447	66,760	67,687	—
Massachusetts	192,650	133,455	59,195	—
Michigan	221,569	138,768	78,651	4,150
Minnesota	91,339	56,040	35,131	168
Mississippi	129,457	82,175	47,282	—
Missouri	273,059	119,196	151,434	2,429
Nebraska	25,932	18,329	7,603	—
Nevada	14,649	8,413	6,236	—
New Hampshire	68,906	37,168	31,425	313
New Jersey	168,467	91,666	76,801	—
New York	829,692	440,758	387,279	1,655
North Carolina	165,163	94,772	70,130	261
Ohio	529,435	281,852	244,320	3,263
Oregon	20,107	11,818	7,742	547
Pennsylvania	561,629	349,589	212,040	—
Rhode Island	18,994	13,665	5,329	—
South Carolina	95,452	72,290	22,699	463
Tennessee	179,046	85,655	93,391	—
Texas	115,700	47,910	67,675	115

State	Total PV	Grant	Greeley	Other
Vermont	52,959	41,480	10,926	553
Virginia	185,195	93,463	91,647	85
West Virginia	62,467	32,320	29,532	615
Wisconsin	192,255	105,012	86,390	853
Total	6,470,674	3,598,468	2,835,315	36,891

Democratic Nomination — 1872

Candidate	ConFB	FB%	ConLB	LB%	PriW	PriV	PriV%
Greeley	686	93.72%	—	—	—	—	—

Republican Nomination — 1872

Candidate	ConFB	FB%	ConLB	LB%	PriW	PriV	PriV%
Grant	752	100.00%	—	—	—	—	—

Equalized Statistics — 1872

Candidate	EVX	PVX	ConFBX	ConLBX	PriVX
Grant	441	55,611,950	1,000	—	—
Greeley	—	43,817,924	937	—	—
Hendricks	65	0	—	—	—
Brown	28	0	—	—	—
Jenkins	3	0	—	—	—
Davis	2	0	—	—	—

Election of 1876

Basics — 1876

Election number — 23
Winner — Rutherford Hayes (R)
Incumbent — Ulysses Grant (R)
U.S. population — 45,750,932
States — 38
Electoral votes — 369
Popular votes — 8,411,618
Voter turnout — 81.8%

Top Candidates — 1876

Rutherford Hayes (CS 77.12)

Samuel Tilden (CS 75.14)

James Blaine (CS 47.05)

Field — 1876

Candidate	PI	Age	State	Position	N	W	CS
Rutherford Hayes (R)	8.3	54.08	Ohio	Governor	X	X	77.12
Samuel Tilden (D)	7.2	62.73	N.Y.	Governor	X	—	75.14
James Blaine (R)	5.1	46.75	Maine	Representative	—	—	47.05
Thomas Hendricks (D)	7.9	57.15	Ind.	Governor	—	—	25.17
Oliver Morton (R)	8.2	53.24	Ind.	Senator	—	—	23.09
Benjamin Bristow (R)	4.0	44.37	Ky.	Cabinet member	—	—	21.90
Roscoe Conkling (R)	8.2	47.01	N.Y.	Senator	—	—	20.46
Winfield Hancock (D)	6.5	52.71	Pa.	General	—	—	18.14
John Hartranft (R)	7.6	45.88	Pa.	Governor	—	—	16.15
William Allen (D)	6.9	72.87	Ohio	Former governor	—	—	15.83
Thomas Bayard (D)	7.1	48.01	Del.	Senator	—	—	13.59

General Election — 1876

Candidate	EV	EV%	SC	PV	PV%
Hayes	185	50.14%	21	4,033,497	47.95%
Tilden	184	49.86%	17	4,288,191	50.98%

Electoral Votes — 1876

Hayes (185) — California (6), Colorado (3), Florida (4), Illinois (21), Iowa (11), Kansas (5), Louisiana (8), Maine (7), Massachusetts (13), Michigan (11), Minnesota (5), Nebraska (3), Nevada (3), New Hampshire (5), Ohio (22), Oregon (3), Pennsylvania (29), Rhode Island (4), South Carolina (7), Vermont (5), Wisconsin (10)

Tilden (184) — Alabama (10), Arkansas (6), Connecticut (6), Delaware (3), Georgia (11), Indiana (15), Kentucky (12), Maryland (8), Mississippi (8), Missouri (15), New Jersey (9), New York (35), North Carolina (10), Tennessee (12), Texas (8), Virginia (11), West Virginia (5)

Popular Votes — 1876

State	Total PV	Tilden	Hayes	Other
Alabama	171,699	102,989	68,708	2
Arkansas	96,946	58,086	38,649	211
California	155,784	76,460	79,258	66
Colorado	—	—	—	
Connecticut	122,134	61,927	59,033	1,174
Delaware	24,133	13,381	10,752	—
Florida	46,776	22,927	23,849	—
Georgia	180,690	130,157	50,533	—
Illinois	554,368	258,611	278,232	17,525
Indiana	430,020	213,516	206,971	9,533
Iowa	293,398	112,121	171,326	9,951
Kansas	124,134	37,902	78,324	7,908
Kentucky	259,614	159,696	97,156	2,762
Louisiana	145,823	70,508	75,315	—
Maine	117,045	49,917	66,300	828
Maryland	163,759	91,779	71,980	—
Massachusetts	259,619	108,777	150,063	779
Michigan	318,426	141,665	166,901	9,860
Minnesota	124,119	48,816	72,982	2,321
Mississippi	164,776	112,173	52,603	—
Missouri	350,610	202,086	145,027	3,497
Nebraska	49,258	17,343	31,915	—
Nevada	19,691	9,308	10,383	—
New Hampshire	80,143	38,510	41,540	93
New Jersey	220,193	115,962	103,517	714
New York	1,015,503	521,949	489,207	4,347
North Carolina	233,911	125,427	108,484	—
Ohio	658,650	323,182	330,698	4,770
Oregon	29,873	14,157	15,207	509
Pennsylvania	758,973	366,204	384,157	8,612
Rhode Island	26,499	10,712	15,787	—
South Carolina	182,683	90,897	91,786	—
Tennessee	222,743	133,177	89,566	—
Texas	151,431	106,372	45,013	46
Vermont	64,460	20,254	44,092	114
Virginia	236,288	140,770	95,518	—
West Virginia	99,647	56,546	41,997	1,104
Wisconsin	257,799	123,927	130,668	3,204
Total	8,411,618	4,288,191	4,033,497	89,930

Democratic Nomination — 1876

Candidate	ConFB	FB%	ConLB[2]	LB%	PriW	PriV	PriV%
Tilden	402	54.40%	535	72.49%	—	—	—
Hendricks	141	19.04%	85	11.52%	—	—	—
Hancock	75	10.16%	58	7.86%	—	—	—
Allen	54	7.32%	54	7.32%	—	—	—
Bayard	33	4.47%	4	0.54%	—	—	—

Republican Nomination — 1876

Candidate	ConFB	FB%	ConLB[7]	LB%	PriW	PriV	PriV%
Hayes	61	8.07%	384	50.79%	—	—	—
Blaine	285	37.70%	351	46.43%	—	—	—
Bristow	113	14.95%	21	2.78%	—	—	—
Morton	124	16.40%	0	0.00%	—	—	—
Conkling	99	13.10%	0	0.00%	—	—	—
Hartranft	58	7.67%	0	0.00%	—	—	—

Equalized Statistics — 1876

Candidate	EVX	PVX	ConFBX	ConLBX	PriVX
Hayes	270	47,951,500	81	508	—
Tilden	268	50,979,384	544	725	—
Blaine	—	—	377	464	—
Hendricks	—	—	190	115	—
Morton	—	—	164	0	—
Bristow	—	—	149	28	—
Conkling	—	—	131	0	—
Hancock	—	—	102	79	—
Hartranft	—	—	77	0	—
Allen	—	—	73	73	—
Bayard	—	—	45	5	—

Election of 1880

Basics — 1880

Election number — 24
Winner — James Garfield (R)
Incumbent — Rutherford Hayes (R)
U.S. population — 50,189,209
States — 38
Electoral votes — 369
Popular votes — 9,220,197
Voter turnout — 79.4%

Top Candidates — 1880

James Garfield (CS 79.77)

Winfield Hancock (CS 72.24)

Ulysses Grant (CS 42.34)

Field — 1880

Candidate	PI	Age	State	Position	N	W	CS
James Garfield (R)	6.6	48.95	Ohio	Representative	X	X	79.77
Winfield Hancock (D)	5.6	56.71	Pa.	General	X	—	72.24
Ulysses Grant (R)	8.5	58.51	Ill.	Former president	—	—	42.34
James Blaine (R)	7.3	50.75	Maine	Senator	—	—	40.02
Thomas Bayard (D)	7.1	52.01	Del.	Senator	—	—	26.61
James Weaver (GBK)	4.2	47.39	Iowa	Representative	—	—	20.66
John Sherman (R)	8.1	57.48	Ohio	Cabinet member	—	—	19.82
Henry Payne (D)	5.6	69.92	Ohio	Former representative	—	—	18.78
Allen Thurman (D)	7.7	66.97	Ohio	Senator	—	—	17.43
Stephen Field (D)	2.3	63.99	Calif.	Supreme Court justice	—	—	17.03
William Morrison (D)	6.5	56.13	Ill.	Representative	—	—	16.71
Thomas Hendricks (D)	7.4	61.15	Ind.	Former governor	—	—	15.35
Samuel Tilden (D)	8.0	66.73	N.Y.	Former nominee	—	—	14.07
George Edmunds (R)	7.3	52.75	Vt.	Senator	—	—	13.59
Elihu Washburne (R)	4.4	64.11	Ill.	Former ambassador	—	—	13.19

General Election — 1880

Candidate	EV	EV%	SC	PV	PV%
Garfield	214	58.00%	19	4,453,611	48.30%
Hancock	155	42.01%	19	4,445,256	48.21%
Weaver	0	0.00%	0	306,921	3.33%

Electoral Votes — 1880

Garfield (214) — California (1), Colorado (3), Connecticut (6), Illinois (21), Indiana (15), Iowa (11), Kansas (5), Maine (7), Massachusetts (13), Michigan (11), Minnesota (5), Nebraska (3), New Hampshire (5), New York (35), Ohio (22), Oregon (3), Pennsylvania (29), Rhode Island (4), Vermont (5), Wisconsin (10)

Hancock (155) — Alabama (10), Arkansas (6), California (5), Delaware (3), Florida (4), Georgia (11), Kentucky (12), Louisiana (8), Maryland (8), Mississippi (8), Missouri (15), Nevada (3), New Jersey (9), North Carolina (10), South Carolina (7), Tennessee (12), Texas (8), Virginia (11), West Virginia (5)

Popular Votes — 1880

State	Total PV	Garfield	Hancock	Weaver	Other
Alabama	151,902	56,350	91,130	4,422	—
Arkansas	108,870	42,436	60,775	4,116	1,543
California	164,218	80,282	80,426	3,381	129
Colorado	53,546	27,450	24,647	1,435	14
Connecticut	132,798	67,071	64,411	868	448
Delaware	29,458	14,148	15,181	129	—
Florida	51,618	23,654	27,964	—	—
Georgia	157,451	54,470	102,981	—	—
Illinois	622,305	318,036	277,321	26,358	590
Indiana	470,758	232,169	225,523	13,066	—
Iowa	323,140	183,904	105,845	32,327	1,064
Kansas	201,054	121,520	59,789	19,710	35
Kentucky	266,884	106,059	149,068	11,499	258
Louisiana	104,462	38,978	65,047	437	—
Maine	143,903	74,052	65,211	4,409	231
Maryland	173,049	78,515	93,706	828	—
Massachusetts	282,505	165,198	111,960	4,548	799
Michigan	353,076	185,335	131,596	34,895	1,250
Minnesota	150,806	93,939	53,314	3,267	286
Mississippi	117,068	34,844	75,750	5,797	677
Missouri	397,289	153,647	208,600	35,042	—
Nebraska	87,355	54,979	28,523	3,853	—
Nevada	18,343	8,732	9,611	—	—
New Hampshire	86,361	44,856	40,797	528	180
New Jersey	245,928	120,555	122,565	2,617	191
New York	1,103,945	555,544	534,511	12,373	1,517
North Carolina	240,946	115,616	124,204	1,126	—
Ohio	724,984	375,048	340,867	6,456	2,613
Oregon	40,841	20,619	19,955	267	—
Pennsylvania	874,783	444,704	407,428	20,667	1,984
Rhode Island	29,235	18,195	10,779	236	25
South Carolina	169,793	57,954	111,236	567	36
Tennessee	243,263	107,677	129,569	6,017	—
Texas	240,659	57,225	155,963	27,471	—
Vermont	65,098	45,567	18,316	1,215	—
Virginia	212,660	83,634	128,647	—	379
West Virginia	112,641	46,243	57,390	9,008	—
Wisconsin	267,202	144,406	114,650	7,986	160
Total	9,220,197	4,453,611	4,445,256	306,921	14,409

Democratic Nomination — 1880

Candidate	ConFB	FB%	ConLB[2]	LB%	PriW	PriV	PriV%
Hancock	171	23.17%	705	95.53%	—	—	—
Hendricks	50	6.71%	30	4.07%	—	—	—
Bayard	154	20.80%	2	0.27%	—	—	—
Tilden	38	5.15%	1	0.14%	—	—	—
Payne	81	10.98%	0	0.00%	—	—	—
Thurman	69	9.28%	0	0.00%	—	—	—
Field	65	8.81%	0	0.00%	—	—	—
Morrison	62	8.40%	0	0.00%	—	—	—

Republican Nomination — 1880

Candidate	ConFB	FB%	ConLB[36]	LB%	PriW	PriV	PriV%
Garfield	0	0.00%	399	52.78%	—	—	—
Grant	304	40.21%	306	40.48%	—	—	—
Blaine	284	37.57%	42	5.56%	—	—	—
Washburne	30	3.97%	5	0.66%	—	—	—
Sherman	93	12.30%	3	0.40%	—	—	—
Edmunds	34	4.50%	0	0.00%	—	—	—

Equalized Statistics — 1880

Candidate	EVX	PVX	ConFBX	ConLBX	PriVX
Garfield	312	48,302,775	0	528	—
Hancock	226	48,212,159	232	955	—
Grant	—	—	402	405	—
Blaine	—	—	376	56	—
Bayard	—	—	208	3	—
Weaver	0	3,328,790	—	—	—
Sherman	—	—	123	4	—
Payne	—	—	110	0	—
Thurman	—	—	93	0	—
Field	—	—	88	0	—
Morrison	—	—	84	0	—
Hendricks	—	—	67	41	—
Tilden	—	—	51	1	—
Edmunds	—	—	45	0	—
Washburne	—	—	40	7	—

Election of 1884

Basics — 1884

Election number — 25
Winner — Grover Cleveland (D)
Incumbent — Chester Arthur (R)
U.S. population — 54,959,987
States — 38
Electoral votes — 401
Popular votes — 10,058,373
Voter turnout — 77.5%

Top Candidates — 1884

Grover Cleveland (CS 78.78)

James Blaine (CS 73.26)

Chester Arthur (CS 37.07)

Field — 1884

Candidate	PI	Age	State	Position	N	W	CS
Grover Cleveland (D)	7.5	47.62	N.Y.	Governor	X	X	78.78
James Blaine (R)	6.7	54.75	Maine	Former senator	X	—	73.26
Chester Arthur (R)	8.8	55.07	N.Y.	President	—	—	37.07
Thomas Bayard (D)	6.2	56.01	Del.	Senator	—	—	26.53
George Edmunds (R)	7.0	56.75	Vt.	Senator	—	—	19.02
Allen Thurman (D)	7.4	70.97	Ohio	Former senator	—	—	18.54
Samuel Randall (D)	6.3	56.06	Pa.	Representative	—	—	17.58
John Logan (R)	8.1	58.73	Ill.	Senator	—	—	16.15
Joseph McDonald (D)	7.3	65.17	Ind.	Former senator	—	—	15.43
Thomas Hendricks (D)	6.4	65.15	Ind.	Former governor	—	—	14.39

General Election — 1884

Candidate	EV	EV%	SC	PV	PV%
Cleveland	219	54.61%	20	4,915,586	48.87%
Blaine	182	45.39%	18	4,852,916	48.25%

Electoral Votes — 1884

Cleveland (219) — Alabama (10), Arkansas (7), Connecticut (6), Delaware (3), Florida (4), Georgia (12), Indiana (15), Kentucky (13), Louisiana (8), Maryland (8), Mississippi (9), Missouri (16), New Jersey (9), New York (36), North Carolina (11), South Carolina (9), Tennessee (12), Texas (13), Virginia (12), West Virginia (6)

Blaine (182) — California (8), Colorado (3), Illinois (22), Iowa (13), Kansas (9), Maine (6), Massachusetts (14), Michigan (13), Minnesota (7), Nebraska (5), Nevada (3), New Hampshire (4), Ohio (23), Oregon (3), Pennsylvania (30), Rhode Island (4), Vermont (4), Wisconsin (11)

Popular Votes — 1884

State	Total PV	Cleveland	Blaine	Other
Alabama	153,624	92,736	59,444	1,444
Arkansas	125,779	72,734	51,198	1,847
California	196,988	89,288	102,369	5,331
Colorado	66,519	27,723	36,084	2,712
Connecticut	137,221	67,167	65,879	4,175
Delaware	29,984	16,957	12,953	74
Florida	59,990	31,769	28,031	190
Georgia	143,610	94,667	48,603	340
Illinois	672,670	312,351	337,469	22,850
Indiana	495,423	245,041	238,511	11,871
Iowa	393,542	177,316	197,089	19,137
Kansas	250,991	90,111	154,410	6,470
Kentucky	276,503	152,894	118,822	4,787
Louisiana	109,399	62,594	46,347	458
Maine	130,489	52,153	72,217	6,119
Maryland	185,838	96,941	85,748	3,149
Massachusetts	303,383	122,352	146,724	34,307
Michigan	401,186	189,361	192,669	19,156
Minnesota	190,236	70,135	111,819	8,282
Mississippi	120,688	77,653	43,035	—
Missouri	441,268	236,023	203,081	2,164
Nebraska	134,202	54,391	76,912	2,899
Nevada	12,779	5,577	7,176	26
New Hampshire	84,586	39,198	43,254	2,134
New Jersey	260,853	127,747	123,436	9,670
New York	1,167,003	563,048	562,001	41,954
North Carolina	268,356	142,905	125,021	430
Ohio	784,620	368,280	400,092	16,248
Oregon	52,683	24,598	26,845	1,240
Pennsylvania	899,563	392,915	474,350	32,298
Rhode Island	32,771	12,391	19,030	1,350
South Carolina	92,812	69,845	21,730	1,237
Tennessee	259,978	133,770	124,101	2,107
Texas	326,458	226,375	93,345	6,738
Vermont	59,409	17,331	39,514	2,564
Virginia	284,977	145,491	139,356	130
West Virginia	132,145	67,311	63,096	1,738
Wisconsin	319,847	146,447	161,155	12,245
Total	10,058,373	4,915,586	4,852,916	289,871

Democratic Nomination — 1884

Candidate	ConFB	FB%	ConLB[2]	LB%	PriW	PriV	PriV%
Cleveland	392	47.81%	683	83.29%	—	—	—
Bayard	170	20.73%	82	9.94%	—	—	—
Hendricks	1	0.12%	46	5.55%	—	—	—
Thurman	88	10.73%	4	0.49%	—	—	—
Randall	78	9.51%	4	0.49%	—	—	—
McDonald	56	6.83%	2	0.24%	—	—	—

Republican Nomination — 1884

Candidate	ConFB	FB%	ConLB[4]	LB%	PriW	PriV	PriV%
Blaine	335	40.79%	541	65.98%	—	—	—
Arthur	278	33.90%	207	25.24%	—	—	—
Edmunds	93	11.34%	41	5.00%	—	—	—
Logan	64	7.74%	7	0.85%	—	—	—

Equalized Statistics — 1884

Candidate	EVX	PVX	ConFBX	ConLBX	PriVX
Cleveland	294	48,870,588	478	833	—
Blaine	244	48,247,525	408	660	—
Arthur	—	—	339	252	—
Bayard	—	—	207	99	—
Edmunds	—	—	113	50	—
Thurman	—	—	107	5	—
Randall	—	—	95	5	—
Logan	—	—	77	9	—
McDonald	—	—	68	2	—
Hendricks	—	—	1	55	—

Election of 1888

Basics — 1888

Election number — 26
Winner — Benjamin Harrison (R)
Incumbent — Grover Cleveland (D)
U.S. population — 60,184,257
States — 38
Electoral votes — 401
Popular votes — 11,395,705
Voter turnout — 79.3%

Top Candidates — 1888

Benjamin Harrison (CS 79.71)

Grover Cleveland (CS 72.27)

John Sherman (CS 31.96)

Field — 1888

Candidate	PI	Age	State	Position	N	W	CS
Benjamin Harrison (R)	7.9	55.20	Ind.	Former senator	X	X	79.71
Grover Cleveland (D)	9.2	51.62	N.Y.	President	X	—	72.27
John Sherman (R)	7.7	65.48	Ohio	Senator	—	—	31.96
Walter Gresham (R)	5.7	56.63	Ind.	Federal judge	—	—	20.30
Russell Alger (R)	7.8	52.68	Mich.	Former governor	—	—	19.58
Chauncey Depew (R)	4.9	54.52	N.Y.	Business executive	—	—	19.50
Clinton Fisk (PRO)	3.8	59.90	N.J.	Former general	—	—	17.02
William Boyd Allison (R)	7.6	59.67	Iowa	Senator	—	—	16.95
James Blaine (R)	6.3	58.75	Maine	Former nominee	—	—	13.35

General Election — 1888

Candidate	EV	EV%	SC	PV	PV%
Harrison	233	58.11%	20	5,449,825	47.82%
Cleveland	168	41.90%	18	5,539,118	48.61%
Fisk	0	0.00%	0	249,913	2.19%

Electoral Votes — 1888

Harrison (233) — California (8), Colorado (3), Illinois (22), Indiana (15), Iowa (13), Kansas (9), Maine (6), Massachusetts (14), Michigan (13), Minnesota (7), Nebraska (5), Nevada (3), New Hampshire (4), New York (36), Ohio (23), Oregon (3), Pennsylvania (30), Rhode Island (4), Vermont (4), Wisconsin (11)

Cleveland (168) — Alabama (10), Arkansas (7), Connecticut (6), Delaware (3), Florida (4), Georgia (12), Kentucky (13), Louisiana (8), Maryland (8), Mississippi (9), Missouri (16), New Jersey (9), North Carolina (11), South Carolina (9), Tennessee (12), Texas (13), Virginia (12), West Virginia (6)

Popular Votes — 1888

State	Total PV	Cleveland	Harrison	Fisk	Other
Alabama	175,085	117,314	57,177	594	—
Arkansas	157,058	86,062	59,752	614	10,630
California	251,339	117,729	124,816	5,761	3,033
Colorado	91,946	37,549	50,772	2,182	1,443
Connecticut	153,978	74,920	74,584	4,234	240
Delaware	29,764	16,414	12,950	399	1
Florida	66,500	39,557	26,529	414	—
Georgia	142,936	100,493	40,499	1,808	136
Illinois	747,813	348,351	370,475	21,703	7,284
Indiana	536,988	260,990	263,366	9,939	2,693
Iowa	404,694	179,876	211,607	3,550	9,661
Kansas	331,133	102,739	182,845	6,774	38,775
Kentucky	344,868	183,830	155,138	5,223	677
Louisiana	115,891	85,032	30,660	160	39
Maine	128,253	50,472	73,730	2,691	1,360
Maryland	210,941	106,188	99,986	4,767	—
Massachusetts	344,243	151,590	183,892	8,701	60
Michigan	475,356	213,469	236,387	20,945	4,555
Minnesota	263,162	104,372	142,492	15,201	1,097
Mississippi	115,786	85,451	30,095	240	—
Missouri	521,359	261,943	236,252	4,539	18,625
Nebraska	202,630	80,552	108,417	9,435	4,226
Nevada	12,573	5,303	7,229	41	—
New Hampshire	90,770	43,382	45,734	1,596	58
New Jersey	303,801	151,508	144,360	7,933	—
New York	1,321,897	635,965	650,338	30,231	5,363
North Carolina	285,946	148,336	134,784	2,789	37
Ohio	839,357	395,456	416,054	24,356	3,491
Oregon	61,889	26,518	33,291	1,676	404
Pennsylvania	997,568	446,633	526,091	20,947	3,897
Rhode Island	40,775	17,530	21,969	1,251	25
South Carolina	79,997	65,824	13,736	—	437
Tennessee	304,313	158,779	139,511	5,975	48
Texas	363,479	236,290	93,991	4,739	28,459
Vermont	63,476	16,788	45,193	1,460	35
Virginia	304,087	152,004	150,399	1,684	—
West Virginia	159,440	78,677	78,171	1,084	1,508
Wisconsin	354,614	155,232	176,553	14,277	8,552
Total	11,395,705	5,539,118	5,449,825	249,913	156,849

Democratic Nomination — 1888

Candidate	ConFB	FB%	ConLB	LB%	PriW	PriV	PriV%
Cleveland	822	100.00%	—	—	—	—	—

Republican Nomination — 1888

Candidate	ConFB	FB%	ConLB[8]	LB%	PriW	PriV	PriV%
Harrison	85	10.22%	544	65.39%	—	—	—
Sherman	229	27.52%	118	14.18%	—	—	—
Alger	84	10.10%	100	12.02%	—	—	—
Gresham	107	12.86%	59	7.09%	—	—	—
Blaine	35	4.21%	5	0.60%	—	—	—
Depew	99	11.90%	0	0.00%	—	—	—
Allison	72	8.65%	0	0.00%	—	—	—

Equalized Statistics — 1888

Candidate	EVX	PVX	ConFBX	ConLBX	PriVX
Harrison	313	47,823,500	102	654	—
Cleveland	225	48,607,067	1,000	—	—
Sherman	—	—	275	142	—
Gresham	—	—	129	71	—
Alger	—	—	101	120	—
Depew	—	—	119	0	—
Fisk	0	2,193,046	—	—	—
Allison	—	—	87	0	—
Blaine	—	—	42	6	—

Election of 1892

Basics — 1892

Election number — 27
Winner — Grover Cleveland (D)
Incumbent — Benjamin Harrison (R)
U.S. population — 65,428,309
States — 44
Electoral votes — 444
Popular votes — 12,071,548
Voter turnout — 74.7%

Top Candidates — 1892

Grover Cleveland (CS 80.73)

Benjamin Harrison (CS 68.40)

James Weaver (CS 38.80)

Field — 1892

Candidate	PI	Age	State	Position	N	W	CS
Grover Cleveland (D)	9.1	55.62	N.Y.	Former president	X	X	80.73
Benjamin Harrison (R)	8.5	59.20	Ind.	President	X	—	68.40
James Weaver (POP)	4.1	59.39	Iowa	Former representative	—	—	38.80
James Blaine (R)	3.7	62.75	Maine	Former nominee	—	—	26.05
William McKinley (R)	8.2	49.76	Ohio	Governor	—	—	26.05
David Hill (D)	8.5	49.17	N.Y.	Senator	—	—	19.98
Horace Boies (D)	6.3	64.90	Iowa	Governor	—	—	19.02
John Bidwell (PRO)	0.4	73.24	Calif.	Movement leader	—	—	17.19
Arthur Gorman (D)	7.4	53.64	Md.	Senator	—	—	13.19

General Election — 1892

Candidate	EV	EV%	SC	PV	PV%
Cleveland	277	62.39%	24	5,554,617	46.01%
Harrison	145	32.66%	17	5,186,793	42.97%
Weaver	22	4.96%	5	1,029,357	8.53%
Bidwell	0	0.00%	0	270,979	2.25%

Electoral Votes — 1892

Cleveland (277) — Alabama (11), Arkansas (8), California (8), Connecticut (6), Delaware (3), Florida (4), Georgia (13), Illinois (24), Indiana (15), Kentucky (13), Louisiana (8), Maryland (8), Michigan (5), Mississippi (9), Missouri (17), New Jersey (10), New York (36), North Carolina (11), North Dakota (1), Ohio (1), South Carolina (9), Tennessee (12), Texas (15), Virginia (12), West Virginia (6), Wisconsin (12)
Harrison (145) — California (1), Iowa (13), Maine (6), Massachusetts (15), Michigan (9), Minnesota (9), Montana (3), Nebraska (8), New Hampshire (4), North Dakota (1), Ohio (22), Oregon (3), Pennsylvania (32), Rhode Island (4), South Dakota (4), Vermont (4), Washington (4), Wyoming (3)
Weaver (22) — Colorado (4), Idaho (3), Kansas (10), Nevada (3), North Dakota (1), Oregon (1)

Popular Votes — 1892

State	Total PV	Cleveland	Harrison	Weaver	Bidwell	Other
Alabama	232,543	138,135	9,184	84,984	240	—
Arkansas	148,117	87,834	47,072	11,831	113	1,267
California	269,585	118,151	118,027	25,311	8,096	—
Colorado	93,881	—	38,620	53,584	1,677	—
Connecticut	164,593	82,395	77,030	809	4,026	333
Delaware	37,235	18,581	18,077	—	564	13
Florida	35,567	30,154	—	4,843	570	—
Georgia	223,961	129,386	48,305	42,937	988	2,345
Idaho	19,407	—	8,599	10,520	288	—
Illinois	873,667	426,281	399,308	22,207	25,871	—
Indiana	553,613	262,740	255,615	22,208	13,050	—
Iowa	443,159	196,367	219,795	20,595	6,402	—
Kansas	323,591	—	156,134	162,888	4,569	—
Kentucky	340,864	175,461	135,462	23,500	6,441	—
Louisiana	118,287	87,922	27,903	2,462	—	—
Maine	116,013	48,024	62,878	2,045	3,062	4
Maryland	213,275	113,866	92,736	796	5,877	—
Massachusetts	391,028	176,813	202,814	3,210	7,539	652
Michigan	466,917	202,396	222,708	20,031	20,857	925
Minnesota	267,461	101,055	122,836	29,336	14,234	—
Mississippi	52,519	40,030	1,398	10,118	973	—
Missouri	541,583	268,400	227,646	41,204	4,333	—
Montana	44,461	17,690	18,871	7,338	562	—
Nebraska	200,205	24,956	87,213	83,134	4,902	—
Nevada	10,826	703	2,811	7,226	86	—
New Hampshire	89,328	42,081	45,658	292	1,297	—
New Jersey	337,485	170,987	156,059	969	8,133	1,337
New York	1,336,793	654,868	609,350	16,429	38,190	17,956
North Carolina	280,270	132,951	100,346	44,336	2,637	—
North Dakota	36,118	—	17,519	17,700	899	—
Ohio	850,164	404,115	405,187	14,850	26,012	—
Oregon	78,378	14,243	35,002	26,875	2,258	—
Pennsylvania	1,003,000	452,264	516,011	8,714	25,123	888
Rhode Island	53,196	24,336	26,975	228	1,654	3
South Carolina	70,504	54,680	13,345	2,407	—	72
South Dakota	70,513	9,081	34,888	26,544	—	—

State	Total PV	Cleveland	Harrison	Weaver	Bidwell	Other
Tennessee	265,732	136,468	100,537	23,918	4,809	—
Texas	422,447	239,148	77,478	99,688	2,165	3,968
Vermont	55,793	16,325	37,992	42	1,424	10
Virginia	292,238	164,136	113,098	12,275	2,729	—
Washington	87,968	29,802	36,459	19,165	2,542	—
West Virginia	171,079	84,467	80,292	4,167	2,153	—
Wisconsin	371,481	177,325	171,101	9,919	13,136	—
Wyoming	16,703	—	8,454	7,722	498	29
Total	12,071,548	5,554,617	5,186,793	1,029,357	270,979	29,802

Democratic Nomination — 1892

Candidate	ConFB	FB%	ConLB	LB%	PriW	PriV	PriV%
Cleveland	617	67.84%	—	—	—	—	—
Hill	114	12.53%	—	—	—	—	—
Boies	103	11.32%	—	—	—	—	—
Gorman	37	4.01%	—	—	—	—	—

Republican Nomination — 1892

Candidate	ConFB	FB%	ConLB	LB%	PriW	PriV	PriV%
Harrison	535	59.07%	—	—	—	—	—
Blaine	182	20.11%	—	—	—	—	—
McKinley	182	20.09%	—	—	—	—	—

Equalized Statistics — 1892

Candidate	EVX	PVX	ConFBX	ConLBX	PriVX
Cleveland	336	46,014,123	678	—	—
Harrison	176	42,967,091	591	—	—
Weaver	27	8,527,133	—	—	—
Blaine	—	—	201	—	—
McKinley	—	—	201	—	—
Hill	—	—	125	—	—
Boies	—	—	113	—	—
Bidwell	0	2,244,774	—	—	—
Gorman	—	—	40	—	—

Election of 1896

Basics — 1896

Election number — 28
Winner — William McKinley (R)
Incumbent — Grover Cleveland (D)
U.S. population — 70,614,681
States — 45
Electoral votes — 447
Popular votes — 13,904,866
Voter turnout — 79.3%

Top Candidates — 1896

William McKinley (CS 81.24)

William Jennings Bryan (CS 70.98)

Richard Bland (CS 30.20)

Field — 1896

Candidate	PI	Age	State	Position	N	W	CS
William McKinley (R)	8.2	53.76	Ohio	Former governor	X	X	81.24
William J. Bryan (D-POP)	4.6	36.62	Nebr.	Former representative	X	—	70.98
Richard Bland (D)	5.5	61.20	Mo.	Former representative	—	—	30.20
Robert Pattison (D)	7.2	45.90	Pa.	Former governor	—	—	18.30
Thomas Reed (R)	5.2	57.04	Maine	Representative	—	—	17.27
Joseph Blackburn (D)	6.2	58.08	Ky.	Senator	—	—	17.03
Horace Boies (D)	6.3	68.90	Iowa	Former governor	—	—	15.75
Matthew Quay (R)	7.5	63.09	Pa.	Senator	—	—	15.35
Levi Morton (R)	7.8	72.46	N.Y.	Governor	—	—	15.03
John R. McLean (D)	5.0	48.12	Ohio	Journalist	—	—	14.63
Claude Matthews (D)	7.3	50.88	Ind.	Governor	—	—	13.19

General Election — 1896

Candidate	EV	EV%	SC	PV	PV%
McKinley	271	60.63%	23	7,105,076	51.10%
Bryan	176	39.37%	22	6,370,897	45.82%

Electoral Votes — 1896

McKinley (271) — California (8), Connecticut (6), Delaware (3), Illinois (24), Indiana (15), Iowa (13), Kentucky (12), Maine (6), Maryland (8), Massachusetts (15), Michigan (14), Minnesota (9), New Hampshire (4), New Jersey (10), New York (36), North Dakota (3), Ohio (23), Oregon (4), Pennsylvania (32), Rhode Island (4), Vermont (4), West Virginia (6), Wisconsin (12)

Bryan (176) — Alabama (11), Arkansas (8), California (1), Colorado (4), Florida (4), Georgia (13), Idaho (3), Kansas (10), Kentucky (1), Louisiana (8), Mississippi (9), Missouri (17), Montana (3), Nebraska (8), Nevada (3), North Carolina (11), South Carolina (9), South Dakota (4), Tennessee (12), Texas (15), Utah (3), Virginia (12), Washington (4), Wyoming (3)

Popular Votes — 1896

State	Total PV	McKinley	Bryan	Other
Alabama	194,580	55,673	130,298	8,609
Arkansas	149,396	37,512	110,103	1,781
California	298,695	146,688	123,143	28,864
Colorado	189,539	26,271	161,005	2,263
Connecticut	174,394	110,285	56,740	7,369
Delaware	31,540	16,883	13,425	1,232
Florida	46,468	11,298	30,683	4,487
Georgia	163,309	60,107	94,733	8,469
Idaho	29,631	6,324	23,135	172
Illinois	1,090,766	607,130	465,593	18,043
Indiana	637,089	323,754	305,538	7,797
Iowa	521,550	289,293	223,744	8,513
Kansas	336,085	159,484	173,049	3,552
Kentucky	445,928	218,171	217,894	9,863
Louisiana	101,046	22,037	77,175	1,834
Maine	118,419	80,403	34,587	3,429
Maryland	250,249	136,959	104,150	9,140
Massachusetts	401,269	278,976	105,414	16,879
Michigan	545,583	293,336	237,164	15,083
Minnesota	341,762	193,503	139,735	8,524
Mississippi	69,591	4,819	63,355	1,417
Missouri	674,032	304,940	363,667	5,425
Montana	53,330	10,509	42,628	193
Nebraska	223,181	103,064	115,007	5,110
Nevada	10,314	1,938	7,802	574
New Hampshire	83,670	57,444	21,271	4,955
New Jersey	371,014	221,367	133,675	15,972
New York	1,423,876	819,838	551,369	52,669
North Carolina	331,337	155,122	174,408	1,807
North Dakota	47,391	26,335	20,686	370
Ohio	1,014,295	525,991	474,882	13,422
Oregon	97,335	48,700	46,739	1,896
Pennsylvania	1,194,355	728,300	427,125	38,930
Rhode Island	54,785	37,437	14,459	2,889
South Carolina	68,938	9,313	58,801	824
South Dakota	82,937	41,040	41,225	672
Tennessee	320,903	148,683	167,168	5,052

State	Total PV	McKinley	Bryan	Other
Texas	515,987	163,413	267,803	84,771
Utah	78,098	13,491	64,607	—
Vermont	63,831	51,127	10,179	2,525
Virginia	294,674	135,379	154,708	4,587
Washington	93,435	39,153	51,646	2,636
West Virginia	201,757	105,379	94,480	1,898
Wisconsin	447,409	268,135	165,523	13,751
Wyoming	21,093	10,072	10,376	645
Total	13,904,866	7,105,076	6,370,897	428,893

Democratic Nomination — 1896

Candidate	ConFB	FB%	ConLB[5]	LB%	PriW	PriV	PriV%
Bryan	137	14.73%	652	70.11%	—	—	—
Pattison	97	10.43%	95	10.22%	—	—	—
Bland	235	25.27%	11	1.18%	—	—	—
Blackburn	82	8.82%	0	0.00%	—	—	—
Boies	67	7.20%	0	0.00%	—	—	—
McLean	54	5.81%	0	0.00%	—	—	—
Matthews	37	3.98%	0	0.00%	—	—	—

Republican Nomination — 1896

Candidate	ConFB	FB%	ConLB	LB%	PriW	PriV	PriV%
McKinley	662	71.59%	—	—	—	—	—
Reed	85	9.15%	—	—	—	—	—
Quay	62	6.66%	—	—	—	—	—
Morton	58	6.28%	—	—	—	—	—

Equalized Statistics — 1896

Candidate	EVX	PVX	ConFBX	ConLBX	PriVX
McKinley	326	51,097,767	716	—	—
Bryan	212	45,817,752	147	701	—
Bland	—	—	253	12	—
Pattison	—	—	104	102	—
Reed	—	—	91	—	—
Blackburn	—	—	88	0	—
Boies	—	—	72	0	—
Quay	—	—	67	—	—
Morton	—	—	63	—	—
McLean	—	—	58	0	—
Matthews	—	—	40	0	—

Election of 1900

Basics — 1900

Election number — 29
Winner — William McKinley (R)
Incumbent — William McKinley (R)
U.S. population — 76,212,168
States — 45
Electoral votes — 447
Popular votes — 13,972,525
Voter turnout — 73.2%

Top Candidates — 1900

William McKinley (CS 82.89)

William Jennings Bryan (CS 69.53)

Field — 1900

Candidate	PI	Age	State	Position	N	W	CS
William McKinley (R)	8.9	57.76	Ohio	President	X	X	82.89
William Jennings Bryan (D)	5.6	40.62	Nebr.	Former nominee	X	—	69.53

General Election — 1900

Candidate	EV	EV%	SC	PV	PV%
McKinley	292	65.32%	28	7,219,193	51.67%
Bryan	155	34.68%	17	6,357,698	45.50%

Electoral Votes — 1900

McKinley (292) — California (9), Connecticut (6), Delaware (3), Illinois (24), Indiana (15), Iowa (13), Kansas (10), Maine (6), Maryland (8), Massachusetts (15), Michigan (14), Minnesota (9), Nebraska (8), New Hampshire (4), New Jersey (10), New York (36), North Dakota (3), Ohio (23), Oregon (4), Pennsylvania (32), Rhode Island (4), South Dakota (4), Utah (3), Vermont (4), Washington (4), West Virginia (6), Wisconsin (12), Wyoming (3)

Bryan (155) — Alabama (11), Arkansas (8), Colorado (4), Florida (4), Georgia (13), Idaho (3), Kentucky (13), Louisiana (8), Mississippi (9), Missouri (17), Montana (3), Nevada (3), North Carolina (11), South Carolina (9), Tennessee (12), Texas (15), Virginia (12)

Popular Votes — 1900

State	Total PV	McKinley	Bryan	Other
Alabama	160,477	55,634	96,368	8,475
Arkansas	127,966	44,800	81,242	1,924
California	302,399	164,755	124,985	12,659
Colorado	220,895	92,701	122,705	5,489
Connecticut	180,195	102,572	74,014	3,609
Delaware	41,989	22,535	18,852	602
Florida	39,777	7,463	28,273	4,041
Georgia	121,410	34,260	81,180	5,970
Idaho	56,760	27,198	28,260	1,302
Illinois	1,131,898	597,985	503,061	30,852
Indiana	664,094	336,063	309,584	18,447
Iowa	530,345	307,799	209,261	13,285
Kansas	353,766	185,955	162,601	5,210
Kentucky	467,580	226,801	234,889	5,890
Louisiana	67,906	14,234	53,668	4
Maine	107,698	66,413	37,822	3,463
Maryland	264,386	136,151	122,237	5,998
Massachusetts	414,804	238,866	156,997	18,941
Michigan	543,789	316,014	211,432	16,343
Minnesota	316,311	190,461	112,901	12,949
Mississippi	59,055	5,707	51,706	1,642
Missouri	683,658	314,092	351,922	17,644
Montana	63,856	25,409	37,311	1,136
Nebraska	241,430	121,835	114,013	5,582
Nevada	10,196	3,849	6,347	—
New Hampshire	92,364	54,799	35,489	2,076
New Jersey	401,050	221,707	164,808	14,535
New York	1,548,043	822,013	678,462	47,568
North Carolina	292,518	132,997	157,733	1,788
North Dakota	57,783	35,898	20,524	1,361
Ohio	1,040,073	543,918	474,882	21,273
Oregon	84,216	46,526	33,385	4,305
Pennsylvania	1,173,210	712,665	424,232	36,313
Rhode Island	56,548	33,784	19,812	2,952
South Carolina	50,698	3,525	47,173	—
South Dakota	96,169	54,574	39,538	2,057
Tennessee	273,860	123,108	145,240	5,512
Texas	424,334	131,174	267,945	25,215
Utah	93,071	47,089	44,949	1,033
Vermont	56,212	42,569	12,849	794
Virginia	264,208	115,769	146,079	2,360
Washington	107,523	57,455	44,833	5,235
West Virginia	220,796	119,829	98,807	2,160
Wisconsin	442,501	265,760	159,163	17,578
Wyoming	24,708	14,482	10,164	62
Total	13,972,525	7,219,193	6,357,698	395,634

Democratic Nomination — 1900

Candidate	ConFB	FB%	ConLB	LB%	PriW	PriV	PriV%
Bryan	936	100.00%	—	—	—	—	—

Republican Nomination — 1900

Candidate	ConFB	FB%	ConLB	LB%	PriW	PriV	PriV%
McKinley	926	100.00%	—	—	—	—	—

Equalized Statistics — 1900

Candidate	EVX	PVX	ConFBX	ConLBX	PriVX
McKinley	351	51,667,061	1,000	—	—
Bryan	187	45,501,425	1,000	—	—

Election of 1904

Basics — 1904

Election number — 30
Winner — Theodore Roosevelt (R)
Incumbent — Theodore Roosevelt (R)
U.S. population — 82,166,000
States — 45
Electoral votes — 476
Popular votes — 13,519,039
Voter turnout — 65.2%

Top Candidates — 1904

Theodore Roosevelt (CS 85.72)

Alton Parker (CS 66.33)

William Randolph Hearst (CS 24.45)

Field — 1904

Candidate	PI	Age	State	Position	N	W	CS
Theodore Roosevelt (R)	8.8	46.01	N.Y.	President	X	X	85.72
Alton Parker (D)	4.9	52.47	N.Y.	State judge	X	—	66.33
William Randolph Hearst (D)	5.5	41.51	N.Y.	Journalist	—	—	24.45
Eugene Debs (SOC)	2.9	48.99	Ind.	Movement leader	—	—	19.53
Francis Cockrell (D)	7.0	70.08	Mo.	Senator	—	—	13.35

General Election — 1904

Candidate	EV	EV%	SC	PV	PV%
Roosevelt	336	70.59%	32	7,625,599	56.41%
Parker	140	29.41%	13	5,083,501	37.60%
Debs	0	0.00%	0	402,490	2.98%

Electoral Votes — 1904

Roosevelt (336) — California (10), Colorado (5), Connecticut (7), Delaware (3), Idaho (3), Illinois (27), Indiana (15), Iowa (13), Kansas (10), Maine (6), Maryland (1), Massachusetts (16), Michigan (14), Minnesota (11), Missouri (18), Montana (3), Nebraska (8), Nevada (3), New Hampshire (4), New Jersey (12), New York (39), North Dakota (4), Ohio (23), Oregon (4), Pennsylvania (34), Rhode Island (4), South Dakota (4), Utah (3), Vermont (4), Washington (5), West Virginia (7), Wisconsin (13), Wyoming (3)

Parker (140) — Alabama (11), Arkansas (9), Florida (5), Georgia (13), Kentucky (13), Louisiana (9), Maryland (7), Mississippi (10), North Carolina (12), South Carolina (9), Tennessee (12), Texas (18), Virginia (12)

Popular Votes — 1904

State	Total PV	Roosevelt	Parker	Debs	Other
Alabama	108,785	22,472	79,797	853	5,663
Arkansas	116,328	46,760	64,434	1,816	3,318
California	331,768	205,226	89,294	29,535	7,713
Colorado	243,667	134,661	100,105	4,304	4,597
Connecticut	191,136	111,089	72,909	4,543	2,595
Delaware	43,856	23,705	19,347	146	658
Florida	39,302	8,314	27,046	2,337	1,605
Georgia	130,986	24,004	83,466	196	23,320
Idaho	72,577	47,783	18,480	4,949	1,365
Illinois	1,076,495	632,645	327,606	69,225	47,019
Indiana	682,206	368,289	274,356	12,023	27,538
Iowa	485,703	307,907	149,141	14,847	13,808
Kansas	329,047	213,455	86,164	15,869	13,559
Kentucky	435,946	205,457	217,170	3,599	9,720
Louisiana	53,908	5,205	47,708	995	—
Maine	96,036	64,438	27,648	2,103	1,847
Maryland	224,229	109,497	109,446	2,247	3,039
Massachusetts	445,100	257,813	165,746	13,604	7,937
Michigan	520,443	361,863	134,163	8,942	15,475
Minnesota	292,860	216,651	55,187	11,692	9,330
Mississippi	58,721	3,280	53,480	462	1,499
Missouri	643,861	321,449	296,312	13,009	13,091
Montana	63,568	33,994	21,816	5,675	2,083
Nebraska	225,732	138,558	52,921	7,412	26,841
Nevada	12,115	6,864	3,982	925	344
New Hampshire	90,151	54,157	34,071	1,090	833
New Jersey	432,547	245,164	164,566	9,587	13,230
New York	1,617,765	859,533	683,981	36,883	37,368
North Carolina	207,818	82,442	124,091	124	1,161
North Dakota	70,179	52,595	14,273	2,009	1,302
Ohio	1,004,395	600,095	344,674	36,260	23,366
Oregon	89,656	60,309	17,327	7,479	4,541
Pennsylvania	1,236,738	840,949	337,998	21,863	35,928
Rhode Island	68,656	41,605	24,839	956	1,256
South Carolina	55,890	2,570	53,320	—	—
South Dakota	101,395	72,083	21,969	3,138	4,205
Tennessee	242,750	105,363	131,653	1,354	4,380

State	Total PV	Roosevelt	Parker	Debs	Other
Texas	233,609	51,307	167,088	2,788	12,426
Utah	101,626	62,446	33,413	5,767	—
Vermont	51,888	40,459	9,777	859	793
Virginia	130,410	48,180	80,649	202	1,379
Washington	145,151	101,540	28,098	10,023	5,490
West Virginia	239,986	132,620	100,855	1,573	4,938
Wisconsin	443,440	280,314	124,205	28,240	10,681
Wyoming	30,614	20,489	8,930	987	208
Total	13,519,039	7,625,599	5,083,501	402,490	407,449

Democratic Nomination — 1904

Candidate	ConFB	FB%	ConLB	LB%	PriW	PriV	PriV%
Parker	679	67.90%	—	—	—	—	—
Hearst	181	18.10%	—	—	—	—	—
Cockrell	42	4.20%	—	—	—	—	—

Republican Nomination — 1904

Candidate	ConFB	FB%	ConLB	LB%	PriW	PriV	PriV%
Roosevelt	994	100.00%	—	—	—	—	—

Equalized Statistics — 1904

Candidate	EVX	PVX	ConFBX	ConLBX	PriVX
Roosevelt	380	56,406,369	1,000	—	—
Parker	158	37,602,532	679	—	—
Hearst	—	—	181	—	—
Debs	0	2,977,209	—	—	—
Cockrell	—	—	42	—	—

Election of 1908

Basics — 1908

Election number — 31
Winner — William Howard Taft (R)
Incumbent — Theodore Roosevelt (R)
U.S. population — 88,710,000
States — 46
Electoral votes — 483
Popular votes — 14,884,098
Voter turnout — 65.4%

Top Candidates — 1908

William Howard Taft (CS 83.31)

William Jennings Bryan (CS 68.65)

Eugene Debs (CS 19.04)

Field — 1908

Candidate	PI	Age	State	Position	N	W	CS
William Howard Taft (R)	6.0	51.13	Ohio	Cabinet member	X	X	83.31
William Jennings Bryan (D)	5.2	48.62	Nebr.	Former nominee	X	—	68.65
Eugene Debs (SOC)	2.9	52.99	Ind.	Movement leader	—	—	19.04
Philander Knox (R)	8.2	55.49	Pa.	Senator	—	—	15.51
Charles Evans Hughes (R)	7.4	46.56	N.Y.	Governor	—	—	15.43
Joseph Cannon (R)	5.3	72.49	Ill.	Representative	—	—	14.71
George Gray (D)	6.3	68.49	Del.	Former senator	—	—	14.71
John Johnson (D)	6.8	47.26	Minn.	Governor	—	—	13.67
Charles Fairbanks (R)	8.8	56.48	Ind.	Vice president	—	—	13.27

General Election — 1908

Candidate	EV	EV%	SC	PV	PV%
Taft	321	66.46%	29	7,676,598	51.58%
Bryan	162	33.54%	17	6,406,874	43.05%
Debs	0	0.00%	0	420,436	2.83%

Electoral Votes — 1908

Taft (321) — California (10), Connecticut (7), Delaware (3), Idaho (3), Illinois (27), Indiana (15), Iowa (13), Kansas (10), Maine (6), Maryland (2), Massachusetts (16), Michigan (14), Minnesota (11), Missouri (18), Montana (3), New Hampshire (4), New Jersey (12), New York (39), North Dakota (4), Ohio (23), Oregon (4), Pennsylvania (34), Rhode Island (4), South Dakota (4), Utah (3), Vermont (4), Washington (5), West Virginia (7), Wisconsin (13), Wyoming (3)

Bryan (162) — Alabama (11), Arkansas (9), Colorado (5), Florida (5), Georgia (13), Kentucky (13), Louisiana (9), Maryland (6), Mississippi (10), Nebraska (8), Nevada (3), North Carolina (12), Oklahoma (7), South Carolina (9), Tennessee (12), Texas (18), Virginia (12)

Popular Votes — 1908

State	Total PV	Taft	Bryan	Debs	Other
Alabama	105,152	25,561	74,391	1,450	3,750
Arkansas	151,845	56,684	87,020	5,842	2,299
California	386,625	214,398	127,492	28,659	16,076
Colorado	263,858	123,693	126,644	7,960	5,561
Connecticut	189,903	112,815	68,255	5,113	3,720
Delaware	48,007	25,014	22,055	239	699
Florida	49,360	10,654	31,104	3,747	3,855
Georgia	132,794	41,692	72,413	584	18,105
Idaho	97,293	52,621	36,162	6,400	2,110
Illinois	1,155,254	629,932	450,810	34,711	39,801
Indiana	721,117	348,993	338,262	13,476	20,386
Iowa	494,770	275,210	200,771	8,287	10,502
Kansas	376,043	197,316	161,209	12,420	5,098
Kentucky	490,719	235,711	244,092	4,093	6,823
Louisiana	75,117	8,958	63,568	2,514	77
Maine	106,335	66,987	35,403	1,758	2,187
Maryland	238,531	116,513	115,908	2,323	3,787
Massachusetts	456,905	265,966	155,533	10,778	24,628
Michigan	538,124	333,313	174,619	11,527	18,665
Minnesota	331,328	195,846	109,411	14,528	11,543
Mississippi	66,904	4,363	60,287	978	1,276
Missouri	715,841	347,203	346,574	15,431	6,633
Montana	69,233	32,471	29,511	5,920	1,331
Nebraska	266,799	126,997	131,099	3,524	5,179
Nevada	24,526	10,775	11,212	2,103	436
New Hampshire	89,595	53,144	33,655	1,299	1,497
New Jersey	467,111	265,298	182,522	10,249	9,042
New York	1,638,350	870,070	667,468	38,451	62,361
North Carolina	252,554	114,887	136,928	372	367
North Dakota	94,524	57,680	32,884	2,421	1,539
Ohio	1,121,552	572,312	502,721	33,795	12,724
Oklahoma	254,260	110,473	122,362	21,425	—
Oregon	110,539	62,454	37,792	7,322	2,971
Pennsylvania	1,267,450	745,779	448,782	33,914	38,975
Rhode Island	72,317	43,942	24,706	1,365	2,304
South Carolina	66,379	3,945	62,288	100	46
South Dakota	114,775	67,536	40,266	2,846	4,127

State	Total PV	Taft	Bryan	Debs	Other
Tennessee	257,180	117,977	135,608	1,870	1,725
Texas	292,913	65,605	216,662	7,779	2,867
Utah	108,757	61,165	42,610	4,890	92
Vermont	52,680	39,552	11,496	—	1,632
Virginia	137,065	52,572	82,946	255	1,292
Washington	183,570	106,062	58,383	14,177	4,948
West Virginia	258,098	137,869	111,410	3,679	5,140
Wisconsin	454,438	247,744	166,662	28,147	11,885
Wyoming	37,608	20,846	14,918	1,715	129
Total	14,884,098	7,676,598	6,406,874	420,436	380,190

Democratic Nomination — 1908

Candidate	ConFB	FB%	ConLB	LB%	PriW	PriV	PriV%
Bryan	889	88.67%	—	—	—	—	—
Gray	60	5.94%	—	—	—	—	—
Johnson	46	4.59%	—	—	—	—	—

Republican Nomination — 1908

Candidate	ConFB	FB%	ConLB	LB%	PriW	PriV	PriV%
Taft	702	71.63%	—	—	—	—	—
Knox	68	6.94%	—	—	—	—	—
Hughes	67	6.84%	—	—	—	—	—
Cannon	58	5.92%	—	—	—	—	—
Fairbanks	40	4.08%	—	—	—	—	—

Equalized Statistics — 1908

Candidate	EVX	PVX	ConFBX	ConLBX	PriVX
Taft	358	51,575,836	716	—	—
Bryan	180	43,045,094	887	—	—
Debs	0	2,824,733	—	—	—
Knox	—	—	69	—	—
Hughes	—	—	68	—	—
Cannon	—	—	59	—	—
Gray	—	—	59	—	—
Johnson	—	—	46	—	—
Fairbanks	—	—	41	—	—

Election of 1912

Basics — 1912

Election number — 32
Winner — Woodrow Wilson (D)
Incumbent — William Howard Taft (R)
U.S. population — 95,335,000
States — 48
Electoral votes — 531
Popular votes — 15,043,030
Voter turnout — 58.8%

Top Candidates — 1912

Woodrow Wilson (CS 86.26)

Theodore Roosevelt (CS 66.37)

William Howard Taft (CS 55.09)

Field — 1912

Candidate	PI	Age	State	Position	N	W	CS
Woodrow Wilson (D)	6.6	55.84	N.J.	Governor	X	X	86.26
Theodore Roosevelt (R/P)	10.0	54.01	N.Y.	Former president	—	—	66.37
William Howard Taft (R)	8.2	55.13	Ohio	President	X	—	55.09
Champ Clark (D)	3.7	62.65	Mo.	Representative	—	—	42.45
Eugene Debs (SOC)	1.5	56.99	Ind.	Movement leader	—	—	29.16
Judson Harmon (D)	5.6	66.74	Ohio	Governor	—	—	20.47
Oscar Underwood (D)	3.0	50.49	Ala.	Representative	—	—	16.41
Robert La Follette (R)	6.3	57.38	Wis.	Senator	—	—	15.18

General Election — 1912

Candidate	EV	EV%	SC	PV	PV%
Wilson	435	81.92%	40	6,294,327	41.84%
Roosevelt	88	16.57%	6	4,120,207	27.39%
Taft	8	1.51%	2	3,486,343	23.18%
Debs	0	0.00%	0	900,370	5.99%

Electoral Votes — 1912

Wilson (435) — Alabama (12), Arizona (3), Arkansas (9), California (2), Colorado (6), Connecticut (7), Delaware (3), Florida (6), Georgia (14), Idaho (4), Illinois (29), Indiana (15), Iowa (13), Kansas (10), Kentucky (13), Louisiana (10), Maine (6), Maryland (8), Massachusetts (18), Mississippi (10), Missouri (18), Montana (4), Nebraska (8), Nevada (3), New Hampshire (4), New Jersey (14), New Mexico (3), New York (45), North Carolina (12), North Dakota (5), Ohio (24), Oklahoma (10), Oregon (5), Rhode Island (5), South Carolina (9), Tennessee (12), Texas (20), Virginia (12), West Virginia (8), Wisconsin (13), Wyoming (3)

Roosevelt (88) — California (11), Michigan (15), Minnesota (12), Pennsylvania (38), South Dakota (5), Washington (7)

Taft (8) — Utah (4), Vermont (4)

Popular Votes — 1912

State	Total PV	Wilson	Roosevelt	Taft	Debs	Other
Alabama	117,959	82,438	22,680	9,807	3,029	5
Arizona	23,687	10,324	6,949	2,986	3,163	265
Arkansas	125,104	68,814	21,644	25,585	8,153	908
California	677,877	283,436	283,610	3,847	79,201	27,783
Colorado	265,954	113,912	71,752	58,386	16,366	5,538
Connecticut	190,404	74,561	34,129	68,324	10,056	3,334
Delaware	48,690	22,631	8,886	15,997	556	620
Florida	51,911	36,417	4,555	4,279	4,806	1,854
Georgia	121,470	93,087	21,985	5,191	1,058	149
Idaho	105,754	33,921	25,527	32,810	11,960	1,536
Illinois	1,146,173	405,048	386,478	253,593	81,278	19,776
Indiana	654,474	281,890	162,007	151,267	36,931	22,379
Iowa	492,353	185,322	161,819	119,805	16,967	8,440
Kansas	365,560	143,663	120,210	74,845	26,779	63
Kentucky	453,707	219,585	102,766	115,520	11,647	4,189
Louisiana	79,248	60,871	9,283	3,833	5,261	—
Maine	129,641	51,113	48,495	26,545	2,541	947
Maryland	231,981	112,674	57,789	54,956	3,996	2,566
Massachusetts	488,056	173,408	142,228	155,948	12,616	3,856
Michigan	547,971	150,201	213,243	151,434	23,060	10,033
Minnesota	334,219	106,426	125,856	64,334	27,505	10,098
Mississippi	64,483	57,324	3,549	1,560	2,050	—
Missouri	698,566	330,746	124,375	207,821	28,466	7,158
Montana	80,256	28,129	22,709	18,575	10,811	32
Nebraska	249,483	109,008	72,681	54,226	10,185	3,383
Nevada	20,115	7,986	5,620	3,196	3,313	—
New Hampshire	87,961	34,724	17,794	32,927	1,981	535
New Jersey	433,663	178,638	145,679	89,066	15,948	4,332
New Mexico	48,807	20,437	8,347	17,164	2,859	—
New York	1,588,315	655,573	390,093	455,487	63,434	23,728
North Carolina	243,776	144,407	69,135	29,129	987	118
North Dakota	86,474	29,549	25,726	22,990	6,966	1,243
Ohio	1,037,114	424,834	229,807	278,168	90,164	14,141
Oklahoma	253,694	119,143	—	90,726	41,630	2,195
Oregon	137,040	47,064	37,600	34,673	13,343	4,360
Pennsylvania	1,217,736	395,637	444,894	273,360	83,614	20,231

State	Total PV	Wilson	Roosevelt	Taft	Debs	Other
Rhode Island	77,894	30,412	16,878	27,703	2,049	852
South Carolina	50,403	48,355	1,293	536	164	55
South Dakota	116,327	48,942	58,811	—	4,664	3,910
Tennessee	251,933	133,021	54,041	60,475	3,564	832
Texas	300,961	218,921	26,715	28,310	24,884	2,131
Utah	112,272	36,576	24,174	42,013	8,999	510
Vermont	62,804	15,350	22,129	23,303	928	1,094
Virginia	136,975	90,332	21,776	23,288	820	759
Washington	322,799	86,840	113,698	70,445	40,134	11,682
West Virginia	268,728	113,097	79,112	56,754	15,248	4,517
Wisconsin	399,975	164,230	62,448	130,596	33,476	9,225
Wyoming	42,283	15,310	9,232	14,560	2,760	421
Total	15,043,030	6,294,327	4,120,207	3,486,343	900,370	241,783

Democratic Nomination — 1912

Candidate	ConFB	FB%	ConLB[46]	LB%	PriW	PriV	PriV%
Wilson	324	29.62%	990	90.49%	5	435,169	44.64%
Clark	441	40.27%	84	7.68%	5	405,537	41.60%
Harmon	148	13.53%	12	1.10%	1	116,294	11.93%
Underwood	118	10.74%	0	0.00%	0	0	0.00%

Republican Nomination — 1912

Candidate	ConFB	FB%	ConLB	LB%	PriW	PriV	PriV%
Taft	556	51.58%	—	—	1	766,326	33.89%
Roosevelt	107	9.93%	—	—	9	1,164,765	51.51%
La Follette	41	3.80%	—	—	2	327,357	14.48%

NOTE: A total of 348 delegates, most of them Roosevelt supporters, abstained.

Equalized Statistics — 1912

Candidate	EVX	PVX	ConFBX	ConLBX	PriVX
Wilson	441	41,842,149	296	905	4,464,302
Roosevelt	89	27,389,475	99	—	5,151,001
Taft	8	23,175,803	516	—	3,388,964
Clark	—	—	403	77	4,160,314
Debs	0	5,985,297	—	—	—
Harmon	—	—	135	11	1,193,034
Underwood	—	—	107	0	0
La Follette	—	—	38	—	1,447,688

Election of 1916

Basics — 1916

Election number — 33
Winner — Woodrow Wilson (D)
Incumbent — Woodrow Wilson (D)
U.S. population — 101,961,000
States — 48
Electoral votes — 531
Popular votes — 18,535,445
Voter turnout — 61.6%

Top Candidates — 1916

Woodrow Wilson (CS 78.07)

Charles Evans Hughes (CS 73.55)

Allan Benson (CS 20.19)

Field — 1916

Candidate	PI	Age	State	Position	N	W	CS
Woodrow Wilson (D)	8.6	59.84	N.J.	President	X	X	78.07
Charles Evans Hughes (R)	8.0	54.56	N.Y.	Supreme Court justice	X	—	73.55
Allan Benson (SOC)	2.7	44.99	N.Y.	Journalist	—	—	20.19
Albert Cummins (R)	5.3	66.71	Iowa	Senator	—	—	17.15
John Weeks (R)	6.5	56.56	Mass.	Senator	—	—	16.35
Charles Fairbanks (R)	4.7	64.48	Ind.	Former vice president	—	—	16.32
Elihu Root (R)	6.0	71.71	N.Y.	Former senator	—	—	16.23
Theodore Burton (R)	5.3	64.87	Ohio	Former senator	—	—	16.00
Lawrence Sherman (R)	6.1	57.98	Ill.	Senator	—	—	15.63
Theodore Roosevelt (R)	9.6	58.01	N.Y.	Former president	—	—	14.78
Henry Ford (R)	3.8	53.26	Mich.	Business executive		—	13.29
Robert La Follette (R)	5.2	61.38	Wis.	Senator	—	—	12.89

General Election — 1916

Candidate	EV	EV%	SC	PV	PV%
Wilson	277	52.17%	30	9,126,063	49.24%
Hughes	254	47.83%	18	8,547,030	46.11%
Benson	0	0.00%	0	590,070	3.18%

Electoral Votes — 1916

Wilson (277) — Alabama (12), Arizona (3), Arkansas (9), California (13), Colorado (6), Florida (6), Georgia (14), Idaho (4), Kansas (10), Kentucky (13), Louisiana (10), Maryland (8), Mississippi (10), Missouri (18), Montana (4), Nebraska (8), Nevada (3), New Hampshire (4), New Mexico (3), North Carolina (12), North Dakota (5), Ohio (24), Oklahoma (10), South Carolina (9), Tennessee (12), Texas (20), Utah (4), Virginia (12), Washington (7), West Virginia (1), Wyoming (3)

Hughes (254) — Connecticut (7), Delaware (3), Illinois (29), Indiana (15), Iowa (13), Maine (6), Massachusetts (18), Michigan (15), Minnesota (12), New Jersey (14), New York (45), Oregon (5), Pennsylvania (38), Rhode Island (5), South Dakota (5), Vermont (4), West Virginia (7), Wisconsin (13)

Popular Votes — 1916

State	Total PV	Wilson	Hughes	Benson	Other
Alabama	131,142	99,409	28,809	1,925	999
Arizona	58,019	33,170	20,522	3,174	1,153
Arkansas	168,348	112,186	47,148	6,999	2,015
California	999,250	465,936	462,516	42,898	27,900
Colorado	294,375	178,816	102,308	10,049	3,202
Connecticut	213,874	99,786	106,514	5,179	2,395
Delaware	51,810	24,753	26,011	480	566
Florida	80,734	55,984	14,611	5,353	4,786
Georgia	158,690	125,845	11,225	967	20,653
Idaho	134,615	70,054	55,368	8,066	1,127
Illinois	2,192,707	950,229	1,152,549	61,394	28,535
Indiana	718,853	334,063	341,005	21,860	21,925
Iowa	518,738	221,699	280,439	10,976	5,624
Kansas	629,813	314,588	277,658	24,685	12,882
Kentucky	520,078	269,990	241,854	4,734	3,500
Louisiana	92,974	79,875	6,466	284	6,349
Maine	136,314	64,033	69,508	2,177	596
Maryland	262,039	138,359	117,347	2,674	3,659
Massachusetts	531,822	247,885	268,784	11,058	4,095
Michigan	646,873	283,993	337,952	16,012	8,916
Minnesota	387,367	179,155	179,544	20,117	8,551
Mississippi	86,679	80,422	4,253	1,484	520
Missouri	786,773	398,032	369,339	14,612	4,790
Montana	178,009	101,104	66,933	9,634	338
Nebraska	287,315	158,827	117,771	7,141	3,576
Nevada	33,314	17,776	12,127	3,065	346
New Hampshire	89,127	43,781	43,725	1,318	303
New Jersey	494,442	211,018	268,982	10,405	4,037
New Mexico	66,879	33,693	31,097	1,977	112
New York	1,706,305	759,426	879,238	45,944	21,697
North Carolina	289,837	168,383	120,890	509	55
North Dakota	115,390	55,206	53,471	5,716	997
Ohio	1,165,091	604,161	514,753	38,092	8,085
Oklahoma	292,327	148,123	97,233	45,091	1,880
Oregon	261,650	120,087	126,813	9,711	5,039
Pennsylvania	1,297,189	521,784	703,823	42,638	28,944
Rhode Island	87,816	40,394	44,858	1,914	650

State	Total PV	Wilson	Hughes	Benson	Other
South Carolina	63,950	61,845	1,550	135	420
South Dakota	128,942	59,191	64,217	3,760	1,774
Tennessee	272,190	153,280	116,223	2,542	145
Texas	372,467	286,514	64,999	18,969	1,985
Utah	143,145	84,145	54,137	4,460	403
Vermont	64,475	22,708	40,250	798	719
Virginia	153,993	102,825	49,358	1,060	750
Washington	380,994	183,388	167,208	22,800	7,598
West Virginia	289,671	140,403	143,124	6,144	—
Wisconsin	447,134	191,363	220,822	27,631	7,318
Wyoming	51,906	28,376	21,698	1,459	373
Total	18,535,445	9,126,063	8,547,030	590,070	272,282

Democratic Nomination — 1916

Candidate	ConFB	FB%	ConLB	LB%	PriW	PriV	PriV%
Wilson	1,092	100.00%	—	—	20	1,173,220	98.78%

Republican Nomination — 1916

Candidate	ConFB	FB%	ConLB[3]	LB%	PriW	PriV	PriV%
Hughes	254	25.68%	950	96.20%	2	80,737	4.20%
Roosevelt	65	6.59%	19	1.87%	1	80,019	4.16%
Weeks	105	10.64%	3	0.30%	0	0	0.00%
La Follette	25	2.53%	3	0.30%	2	133,426	6.94%
Root	103	10.44%	0	0.00%	0	0	0.00%
Cummins	85	8.61%	0	0.00%	5	191,950	9.98%
Burton	78	7.85%	0	0.00%	2	122,165	6.35%
Fairbanks	75	7.55%	0	0.00%	1	176,078	9.16%
Sherman	66	6.69%	0	0.00%	1	155,945	8.11%
Ford	32	3.24%	0	0.00%	1	131,889	6.86%

Equalized Statistics — 1916

Candidate	EVX	PVX	ConFBX	ConLBX	PriVX
Wilson	281	49,235,737	1,000	—	9,878,159
Hughes	257	46,111,814	257	962	419,768
Benson	0	3,183,468	—	—	—
Cummins	—	—	86	0	997,986
Weeks	—	—	106	3	0
Fairbanks	—	—	75	0	915,464
Root	—	—	104	0	0
Burton	—	—	79	0	635,160
Sherman	—	—	67	0	810,789
Roosevelt	—	—	66	19	416,035
Ford	—	—	32	0	685,717
La Follette	—	—	25	3	693,708

Election of 1920

Basics — 1920

Election number — 34
Winner — Warren Harding (R)
Incumbent — Woodrow Wilson (D)
U.S. population — 106,021,537
States — 48
Electoral votes — 531
Popular votes — 26,768,457
Voter turnout — 49.2%

Top Candidates — 1920

Warren Harding (CS 88.37)

James Cox (CS 64.01)

Leonard Wood (CS 31.95)

Field — 1920

Candidate	PI	Age	State	Position	N	W	CS
Warren Harding (R)	6.0	55.00	Ohio	Senator	X	X	88.37
James Cox (D)	5.9	50.59	Ohio	Governor	X	—	64.01
Leonard Wood (R)	4.3	60.06	N.H.	General	—	—	31.95
William Gibbs McAdoo (D)	6.3	57.00	N.Y.	Former Cabinet member	—	—	27.41
Mitchell Palmer (D)	4.9	48.49	Pa.	Cabinet member	—	—	27.09
Frank Lowden (R)	6.3	59.77	Ill.	Governor	—	—	25.31
Hiram Johnson (R)	5.8	54.16	Calif.	Senator	—	—	24.20
Eugene Debs (SOC)	0.1	64.99	Ind.	Movement leader	—	—	20.94
Alfred Smith (D)	6.5	46.84	N.Y.	Governor	—	—	15.99
William Sproul (R)	6.4	50.13	Pa.	Governor	—	—	15.09
Nicholas Murray Butler (R)	5.9	58.58	N.Y.	College president	—	—	14.25
Edward Edwards (D)	6.6	56.92	N.J.	Governor	—	—	13.28
John Davis (D)	3.7	47.55	W.Va.	Ambassador	—	—	12.87
Herbert Hoover (R)	2.6	46.23	Calif.	Business executive	—	—	12.56

General Election — 1920

Candidate	EV	EV%	SC	PV	PV%
Harding	404	76.08%	37	16,151,916	60.34%
Cox	127	23.92%	11	9,134,074	34.12%
Debs	0	0.00%	0	915,511	3.42%

Electoral Votes — 1920

Harding (404) — Arizona (3), California (13), Colorado (6), Connecticut (7), Delaware (3), Idaho (4), Illinois (29), Indiana (15), Iowa (13), Kansas (10), Maine (6), Maryland (8), Massachusetts (18), Michigan (15), Minnesota (12), Missouri (18), Montana (4), Nebraska (8), Nevada (3), New Hampshire (4), New Jersey (14), New Mexico (3), New York (45), North Dakota (5), Ohio (24), Oklahoma (10), Oregon (5), Pennsylvania (38), Rhode Island (5), South Dakota (5), Tennessee (12), Utah (4), Vermont (4), Washington (7), West Virginia (8), Wisconsin (13), Wyoming (3)

Cox (127) — Alabama (12), Arkansas (9), Florida (6), Georgia (14), Kentucky (13), Louisiana (10), Mississippi (10), North Carolina (12), South Carolina (9), Texas (20), Virginia (12)

Popular Votes — 1920

State	Total PV	Harding	Cox	Debs	Other
Alabama	233,951	74,719	156,064	2,402	766
Arizona	66,803	37,016	29,546	222	19
Arkansas	183,637	71,117	107,409	5,111	—
California	943,463	624,992	229,191	64,076	25,204
Colorado	292,053	173,248	104,936	8,046	5,823
Connecticut	365,518	229,238	120,721	10,350	5,209
Delaware	94,875	52,858	39,911	988	1,118
Florida	145,684	44,853	90,515	5,189	5,127
Georgia	149,558	42,981	106,112	465	—
Idaho	138,359	91,351	46,930	38	40
Illinois	2,094,714	1,420,480	534,395	74,747	65,092
Indiana	1,262,974	696,370	511,364	24,713	30,527
Iowa	894,959	634,674	227,804	16,981	15,500
Kansas	570,243	369,268	185,464	15,511	—
Kentucky	918,636	452,480	456,497	6,409	3,250
Louisiana	126,397	38,539	87,519	—	339
Maine	197,840	136,355	58,961	2,214	310
Maryland	428,443	236,117	180,626	8,876	2,824
Massachusetts	993,718	681,153	276,691	32,267	3,607
Michigan	1,048,411	762,865	233,450	28,947	23,149
Minnesota	735,838	519,421	142,994	56,106	17,317
Mississippi	82,351	11,576	69,136	1,639	—
Missouri	1,332,140	727,252	574,699	20,342	9,847
Montana	179,006	109,430	57,372	—	12,204
Nebraska	382,743	247,498	119,608	9,600	6,037
Nevada	27,194	15,479	9,851	1,864	—
New Hampshire	159,092	95,196	62,662	1,234	—
New Jersey	910,251	615,333	258,761	27,385	8,772
New Mexico	105,412	57,634	46,668	2	1,108
New York	2,898,513	1,871,167	781,238	203,201	42,907
North Carolina	538,649	232,819	305,367	446	17
North Dakota	205,786	160,082	37,422	8,282	—
Ohio	2,021,653	1,182,022	780,037	57,147	2,447
Oklahoma	485,678	243,840	216,122	25,716	—
Oregon	238,522	143,592	80,019	9,801	5,110
Pennsylvania	1,851,248	1,218,215	503,202	70,021	59,810
Rhode Island	167,981	107,463	55,062	4,351	1,105
South Carolina	66,808	2,610	64,170	28	—

State	Total PV	Harding	Cox	Debs	Other
South Dakota	182,237	110,692	35,938	—	35,607
Tennessee	428,036	219,229	206,558	2,249	—
Texas	486,109	114,658	287,920	8,124	75,407
Utah	145,828	81,555	56,639	3,159	4,475
Vermont	89,961	68,212	20,919	—	830
Virginia	231,000	87,456	141,670	808	1,066
Washington	398,715	223,137	84,298	8,913	82,367
West Virginia	509,936	282,007	220,785	5,618	1,526
Wisconsin	701,281	498,576	113,422	80,635	8,648
Wyoming	56,253	35,091	17,429	1,288	2,445
Total	26,768,457	16,151,916	9,134,074	915,511	566,956

Democratic Nomination — 1920

Candidate	ConFB	FB%	ConLB[44]	LB%	PriW	PriV	PriV%
Cox	134	12.25%	700	63.94%	1	86,194	15.08%
McAdoo	266	24.31%	270	24.68%	3	74,987	13.12%
Davis	32	2.93%	52	4.75%	0	0	0.00%
Palmer	254	23.22%	1	0.09%	1	91,543	16.01%
Smith	109	9.96%	0	0.00%	0	0	0.00%
Edwards	42	3.84%	0	0.00%	2	28,470	4.98%

Republican Nomination — 1920

Candidate	ConFB	FB%	ConLB[10]	LB%	PriW	PriV	PriV%
Harding	66	6.66%	645	65.52%	1	144,762	4.54%
Wood	288	29.22%	182	18.45%	8	710,863	22.31%
Johnson	134	13.57%	81	8.21%	7	965,651	30.31%
Lowden	212	21.49%	28	2.85%	1	389,127	12.21%
Hoover	6	0.56%	11	1.07%	0	303,212	9.52%
Butler	70	7.06%	2	0.20%	0	0	0.00%
Sproul	84	8.54%	0	0.00%	0	0	0.00%

Equalized Statistics — 1920

Candidate	EVX	PVX	ConFBX	ConLBX	PriVX
Harding	409	60,339,361	67	655	454,334
Cox	129	34,122,527	122	639	1,507,755
Wood	—	—	292	184	2,231,035
McAdoo	—	—	243	247	1,311,716
Palmer	—	—	232	1	1,601,323
Lowden	—	—	215	28	1,221,270
Johnson	—	—	136	82	3,030,684
Debs	0	3,420,111	—	—	—
Smith	—	—	100	0	0
Sproul	—	—	85	0	0
Butler	—	—	71	2	0
Edwards	—	—	38	0	498,014
Davis	—	—	29	48	0
Hoover	—	—	6	11	951,627

Election of 1924

Basics — 1924

Election number — 35
Winner — Calvin Coolidge (R)
Incumbent — Calvin Coolidge (R)
U.S. population — 114,109,000
States — 48
Electoral votes — 531
Popular votes — 29,099,121
Voter turnout — 48.9%

Top Candidates — 1924

Calvin Coolidge (CS 85.63)

John Davis (CS 63.46)

Robert La Follette (CS 46.37)

Field — 1924

Candidate	PI	Age	State	Position	N	W	CS
Calvin Coolidge (R)	9.1	52.33	Mass.	President	X	X	85.63
John Davis (D)	4.4	51.55	W.Va.	Former ambassador	X	—	63.46
Robert La Follette (R/P)	2.2	69.38	Wis.	Senator	—	—	46.37
William Gibbs McAdoo (D)	3.6	61.00	Calif.	Former Cabinet member	—	—	43.53
Alfred Smith (D)	7.0	50.84	N.Y.	Governor	—	—	23.54
Hiram Johnson (R)	5.4	58.16	Calif.	Senator	—	—	16.26
Oscar Underwood (D)	4.5	62.49	Ala.	Senator	—	—	15.57
James Cox (D)	7.5	54.59	Ohio	Former nominee	—	—	15.17
Thomas Walsh (D)	4.0	65.39	Mont.	Senator	—	—	13.17
Pat Harrison (D)	3.4	43.17	Miss.	Senator	—	—	12.40

General Election — 1924

Candidate	EV	EV%	SC	PV	PV%
Coolidge	382	71.94%	35	15,724,310	54.04%
Davis	136	25.61%	12	8,386,532	28.82%
La Follette	13	2.45%	1	4,827,184	16.59%

Electoral Votes — 1924

Coolidge (382) — Arizona (3), California (13), Colorado (6), Connecticut (7), Delaware (3), Idaho (4), Illinois (29), Indiana (15), Iowa (13), Kansas (10), Kentucky (13), Maine (6), Maryland (8), Massachusetts (18), Michigan (15), Minnesota (12), Missouri (18), Montana (4), Nebraska (8), Nevada (3), New Hampshire (4), New Jersey (14), New Mexico (3), New York (45), North Dakota (5), Ohio (24), Oregon (5), Pennsylvania (38), Rhode Island (5), South Dakota (5), Utah (4), Vermont (4), Washington (7), West Virginia (8), Wyoming (3)

Davis (136) — Alabama (12), Arkansas (9), Florida (6), Georgia (14), Louisiana (10), Mississippi (10), North Carolina (12), Oklahoma (10), South Carolina (9), Tennessee (12), Texas (20), Virginia (12)

La Follette (13) — Wisconsin (13)

Popular Votes — 1924

State	Total PV	Coolidge	Davis	La Follette	Other
Alabama	166,593	45,005	112,966	8,084	538
Arizona	73,961	30,516	26,235	17,210	—
Arkansas	138,540	40,583	84,790	13,167	—
California	1,281,778	733,250	105,514	424,649	18,365
Colorado	342,260	195,171	75,238	69,945	1,906
Connecticut	400,396	246,322	110,184	42,416	1,474
Delaware	90,885	52,441	33,445	4,979	20
Florida	109,158	30,633	62,083	8,625	7,817
Georgia	166,635	30,300	123,262	12,687	386
Idaho	147,690	69,791	23,951	53,948	—
Illinois	2,470,067	1,453,321	576,975	432,027	7,744
Indiana	1,272,390	703,042	492,245	71,700	5,403
Iowa	976,770	537,458	160,382	274,448	4,482
Kansas	662,456	407,671	156,320	98,461	4
Kentucky	816,070	398,966	375,593	38,465	3,046
Louisiana	121,951	24,670	93,218	—	4,063
Maine	192,192	138,440	41,964	11,382	406
Maryland	358,630	162,414	148,072	47,157	987
Massachusetts	1,129,837	703,476	280,831	141,225	4,305
Michigan	1,160,419	874,631	152,359	122,014	11,415
Minnesota	822,146	420,759	55,913	339,192	6,282
Mississippi	112,442	8,494	100,474	3,474	—
Missouri	1,310,085	648,488	574,962	83,986	2,649
Montana	174,177	74,138	33,805	65,876	358
Nebraska	463,559	218,985	137,299	105,681	1,594
Nevada	26,921	11,243	5,909	9,769	—
New Hampshire	164,769	98,575	57,201	8,993	—
New Jersey	1,088,054	676,277	298,043	109,028	4,706
New Mexico	112,830	54,745	48,542	9,543	—
New York	3,263,939	1,820,058	950,796	474,913	18,172
North Carolina	481,608	190,754	284,190	6,651	13
North Dakota	199,081	94,931	13,858	89,922	370
Ohio	2,016,296	1,176,130	477,887	358,008	4,271
Oklahoma	527,928	225,755	255,798	41,141	5,234
Oregon	279,488	142,579	67,589	68,403	917
Pennsylvania	2,144,850	1,401,481	409,192	307,567	26,610

State	Total PV	Coolidge	Davis	La Follette	Other
Rhode Island	210,115	125,286	76,606	7,628	595
South Carolina	50,755	1,123	49,008	623	1
South Dakota	203,868	101,299	27,214	75,355	—
Tennessee	301,030	130,831	159,339	10,666	194
Texas	657,054	130,794	483,381	42,879	—
Utah	156,990	77,327	47,001	32,662	—
Vermont	102,917	80,498	16,124	5,964	331
Virginia	223,603	73,328	139,717	10,369	189
Washington	421,549	220,224	42,842	150,727	7,756
West Virginia	583,662	288,635	257,232	36,723	1,072
Wisconsin	840,827	311,614	68,115	453,678	7,420
Wyoming	79,900	41,858	12,868	25,174	—
Total	29,099,121	15,724,310	8,386,532	4,827,184	161,095

Democratic Nomination — 1924

Candidate	ConFB	FB%	ConLB[103]	LB%	PriW	PriV	PriV%
Davis	31	2.82%	844	76.87%	0	0	0.00%
Underwood	43	3.87%	103	9.34%	0	0	0.00%
Walsh	0	0.00%	58	5.28%	0	0	0.00%
McAdoo	432	39.30%	12	1.05%	9	456,733	59.79%
Smith	241	21.95%	8	0.68%	0	16,459	2.16%
Cox	59	5.37%	0	0.00%	1	74,183	9.71%
Harrison	44	3.96%	0	0.00%	0	0	0.00%

Republican Nomination — 1924

Candidate	ConFB	FB%	ConLB	LB%	PriW	PriV	PriV%
Coolidge	1,065	96.03%	—	—	15	2,410,363	68.38%
La Follette	34	3.07%	—	—	1	82,492	2.34%
Johnson	10	0.90%	—	—	1	1,007,833	28.59%

Equalized Statistics — 1924

Candidate	EVX	PVX	ConFBX	ConLBX	PriVX
Coolidge	387	54,037,062	960	—	6,837,550
Davis	138	28,820,568	28	769	0
La Follette	13	16,588,762	31	—	234,008
McAdoo	—	—	393	10	5,979,292
Smith	—	—	219	7	215,472
Johnson	—	—	9	—	2,858,951
Underwood	—	—	39	93	0
Cox	—	—	54	0	971,162
Walsh	—	—	0	53	0
Harrison	—	—	40	0	0

Election of 1928

Basics — 1928

Election number — 36
Winner — Herbert Hoover (R)
Incumbent — Calvin Coolidge (R)
U.S. population — 120,509,000
States — 48
Electoral votes — 531
Popular votes — 36,801,510
Voter turnout — 56.9%

Top Candidates — 1928

Herbert Hoover (CS 90.41)

Alfred Smith (CS 63.06)

Frank Lowden (CS 20.32)

Field — 1928

Candidate	PI	Age	State	Position	N	W	CS
Herbert Hoover (R)	4.0	54.23	Calif.	Cabinet member	X	X	90.41
Alfred Smith (D)	6.9	54.84	N.Y.	Governor	X	—	63.06
Frank Lowden (R)	5.7	67.77	Ill.	Former governor	—	—	20.32
James Reed (D)	4.8	66.98	Mo.	Senator	—	—	16.09
James Watson (R)	5.1	64.00	Ind.	Senator	—	—	13.57
Charles Curtis (R)	4.1	68.77	Kan.	Senator	—	—	13.53
Walter George (D)	4.4	50.76	Ga.	Senator	—	—	12.87
Cordell Hull (D)	3.7	57.08	Tenn.	Representative	—	—	12.75
George Norris (R)	4.3	67.31	Nebr.	Senator	—	—	12.58
Thomas Walsh (D)	3.5	69.39	Mont.	Senator	—	—	10.95

General Election — 1928

Candidate	EV	EV%	SC	PV	PV%
Hoover	444	83.62%	40	21,432,823	58.24%
Smith	87	16.38%	8	15,004,336	40.77%

Electoral Votes — 1928

Hoover (444) — Arizona (3), California (13), Colorado (6), Connecticut (7), Delaware (3), Florida (6), Idaho (4), Illinois (29), Indiana (15), Iowa (13), Kansas (10), Kentucky (13), Maine (6), Maryland (8), Michigan (15), Minnesota (12), Missouri (18), Montana (4), Nebraska (8), Nevada (3), New Hampshire (4), New Jersey (14), New Mexico (3), New York (45), North Carolina (12), North Dakota (5), Ohio (24), Oklahoma (10), Oregon (5), Pennsylvania (38), South Dakota (5), Tennessee (12), Texas (20), Utah (4), Vermont (4), Virginia (12), Washington (7), West Virginia (8), Wisconsin (13), Wyoming (3)

Smith (87) — Alabama (12), Arkansas (9), Georgia (14), Louisiana (10), Massachusetts (18), Mississippi (10), Rhode Island (5), South Carolina (9)

Popular Votes — 1928

State	Total PV	Hoover	Smith	Other
Alabama	248,981	120,725	127,796	460
Arizona	91,254	52,533	38,537	184
Arkansas	197,726	77,784	119,196	746
California	1,796,656	1,162,323	614,365	19,968
Colorado	392,242	253,872	133,131	5,239
Connecticut	553,118	296,641	252,085	4,392
Delaware	104,602	68,860	35,354	388
Florida	253,672	144,168	101,764	7,740
Georgia	231,592	101,800	129,604	188
Idaho	154,230	99,848	53,074	1,308
Illinois	3,107,489	1,769,141	1,313,817	24,531
Indiana	1,421,314	848,290	562,691	10,333
Iowa	1,009,189	623,570	379,011	6,608
Kansas	713,200	513,672	193,003	6,525
Kentucky	940,521	558,064	381,070	1,387
Louisiana	215,833	51,160	164,655	18
Maine	262,170	179,923	81,179	1,068
Maryland	528,348	301,479	223,626	3,243
Massachusetts	1,577,823	775,566	792,758	9,499
Michigan	1,372,082	965,396	396,762	9,924
Minnesota	970,976	560,977	396,451	13,548
Mississippi	151,568	27,030	124,538	—
Missouri	1,500,845	834,080	662,684	4,081
Montana	194,108	113,300	78,578	2,230
Nebraska	547,128	345,745	197,950	3,433
Nevada	32,417	18,327	14,090	—
New Hampshire	196,757	115,404	80,715	638
New Jersey	1,549,381	926,050	616,517	6,814
New Mexico	118,077	69,708	48,211	158
New York	4,405,626	2,193,344	2,089,863	122,419
North Carolina	635,150	348,923	286,227	—
North Dakota	239,845	131,419	106,648	1,778
Ohio	2,508,346	1,627,546	864,210	16,590
Oklahoma	618,427	394,046	219,174	5,207
Oregon	319,942	205,341	109,223	5,378
Pennsylvania	3,150,612	2,055,382	1,067,586	27,644
Rhode Island	237,194	117,522	118,973	699
South Carolina	68,605	5,858	62,700	47

State	Total PV	Hoover	Smith	Other
South Dakota	261,857	157,603	102,660	1,594
Tennessee	353,192	195,388	157,143	661
Texas	708,999	367,036	341,032	931
Utah	176,603	94,618	80,985	1,000
Vermont	135,191	90,404	44,440	347
Virginia	305,364	164,609	140,146	609
Washington	500,840	335,844	156,772	8,224
West Virginia	642,752	375,551	263,784	3,417
Wisconsin	1,016,831	544,205	450,259	22,367
Wyoming	82,835	52,748	29,299	788
Total	36,801,510	21,432,823	15,004,336	364,351

Democratic Nomination — 1928

Candidate	ConFB	FB%	ConLB	LB%	PriW	PriV	PriV%
Smith	850	77.24%	—	—	9	499,452	39.51%
George	53	4.77%	—	—	0	0	0.00%
Reed	52	4.73%	—	—	1	207,367	16.40%
Hull	51	4.62%	—	—	0	0	0.00%
Walsh	0	0.00%	—	—	0	59,871	4.74%

Republican Nomination — 1928

Candidate	ConFB	FB%	ConLB	LB%	PriW	PriV	PriV%
Hoover	837	76.86%	—	—	7	2,020,325	49.15%
Lowden	74	6.80%	—	—	2	1,283,535	31.23%
Curtis	64	5.88%	—	—	0	0	0.00%
Watson	45	4.13%	—	—	1	228,795	5.57%
Norris	24	2.20%	—	—	2	259,548	6.32%

Equalized Statistics — 1928

Candidate	EVX	PVX	ConFBX	ConLBX	PriVX
Hoover	450	58,238,977	769	—	4,915,288
Smith	88	40,770,979	772	—	3,950,673
Lowden	—	—	68	—	3,122,737
Reed	—	—	47	—	1,640,276
Watson	—	—	41	—	556,640
Curtis	—	—	59	—	0
George	—	—	48	—	0
Hull	—	—	46	—	0
Norris	—	—	22	—	631,459
Walsh	—	—	0	—	473,581

Election of 1932

Basics — 1932

Election number — 37
Winner — Franklin Roosevelt (D)
Incumbent — Herbert Hoover (R)
U.S. population — 124,840,471
States — 48
Electoral votes — 531
Popular votes — 39,747,783
Voter turnout — 52.6%

Top Candidates — 1932

Franklin Roosevelt (CS 91.94)

Herbert Hoover (CS 61.28)

Alfred Smith (CS 23.23)

Field — 1932

Candidate	PI	Age	State	Position	N	W	CS
Franklin Roosevelt (D)	8.3	50.75	N.Y.	Governor	X	X	91.94
Herbert Hoover (R)	7.3	58.23	Calif.	President	X	—	61.28
Alfred Smith (D)	6.6	58.84	N.Y.	Former nominee	—	—	23.23
Joseph France (R)	5.6	59.06	Md.	Former senator	—	—	19.88
Norman Thomas (SOC)	3.0	47.95	N.Y.	Movement leader	—	—	17.13
John Nance Garner (D)	3.3	63.94	Texas	Representative	—	—	16.36
William Murray (D)	5.1	62.95	Okla.	Governor	—	—	12.73
George White (D)	6.1	60.20	Ohio	Governor	—	—	12.70
Jacob Coxey (R/FL)	2.5	78.54	Ohio	Mayor	—	—	10.92

General Election — 1932

Candidate	EV	EV%	SC	PV	PV%
Roosevelt	472	88.89%	42	22,818,740	57.41%
Hoover	59	11.11%	6	15,760,425	39.65%
Thomas	0	0.00%	0	884,685	2.23%
Coxey	0	0.00%	0	7,431	0.02%

Electoral Votes — 1932

Roosevelt (472) — Alabama (11), Arizona (3), Arkansas (9), California (22), Colorado (6), Florida (7), Georgia (12), Idaho (4), Illinois (29), Indiana (14), Iowa (11), Kansas (9), Kentucky (11), Louisiana (10), Maryland (8), Massachusetts (17), Michigan (19), Minnesota (11), Mississippi (9), Missouri (15), Montana (4), Nebraska (7), Nevada (3), New Jersey (16), New Mexico (3), New York (47), North Carolina (13), North Dakota (4), Ohio (26), Oklahoma (11), Oregon (5), Rhode Island (4), South Carolina (8), South Dakota (4), Tennessee (11), Texas (23), Utah (4), Virginia (11), Washington (8), West Virginia (8), Wisconsin (12), Wyoming (3)

Hoover (59) — Connecticut (8), Delaware (3), Maine (5), New Hampshire (4), Pennsylvania (36), Vermont (3)

Popular Votes — 1932

State	Total PV	Roosevelt	Hoover	Thomas	Other
Alabama	245,303	207,910	34,675	2,030	688
Arizona	118,251	79,264	36,104	2,618	265
Arkansas	216,569	186,829	27,465	1,166	1,109
California	2,266,972	1,324,157	847,902	63,299	31,614
Colorado	457,696	250,877	189,617	13,591	3,611
Connecticut	594,183	281,632	288,420	20,480	3,651
Delaware	112,901	54,319	57,073	1,376	133
Florida	276,943	206,307	69,170	775	691
Georgia	255,590	234,118	19,863	461	1,148
Idaho	186,520	109,479	71,312	526	5,203
Illinois	3,407,926	1,882,304	1,432,756	67,258	25,608
Indiana	1,576,927	862,054	677,184	21,388	16,301
Iowa	1,036,687	598,019	414,433	20,467	3,768
Kansas	791,978	424,204	349,498	18,276	—
Kentucky	983,059	580,574	394,716	3,853	3,916
Louisiana	268,804	249,418	18,853	—	533
Maine	298,444	128,907	166,631	2,489	417
Maryland	511,054	314,314	184,184	10,489	2,067
Massachusetts	1,580,114	800,148	736,959	34,305	8,702
Michigan	1,664,765	871,700	739,894	39,205	13,966
Minnesota	1,002,843	600,806	363,959	25,476	12,602
Mississippi	146,034	140,168	5,180	686	—
Missouri	1,609,894	1,025,406	564,713	16,374	3,401
Montana	216,479	127,286	78,078	7,891	3,224
Nebraska	570,135	359,082	201,177	9,876	—
Nevada	41,430	28,756	12,674	—	—
New Hampshire	205,520	100,680	103,629	947	264
New Jersey	1,630,063	806,630	775,684	42,998	4,751
New Mexico	151,606	95,089	54,217	1,776	524
New York	4,688,614	2,534,959	1,937,963	177,397	38,295
North Carolina	711,498	497,566	208,344	5,588	—
North Dakota	256,290	178,350	71,772	3,521	2,647
Ohio	2,609,728	1,301,695	1,227,319	64,094	16,620
Oklahoma	704,633	516,468	188,165	—	—
Oregon	368,751	213,871	136,019	15,450	3,411
Pennsylvania	2,859,021	1,295,948	1,453,540	91,119	18,414
Rhode Island	266,170	146,604	115,266	3,138	1,162

State	Total PV	Roosevelt	Hoover	Thomas	Other
South Carolina	104,407	102,347	1,978	82	—
South Dakota	288,438	183,515	99,212	1,551	4,160
Tennessee	390,273	259,473	126,752	1,796	2,252
Texas	863,406	760,348	97,959	4,450	649
Utah	206,578	116,750	84,795	4,087	946
Vermont	136,980	56,266	78,984	1,533	197
Virginia	297,942	203,979	89,637	2,382	1,944
Washington	614,814	353,260	208,645	17,080	35,829
West Virginia	743,774	405,124	330,731	5,133	2,786
Wisconsin	1,114,814	707,410	347,741	53,379	6,284
Wyoming	96,962	54,370	39,583	2,829	180
Total	39,747,783	22,818,740	15,760,425	884,685	283,933

Democratic Nomination — 1932

Candidate	ConFB	FB%	ConLB[4]	LB%	PriW	PriV	PriV%
Roosevelt	666	57.73%	945	81.89%	9	1,314,366	44.51%
Smith	202	17.48%	191	16.51%	2	406,162	13.76%
White	52	4.51%	3	0.26%	0	834	0.03%
Garner	90	7.82%	0	0.00%	1	249,816	8.46%
Murray	23	1.99%	0	0.00%	1	226,392	7.67%

Republican Nomination — 1932

Candidate	ConFB	FB%	ConLB	LB%	PriW	PriV	PriV%
Hoover	1,127	97.62%	—	—	2	781,165	33.28%
France	4	0.35%	—	—	7	1,137,948	48.49%
Coxey	0	0.00%	—	—	1	100,844	4.30%

Equalized Statistics — 1932

Candidate	EVX	PVX	ConFBX	ConLBX	PriVX
Roosevelt	478	57,408,837	577	819	4,451,053
Hoover	60	39,651,079	976	—	3,328,361
Smith	—	—	175	165	1,375,453
France	—	—	3	—	4,848,530
Thomas	0	2,225,747	—	—	—
Garner	—	—	78	0	845,993
Murray	—	—	20	0	766,668
White	—	—	45	3	2,824
Coxey	0	18,695	0	—	429,673

Election of 1936

Basics — 1936

Election number — 38
Winner — Franklin Roosevelt (D)
Incumbent — Franklin Roosevelt (D)
U.S. population — 128,053,180
States — 48
Electoral votes — 531
Popular votes — 45,646,991
Voter turnout — 56.9%

Top Candidates — 1936

Franklin Roosevelt (CS 95.88)

Alfred Landon (CS 57.76)

William Borah (CS 20.02)

Field — 1936

Candidate	PI	Age	State	Position	N	W	CS
Franklin Roosevelt (D)	10.0	54.75	N.Y.	President	X	X	95.88
Alfred Landon (R)	4.8	49.14	Kan.	Governor	X	—	57.76
William Borah (R)	3.3	71.34	Idaho	Senator	—	—	20.02
William Lemke (U)	1.8	58.22	N.D.	Representative	—	—	16.26
Frank Knox (R)	3.5	62.83	Ill.	Journalist	—	—	12.97

General Election — 1936

Candidate	EV	EV%	SC	PV	PV%
Roosevelt	523	98.49%	46	27,750,866	60.80%
Landon	8	1.51%	2	16,679,683	36.54%
Lemke	0	0.00%	0	892,361	1.96%

Electoral Votes — 1936

Roosevelt (523) — Alabama (11), Arizona (3), Arkansas (9), California (22), Colorado (6), Connecticut (8), Delaware (3), Florida (7), Georgia (12), Idaho (4), Illinois (29), Indiana (14), Iowa (11), Kansas (9), Kentucky (11), Louisiana (10), Maryland (8), Massachusetts (17), Michigan (19), Minnesota (11), Mississippi (9), Missouri (15), Montana (4), Nebraska (7), Nevada (3), New Hampshire (4), New Jersey (16), New Mexico (3), New York (47), North Carolina (13), North Dakota (4), Ohio (26), Oklahoma (11), Oregon (5), Pennsylvania (36), Rhode Island (4), South Carolina (8), South Dakota (4), Tennessee (11), Texas (23), Utah (4), Virginia (11), Washington (8), West Virginia (8), Wisconsin (12), Wyoming (3)

Landon (8) — Maine (5), Vermont (3)

Popular Votes — 1936

State	Total PV	Roosevelt	Landon	Lemke	Other
Alabama	275,744	238,196	35,358	551	1,639
Arizona	124,163	86,722	33,433	3,307	701
Arkansas	179,431	146,765	32,049	4	613
California	2,638,882	1,766,836	836,431	—	35,615
Colorado	488,685	295,021	181,267	9,962	2,435
Connecticut	690,723	382,129	278,685	21,805	8,104
Delaware	127,603	69,702	54,014	442	3,445
Florida	327,436	249,117	78,248	—	71
Georgia	293,170	255,363	36,943	136	728
Idaho	199,617	125,683	66,256	7,678	—
Illinois	3,956,522	2,282,999	1,570,393	89,439	13,691
Indiana	1,650,897	934,974	691,570	19,407	4,946
Iowa	1,142,737	621,756	487,977	29,687	3,317
Kansas	865,507	464,520	397,727	494	2,766
Kentucky	926,214	541,944	369,702	12,501	2,067
Louisiana	329,778	292,894	36,791	—	93
Maine	304,240	126,333	168,823	7,581	1,503
Maryland	624,896	389,612	231,435	—	3,849
Massachusetts	1,840,357	942,716	768,613	118,639	10,389
Michigan	1,805,098	1,016,794	699,733	75,795	12,776
Minnesota	1,129,975	698,811	350,461	74,296	6,407
Mississippi	162,142	157,333	4,467	—	342
Missouri	1,828,635	1,111,043	697,891	14,630	5,071
Montana	230,502	159,690	63,598	5,539	1,675
Nebraska	608,023	347,445	247,731	12,847	
Nevada	43,848	31,925	11,923	—	—
New Hampshire	218,114	108,460	104,642	4,819	193
New Jersey	1,820,437	1,083,850	720,322	9,407	6,858
New Mexico	169,135	106,037	61,727	924	447
New York	5,596,398	3,293,222	2,180,670	—	122,506
North Carolina	839,475	616,141	223,294	2	38
North Dakota	273,716	163,148	72,751	36,708	1,109
Ohio	3,012,660	1,747,140	1,127,855	132,212	5,453
Oklahoma	749,740	501,069	245,122	—	3,549
Oregon	414,021	266,733	122,706	21,831	2,751
Pennsylvania	4,138,105	2,353,788	1,690,300	67,467	26,550
Rhode Island	310,278	164,338	125,031	19,569	1,340

State	Total PV	Roosevelt	Landon	Lemke	Other
South Carolina	115,437	113,791	1,646	—	—
South Dakota	296,452	160,137	125,977	10,338	—
Tennessee	475,533	327,083	146,516	296	1,638
Texas	843,482	734,485	103,874	3,281	1,842
Utah	216,679	150,248	64,555	1,121	755
Vermont	143,689	62,124	81,023	—	542
Virginia	334,590	234,980	98,336	233	1,041
Washington	692,338	459,579	206,892	17,463	8,404
West Virginia	829,945	502,582	325,358	—	2,005
Wisconsin	1,258,560	802,984	380,828	60,297	14,451
Wyoming	103,382	62,624	38,739	1,653	366
Total	45,646,991	27,750,866	16,679,683	892,361	324,081

Democratic Nomination — 1936

Candidate	ConFB	FB%	ConLB	LB%	PriW	PriV	PriV%
Roosevelt	1,100	100.00%	—	—	12	4,814,978	92.92%

Republican Nomination — 1936

Candidate	ConFB	FB%	ConLB	LB%	PriW	PriV	PriV%
Landon	984	98.11%	—	—	2	729,908	21.99%
Borah	19	1.89%	—	—	5	1,474,152	44.41%
Knox	0	0.00%	—	—	1	493,562	14.87%

Equalized Statistics — 1936

Candidate	EVX	PVX	ConFBX	ConLBX	PriVX
Roosevelt	530	60,794,513	1,000	—	9,292,081
Landon	8	36,540,597	981	—	2,198,644
Borah	—	—	19	—	4,440,471
Lemke	0	1,954,917	—	—	—
Knox	—	—	0	—	1,486,718

Election of 1940

Basics — 1940

Election number — 39
Winner — Franklin Roosevelt (D)
Incumbent — Franklin Roosevelt (D)
U.S. population — 132,164,569
States — 48
Electoral votes — 531
Popular votes — 49,817,149
Voter turnout — 58.8%

Top Candidates — 1940

Franklin Roosevelt (CS 89.94)

Wendell Willkie (CS 63.60)

Thomas Dewey (CS 41.51)

Field — 1940

Candidate	PI	Age	State	Position	N	W	CS
Franklin Roosevelt (D)	9.6	58.75	N.Y.	President	X	X	89.94
Wendell Willkie (R)	4.7	48.70	N.Y.	Business executive	X	—	63.60
Thomas Dewey (R)	4.0	38.61	N.Y.	District attorney	—	—	41.51
Robert Taft (R)	5.8	51.15	Ohio	Senator	—	—	32.24
John Nance Garner (D)	3.5	71.94	Texas	Vice president	—	—	15.20
Arthur Vandenberg (R)	5.8	56.61	Mich.	Senator	—	—	15.17
Arthur James (R)	7.1	57.30	Pa.	Governor	—	—	14.48
James Farley (D)	6.3	52.42	N.Y.	Cabinet member	—	—	13.95
Joseph Martin (R)	5.1	55.99	Mass.	Representative	—	—	12.63

General Election — 1940

Candidate	EV	EV%	SC	PV	PV%
Roosevelt	449	84.56%	38	27,243,218	54.69%
Willkie	82	15.44%	10	22,334,940	44.83%

Electoral Votes — 1940

Roosevelt (449) — Alabama (11), Arizona (3), Arkansas (9), California (22), Connecticut (8), Delaware (3), Florida (7), Georgia (12), Idaho (4), Illinois (29), Kentucky (11), Louisiana (10), Maryland (8), Massachusetts (17), Minnesota (11), Mississippi (9), Missouri (15), Montana (4), Nevada (3), New Hampshire (4), New Jersey (16), New Mexico (3), New York (47), North Carolina (13), Ohio (26), Oklahoma (11), Oregon (5), Pennsylvania (36), Rhode Island (4), South Carolina (8), Tennessee (11), Texas (23), Utah (4), Virginia (11), Washington (8), West Virginia (8), Wisconsin (12), Wyoming (3)
Willkie (82) — Colorado (6), Indiana (14), Iowa (11), Kansas (9), Maine (5), Michigan (19), Nebraska (7), North Dakota (4), South Dakota (4), Vermont (3)

Popular Votes — 1940

State	Total PV	Roosevelt	Willkie	Other
Alabama	294,219	250,726	42,184	1,309
Arizona	150,039	95,267	54,030	742
Arkansas	200,429	157,213	42,122	1,094
California	3,268,791	1,877,618	1,351,419	39,754
Colorado	549,004	265,554	279,576	3,874
Connecticut	781,502	417,621	361,819	2,062
Delaware	136,374	74,599	61,440	335
Florida	485,640	359,334	126,158	148
Georgia	312,686	265,194	46,495	997
Idaho	235,168	127,842	106,553	773
Illinois	4,217,935	2,149,934	2,047,240	20,761
Indiana	1,782,747	874,063	899,466	9,218
Iowa	1,215,432	578,802	632,370	4,260
Kansas	860,297	364,725	489,169	6,403
Kentucky	970,163	557,322	410,384	2,457
Louisiana	372,305	319,751	52,446	108
Maine	320,840	156,478	163,951	411
Maryland	660,104	384,546	269,534	6,024
Massachusetts	2,026,993	1,076,522	939,700	10,771
Michigan	2,085,929	1,032,991	1,039,917	13,021
Minnesota	1,251,188	644,196	596,274	10,718
Mississippi	175,824	168,267	7,364	193
Missouri	1,833,729	958,476	871,009	4,244
Montana	247,873	145,698	99,579	2,596
Nebraska	615,878	263,677	352,201	—
Nevada	53,174	31,945	21,229	—
New Hampshire	235,419	125,292	110,127	—
New Jersey	1,972,552	1,016,808	945,475	10,269
New Mexico	183,258	103,699	79,315	244
New York	6,301,596	3,251,918	3,027,478	22,200
North Carolina	822,648	609,015	213,633	—
North Dakota	280,775	124,036	154,590	2,149
Ohio	3,319,912	1,733,139	1,586,773	—
Oklahoma	826,212	474,313	348,872	3,027
Oregon	481,240	258,415	219,555	3,270
Pennsylvania	4,078,714	2,171,035	1,889,848	17,831
Rhode Island	321,152	182,181	138,654	317
South Carolina	99,830	95,470	4,360	—

State	Total PV	Roosevelt	Willkie	Other
South Dakota	308,427	131,362	177,065	—
Tennessee	522,823	351,601	169,153	2,069
Texas	1,041,168	840,151	199,152	1,865
Utah	247,819	154,277	93,151	391
Vermont	143,062	64,269	78,371	422
Virginia	346,608	235,961	109,363	1,284
Washington	793,833	462,145	322,123	9,565
West Virginia	868,076	495,662	372,414	—
Wisconsin	1,405,522	704,821	679,206	21,495
Wyoming	112,240	59,287	52,633	320
Total	49,817,149	27,243,218	22,334,940	238,991

Democratic Nomination — 1940

Candidate	ConFB	FB%	ConLB	LB%	PriW	PriV	PriV%
Roosevelt	946	86.04%	—	—	7	3,204,054	71.70%
Farley	73	6.63%	—	—	0	0	0.00%
Garner	61	5.55%	—	—	0	426,641	9.55%

Republican Nomination — 1940

Candidate	ConFB	FB%	ConLB[6]	LB%	PriW	PriV	PriV%
Willkie	105	10.50%	655	65.50%	0	21,140	0.66%
Taft	189	18.90%	318	31.80%	1	516,428	16.00%
Dewey	360	36.00%	11	1.10%	6	1,605,754	49.75%
Vandenberg	76	7.60%	0	0.00%	0	100,651	3.12%
James	74	7.40%	0	0.00%	0	8,172	0.25%
Martin	44	4.40%	0	0.00%	0	0	0.00%

Equalized Statistics — 1940

Candidate	EVX	PVX	ConFBX	ConLBX	PriVX
Roosevelt	455	54,686,425	860	—	7,170,102
Willkie	83	44,833,838	105	655	65,492
Dewey	—	—	360	11	4,974,647
Taft	—	—	189	318	1,599,901
Garner	—	—	55	—	954,747
Vandenberg	—	—	76	0	311,818
James	—	—	74	0	25,317
Farley	—	—	66	—	0
Martin	—	—	44	0	0

Election of 1944

Basics — 1944

Election number — 40
Winner — Franklin Roosevelt (D)
Incumbent — Franklin Roosevelt (D)
U.S. population — 138,397,345
States — 48
Electoral votes — 531
Popular votes — 47,976,649
Voter turnout — 56.1%

Top Candidates — 1944

Franklin Roosevelt (CS 88.61)

Thomas Dewey (CS 64.76)

Douglas MacArthur (CS 15.89)

Field — 1944

Candidate	PI	Age	State	Position	N	W	CS
Franklin Roosevelt (D)	9.4	62.75	N.Y.	President	X	X	88.61
Thomas Dewey (R)	6.3	42.61	N.Y.	Governor	X	—	64.76
Douglas MacArthur (R)	3.9	64.77	Wis.	General	—	—	15.89
Harry Byrd (D)	5.1	57.39	Va.	Senator	—	—	14.55

General Election — 1944

Candidate	EV	EV%	SC	PV	PV%
Roosevelt	432	81.36%	36	25,612,610	53.39%
Dewey	99	18.64%	12	22,014,160	45.89%

Electoral Votes — 1944

Roosevelt (432) — Alabama (11), Arizona (4), Arkansas (9), California (25), Connecticut (8), Delaware (3), Florida (8), Georgia (12), Idaho (4), Illinois (28), Kentucky (11), Louisiana (10), Maryland (8), Massachusetts (16), Michigan (19), Minnesota (11), Mississippi (9), Missouri (15), Montana (4), Nevada (3), New Hampshire (4), New Jersey (16), New Mexico (4), New York (47), North Carolina (14), Oklahoma (10), Oregon (6), Pennsylvania (35), Rhode Island (4), South Carolina (8), Tennessee (12), Texas (23), Utah (4), Virginia (11), Washington (8), West Virginia (8)

Dewey (99) — Colorado (6), Indiana (13), Iowa (10), Kansas (8), Maine (5), Nebraska (6), North Dakota (4), Ohio (25), South Dakota (4), Vermont (3), Wisconsin (12), Wyoming (3)

Popular Votes — 1944

State	Total PV	Roosevelt	Dewey	Other
Alabama	244,743	198,918	44,540	1,285
Arizona	137,634	80,926	56,287	421
Arkansas	212,954	148,965	63,551	438
California	3,520,875	1,988,564	1,512,965	19,346
Colorado	505,039	234,331	268,731	1,977
Connecticut	831,990	435,146	390,527	6,317
Delaware	125,361	68,166	56,747	448
Florida	482,803	339,377	143,215	211
Georgia	328,108	268,187	56,506	3,415
Idaho	208,321	107,399	100,137	785
Illinois	4,036,061	2,079,479	1,939,314	17,268
Indiana	1,672,091	781,403	875,891	14,797
Iowa	1,052,599	499,876	547,267	5,456
Kansas	733,776	287,458	442,096	4,222
Kentucky	867,924	472,589	392,448	2,887
Louisiana	349,383	281,564	67,750	69
Maine	296,400	140,631	155,434	335
Maryland	608,439	315,490	292,949	—
Massachusetts	1,960,665	1,035,296	921,350	4,019
Michigan	2,205,223	1,106,899	1,084,423	13,901
Minnesota	1,125,504	589,864	527,416	8,224
Mississippi	180,234	168,621	11,613	—
Missouri	1,571,697	807,356	761,175	3,166
Montana	207,355	112,556	93,163	1,636
Nebraska	563,126	233,246	329,880	—
Nevada	54,234	29,623	24,611	—
New Hampshire	229,625	119,663	109,916	46
New Jersey	1,963,761	987,874	961,335	14,552
New Mexico	152,225	81,389	70,688	148
New York	6,316,790	3,304,238	2,987,647	24,905
North Carolina	790,554	527,399	263,155	—
North Dakota	220,182	100,144	118,535	1,503
Ohio	3,153,056	1,570,763	1,582,293	—
Oklahoma	722,636	401,549	319,424	1,663
Oregon	480,147	248,635	225,365	6,147
Pennsylvania	3,794,793	1,940,479	1,835,054	19,260
Rhode Island	299,276	175,356	123,487	433
South Carolina	103,382	90,601	4,554	8,227
South Dakota	232,076	96,711	135,365	—
Tennessee	510,692	308,707	200,311	1,674
Texas	1,150,334	821,605	191,423	137,306
Utah	248,319	150,088	97,891	340
Vermont	125,361	53,820	71,527	14
Virginia	388,485	242,276	145,243	966
Washington	856,328	486,774	361,689	7,865
West Virginia	715,596	392,777	322,819	—
Wisconsin	1,339,152	650,413	674,532	14,207
Wyoming	101,340	49,419	51,921	—
Total	47,976,649	25,612,610	22,014,160	349,879

Democratic Nomination — 1944

Candidate	ConFB	FB%	ConLB	LB%	PriW	PriV	PriV%
Roosevelt	1,086	92.35%	—	—	7	1,324,006	70.89%
Byrd	89	7.57%	—	—	0	0	0.00%

Republican Nomination — 1944

Candidate	ConFB	FB%	ConLB	LB%	PriW	PriV	PriV%
Dewey	1,056	99.72%	—	—	3	262,746	11.57%
MacArthur	1	0.09%	—	—	2	662,127	29.15%

Equalized Statistics — 1944

Candidate	EVX	PVX	ConFBX	ConLBX	PriVX
Roosevelt	438	53,385,575	923	—	7,089,310
Dewey	100	45,885,156	997	—	1,156,654
MacArthur	—	—	1	—	2,914,798
Byrd	—	—	76	—	0

Election of 1948

Basics — 1948

Election number — 41
Winner — Harry Truman (D)
Incumbent — Harry Truman (D)
U.S. population — 146,631,302
States — 48
Electoral votes — 531
Popular votes — 48,691,494
Voter turnout — 51.1%

Top Candidates — 1948

Harry Truman (CS 79.72)

Thomas Dewey (CS 69.67)

Strom Thurmond (CS 34.75)

Field — 1948

Candidate	PI	Age	State	Position	N	W	CS
Harry Truman (D)	7.6	64.48	Mo.	President	X	X	79.72
Thomas Dewey (R)	6.6	46.61	N.Y.	Former nominee	X	—	69.67
Strom Thurmond (SRD)	2.2	45.91	S.C.	Governor	—	—	34.75
Richard Russell (D)	4.4	51.00	Ga.	Senator	—	—	22.93
Robert Taft (R)	5.6	59.15	Ohio	Senator	—	—	22.57
Harold Stassen (R)	4.5	41.55	Minn.	Former governor	—	—	22.01
Earl Warren (R)	5.7	57.62	Calif.	Governor	—	—	19.04
Henry Wallace (D/P)	3.1	60.07	Iowa	Former vice president	—	—	17.65
Arthur Vandenberg (R)	5.1	64.61	Mich.	Senator	—	—	13.55
Dwight Green (R)	6.5	51.81	Ill.	Governor	—	—	13.05

General Election — 1948

Candidate	EV	EV%	SC	PV	PV%
Truman	303	57.06%	28	24,105,810	49.51%
Dewey	189	35.59%	16	21,970,064	45.12%
Thurmond	39	7.35%	4	1,169,156	2.40%
Wallace	0	0.00%	0	1,157,172	2.38%

Electoral Votes — 1948

Truman (303) — Arizona (4), Arkansas (9), California (25), Colorado (6), Florida (8), Georgia (12), Idaho (4), Illinois (28), Iowa (10), Kentucky (11), Massachusetts (16), Minnesota (11), Missouri (15), Montana (4), Nevada (3), New Mexico (4), North Carolina (14), Ohio (25), Oklahoma (10), Rhode Island (4), Tennessee (11), Texas (23), Utah (4), Virginia (11), Washington (8), West Virginia (8), Wisconsin (12), Wyoming (3)

Dewey (189) — Connecticut (8), Delaware (3), Indiana (13), Kansas (8), Maine (5), Maryland (8), Michigan (19), Nebraska (6), New Hampshire (4), New Jersey (16), New York (47), North Dakota (4), Oregon (6), Pennsylvania (35), South Dakota (4), Vermont (3)

Thurmond (39) — Alabama (11), Louisiana (10), Mississippi (9), South Carolina (8), Tennessee (1)

Popular Votes — 1948

State	Total PV	Truman	Dewey	Thurmond	Wallace	Other
Alabama	214,980	—	40,930	171,443	1,522	1,085
Arizona	177,065	95,251	77,597	—	3,310	907
Arkansas	242,475	149,659	50,959	40,068	751	1,038
California	4,021,538	1,913,134	1,895,269	1,228	190,381	21,526
Colorado	515,237	267,288	239,714	—	6,115	2,120
Connecticut	883,518	423,297	437,754	—	13,713	8,754
Delaware	139,073	67,813	69,588	—	1,050	622
Florida	577,643	281,988	194,280	89,755	11,620	—
Georgia	418,844	254,646	76,691	85,135	1,636	736
Idaho	214,816	107,370	101,514	—	4,972	960
Illinois	3,984,046	1,994,715	1,961,103	—	—	28,228
Indiana	1,656,212	807,831	821,079	—	9,649	17,653
Iowa	1,038,264	522,380	494,018	—	12,125	9,741
Kansas	788,819	351,902	423,039	—	4,603	9,275
Kentucky	822,658	466,756	341,210	10,411	1,567	2,714
Louisiana	416,336	136,344	72,657	204,290	3,035	10
Maine	264,787	111,916	150,234	—	1,884	753
Maryland	596,748	286,521	294,814	2,489	9,983	2,941
Massachusetts	2,107,146	1,151,788	909,370	—	38,157	7,831
Michigan	2,109,609	1,003,448	1,038,595	—	46,515	21,051
Minnesota	1,212,226	692,966	483,617	—	27,866	7,777
Mississippi	192,190	19,384	5,043	167,538	225	—
Missouri	1,578,628	917,315	655,039	42	3,998	2,234
Montana	224,278	119,071	96,770	—	7,313	1,124
Nebraska	488,940	224,165	264,774	—	—	1
Nevada	62,117	31,291	29,357	—	1,469	—
New Hampshire	231,440	107,995	121,299	7	1,970	169
New Jersey	1,949,555	895,455	981,124	—	42,683	30,293
New Mexico	187,063	105,464	80,303	—	1,037	259
New York	6,177,337	2,780,204	2,841,163	—	509,559	46,411
North Carolina	791,209	459,070	258,572	69,652	3,915	—
North Dakota	220,716	95,812	115,139	374	8,391	1,000
Ohio	2,936,071	1,452,791	1,445,684	—	37,596	—
Oklahoma	721,599	452,782	268,817	—	—	—
Oregon	524,080	243,147	260,904	—	14,978	5,051
Pennsylvania	3,735,348	1,752,426	1,902,197	—	55,161	25,564

State	Total PV	Truman	Dewey	Thurmond	Wallace	Other
Rhode Island	327,702	188,736	135,787	—	2,619	560
South Carolina	142,571	34,423	5,386	102,607	154	1
South Dakota	250,105	117,653	129,651	—	2,801	—
Tennessee	550,283	270,402	202,914	73,815	1,864	1,288
Texas	1,147,245	750,700	282,240	106,909	3,764	3,632
Utah	276,306	149,151	124,402	—	2,679	74
Vermont	123,382	45,557	75,926	—	1,279	620
Virginia	419,256	200,786	172,070	43,393	2,047	960
Washington	905,058	476,165	386,314	—	31,692	10,887
West Virginia	748,750	429,188	316,251	—	3,311	—
Wisconsin	1,276,800	647,310	590,959	—	25,282	13,249
Wyoming	101,425	52,354	47,947	—	931	193
Total	48,691,494	24,105,810	21,970,064	1,169,156	1,157,172	289,292

Democratic Nomination — 1948

Candidate	ConFB	FB%	ConLB	LB%	PriW	PriV	PriV%
Truman	926	75.04%	—	—	8	1,375,452	63.92%
Russell	266	21.56%	—	—	0	0	0.00%
Wallace	0	0.00%	—	—	0	4,416	0.21%

Republican Nomination — 1948

Candidate	ConFB	FB%	ConLB[3]	LB%	PriW	PriV	PriV%
Dewey	434	39.67%	1,094	100.00%	2	304,394	11.47%
Taft	224	20.48%	0	0.00%	0	37,974	1.43%
Stassen	157	14.35%	0	0.00%	4	449,713	16.95%
Vandenberg	62	5.67%	0	0.00%	0	18,924	0.71%
Warren	59	5.39%	0	0.00%	1	771,295	29.07%
Green	56	5.12%	0	0.00%	0	0	0.00%

Equalized Statistics — 1948

Candidate	EVX	PVX	ConFBX	ConLBX	PriVX
Truman	307	49,507,230	750	—	6,391,907
Dewey	191	45,120,949	397	1,000	1,147,247
Thurmond	40	2,401,150	—	—	—
Russell	—	—	216	—	0
Taft	—	—	205	0	143,122
Stassen	—	—	144	0	1,694,948
Warren	—	—	54	0	2,906,977
Wallace	0	2,376,538	0	—	20,522
Vandenberg	—	—	57	0	71,324
Green	—	—	51	0	0

Election of 1952

Basics — 1952

Election number — 42
Winner — Dwight Eisenhower (R)
Incumbent — Harry Truman (D)
U.S. population — 157,552,740
States — 48
Electoral votes — 531
Popular votes — 61,550,918
Voter turnout — 61.6%

Top Candidates — 1952

Dwight Eisenhower (CS 89.56)

Adlai Stevenson (CS 63.90)

Estes Kefauver (CS 38.77)

Field — 1952

Candidate	PI	Age	State	Position	N	W	CS
Dwight Eisenhower (R)	5.6	62.05	N.Y.	General	X	X	89.56
Adlai Stevenson (D)	6.7	52.74	Ill.	Governor	X	—	63.90
Estes Kefauver (D)	4.4	49.27	Tenn.	Senator	—	—	38.77
Robert Taft (R)	4.6	63.15	Ohio	Senator	—	—	32.33
Richard Russell (D)	5.1	55.00	Ga.	Senator	—	—	23.13
Earl Warren (R)	6.2	61.62	Calif.	Governor	—	—	18.38
Averell Harriman (D)	5.8	60.96	N.Y.	Former Cabinet member	—	—	15.10
Harold Stassen (R)	3.9	45.55	Pa.	College president	—	—	13.39
Robert Kerr (D)	5.3	56.14	Okla.	Senator	—	—	12.90
Alben Barkley (D)	4.2	74.94	Ky.	Vice president	—	—	12.74

General Election — 1952

Candidate	EV	EV%	SC	PV	PV%
Eisenhower	442	83.24%	39	33,777,945	54.88%
Stevenson	89	16.76%	9	27,314,992	44.38%

Electoral Votes — 1952

Eisenhower (442) — Arizona (4), California (32), Colorado (6), Connecticut (8), Delaware (3), Florida (10), Idaho (4), Illinois (27), Indiana (13), Iowa (10), Kansas (8), Maine (5), Maryland (9), Massachusetts (16), Michigan (20), Minnesota (11), Missouri (13), Montana (4), Nebraska (6), Nevada (3), New Hampshire (4), New Jersey (16), New Mexico (4), New York (45), North Dakota (4), Ohio (25), Oklahoma (8), Oregon (6), Pennsylvania (32), Rhode Island (4), South Dakota (4), Tennessee (11), Texas (24), Utah (4), Vermont (3), Virginia (12), Washington (9), Wisconsin (12), Wyoming (3)

Stevenson (89) — Alabama (11), Arkansas (8), Georgia (12), Kentucky (10), Louisiana (10), Mississippi (8), North Carolina (14), South Carolina (8), West Virginia (8)

Popular Votes — 1952

State	Total PV	Eisenhower	Stevenson	Other
Alabama	426,120	149,231	275,075	1,814
Arizona	260,570	152,042	108,528	—
Arkansas	404,800	177,155	226,300	1,345
California	5,141,849	2,897,310	2,197,548	46,991
Colorado	630,103	379,782	245,504	4,817
Connecticut	1,096,911	611,012	481,649	4,250
Delaware	174,025	90,059	83,315	651
Florida	989,337	544,036	444,950	351
Georgia	655,785	198,961	456,823	1
Idaho	276,254	180,707	95,081	466
Illinois	4,481,058	2,457,327	2,013,920	9,811
Indiana	1,955,049	1,136,259	801,530	17,260
Iowa	1,268,773	808,906	451,513	8,354
Kansas	896,166	616,302	273,296	6,568
Kentucky	993,148	495,029	495,729	2,390
Louisiana	651,952	306,925	345,027	—
Maine	351,786	232,353	118,806	627
Maryland	902,074	499,424	395,337	7,313
Massachusetts	2,383,398	1,292,325	1,083,525	7,548
Michigan	2,798,592	1,551,529	1,230,657	16,406
Minnesota	1,379,483	763,211	608,458	7,814
Mississippi	285,532	112,966	172,566	—
Missouri	1,892,062	959,429	929,830	2,803
Montana	265,037	157,394	106,213	1,430
Nebraska	609,660	421,603	188,057	—
Nevada	82,190	50,502	31,688	
New Hampshire	272,950	166,287	106,663	—
New Jersey	2,418,554	1,373,613	1,015,902	29,039
New Mexico	238,608	132,170	105,661	777
New York	7,128,239	3,952,813	3,104,601	70,825
North Carolina	1,210,910	558,107	652,803	—
North Dakota	270,127	191,712	76,694	1,721
Ohio	3,700,758	2,100,391	1,600,367	—
Oklahoma	948,984	518,045	430,939	—
Oregon	695,059	420,815	270,579	3,665
Pennsylvania	4,580,969	2,415,789	2,146,269	18,911
Rhode Island	414,498	210,935	203,293	270
South Carolina	341,087	9,793	173,004	158,290

State	Total PV	Eisenhower	Stevenson	Other
South Dakota	294,283	203,857	90,426	—
Tennessee	892,553	446,147	443,710	2,696
Texas	2,075,946	1,102,878	969,228	3,840
Utah	329,554	194,190	135,364	—
Vermont	153,557	109,717	43,355	485
Virginia	619,689	349,037	268,677	1,975
Washington	1,102,708	599,107	492,845	10,756
West Virginia	873,548	419,970	453,578	—
Wisconsin	1,607,370	979,744	622,175	5,451
Wyoming	129,253	81,049	47,934	270
Total	61,550,918	33,777,945	27,314,992	457,981

Democratic Nomination — 1952

Candidate	ConFB	FB%	ConLB[3]	LB%	PriW	PriV	PriV%
Stevenson	273	22.20%	618	50.20%	0	78,583	1.60%
Kefauver	340	27.64%	276	22.40%	12	3,169,448	64.32%
Russell	268	21.79%	261	21.22%	1	369,671	7.50%
Barkley	49	3.94%	68	5.49%	0	0	0.00%
Harriman	124	10.04%	0	0.00%	0	17,820	0.36%
Kerr	65	5.29%	0	0.00%	0	42,467	0.86%

Republican Nomination — 1952

Candidate	ConFB	FB%	ConLB	LB%	PriW	PriV	PriV%
Eisenhower	845	70.07%	—	—	5	2,114,588	27.11%
Taft	280	23.22%	—	—	6	2,794,736	35.82%
Warren	77	6.39%	—	—	1	1,349,036	17.29%
Stassen	0	0.00%	—	—	1	881,702	11.30%

Equalized Statistics — 1952

Candidate	EVX	PVX	ConFBX	ConLBX	PriVX
Eisenhower	448	54,878,052	701	—	2,710,519
Stevenson	90	44,377,879	222	502	159,462
Kefauver	—	—	276	224	6,431,502
Taft	—	—	232	—	3,582,346
Russell	—	—	218	212	750,143
Warren	—	—	64	—	1,729,220
Harriman	—	—	100	0	36,161
Stassen	—	—	0	—	1,130,182
Kerr	—	—	53	0	86,175
Barkley	—	—	39	55	0

Election of 1956

Basics — 1956

Election number — 43
Winner — Dwight Eisenhower (R)
Incumbent — Dwight Eisenhower (R)
U.S. population — 168,903,031
States — 48
Electoral votes — 531
Popular votes — 62,026,908
Voter turnout — 59.3%

Top Candidates — 1956

Dwight Eisenhower (CS 91.03)

Adlai Stevenson (CS 62.52)

Estes Kefauver (CS 21.72)

Field — 1956

Candidate	PI	Age	State	Position	N	W	CS
Dwight Eisenhower (R)	8.7	66.05	N.Y.	President	X	X	91.03
Adlai Stevenson (D)	7.6	56.74	Ill.	Former nominee	X	—	62.52
Estes Kefauver (D)	5.1	53.27	Tenn.	Senator	—	—	21.72
Averell Harriman (D)	7.4	64.96	N.Y.	Governor	—	—	17.64
Lyndon Johnson (D)	4.5	48.18	Texas	Senator	—	—	12.89
Frank Lausche (D)	5.7	60.96	Ohio	Governor	—	—	11.62
Walter Jones (D)	1.9	68.04	Ala.	State judge	—	—	10.62

General Election — 1956

Candidate	EV	EV%	SC	PV	PV%
Eisenhower	457	86.06%	41	35,590,472	57.38%
Stevenson	73	13.75%	7	26,022,752	41.95%
Jones	1	0.19%	0	0	0.00%

Electoral Votes — 1956

Eisenhower (457) — Arizona (4), California (32), Colorado (6), Connecticut (8), Delaware (3), Florida (10), Idaho (4), Illinois (27), Indiana (13), Iowa (10), Kansas (8), Kentucky (10), Louisiana (10), Maine (5), Maryland (9), Massachusetts (16), Michigan (20), Minnesota (11), Montana (4), Nebraska (6), Nevada (3), New Hampshire (4), New Jersey (16), New Mexico (4), New York (45), North Dakota (4), Ohio (25), Oklahoma (8), Oregon (6), Pennsylvania (32), Rhode Island (4), South Dakota (4), Tennessee (11), Texas (24), Utah (4), Vermont (3), Virginia (12), Washington (9), West Virginia (8), Wisconsin (12), Wyoming (3)

Stevenson (73) — Alabama (10), Arkansas (8), Georgia (12), Mississippi (8), Missouri (13), North Carolina (14), South Carolina (8)

Jones (1) — Alabama (1)

Popular Votes — 1956

State	Total PV	Eisenhower	Stevenson	Other
Alabama	496,861	195,694	280,844	20,323
Arizona	290,173	176,990	112,880	303
Arkansas	406,572	186,287	213,277	7,008
California	5,466,355	3,027,668	2,420,135	18,552
Colorado	657,074	394,479	257,997	4,598
Connecticut	1,117,121	711,837	405,079	205
Delaware	177,988	98,057	79,421	510
Florida	1,125,762	643,849	480,371	1,542
Georgia	669,655	222,778	444,688	2,189
Idaho	272,989	166,979	105,868	142
Illinois	4,407,407	2,623,327	1,775,682	8,398
Indiana	1,974,607	1,182,811	783,908	7,888
Iowa	1,234,564	729,187	501,858	3,519
Kansas	866,243	566,878	296,317	3,048
Kentucky	1,053,805	572,192	476,453	5,160
Louisiana	617,544	329,047	243,977	44,520
Maine	351,706	249,238	102,468	—
Maryland	932,827	559,738	372,613	476
Massachusetts	2,348,506	1,393,197	948,190	7,119
Michigan	3,080,468	1,713,647	1,359,898	6,923
Minnesota	1,340,005	719,302	617,525	3,178
Mississippi	248,104	60,685	144,453	42,966
Missouri	1,832,562	914,289	918,273	—
Montana	271,171	154,933	116,238	—
Nebraska	577,137	378,108	199,029	—
Nevada	96,689	56,049	40,640	—
New Hampshire	266,994	176,519	90,364	111
New Jersey	2,484,312	1,606,942	850,337	27,033
New Mexico	253,926	146,788	106,098	1,040
New York	7,095,971	4,345,506	2,747,944	2,521
North Carolina	1,165,592	575,062	590,530	—
North Dakota	253,991	156,766	96,742	483
Ohio	3,702,265	2,262,610	1,439,655	—
Oklahoma	859,350	473,769	385,581	—
Oregon	736,132	406,393	329,204	535
Pennsylvania	4,576,503	2,585,252	1,981,769	9,482

State	Total PV	Eisenhower	Stevenson	Other
Rhode Island	387,609	225,819	161,790	—
South Carolina	300,583	75,700	136,372	88,511
South Dakota	293,857	171,569	122,288	—
Tennessee	939,404	462,288	456,507	20,609
Texas	1,955,168	1,080,619	859,958	14,591
Utah	333,995	215,631	118,364	—
Vermont	152,978	110,390	42,549	39
Virginia	697,978	386,459	267,760	43,759
Washington	1,150,889	620,430	523,002	7,457
West Virginia	830,831	449,297	381,534	—
Wisconsin	1,550,558	954,844	586,768	8,946
Wyoming	124,127	74,573	49,554	—
Total	62,026,908	35,590,472	26,022,752	413,684

Democratic Nomination — 1956

Candidate	ConFB	FB%	ConLB	LB%	PriW	PriV	PriV%
Stevenson	906	66.00%	—	—	7	3,058,470	52.33%
Harriman	210	15.31%	—	—	0	2,281	0.04%
Johnson	80	5.83%	—	—	0	0	0.00%
Lausche	6	0.40%	—	—	1	276,923	4.74%
Kefauver	0	0.00%	—	—	9	2,283,172	39.07%

Republican Nomination — 1956

Candidate	ConFB	FB%	ConLB	LB%	PriW	PriV	PriV%
Eisenhower	1,323	100.00%	—	—	15	5,007,970	85.93%

Equalized Statistics — 1956

Candidate	EVX	PVX	ConFBX	ConLBX	PriVX
Eisenhower	463	57,379,085	1,000	—	8,592,547
Stevenson	74	41,953,973	660	—	5,233,297
Kefauver	—	—	0	—	3,906,697
Harriman	—	—	153	—	3,903
Johnson	—	—	58	—	0
Lausche	—	—	4	—	473,838
Jones	1	0	—	—	—

Election of 1960

Basics — 1960

Election number — 44
Winner — John Kennedy (D)
Incumbent — Dwight Eisenhower (R)
U.S. population — 179,323,175
States — 50
Electoral votes — 537
Popular votes — 68,838,219
Voter turnout — 62.8%

Top Candidates — 1960

John Kennedy (CS 79.58)

Richard Nixon (CS 72.12)

Lyndon Johnson (CS 23.50)

Field — 1960

Candidate	PI	Age	State	Position	N	W	CS
John Kennedy (D)	6.2	43.43	Mass.	Senator	X	X	79.58
Richard Nixon (R)	8.0	47.81	Calif.	Vice president	X	—	72.12
Lyndon Johnson (D)	8.1	52.18	Texas	Senator	—	—	23.50
Harry Byrd (D)	6.9	73.39	Va.	Senator	—	—	19.25
Hubert Humphrey (D)	7.1	49.43	Minn.	Senator	—	—	14.46
Stuart Symington (D)	6.9	59.35	Mo.	Senator	—	—	13.00
Adlai Stevenson (D)	7.2	60.74	Ill.	Former nominee	—	—	12.86

General Election — 1960

Candidate	EV	EV%	SC	PV	PV%
Kennedy	303	56.43%	22	34,226,731	49.72%
Nixon	219	40.78%	26	34,108,157	49.55%
Byrd	15	2.79%	2	116,248	0.17%

NOTE: The popular votes listed for Byrd were cast for unpledged electors who declared their support for him after the general election.

Electoral Votes — 1960

Kennedy (303) — Alabama (5), Arkansas (8), Connecticut (8), Delaware (3), Georgia (12), Hawaii (3), Illinois (27), Louisiana (10), Maryland (9), Massachusetts (16), Michigan (20), Minnesota (11), Missouri (13), Nevada (3), New Jersey (16), New Mexico (4), New York (45), North Carolina (14), Pennsylvania (32), Rhode Island (4), South Carolina (8), Texas (24), West Virginia (8)

Nixon (219) — Alaska (3), Arizona (4), California (32), Colorado (6), Florida (10), Idaho (4), Indiana (13), Iowa (10), Kansas (8), Kentucky (10), Maine (5), Montana (4), Nebraska (6), New Hampshire (4), North Dakota (4), Ohio (25), Oklahoma (7), Oregon (6), South Dakota (4), Tennessee (11), Utah (4), Vermont (3), Virginia (12), Washington (9), Wisconsin (12), Wyoming (3)

Byrd (15) — Alabama (6), Mississippi (8), Oklahoma (1)

Popular Votes — 1960

State	Total PV	Kennedy	Nixon	Other
Alabama	570,225	324,050	237,981	8,194
Alaska	60,762	29,809	30,953	—
Arizona	398,491	176,781	221,241	469
Arkansas	428,509	215,049	184,508	28,952
California	6,506,578	3,224,099	3,259,722	22,757
Colorado	736,236	330,629	402,242	3,365
Connecticut	1,222,883	657,055	565,813	15
Delaware	196,683	99,590	96,373	720
Florida	1,544,176	748,700	795,476	—
Georgia	733,349	458,638	274,472	239
Hawaii	184,705	92,410	92,295	—
Idaho	300,450	138,853	161,597	—
Illinois	4,757,409	2,377,846	2,368,988	10,575
Indiana	2,135,360	952,358	1,175,120	7,882
Iowa	1,273,810	550,565	722,381	864
Kansas	928,825	363,213	561,474	4,138
Kentucky	1,124,462	521,855	602,607	—
Louisiana	807,891	407,339	230,980	169,572
Maine	421,767	181,159	240,608	—
Maryland	1,055,349	565,808	489,538	3
Massachusetts	2,469,480	1,487,174	976,750	5,556
Michigan	3,318,097	1,687,269	1,620,428	10,400
Minnesota	1,541,887	779,933	757,915	4,039
Mississippi	298,171	108,362	73,561	116,248
Missouri	1,934,422	972,201	962,221	—
Montana	277,579	134,891	141,841	847
Nebraska	613,095	232,542	380,553	—
Nevada	107,267	54,880	52,387	—
New Hampshire	295,761	137,772	157,989	—
New Jersey	2,773,111	1,385,415	1,363,324	24,372
New Mexico	311,107	156,027	153,733	1,347
New York	7,291,079	3,830,085	3,446,419	14,575
North Carolina	1,368,556	713,136	655,420	—
North Dakota	278,431	123,963	154,310	158
Ohio	4,161,859	1,944,248	2,217,611	—
Oklahoma	903,150	370,111	533,039	—

State	Total PV	Kennedy	Nixon	Other
Oregon	776,421	367,402	408,060	959
Pennsylvania	5,006,541	2,556,282	2,439,956	10,303
Rhode Island	405,535	258,032	147,502	1
South Carolina	386,688	198,129	188,558	1
South Dakota	306,487	128,070	178,417	—
Tennessee	1,051,792	481,453	556,577	13,762
Texas	2,311,084	1,167,567	1,121,310	22,207
Utah	374,709	169,248	205,361	100
Vermont	167,324	69,186	98,131	7
Virginia	771,449	362,327	404,521	4,601
Washington	1,241,572	599,298	629,273	13,001
West Virginia	837,781	441,786	395,995	—
Wisconsin	1,729,082	830,805	895,175	3,102
Wyoming	140,782	63,331	77,451	—
Total	68,838,219	34,226,731	34,108,157	503,331

Democratic Nomination — 1960

Candidate	ConFB	FB%	ConLB	LB%	PriW	PriV	PriV%
Kennedy	806	52.99%	—	—	10	1,847,259	32.48%
Johnson	409	26.89%	—	—	0	15,691	0.28%
Symington	86	5.65%	—	—	0	29,557	0.52%
Stevenson	80	5.23%	—	—	0	51,665	0.91%
Humphrey	42	2.73%	—	—	2	590,410	10.38%

Republican Nomination — 1960

Candidate	ConFB	FB%	ConLB	LB%	PriW	PriV	PriV%
Nixon	1,321	99.25%	—	—	11	4,975,938	89.85%

Equalized Statistics — 1960

Candidate	EVX	PVX	ConFBX	ConLBX	PriVX
Kennedy	304	49,720,535	530	—	3,247,790
Nixon	219	49,548,285	992	—	8,985,135
Johnson	—	—	269	—	27,587
Byrd	15	168,871	—	—	—
Humphrey	—	—	27	—	1,038,039
Symington	—	—	57	—	51,966
Stevenson	—	—	52	—	90,836

Election of 1964

Basics — 1964

Election number — 45
Winner — Lyndon Johnson (D)
Incumbent — Lyndon Johnson (D)
U.S. population — 191,888,791
States — 51
Electoral votes — 538
Popular votes — 70,644,592
Voter turnout — 61.4%

Top Candidates — 1964

Lyndon Johnson (CS 93.24)

Barry Goldwater (CS 60.59)

Nelson Rockefeller (CS 20.93)

Field — 1964

Candidate	PI	Age	State	Position	N	W	CS
Lyndon Johnson (D)	9.3	56.18	Texas	President	X	X	93.24
Barry Goldwater (R)	6.6	55.83	Ariz.	Senator	X	—	60.59
Nelson Rockefeller (R)	7.6	56.32	N.Y.	Governor	—	—	20.93
William Scranton (R)	6.9	47.29	Pa.	Governor	—	—	19.42
George Wallace (D)	6.4	45.19	Ala.	Governor	—	—	13.23
Henry Cabot Lodge (R)	4.8	62.33	Mass.	Former v.p. nominee	—	—	12.05
Richard Nixon (R)	6.7	51.81	N.Y.	Former nominee	—	—	11.00

General Election — 1964

Candidate	EV	EV%	SC	PV	PV%
Johnson	486	90.34%	45	43,129,566	61.05%
Goldwater	52	9.67%	6	27,178,188	38.47%

Electoral Votes — 1964

Johnson (486) — Alaska (3), Arkansas (6), California (40), Colorado (6), Connecticut (8), Delaware (3), District of Columbia (3), Florida (14), Hawaii (4), Idaho (4), Illinois (26), Indiana (13), Iowa (9), Kansas (7), Kentucky (9), Maine (4), Maryland (10), Massachusetts (14), Michigan (21), Minnesota (10), Missouri (12), Montana (4), Nebraska (5), Nevada (3), New Hampshire (4), New Jersey (17), New Mexico (4), New York (43), North Carolina (13), North Dakota (4), Ohio (26), Oklahoma (8), Oregon (6), Pennsylvania (29), Rhode Island (4), South Dakota (4), Tennessee (11), Texas (25), Utah (4), Vermont (3), Virginia (12), Washington (9), West Virginia (7), Wisconsin (12), Wyoming (3)

Goldwater (52) — Alabama (10), Arizona (5), Georgia (12), Louisiana (10), Mississippi (7), South Carolina (8)

Popular Votes — 1964

State	Total PV	Johnson	Goldwater	Other
Alabama	689,818	—	479,085	210,733
Alaska	67,259	44,329	22,930	—
Arizona	480,770	237,753	242,535	482
Arkansas	560,426	314,197	243,264	2,965
California	7,057,586	4,171,877	2,879,108	6,601
Colorado	776,986	476,024	296,767	4,195
Connecticut	1,218,578	826,269	390,996	1,313
Delaware	201,320	122,704	78,078	538
District of Columbia	198,597	169,796	28,801	—
Florida	1,854,481	948,540	905,941	—
Georgia	1,139,335	522,556	616,584	195
Hawaii	207,271	163,249	44,022	—
Idaho	292,477	148,920	143,557	—
Illinois	4,702,841	2,796,833	1,905,946	62
Indiana	2,091,606	1,170,848	911,118	9,640
Iowa	1,184,539	733,030	449,148	2,361
Kansas	857,901	464,028	386,579	7,294
Kentucky	1,046,105	669,659	372,977	3,469
Louisiana	896,293	387,068	509,225	—
Maine	380,965	262,264	118,701	—
Maryland	1,116,457	730,912	385,495	50
Massachusetts	2,344,798	1,786,422	549,727	8,649
Michigan	3,203,102	2,136,615	1,060,152	6,335
Minnesota	1,554,462	991,117	559,624	3,721
Mississippi	409,146	52,618	356,528	—
Missouri	1,817,879	1,164,344	653,535	—
Montana	278,628	164,246	113,032	1,350
Nebraska	584,154	307,307	276,847	—
Nevada	135,433	79,339	56,094	—
New Hampshire	288,093	184,064	104,029	—
New Jersey	2,847,663	1,868,231	964,174	15,258
New Mexico	328,645	194,015	132,838	1,792
New York	7,166,275	4,913,102	2,243,559	9,614
North Carolina	1,424,983	800,139	624,844	—
North Dakota	258,389	149,784	108,207	398
Ohio	3,969,196	2,498,331	1,470,865	—

State	Total PV	Johnson	Goldwater	Other
Oklahoma	932,499	519,834	412,665	—
Oregon	786,305	501,017	282,779	2,509
Pennsylvania	4,822,690	3,130,954	1,673,657	18,079
Rhode Island	390,091	315,463	74,615	13
South Carolina	524,779	215,723	309,048	8
South Dakota	293,118	163,010	130,108	—
Tennessee	1,143,946	634,947	508,965	34
Texas	2,626,811	1,663,185	958,566	5,060
Utah	401,413	219,628	181,785	—
Vermont	163,089	108,127	54,942	20
Virginia	1,042,267	558,038	481,334	2,895
Washington	1,258,556	779,881	470,366	8,309
West Virginia	792,040	538,087	253,953	—
Wisconsin	1,691,815	1,050,424	638,495	2,896
Wyoming	142,716	80,718	61,998	—
Total	70,644,592	43,129,566	27,178,188	336,838

Democratic Nomination — 1964

Candidate	ConFB	FB%	ConLB	LB%	PriW	PriV	PriV%
Johnson	2,318	100.00%	—	—	8	1,106,999	17.72%
Wallace	0	0.00%	—	—	0	672,984	10.77%

Republican Nomination — 1964

Candidate	ConFB	FB%	ConLB	LB%	PriW	PriV	PriV%
Goldwater	883	67.51%	—	—	5	2,267,079	38.20%
Scranton	214	16.36%	—	—	1	245,401	4.14%
Rockefeller	114	8.72%	—	—	2	1,304,204	21.97%
Lodge	2	0.15%	—	—	3	386,661	6.52%
Nixon	0	0.00%	—	—	0	197,212	3.32%

Equalized Statistics — 1964

Candidate	EVX	PVX	ConFBX	ConLBX	PriVX
Johnson	486	61,051,476	1,000	—	1,771,926
Goldwater	52	38,471,718	675	—	3,819,628
Rockefeller	—	—	87	—	2,197,354
Scranton	—	—	164	—	413,457
Wallace		—	0	—	1,077,216
Lodge	—	—	2	—	651,456
Nixon	—	—	0	—	332,267

Election of 1968

Basics — 1968

Election number — 46
Winner — Richard Nixon (R)
Incumbent — Lyndon Johnson (D)
U.S. population — 200,706,052
States — 51
Electoral votes — 538
Popular votes — 73,211,875
Voter turnout — 60.7%

Top Candidates — 1968

Richard Nixon (CS 78.01)

Hubert Humphrey (CS 69.19)

George Wallace (CS 45.41)

Field — 1968

Candidate	PI	Age	State	Position	N	W	CS
Richard Nixon (R)	6.2	55.81	N.Y.	Former nominee	X	X	78.01
Hubert Humphrey (D)	7.8	57.43	Minn.	Vice president	X	—	69.19
George Wallace (D/AI)	5.4	49.19	Ala.	Former governor	—	—	45.41
Eugene McCarthy (D)	6.9	52.59	Minn.	Senator	—	—	33.16
Ronald Reagan (R)	7.3	57.73	Calif.	Governor	—	—	28.22
Nelson Rockefeller (R)	7.1	60.32	N.Y.	Governor	—	—	21.48
Robert Kennedy (D)	6.6	42.95	N.Y.	Senator	—	—	19.18
James Rhodes (R)	6.6	59.13	Ohio	Governor	—	—	16.17
George McGovern (D)	6.0	46.29	S.D.	Senator	—	—	12.79
Lyndon Johnson (D)	8.7	60.18	Texas	President	—	—	11.53

General Election — 1968

Candidate	EV	EV%	SC	PV	PV%
Nixon	301	55.95%	32	31,785,480	43.42%
Humphrey	191	35.50%	14	31,275,166	42.72%
Wallace	46	8.55%	5	9,906,473	13.53%
McCarthy	0	0.00%	0	25,552	0.04%

Electoral Votes — 1968

Nixon (301) — Alaska (3), Arizona (5), California (40), Colorado (6), Delaware (3), Florida (14), Idaho (4), Illinois (26), Indiana (13), Iowa (9), Kansas (7), Kentucky (9), Missouri (12), Montana (4), Nebraska (5), Nevada (3), New Hampshire (4), New Jersey (17), New Mexico (4), North Carolina (12), North Dakota (4), Ohio (26), Oklahoma (8), Oregon (6), South Carolina (8), South Dakota (4), Tennessee (11), Utah (4), Vermont (3), Virginia (12), Wisconsin (12), Wyoming (3)

Humphrey (191) — Connecticut (8), District of Columbia (3), Hawaii (4), Maine (4), Maryland (10), Massachusetts (14), Michigan (21), Minnesota (10), New York (43), Pennsylvania (29), Rhode Island (4), Texas (25), Washington (9), West Virginia (7)

Wallace (46) — Alabama (10), Arkansas (6), Georgia (12), Louisiana (10), Mississippi (7), North Carolina (1)

Popular Votes — 1968

State	Total PV	Nixon	Humphrey	Wallace	Other
Alabama	1,049,922	146,923	196,579	691,425	14,995
Alaska	83,035	37,600	35,411	10,024	—
Arizona	486,936	266,721	170,514	46,573	3,128
Arkansas	619,969	190,759	188,228	240,982	—
California	7,251,587	3,467,664	3,244,318	487,270	52,335
Colorado	811,199	409,345	335,174	60,813	5,867
Connecticut	1,256,232	556,721	621,561	76,650	1,300
Delaware	214,367	96,714	89,194	28,459	—
District of Columbia	170,578	31,012	139,566	—	—
Florida	2,187,805	886,804	676,794	624,207	—
Georgia	1,250,266	380,111	334,440	535,550	165
Hawaii	236,218	91,425	141,324	3,469	—
Idaho	291,183	165,369	89,273	36,541	—
Illinois	4,619,749	2,174,774	2,039,814	390,958	14,203
Indiana	2,123,597	1,067,885	806,659	243,108	5,945
Iowa	1,167,931	619,106	476,699	66,422	5,704
Kansas	872,783	478,674	302,996	88,921	2,192
Kentucky	1,055,893	462,411	397,541	193,098	2,843
Louisiana	1,097,450	257,535	309,615	530,300	—
Maine	392,936	169,254	217,312	6,370	—
Maryland	1,235,039	517,995	538,310	178,734	—
Massachusetts	2,331,752	766,844	1,469,218	87,088	8,602
Michigan	3,306,250	1,370,665	1,593,082	331,968	10,535
Minnesota	1,588,506	658,643	857,738	68,931	3,194
Mississippi	654,509	88,516	150,644	415,349	—
Missouri	1,809,502	811,932	791,444	206,126	—
Montana	274,404	138,835	114,117	20,015	1,437
Nebraska	536,851	321,163	170,784	44,904	—
Nevada	154,218	73,188	60,598	20,432	—
New Hampshire	297,298	154,903	130,589	11,173	633
New Jersey	2,875,395	1,325,467	1,264,206	262,187	23,535
New Mexico	327,350	169,692	130,081	25,737	1,840
New York	6,791,688	3,007,932	3,378,470	358,864	46,422
North Carolina	1,587,493	627,192	464,113	496,188	—
North Dakota	247,882	138,669	94,769	14,244	200
Ohio	3,959,698	1,791,014	1,700,586	467,495	603

State	Total PV	Nixon	Humphrey	Wallace	Other
Oklahoma	943,086	449,697	301,658	191,731	—
Oregon	819,622	408,433	358,866	49,683	2,640
Pennsylvania	4,747,928	2,090,017	2,259,405	378,582	19,924
Rhode Island	385,000	122,359	246,518	15,678	445
South Carolina	666,978	254,062	197,486	215,430	—
South Dakota	281,264	149,841	118,023	13,400	—
Tennessee	1,248,617	472,592	351,233	424,792	—
Texas	3,079,216	1,227,844	1,266,804	584,269	299
Utah	422,568	238,728	156,665	26,906	269
Vermont	161,404	85,142	70,255	5,104	903
Virginia	1,361,491	590,319	442,387	321,833	6,952
Washington	1,304,281	588,510	616,037	96,990	2,744
West Virginia	754,206	307,555	374,091	72,560	—
Wisconsin	1,691,538	809,997	748,804	127,835	4,902
Wyoming	127,205	70,927	45,173	11,105	—
Total	73,211,875	31,785,480	31,275,166	9,906,473	244,756

Democratic Nomination — 1968

Candidate	ConFB	FB%	ConLB	LB%	PriW	PriV	PriV%
Humphrey	1,759	67.10%	—	—	0	166,463	2.21%
McCarthy	601	22.92%	—	—	6	2,914,933	38.69%
McGovern	147	5.59%	—	—	0	0	0.00%
Wallace	1	0.02%	—	—	0	33,520	0.45%
Johnson	0	0.00%	—	—	1	383,048	5.08%
Kennedy	—	—	—	—	5	2,304,542	30.58%

Republican Nomination — 1968

Candidate	ConFB	FB%	ConLB	LB%	PriW	PriV	PriV%
Nixon	692	51.91%	—	—	9	1,679,443	37.54%
Rockefeller	277	20.78%	—	—	1	164,340	3.67%
Reagan	182	13.65%	—	—	1	1,696,270	37.92%
Rhodes	55	4.13%	—	—	1	614,492	13.74%

Equalized Statistics — 1968

Candidate	EVX	PVX	ConFBX	ConLBX	PriVX
Nixon	301	43,415,744	519	—	3,754,161
Humphrey	191	42,718,706	671	—	220,918
Wallace	46	13,531,238	0	—	44,485
McCarthy	0	34,901	229	—	3,868,489
Reagan	—	—	137	—	3,791,775
Rockefeller	—	—	208	—	367,359
Kennedy	—	—	—	—	3,058,422
Rhodes	—	—	41	—	1,373,611
McGovern	—	—	56	—	0
Johnson	—	—	0	—	508,354

Election of 1972

Basics — 1972

Election number — 47
Winner — Richard Nixon (R)
Incumbent — Richard Nixon (R)
U.S. population — 209,896,021
States — 51
Electoral votes — 538
Popular votes — 77,718,554
Voter turnout — 55.1%

Top Candidates — 1972

Richard Nixon (CS 95.25)

George McGovern (CS 58.46)

George Wallace (CS 26.62)

Field — 1972

Candidate	PI	Age	State	Position	N	W	CS
Richard Nixon (R)	8.8	59.81	Calif.	President	X	X	95.25
George McGovern (D)	6.4	50.29	S.D.	Senator	X	—	58.46
George Wallace (D)	6.5	53.19	Ala.	Governor	—	—	26.62
Hubert Humphrey (D)	6.5	61.43	Minn.	Former nominee	—	—	25.90
Edmund Muskie (D)	7.2	58.60	Maine	Senator	—	—	17.06
Henry Jackson (D)	6.3	60.42	Wash.	Senator	—	—	15.37
John Ashbrook (R)	4.2	44.11	Ohio	Representative	—	—	13.02
Shirley Chisholm (D)	4.5	47.92	N.Y.	Representative	—	—	12.62
Paul McCloskey (R)	4.7	45.09	Calif.	Representative	—	—	11.31
John Hospers (LIB)	3.3	54.40	Calif.	Movement leader	—	—	10.62
Wilbur Mills (D)	4.3	63.44	Ark.	Representative	—	—	10.36
Sam Yorty (D)	4.3	63.08	Calif.	Mayor	—	—	10.30

General Election — 1972

Candidate	EV	EV%	SC	PV	PV%
Nixon	520	96.65%	49	47,169,911	60.69%
McGovern	17	3.16%	2	29,170,383	37.53%
Hospers	1	0.19%	0	3,673	0.01%

Electoral Votes — 1972

Nixon (520) — Alabama (9), Alaska (3), Arizona (6), Arkansas (6), California (45), Colorado (7), Connecticut (8), Delaware (3), Florida (17), Georgia (12), Hawaii (4), Idaho (4), Illinois (26), Indiana (13), Iowa (8), Kansas (7), Kentucky (9), Louisiana (10), Maine (4), Maryland (10), Michigan (21), Minnesota (10), Mississippi (7), Missouri (12), Montana (4), Nebraska (5), Nevada (3), New Hampshire (4), New Jersey (17), New Mexico (4), New York (41), North Carolina (13), North Dakota (3), Ohio (25), Oklahoma (8), Oregon (6), Pennsylvania (27), Rhode Island (4), South Carolina (8), South Dakota (4), Tennessee (10), Texas (26), Utah (4), Vermont (3), Virginia (11), Washington (9), West Virginia (6), Wisconsin (11), Wyoming (3)

McGovern (17) — District of Columbia (3), Massachusetts (14)

Hospers (1) — Virginia (1)

Popular Votes — 1972

State	Total PV	Nixon	McGovern	Other
Alabama	1,006,111	728,701	256,923	20,487
Alaska	95,219	55,349	32,967	6,903
Arizona	622,926	402,812	198,540	21,574
Arkansas	651,320	448,541	199,892	2,887
California	8,367,862	4,602,096	3,475,847	289,919
Colorado	953,884	597,189	329,980	26,715
Connecticut	1,384,277	810,763	555,498	18,016
Delaware	235,516	140,357	92,283	2,876
District of Columbia	163,421	35,226	127,627	568
Florida	2,583,283	1,857,759	718,117	7,407
Georgia	1,174,772	881,496	289,529	3,747
Hawaii	270,274	168,865	101,409	—
Idaho	310,379	199,384	80,826	30,169
Illinois	4,723,236	2,788,179	1,913,472	21,585
Indiana	2,125,529	1,405,154	708,568	11,807
Iowa	1,225,944	706,207	496,206	23,531
Kansas	916,095	619,812	270,287	25,996
Kentucky	1,067,499	676,446	371,159	19,894
Louisiana	1,051,491	686,852	298,142	66,497
Maine	417,042	256,458	160,584	—
Maryland	1,353,812	829,305	505,781	18,726
Massachusetts	2,458,756	1,112,078	1,332,540	14,138
Michigan	3,489,727	1,961,721	1,459,435	68,571
Minnesota	1,741,652	898,269	802,346	41,037
Mississippi	645,963	505,125	126,782	14,056
Missouri	1,855,803	1,153,852	697,147	4,804
Montana	317,603	183,976	120,197	13,430
Nebraska	576,289	406,298	169,991	—
Nevada	181,766	115,750	66,016	—
New Hampshire	334,055	213,724	116,435	3,896
New Jersey	2,997,229	1,845,502	1,102,211	49,516
New Mexico	386,241	235,606	141,084	9,551
New York	7,165,919	4,192,778	2,951,084	22,057
North Carolina	1,518,612	1,054,889	438,705	25,018
North Dakota	280,514	174,109	100,384	6,021
Ohio	4,094,787	2,441,827	1,558,889	94,071

State	Total PV	Nixon	McGovern	Other
Oklahoma	1,029,900	759,025	247,147	23,728
Oregon	927,946	486,686	392,760	48,500
Pennsylvania	4,592,106	2,714,521	1,796,951	80,634
Rhode Island	415,808	220,383	194,645	780
South Carolina	673,960	477,044	186,824	10,092
South Dakota	307,415	166,476	139,945	994
Tennessee	1,201,182	813,147	357,293	30,742
Texas	3,471,281	2,298,896	1,154,289	18,096
Utah	478,476	323,643	126,284	28,549
Vermont	186,947	117,149	68,174	1,624
Virginia	1,457,019	988,493	438,887	29,639
Washington	1,470,847	837,135	568,334	65,378
West Virginia	762,399	484,964	277,435	—
Wisconsin	1,852,890	989,430	810,174	53,286
Wyoming	145,570	100,464	44,358	748
Total	77,718,554	47,169,911	29,170,383	1,378,260

Democratic Nomination — 1972

Candidate	ConFB	FB%	ConLB	LB%	PriW	PriV	PriV%
McGovern	1,728	57.31%	—	—	8	4,053,451	25.34%
Jackson	525	17.41%	—	—	0	505,198	3.16%
Wallace	382	12.66%	—	—	5	3,755,424	23.48%
Chisholm	152	5.04%	—	—	1	430,703	2.69%
Humphrey	67	2.21%	—	—	4	4,121,372	25.77%
Mills	34	1.12%	—	—	0	37,401	0.23%
Muskie	24	0.81%	—	—	2	1,840,217	11.51%
Yorty	0	0.00%	—	—	0	79,446	0.50%

Republican Nomination — 1972

Candidate	ConFB	FB%	ConLB	LB%	PriW	PriV	PriV%
Nixon	1,347	99.93%	—	—	18	5,378,704	86.92%
McCloskey	1	0.07%	—	—	0	132,731	2.15%
Ashbrook	0	0.00%	—	—	0	311,543	5.03%

Equalized Statistics — 1972

Candidate	EVX	PVX	ConFBX	ConLBX	PriVX
Nixon	520	60,693,243	999	—	8,691,758
McGovern	17	37,533,358	573	—	2,534,363
Wallace	—	—	127	—	2,348,026
Humphrey	—	—	22	—	2,576,829
Muskie	—	—	8	—	1,150,570
Jackson	—	—	174	—	315,868
Ashbrook	—	—	0	—	503,440
Chisholm	—	—	50	—	269,291
McCloskey	—	—	1	—	214,488
Hospers	1	4,726	—	—	—
Mills	—	—	11	—	23,384
Yorty	—	—	0	—	49,672

Election of 1976

Basics — 1976

Election number — 48
Winner — Jimmy Carter (D)
Incumbent — Gerald Ford (R)
U.S. population — 218,035,164
States — 51
Electoral votes — 538
Popular votes — 81,555,889
Voter turnout — 53.6%

Top Candidates — 1976

Jimmy Carter (CS 79.23)

Gerald Ford (CS 72.98)

Ronald Reagan (CS 47.60)

Field — 1976

Candidate	PI	Age	State	Position	N	W	CS
Jimmy Carter (D)	7.4	52.08	Ga.	Former governor	X	X	79.23
Gerald Ford (R)	6.6	63.30	Mich.	President	X	—	72.98
Ronald Reagan (R)	6.7	65.73	Calif.	Former governor	—	—	47.60
Jerry Brown (D)	6.2	38.57	Calif.	Governor	—	—	21.16
Morris Udall (D)	4.3	54.38	Ariz.	Representative	—	—	18.22
George Wallace (D)	5.6	57.19	Ala.	Governor	—	—	17.84
Henry Jackson (D)	6.2	64.42	Wash.	Senator	—	—	14.30
Frank Church (D)	6.5	52.27	Idaho	Senator	—	—	13.23
Sargent Shriver (D)	4.2	60.98	Md.	Former v.p. nominee	—	—	11.14
Fred Harris (D)	6.9	45.97	Okla.	Former senator	—	—	10.94
Birch Bayh (D)	6.9	48.78	Ind.	Senator	—	—	10.32
Hubert Humphrey (D)	5.5	65.43	Minn.	Former nominee	—	—	10.29

General Election — 1976

Candidate	EV	EV%	SC	PV	PV%
Carter	297	55.20%	24	40,830,763	50.07%
Ford	240	44.61%	27	39,147,793	48.00%
Reagan	1	0.19%	0	0	0.00%

Electoral Votes — 1976

Carter (297) — Alabama (9), Arkansas (6), Delaware (3), District of Columbia (3), Florida (17), Georgia (12), Hawaii (4), Kentucky (9), Louisiana (10), Maryland (10), Massachusetts (14), Minnesota (10), Mississippi (7), Missouri (12), New York (41), North Carolina (13), Ohio (25), Pennsylvania (27), Rhode Island (4), South Carolina (8), Tennessee (10), Texas (26), West Virginia (6), Wisconsin (11)

Ford (240) — Alaska (3), Arizona (6), California (45), Colorado (7), Connecticut (8), Idaho (4), Illinois (26), Indiana (13), Iowa (8), Kansas (7), Maine (4), Michigan (21), Montana (4), Nebraska (5), Nevada (3), New Hampshire (4), New Jersey (17), New Mexico (4), North Dakota (3), Oklahoma (8), Oregon (6), South Dakota (4), Utah (4), Vermont (3), Virginia (12), Washington (8), Wyoming (3)

Reagan (1) — Washington (1)

Popular Votes — 1976

State	Total PV	Carter	Ford	Other
Alabama	1,182,850	659,170	504,070	19,610
Alaska	123,574	44,058	71,555	7,961
Arizona	742,719	295,602	418,642	28,475
Arkansas	767,535	498,604	267,903	1,028
California	7,867,117	3,742,284	3,882,244	242,589
Colorado	1,081,554	460,353	584,367	36,834
Connecticut	1,381,526	647,895	719,261	14,370
Delaware	235,834	122,596	109,831	3,407
District of Columbia	168,830	137,818	27,873	3,139
Florida	3,150,631	1,636,000	1,469,531	45,100
Georgia	1,467,458	979,409	483,743	4,306
Hawaii	291,301	147,375	140,003	3,923
Idaho	344,071	126,549	204,151	13,371
Illinois	4,718,914	2,271,295	2,364,269	83,350
Indiana	2,220,362	1,014,714	1,183,958	21,690
Iowa	1,279,306	619,931	632,863	26,512
Kansas	957,845	430,421	502,752	24,672
Kentucky	1,167,142	615,717	531,852	19,573
Louisiana	1,278,439	661,365	587,446	29,628
Maine	483,216	232,279	236,320	14,617
Maryland	1,439,897	759,612	672,661	7,624
Massachusetts	2,547,558	1,429,475	1,030,276	87,807
Michigan	3,653,749	1,696,714	1,893,742	63,293
Minnesota	1,949,931	1,070,440	819,395	60,096
Mississippi	769,361	381,309	366,846	21,206
Missouri	1,953,600	998,387	927,443	27,770
Montana	328,734	149,259	173,703	5,772
Nebraska	607,668	233,692	359,705	14,271
Nevada	201,876	92,479	101,273	8,124
New Hampshire	339,618	147,635	185,935	6,048
New Jersey	3,014,472	1,444,653	1,509,688	60,131
New Mexico	418,409	201,148	211,419	5,842
New York	6,534,170	3,389,558	3,100,791	43,821
North Carolina	1,678,914	927,365	741,960	9,589
North Dakota	297,188	136,078	153,470	7,640
Ohio	4,111,873	2,011,621	2,000,505	99,747

State	Total PV	Carter	Ford	Other
Oklahoma	1,092,251	532,442	545,708	14,101
Oregon	1,029,876	490,407	492,120	47,349
Pennsylvania	4,620,787	2,328,677	2,205,604	86,506
Rhode Island	411,170	227,636	181,249	2,285
South Carolina	802,583	450,807	346,149	5,627
South Dakota	300,678	147,068	151,505	2,105
Tennessee	1,476,345	825,879	633,969	16,497
Texas	4,071,884	2,082,319	1,953,300	36,265
Utah	541,198	182,110	337,908	21,180
Vermont	187,765	80,954	102,085	4,726
Virginia	1,697,094	813,896	836,554	46,644
Washington	1,555,534	717,323	777,732	60,479
West Virginia	750,964	435,914	314,760	290
Wisconsin	2,104,175	1,040,232	1,004,987	58,956
Wyoming	156,343	62,239	92,717	1,387
Total	81,555,889	40,830,763	39,147,793	1,577,333

Democratic Nomination — 1976

Candidate	ConFB	FB%	ConLB	LB%	PriW	PriV	PriV%
Carter	2,239	74.42%	—	—	17	6,235,609	38.85%
Udall	330	10.95%	—	—	0	1,611,754	10.04%
Brown	301	9.99%	—	—	3	2,449,374	15.26%
Wallace	57	1.90%	—	—	0	1,995,388	12.43%
Church	19	0.63%	—	—	4	830,818	5.18%
Jackson	10	0.33%	—	—	1	1,134,375	7.07%
Humphrey	10	0.33%	—	—	0	61,992	0.39%
Harris	9	0.30%	—	—	0	234,568	1.46%
Shriver	0	0.00%	—	—	0	304,399	1.90%
Bayh	0	0.00%	—	—	0	86,438	0.54%

Republican Nomination — 1976

Candidate	ConFB	FB%	ConLB	LB%	PriW	PriV	PriV%
Ford	1,187	52.55%	—	—	16	5,529,899	53.31%
Reagan	1,070	47.37%	—	—	10	4,758,325	45.87%

Equalized Statistics — 1976

Candidate	EVX	PVX	ConFBX	ConLBX	PriVX
Carter	297	50,064,764	744	—	3,884,473
Ford	240	48,001,185	525	—	5,330,473
Reagan	1	0	474	—	4,586,724
Brown	—	—	100	—	1,525,838
Udall	—	—	110	—	1,004,042
Wallace	—	—	19	—	1,243,027
Jackson	—	—	3	—	706,659
Church	—	—	6	—	517,558
Shriver	—	—	0	—	189,625
Harris	—	—	3	—	146,124
Bayh	—	—	0	—	53,847
Humphrey	—	—	3	—	38,618

Election of 1980

Basics — 1980

Election number — 49
Winner — Ronald Reagan (R)
Incumbent — Jimmy Carter (D)
U.S. population — 226,545,805
States — 51
Electoral votes — 538
Popular votes — 86,513,813
Voter turnout — 52.8%

Top Candidates — 1980

Ronald Reagan (CS 91.16)

Jimmy Carter (CS 60.93)

Edward Kennedy (CS 39.18)

Field — 1980

Candidate	PI	Age	State	Position	N	W	CS
Ronald Reagan (R)	5.7	69.73	Calif.	Former governor	X	X	91.16
Jimmy Carter (D)	9.0	56.08	Ga.	President	X	—	60.93
Edward Kennedy (D)	6.8	48.69	Mass.	Senator	—	—	39.18
John Anderson (R/NU)	4.7	58.71	Ill.	Representative	—	—	38.97
George H.W. Bush (R)	5.2	56.39	Texas	Former ambassador	—	—	24.15
Jerry Brown (D)	6.4	42.57	Calif.	Governor	—	—	11.84
Howard Baker (R)	7.7	54.96	Tenn.	Senator	—	—	10.51
Phil Crane (R)	4.7	49.99	Ill.	Representative	—	—	10.46
John Connally (R)	7.4	63.68	Texas	Former governor	—	—	10.38

General Election — 1980

Candidate	EV	EV%	SC	PV	PV%
Reagan	489	90.89%	44	43,904,153	50.75%
Carter	49	9.11%	7	35,483,883	41.02%
Anderson	0	0.00%	0	5,720,060	6.61%

Electoral Votes — 1980

Reagan (489) — Alabama (9), Alaska (3), Arizona (6), Arkansas (6), California (45), Colorado (7), Connecticut (8), Delaware (3), Florida (17), Idaho (4), Illinois (26), Indiana (13), Iowa (8), Kansas (7), Kentucky (9), Louisiana (10), Maine (4), Massachusetts (14), Michigan (21), Mississippi (7), Missouri (12), Montana (4), Nebraska (5), Nevada (3), New Hampshire (4), New Jersey (17), New Mexico (4), New York (41), North Carolina (13), North Dakota (3), Ohio (25), Oklahoma (8), Oregon (6), Pennsylvania (27), South Carolina (8), South Dakota (4), Tennessee (10), Texas (26), Utah (4), Vermont (3), Virginia (12), Washington (9), Wisconsin (11), Wyoming (3)
Carter (49) — District of Columbia (3), Georgia (12), Hawaii (4), Maryland (10), Minnesota (10), Rhode Island (4), West Virginia (6)

Popular Votes — 1980

State	Total PV	Reagan	Carter	Anderson	Other
Alabama	1,341,929	654,192	636,730	16,481	34,526
Alaska	158,445	86,112	41,842	11,155	19,336
Arizona	873,945	529,688	246,843	76,952	20,462
Arkansas	837,582	403,164	398,041	22,468	13,909
California	8,587,063	4,524,858	3,083,661	739,833	238,711
Colorado	1,184,415	652,264	367,973	130,633	33,545
Connecticut	1,406,285	677,210	541,732	171,807	15,536
Delaware	235,900	111,252	105,754	16,288	2,606
District of Columbia	175,237	23,545	131,113	16,337	4,242
Florida	3,686,930	2,046,951	1,419,475	189,692	30,812
Georgia	1,596,695	654,168	890,733	36,055	15,739
Hawaii	303,287	130,112	135,879	32,021	5,275
Idaho	437,431	290,699	110,192	27,058	9,482
Illinois	4,749,721	2,358,049	1,981,413	346,754	63,505
Indiana	2,242,033	1,255,656	844,197	111,639	30,541
Iowa	1,317,661	676,026	508,672	115,633	17,330
Kansas	979,795	566,812	326,150	68,231	18,602
Kentucky	1,294,627	635,274	616,417	31,127	11,809
Louisiana	1,548,591	792,853	708,453	26,345	20,940
Maine	523,011	238,522	220,974	53,327	10,188
Maryland	1,540,496	680,606	726,161	119,537	14,192
Massachusetts	2,522,890	1,057,631	1,053,802	382,539	28,918
Michigan	3,909,725	1,915,225	1,661,532	275,223	57,745
Minnesota	2,051,980	873,268	954,174	174,990	49,548
Mississippi	892,620	441,089	429,281	12,036	10,214
Missouri	2,099,824	1,074,181	931,182	77,920	16,541
Montana	363,952	206,814	118,032	29,281	9,825
Nebraska	640,854	419,937	166,851	44,993	9,073
Nevada	247,885	155,017	66,666	17,651	8,551
New Hampshire	383,990	221,705	108,864	49,693	3,728
New Jersey	2,975,684	1,546,557	1,147,364	234,632	47,131
New Mexico	456,971	250,779	167,826	29,459	8,907
New York	6,201,959	2,893,831	2,728,372	467,801	111,955
North Carolina	1,855,833	915,018	875,635	52,800	12,380
North Dakota	301,545	193,695	79,189	23,640	5,021
Ohio	4,283,603	2,206,545	1,752,414	254,472	70,172
Oklahoma	1,149,708	695,570	402,026	38,284	13,828

State	Total PV	Reagan	Carter	Anderson	Other
Oregon	1,181,516	571,044	456,890	112,389	41,193
Pennsylvania	4,561,501	2,261,872	1,937,540	292,921	69,168
Rhode Island	416,072	154,793	198,342	59,819	3,118
South Carolina	894,071	441,841	430,385	14,153	7,692
South Dakota	327,703	198,343	103,855	21,431	4,074
Tennessee	1,617,616	787,761	783,051	35,991	10,813
Texas	4,541,636	2,510,705	1,881,147	111,613	38,171
Utah	604,222	439,687	124,266	30,284	9,985
Vermont	213,299	94,628	81,952	31,761	4,958
Virginia	1,866,032	989,609	752,174	95,418	28,831
Washington	1,742,394	865,244	650,193	185,073	41,884
West Virginia	737,715	334,206	367,462	31,691	4,356
Wisconsin	2,273,221	1,088,845	981,584	160,657	42,135
Wyoming	176,713	110,700	49,427	12,072	4,514
Total	86,513,813	43,904,153	35,483,883	5,720,060	1,405,717

Democratic Nomination — 1980

Candidate	ConFB	FB%	ConLB	LB%	PriW	PriV	PriV%
Carter	2,123	63.74%	—	—	23	9,593,335	51.17%
Kennedy	1,150	34.54%	—	—	10	6,963,625	37.15%
Brown	1	0.03%	—	—	0	573,994	3.06%

Republican Nomination — 1980

Candidate	ConFB	FB%	ConLB	LB%	PriW	PriV	PriV%
Reagan	1,939	97.24%	—	—	29	7,709,793	60.76%
Anderson	37	1.86%	—	—	0	1,572,174	12.39%
Bush	13	0.65%	—	—	5	2,963,509	23.35%
Baker	0	0.00%	—	—	0	106,819	0.84%
Crane	0	0.00%	—	—	0	97,793	0.77%
Connally	0	0.00%	—	—	0	80,662	0.64%

Equalized Statistics — 1980

Candidate	EVX	PVX	ConFBX	ConLBX	PriVX
Reagan	489	50,748,142	972	—	6,075,833
Carter	49	41,015,280	637	—	5,117,434
Kennedy	—	—	345	—	3,714,651
Anderson	0	6,611,730	19	—	1,238,978
Bush	—	—	7	—	2,335,444
Brown	—	—	0	—	306,189
Baker	—	—	0	—	84,181
Crane	—	—	0	—	77,067
Connally	—	—	0	—	63,567

Election of 1984

Basics — 1984

Election number — 50
Winner — Ronald Reagan (R)
Incumbent — Ronald Reagan (R)
U.S. population — 235,824,902
States — 51
Electoral votes — 538
Popular votes — 92,652,842
Voter turnout — 53.3%

Top Candidates — 1984

Ronald Reagan (CS 95.13)

Walter Mondale (CS 58.83)

Gary Hart (CS 37.76)

Field — 1984

Candidate	PI	Age	State	Position	N	W	CS
Ronald Reagan (R)	8.1	73.73	Calif.	President	X	X	95.13
Walter Mondale (D)	7.8	56.82	Minn.	Former vice president	X	—	58.83
Gary Hart (D)	6.3	47.93	Colo.	Senator	—	—	37.76
Jesse Jackson (D)	3.3	43.07	Ill.	Movement leader	—	—	23.30
John Glenn (D)	6.8	63.29	Ohio	Senator	—	—	12.08
George McGovern (D)	6.2	62.29	S.D.	Former nominee	—	—	11.14
Alan Cranston (D)	7.0	70.37	Calif.	Senator	—	—	10.17

General Election — 1984

Candidate	EV	EV%	SC	PV	PV%
Reagan	525	97.58%	49	54,455,075	58.77%
Mondale	13	2.42%	2	37,577,185	40.56%

Electoral Votes — 1984

Reagan (525) — Alabama (9), Alaska (3), Arizona (7), Arkansas (6), California (47), Colorado (8), Connecticut (8), Delaware (3), Florida (21), Georgia (12), Hawaii (4), Idaho (4), Illinois (24), Indiana (12), Iowa (8), Kansas (7), Kentucky (9), Louisiana (10), Maine (4), Maryland (10), Massachusetts (13), Michigan (20), Mississippi (7), Missouri (11), Montana (4), Nebraska (5), Nevada (4), New Hampshire (4), New Jersey (16), New Mexico (5), New York (36), North Carolina (13), North Dakota (3), Ohio (23), Oklahoma (8), Oregon (7), Pennsylvania (25), Rhode Island (4), South Carolina (8), South Dakota (3), Tennessee (11), Texas (29), Utah (5), Vermont (3), Virginia (12), Washington (10), West Virginia (6), Wisconsin (11), Wyoming (3)
Mondale (13) — District of Columbia (3), Minnesota (10)

Popular Votes — 1984

State	Total PV	Reagan	Mondale	Other
Alabama	1,441,713	872,849	551,899	16,965
Alaska	207,605	138,377	62,007	7,221
Arizona	1,025,897	681,416	333,854	10,627
Arkansas	884,406	534,774	338,646	10,986
California	9,505,423	5,467,009	3,922,519	115,895
Colorado	1,295,380	821,817	454,975	18,588
Connecticut	1,466,900	890,877	569,597	6,426
Delaware	254,572	152,190	101,656	726
District of Columbia	211,288	29,009	180,408	1,871
Florida	4,180,051	2,730,350	1,448,816	885
Georgia	1,776,120	1,068,722	706,628	770
Hawaii	335,846	185,050	147,154	3,642
Idaho	411,144	297,523	108,510	5,111
Illinois	4,819,088	2,707,103	2,086,499	25,486
Indiana	2,233,069	1,377,230	841,481	14,358
Iowa	1,319,805	703,088	605,620	11,097
Kansas	1,021,991	677,296	333,149	11,546
Kentucky	1,369,345	821,702	539,539	8,104
Louisiana	1,706,822	1,037,299	651,586	17,937
Maine	553,144	336,500	214,515	2,129
Maryland	1,675,873	879,918	787,935	8,020
Massachusetts	2,559,453	1,310,936	1,239,606	8,911
Michigan	3,801,658	2,251,571	1,529,638	20,449
Minnesota	2,084,449	1,032,603	1,036,364	15,482
Mississippi	941,104	582,377	352,192	6,535
Missouri	2,122,783	1,274,188	848,583	12
Montana	384,377	232,450	146,742	5,185
Nebraska	652,090	460,054	187,866	4,170
Nevada	286,667	188,770	91,655	6,242
New Hampshire	389,066	267,051	120,395	1,620
New Jersey	3,217,862	1,933,630	1,261,323	22,909
New Mexico	514,370	307,101	201,769	5,500
New York	6,806,810	3,664,763	3,119,609	22,438
North Carolina	2,175,361	1,346,481	824,287	4,593
North Dakota	308,971	200,336	104,429	4,206
Ohio	4,547,619	2,678,560	1,825,440	43,619
Oklahoma	1,255,676	861,530	385,080	9,066

State	Total PV	Reagan	Mondale	Other
Oregon	1,226,527	685,700	536,479	4,348
Pennsylvania	4,844,903	2,584,323	2,228,131	32,449
Rhode Island	410,492	212,080	197,106	1,306
South Carolina	968,529	615,539	344,459	8,531
South Dakota	317,867	200,267	116,113	1,487
Tennessee	1,711,994	990,212	711,714	10,068
Texas	5,397,571	3,433,428	1,949,276	14,867
Utah	629,656	469,105	155,369	5,182
Vermont	234,561	135,865	95,730	2,966
Virginia	2,146,635	1,337,078	796,250	13,307
Washington	1,883,910	1,051,670	807,352	24,888
West Virginia	735,742	405,483	328,125	2,134
Wisconsin	2,211,689	1,198,584	995,740	17,365
Wyoming	188,968	133,241	53,370	2,357
Total	92,652,842	54,455,075	37,577,185	620,582

Democratic Nomination — 1984

Candidate	ConFB	FB%	ConLB	LB%	PriW	PriV	PriV%
Mondale	2,191	55.71%	—	—	10	6,811,214	37.82%
Hart	1,201	30.52%	—	—	16	6,503,968	36.12%
Jackson	466	11.84%	—	—	2	3,282,380	18.23%
McGovern	4	0.10%	—	—	0	334,801	1.86%
Glenn	2	0.05%	—	—	0	617,473	3.43%
Cranston	0	0.00%	—	—	0	51,437	0.29%

Republican Nomination — 1984

Candidate	ConFB	FB%	ConLB	LB%	PriW	PriV	PriV%
Reagan	2,233	99.91%	—	—	25	6,484,987	98.62%

Equalized Statistics — 1984

Candidate	EVX	PVX	ConFBX	ConLBX	PriVX
Reagan	525	58,773,238	999	—	9,862,122
Mondale	13	40,556,970	557	—	3,782,076
Hart	—	—	305	—	3,611,471
Jackson	—	—	118	—	1,822,614
Glenn	—	—	1	—	342,865
McGovern	—	—	1	—	185,906
Cranston	—	—	0	—	28,562

Election of 1988

Basics — 1988

Election number — 51
Winner — George H.W. Bush (R)
Incumbent — Ronald Reagan (R)
U.S. population — 244,498,982
States — 51
Electoral votes — 538
Popular votes — 91,594,809
Voter turnout — 50.3%

Top Candidates — 1988

George H.W. Bush (CS 87.86)

Michael Dukakis (CS 65.32)

Jesse Jackson (CS 33.32)

Field — 1988

Candidate	PI	Age	State	Position	N	W	CS
George H.W. Bush (R)	6.5	64.39	Texas	Vice president	X	X	87.86
Michael Dukakis (D)	6.7	54.99	Mass.	Governor	X	—	65.32
Jesse Jackson (D)	3.6	47.07	Ill.	Movement leader	—	—	33.32
Bob Dole (R)	7.0	65.28	Kan.	Senator	—	—	21.51
Al Gore (D)	6.8	40.59	Tenn.	Senator	—	—	18.19
Pat Robertson (R)	4.5	58.61	Va.	Movement leader	—	—	15.41
Richard Gephardt (D)	4.0	47.75	Mo.	Representative	—	—	13.63
Paul Simon (D)	7.1	59.92	Ill.	Senator	—	—	12.66
Jack Kemp (R)	5.2	53.30	N.Y.	Representative	—	—	11.63
Gary Hart (D)	6.7	51.93	Colo.	Former senator	—	—	11.02
Lloyd Bentsen (D)	7.6	67.72	Texas	Senator	—	—	10.62
Pete du Pont (R)	6.6	53.78	Del.	Former governor	—	—	10.25
Bruce Babbitt (D)	6.2	50.35	Ariz.	Former governor	—	—	10.20

General Election — 1988

Candidate	EV	EV%	SC	PV	PV%
Bush	426	79.18%	40	48,886,106	53.37%
Dukakis	111	20.63%	11	41,809,065	45.65%
Bentsen	1	0.19%	0	0	0.00%

Electoral Votes — 1988

Bush (426) — Alabama (9), Alaska (3), Arizona (7), Arkansas (6), California (47), Colorado (8), Connecticut (8), Delaware (3), Florida (21), Georgia (12), Idaho (4), Illinois (24), Indiana (12), Kansas (7), Kentucky (9), Louisiana (10), Maine (4), Maryland (10), Michigan (20), Mississippi (7), Missouri (11), Montana (4), Nebraska (5), Nevada (4), New Hampshire (4), New Jersey (16), New Mexico (5), North Carolina (13), North Dakota (3), Ohio (23), Oklahoma (8), Pennsylvania (25), South Carolina (8), South Dakota (3), Tennessee (11), Texas (29), Utah (5), Vermont (3), Virginia (12), Wyoming (3)

Dukakis (111) — District of Columbia (3), Hawaii (4), Iowa (8), Massachusetts (13), Minnesota (10), New York (36), Oregon (7), Rhode Island (4), Washington (10), West Virginia (5), Wisconsin (11)

Bentsen (1) — West Virginia (1)

Popular Votes — 1988

State	Total PV	Bush	Dukakis	Other
Alabama	1,378,476	815,576	549,506	13,394
Alaska	200,116	119,251	72,584	8,281
Arizona	1,171,873	702,541	454,029	15,303
Arkansas	827,738	466,578	349,237	11,923
California	9,887,065	5,054,917	4,702,233	129,915
Colorado	1,372,394	728,177	621,453	22,764
Connecticut	1,443,394	750,241	676,584	16,569
Delaware	249,891	139,639	108,647	1,605
District of Columbia	192,877	27,590	159,407	5,880
Florida	4,302,313	2,618,885	1,656,701	26,727
Georgia	1,809,672	1,081,331	714,792	13,549
Hawaii	354,461	158,625	192,364	3,472
Idaho	408,968	253,881	147,272	7,815
Illinois	4,559,120	2,310,939	2,215,940	32,241
Indiana	2,168,621	1,297,763	860,643	10,215
Iowa	1,225,614	545,355	670,557	9,702
Kansas	993,044	554,049	422,636	16,359
Kentucky	1,322,517	734,281	580,368	7,868
Louisiana	1,628,202	883,702	717,460	27,040
Maine	555,035	307,131	243,569	4,335
Maryland	1,714,358	876,167	826,304	11,887
Massachusetts	2,632,805	1,194,644	1,401,406	36,755
Michigan	3,669,163	1,965,486	1,675,783	27,894
Minnesota	2,096,790	962,337	1,109,471	24,982
Mississippi	931,527	557,890	363,921	9,716
Missouri	2,093,713	1,084,953	1,001,619	7,141
Montana	365,674	190,412	168,936	6,326
Nebraska	661,465	397,956	259,235	4,274
Nevada	350,067	206,040	132,738	11,289
New Hampshire	451,074	281,537	163,696	5,841
New Jersey	3,099,553	1,743,192	1,320,352	36,009
New Mexico	521,287	270,341	244,497	6,449
New York	6,485,683	3,081,871	3,347,882	55,930
North Carolina	2,134,370	1,237,258	890,167	6,945
North Dakota	297,261	166,559	127,739	2,963

State	Total PV	Bush	Dukakis	Other
Ohio	4,393,699	2,416,549	1,939,629	37,521
Oklahoma	1,171,036	678,367	483,423	9,246
Oregon	1,201,694	560,126	616,206	25,362
Pennsylvania	4,536,251	2,300,087	2,194,944	41,220
Rhode Island	404,620	177,761	225,123	1,736
South Carolina	986,009	606,443	370,554	9,012
South Dakota	312,991	165,415	145,560	2,016
Tennessee	1,636,250	947,233	679,794	9,223
Texas	5,427,410	3,036,829	2,352,748	37,833
Utah	647,008	428,442	207,343	11,223
Vermont	243,328	124,331	115,775	3,222
Virginia	2,191,609	1,309,162	859,799	22,648
Washington	1,865,253	903,835	933,516	27,902
West Virginia	653,311	310,065	341,016	2,230
Wisconsin	2,191,608	1,047,499	1,126,794	17,315
Wyoming	176,551	106,867	67,113	2,571
Total	91,594,809	48,886,106	41,809,065	899,638

Democratic Nomination — 1988

Candidate	ConFB	FB%	ConLB	LB%	PriW	PriV	PriV%
Dukakis	2,876	69.12%	—	—	22	9,817,185	42.75%
Jackson	1,219	29.28%	—	—	6	6,685,699	29.12%
Gephardt	2	0.05%	—	—	2	1,388,356	6.05%
Hart	1	0.02%	—	—	0	389,003	1.69%
Bentsen	1	0.02%	—	—	0	0	0.00%
Gore	0	0.00%	—	—	5	3,134,516	13.65%
Simon	0	0.00%	—	—	1	1,018,136	4.43%
Babbitt	0	0.00%	—	—	0	77,780	0.34%

Republican Nomination — 1988

Candidate	ConFB	FB%	ConLB	LB%	PriW	PriV	PriV%
Bush	2,277	100.00%	—	—	35	8,254,654	67.86%
Dole	0	0.00%	—	—	1	2,333,268	19.18%
Robertson	0	0.00%	—	—	0	1,097,442	9.02%
Kemp	0	0.00%	—	—	0	331,333	2.72%
du Pont	0	0.00%	—	—	0	49,781	0.41%

Equalized Statistics — 1988

Candidate	EVX	PVX	ConFBX	ConLBX	PriVX
Bush	426	53,372,136	1,000	—	6,785,513
Dukakis	111	45,645,671	691	—	4,275,417
Jackson	—	—	293	—	2,911,644
Dole	—	—	0	—	1,917,999
Gore	—	—	0	—	1,365,092
Robertson	—	—	0	—	902,122
Gephardt	—	—	0	—	604,634
Simon	—	—	0	—	443,402
Kemp	—	—	0	—	272,363
Hart	—	—	0	—	169,412
Bentsen	1	0	0	—	0
du Pont	—	—	0	—	40,921
Babbitt	—	—	0	—	33,873

Election of 1992

Basics — 1992

Election number — 52
Winner — Bill Clinton (D)
Incumbent — George H.W. Bush (R)
U.S. population — 256,514,224
States — 51
Electoral votes — 538
Popular votes — 104,425,014
Voter turnout — 55.2%

Top Candidates — 1992

Bill Clinton (CS 82.15)

George H.W. Bush (CS 66.86)

Ross Perot (CS 43.78)

Field — 1992

Candidate	PI	Age	State	Position	N	W	CS
Bill Clinton (D)	6.5	46.20	Ark.	Governor	X	X	82.15
George H.W. Bush (R)	8.2	68.39	Texas	President	X	—	66.86
Ross Perot (I)	2.9	62.35	Texas	Business executive	—	—	43.78
Jerry Brown (D)	6.8	54.57	Calif.	Former governor	—	—	24.83
Pat Buchanan (R)	5.2	54.00	Va.	Journalist	—	—	23.85
Paul Tsongas (D)	7.0	51.71	Mass.	Former senator	—	—	21.82
Bob Kerrey (D)	6.4	49.18	Nebr.	Senator	—	—	10.95
Tom Harkin (D)	6.9	52.95	Iowa	Senator	—	—	10.83

General Election — 1992

Candidate	EV	EV%	SC	PV	PV%
Clinton	370	68.77%	33	44,909,326	43.01%
Bush	168	31.23%	18	39,103,882	37.45%
Perot	0	0.00%	0	19,741,657	18.91%

Electoral Votes — 1992

Clinton (370) — Arkansas (6), California (54), Colorado (8), Connecticut (8), Delaware (3), District of Columbia (3), Georgia (13), Hawaii (4), Illinois (22), Iowa (7), Kentucky (8), Louisiana (9), Maine (4), Maryland (10), Massachusetts (12), Michigan (18), Minnesota (10), Missouri (11), Montana (3), Nevada (4), New Hampshire (4), New Jersey (15), New Mexico (5), New York (33), Ohio (21), Oregon (7), Pennsylvania (23), Rhode Island (4), Tennessee (11), Vermont (3), Washington (11), West Virginia (5), Wisconsin (11)

Bush (168) — Alabama (9), Alaska (3), Arizona (8), Florida (25), Idaho (4), Indiana (12), Kansas (6), Mississippi (7), Nebraska (5), North Carolina (14), North Dakota (3), Oklahoma (8), South Carolina (8), South Dakota (3), Texas (32), Utah (5), Virginia (13), Wyoming (3)

Popular Votes — 1992

State	Total PV	Clinton	Bush	Perot	Other
Alabama	1,688,060	690,080	804,283	183,109	10,588
Alaska	258,506	78,294	102,000	73,481	4,731
Arizona	1,486,975	543,050	572,086	353,741	18,098
Arkansas	950,653	505,823	337,324	99,132	8,374
California	11,131,721	5,121,325	3,630,574	2,296,006	83,816
Colorado	1,569,180	629,681	562,850	366,010	10,639
Connecticut	1,616,332	682,318	578,313	348,771	6,930
Delaware	289,735	126,054	102,313	59,213	2,155
District of Columbia	227,572	192,619	20,698	9,681	4,574
Florida	5,314,392	2,072,698	2,173,310	1,053,067	15,317
Georgia	2,321,125	1,008,966	995,252	309,657	7,250
Hawaii	372,842	179,310	136,822	53,003	3,707
Idaho	482,142	137,013	202,645	130,395	12,089
Illinois	5,050,157	2,453,350	1,734,096	840,515	22,196
Indiana	2,305,871	848,420	989,375	455,934	12,142
Iowa	1,354,607	586,353	504,891	253,468	9,895
Kansas	1,157,335	390,434	449,951	312,358	4,592
Kentucky	1,492,900	665,104	617,178	203,944	6,674
Louisiana	1,790,017	815,971	733,386	211,478	29,182
Maine	679,499	263,420	206,504	206,820	2,755
Maryland	1,985,046	988,571	707,094	281,414	7,967
Massachusetts	2,773,700	1,318,662	805,049	630,731	19,258
Michigan	4,274,673	1,871,182	1,554,940	824,813	23,738
Minnesota	2,347,948	1,020,997	747,841	562,506	16,604
Mississippi	981,793	400,258	487,793	85,626	8,116
Missouri	2,391,565	1,053,873	811,159	518,741	7,792
Montana	410,611	154,507	144,207	107,225	4,672
Nebraska	737,546	216,864	343,678	174,104	2,900
Nevada	506,318	189,148	175,828	132,580	8,762
New Hampshire	537,943	209,040	202,484	121,337	5,082
New Jersey	3,343,594	1,436,206	1,356,865	521,829	28,694
New Mexico	569,986	261,617	212,824	91,895	3,650
New York	6,926,925	3,444,450	2,346,649	1,090,721	45,105
North Carolina	2,611,850	1,114,042	1,134,661	357,864	5,283
North Dakota	308,133	99,168	136,244	71,084	1,637
Ohio	4,939,967	1,984,942	1,894,310	1,036,426	24,289

State	Total PV	Clinton	Bush	Perot	Other
Oklahoma	1,390,359	473,066	592,929	319,878	4,486
Oregon	1,462,643	621,314	475,757	354,091	11,481
Pennsylvania	4,959,810	2,239,164	1,791,841	902,667	26,138
Rhode Island	453,477	213,299	131,601	105,045	3,532
South Carolina	1,202,527	479,514	577,507	138,872	6,634
South Dakota	336,254	124,888	136,718	73,295	1,353
Tennessee	1,982,638	933,521	841,300	199,968	7,849
Texas	6,154,018	2,281,815	2,496,071	1,354,781	21,351
Utah	743,999	183,429	322,632	203,400	34,538
Vermont	289,701	133,592	88,122	65,991	1,996
Virginia	2,558,665	1,038,650	1,150,517	348,639	20,859
Washington	2,288,230	993,037	731,234	541,780	22,179
West Virginia	683,762	331,001	241,974	108,829	1,958
Wisconsin	2,531,114	1,041,066	930,855	544,479	14,714
Wyoming	200,598	68,160	79,347	51,263	1,828
Total	104,425,014	44,909,326	39,103,882	19,741,657	670,149

Democratic Nomination — 1992

Candidate	ConFB	FB%	ConLB	LB%	PriW	PriV	PriV%
Clinton	3,372	78.64%	—	—	31	10,503,503	51.73%
Brown	596	13.90%	—	—	2	4,081,036	20.10%
Tsongas	209	4.87%	—	—	5	3,666,618	18.06%
Kerrey	0	0.00%	—	—	1	321,913	1.59%
Harkin	0	0.00%	—	—	0	281,584	1.39%

Republican Nomination — 1992

Candidate	ConFB	FB%	ConLB	LB%	PriW	PriV	PriV%
Bush	2,166	98.01%	—	—	38	9,199,504	72.41%
Buchanan	18	0.81%	—	—	0	2,899,508	22.82%

Equalized Statistics — 1992

Candidate	EVX	PVX	ConFBX	ConLBX	PriVX
Clinton	370	43,006,292	786	—	5,173,108
Bush	168	37,446,853	980	—	7,240,463
Perot	0	18,905,104	—	—	—
Brown	—	—	139	—	2,009,962
Buchanan	—	—	8	—	2,282,056
Tsongas	—	—	49	—	1,805,856
Kerrey	—	—	0	—	158,546
Harkin	—	—	0	—	138,684

Election of 1996

Basics — 1996

Election number — 53
Winner — Bill Clinton (D)
Incumbent — Bill Clinton (D)
U.S. population — 269,394,284
States — 51
Electoral votes — 538
Popular votes — 96,277,223
Voter turnout — 49.0%

Top Candidates — 1996

Bill Clinton (CS 84.08)

Bob Dole (CS 67.01)

Ross Perot (CS 36.87)

Field — 1996

Candidate	PI	Age	State	Position	N	W	CS
Bill Clinton (D)	8.5	50.20	Ark.	President	X	X	84.08
Bob Dole (R)	6.8	73.28	Kan.	Senator	X	—	67.01
Ross Perot (REF)	2.6	66.35	Texas	Business executive	—	—	36.87
Pat Buchanan (R)	5.0	58.00	Va.	Journalist	—	—	23.11
Steve Forbes (R)	3.6	49.29	N.J.	Journalist	—	—	16.96
Lyndon LaRouche (D)	3.6	74.15	Va.	Movement leader	—	—	13.27
Lamar Alexander (R)	7.8	56.33	Tenn.	Former governor	—	—	11.97
Alan Keyes (R)	3.2	46.23	Md.	Former ambassador	—	—	11.81
Richard Lugar (R)	6.5	64.58	Ind.	Senator	—	—	10.51
Phil Gramm (R)	8.4	54.32	Texas	Senator	—	—	10.30

General Election — 1996

Candidate	EV	EV%	SC	PV	PV%
Clinton	379	70.45%	32	47,402,357	49.24%
Dole	159	29.55%	19	39,198,755	40.71%
Perot	0	0.00%	0	8,085,402	8.40%

Electoral Votes — 1996

Clinton (379) — Arizona (8), Arkansas (6), California (54), Connecticut (8), Delaware (3), District of Columbia (3), Florida (25), Hawaii (4), Illinois (22), Iowa (7), Kentucky (8), Louisiana (9), Maine (4), Maryland (10), Massachusetts (12), Michigan (18), Minnesota (10), Missouri (11), Nevada (4), New Hampshire (4), New Jersey (15), New Mexico (5), New York (33), Ohio (21), Oregon (7), Pennsylvania (23), Rhode Island (4), Tennessee (11), Vermont (3), Washington (11), West Virginia (5), Wisconsin (11)

Dole (159) — Alabama (9), Alaska (3), Colorado (8), Georgia (13), Idaho (4), Indiana (12), Kansas (6), Mississippi (7), Montana (3), Nebraska (5), North Carolina (14), North Dakota (3), Oklahoma (8), South Carolina (8), South Dakota (3), Texas (32), Utah (5), Virginia (13), Wyoming (3)

Popular Votes — 1996

State	Total PV	Clinton	Dole	Perot	Other
Alabama	1,534,349	662,165	769,044	92,149	10,991
Alaska	241,620	80,380	122,746	26,333	12,161
Arizona	1,404,405	653,288	622,073	112,072	16,972
Arkansas	884,262	475,171	325,416	69,884	13,791
California	10,019,484	5,119,835	3,828,380	697,847	373,422
Colorado	1,510,704	671,152	691,848	99,629	48,075
Connecticut	1,392,614	735,740	483,109	139,523	34,242
Delaware	270,845	140,355	99,062	28,719	2,709
District of Columbia	185,726	158,220	17,339	3,611	6,556
Florida	5,303,794	2,546,870	2,244,536	483,870	28,518
Georgia	2,299,071	1,053,849	1,080,843	146,337	18,042
Hawaii	360,120	205,012	113,943	27,358	13,807
Idaho	491,719	165,443	256,595	62,518	7,163
Illinois	4,311,391	2,341,744	1,587,021	346,408	36,218
Indiana	2,135,431	887,424	1,006,693	224,299	17,015
Iowa	1,234,075	620,258	492,644	105,159	16,014
Kansas	1,074,300	387,659	583,245	92,639	10,757
Kentucky	1,388,708	636,614	623,283	120,396	8,415
Louisiana	1,783,959	927,837	712,586	123,293	20,243
Maine	605,897	312,788	186,378	85,970	20,761
Maryland	1,780,870	966,207	681,530	115,812	17,321
Massachusetts	2,556,786	1,571,763	718,107	227,217	39,699
Michigan	3,848,844	1,989,653	1,481,212	336,670	41,309
Minnesota	2,192,640	1,120,438	766,476	257,704	48,022
Mississippi	893,857	394,022	439,838	52,222	7,775
Missouri	2,158,065	1,025,935	890,016	217,188	24,926
Montana	407,261	167,922	179,652	55,229	4,458
Nebraska	677,415	236,761	363,467	71,278	5,909
Nevada	464,279	203,974	199,244	43,986	17,075
New Hampshire	499,175	246,214	196,532	48,390	8,039
New Jersey	3,075,807	1,652,329	1,103,078	262,134	58,266
New Mexico	556,074	273,495	232,751	32,257	17,571
New York	6,316,129	3,756,177	1,933,492	503,458	123,002
North Carolina	2,515,807	1,107,849	1,225,938	168,059	13,961
North Dakota	266,411	106,905	125,050	32,515	1,941
Ohio	4,534,434	2,148,222	1,859,883	483,207	43,122
Oklahoma	1,206,713	488,105	582,315	130,788	5,505

State	Total PV	Clinton	Dole	Perot	Other
Oregon	1,377,760	649,641	538,152	121,221	68,746
Pennsylvania	4,506,118	2,215,819	1,801,169	430,984	58,146
Rhode Island	390,284	233,050	104,683	43,723	8,828
South Carolina	1,151,689	506,283	573,458	64,386	7,562
South Dakota	323,826	139,333	150,543	31,250	2,700
Tennessee	1,894,105	909,146	863,530	105,918	15,511
Texas	5,611,644	2,459,683	2,736,167	378,537	37,257
Utah	665,629	221,633	361,911	66,461	15,624
Vermont	258,449	137,894	80,352	31,024	9,179
Virginia	2,416,642	1,091,060	1,138,350	159,861	27,371
Washington	2,253,837	1,123,323	840,712	201,003	88,799
West Virginia	636,459	327,812	233,946	71,639	3,062
Wisconsin	2,196,169	1,071,971	845,029	227,339	51,830
Wyoming	211,571	77,934	105,388	25,928	2,321
Total	96,277,223	47,402,357	39,198,755	8,085,402	1,590,709

Democratic Nomination — 1996

Candidate	ConFB	FB%	ConLB	LB%	PriW	PriV	PriV%
Clinton	4,277	99.72%	—	—	34	9,706,802	88.57%
LaRouche	0	0.00%	—	—	0	596,422	5.44%

Republican Nomination — 1996

Candidate	ConFB	FB%	ConLB	LB%	PriW	PriV	PriV%
Dole	1,928	96.88%	—	—	39	8,791,000	58.30%
Buchanan	43	2.16%	—	—	1	3,184,099	21.12%
Gramm	2	0.10%	—	—	0	70,002	0.46%
Keyes	1	0.05%	—	—	0	449,459	2.98%
Forbes	0	0.00%	—	—	2	1,750,109	11.61%
Alexander	0	0.00%	—	—	0	494,317	3.28%
Lugar	0	0.00%	—	—	0	127,111	0.84%

Equalized Statistics — 1996

Candidate	EVX	PVX	ConFBX	ConLBX	PriVX
Clinton	379	49,235,277	997	—	8,856,803
Dole	159	40,714,464	969	—	5,829,662
Perot	0	8,398,042	—	—	—
Buchanan	—	—	22	—	2,111,503
Forbes	—	—	0	—	1,160,567
LaRouche	—	—	0	—	544,195
Alexander	—	—	0	—	327,801
Keyes	—	—	1	—	298,054
Lugar	—	—	0	—	84,292
Gramm	—	—	1	—	46,421

Election of 2000

Basics — 2000

Election number — 54
Winner — George W. Bush (R)
Incumbent — Bill Clinton (D)
U.S. population — 281,421,906
States — 51
Electoral votes — 537
Popular votes — 105,405,100
Voter turnout — 50.3%

Top Candidates — 2000

George W. Bush (CS 77.21)

Al Gore (CS 74.51)

John McCain (CS 29.92)

Field — 2000

Candidate	PI	Age	State	Position	N	W	CS
George W. Bush (R)	7.9	54.32	Texas	Governor	X	X	77.21
Al Gore (D)	8.8	52.59	Tenn.	Vice president	X	—	74.51
John McCain (R)	6.2	64.17	Ariz.	Senator	—	—	29.92
Bill Bradley (D)	7.1	57.26	N.J.	Former senator	—	—	22.10
Ralph Nader (GRN)	1.3	66.68	Conn.	Movement leader	—	—	18.76
Alan Keyes (R)	3.7	50.23	Md.	Former ambassador	—	—	13.04
Steve Forbes (R)	4.0	53.29	N.J.	Journalist	—	—	10.52
Gary Bauer (R)	5.1	54.49	Va.	Movement leader	—	—	10.19

General Election — 2000

Candidate	EV	EV%	SC	PV	PV%
Bush	271	50.47%	30	50,456,002	47.87%
Gore	266	49.53%	21	50,999,897	48.39%
Nader	0	0.00%	0	2,882,955	2.74%

Electoral Votes — 2000

Bush (271) — Alabama (9), Alaska (3), Arizona (8), Arkansas (6), Colorado (8), Florida (25), Georgia (13), Idaho (4), Indiana (12), Kansas (6), Kentucky (8), Louisiana (9), Mississippi (7), Missouri (11), Montana (3), Nebraska (5), Nevada (4), New Hampshire (4), North Carolina (14), North Dakota (3), Ohio (21), Oklahoma (8), South Carolina (8), South Dakota (3), Tennessee (11), Texas (32), Utah (5), Virginia (13), West Virginia (5), Wyoming (3)

Gore (266) — California (54), Connecticut (8), Delaware (3), District of Columbia (2), Hawaii (4), Illinois (22), Iowa (7), Maine (4), Maryland (10), Massachusetts (12), Michigan (18), Minnesota (10), New Jersey (15), New Mexico (5), New York (33), Oregon (7), Pennsylvania (23), Rhode Island (4), Vermont (3), Washington (11), Wisconsin (11)

Popular Votes — 2000

State	Total PV	Gore	Bush	Nader	Other
Alabama	1,666,272	692,611	941,173	18,323	14,165
Alaska	285,560	79,004	167,398	28,747	10,411
Arizona	1,532,016	685,341	781,652	45,645	19,378
Arkansas	921,781	422,768	472,940	13,421	12,652
California	10,965,856	5,861,203	4,567,429	418,707	118,517
Colorado	1,741,368	738,227	883,748	91,434	27,959
Connecticut	1,459,525	816,015	561,094	64,452	17,964
Delaware	327,622	180,068	137,288	8,307	1,959
District of Columbia	201,894	171,923	18,073	10,576	1,322
Florida	5,963,110	2,912,253	2,912,790	97,488	40,579
Georgia	2,596,804	1,116,230	1,419,720	13,432	47,422
Hawaii	367,951	205,286	137,845	21,623	3,197
Idaho	501,621	138,637	336,937	12,292	13,755
Illinois	4,742,123	2,589,026	2,019,421	103,759	29,917
Indiana	2,199,302	901,980	1,245,836	18,531	32,955
Iowa	1,315,563	638,517	634,373	29,374	13,299
Kansas	1,072,218	399,276	622,332	36,086	14,524
Kentucky	1,544,187	638,898	872,492	23,192	9,605
Louisiana	1,765,656	792,344	927,871	20,473	24,968
Maine	651,817	319,951	286,616	37,127	8,123
Maryland	2,025,480	1,145,782	813,797	53,768	12,133
Massachusetts	2,702,984	1,616,487	878,502	173,564	34,431
Michigan	4,232,501	2,170,418	1,953,139	84,165	24,779
Minnesota	2,438,685	1,168,266	1,109,659	126,696	34,064
Mississippi	994,184	404,614	572,844	8,122	8,604
Missouri	2,359,892	1,111,138	1,189,924	38,515	20,315
Montana	410,997	137,126	240,178	24,437	9,256
Nebraska	697,019	231,780	433,862	24,540	6,837
Nevada	608,970	279,978	301,575	15,008	12,409
New Hampshire	569,081	266,348	273,559	22,198	6,976
New Jersey	3,187,226	1,788,850	1,284,173	94,554	19,649
New Mexico	598,605	286,783	286,417	21,251	4,154
New York	6,821,999	4,107,697	2,403,374	244,030	66,898
North Carolina	2,911,262	1,257,692	1,631,163	—	22,407
North Dakota	288,256	95,284	174,852	9,486	8,634
Ohio	4,705,457	2,186,190	2,351,209	117,857	50,201
Oklahoma	1,234,229	474,276	744,337	—	15,616
Oregon	1,533,968	720,342	713,577	77,357	22,692
Pennsylvania	4,913,119	2,485,967	2,281,127	103,392	42,633
Rhode Island	409,112	249,508	130,555	25,052	3,997
South Carolina	1,382,717	565,561	785,937	20,200	11,019
South Dakota	316,269	118,804	190,700	—	6,765
Tennessee	2,076,181	981,720	1,061,949	19,781	12,731
Texas	6,407,637	2,433,746	3,799,639	137,994	36,258

State	Total PV	Gore	Bush	Nader	Other
Utah	770,754	203,053	515,096	35,850	16,755
Vermont	294,308	149,022	119,775	20,374	5,137
Virginia	2,739,447	1,217,290	1,437,490	59,398	25,269
Washington	2,487,433	1,247,652	1,108,864	103,002	27,915
West Virginia	648,124	295,497	336,475	10,680	5,472
Wisconsin	2,598,607	1,242,987	1,237,279	94,070	24,271
Wyoming	218,351	60,481	147,947	4,625	5,298
Total	105,405,100	50,999,897	50,456,002	2,882,955	1,066,246

Democratic Nomination — 2000

Candidate	ConFB	FB%	ConLB	LB%	PriW	PriV	PriV%
Gore	4,339	100.00%	—	—	39	11,081,274	75.56%
Bradley	0	0.00%	—	—	0	2,958,074	20.17%

Republican Nomination — 2000

Candidate	ConFB	FB%	ConLB	LB%	PriW	PriV	PriV%
Bush	2,066	100.00%	—	—	36	12,390,575	60.08%
McCain	0	0.00%	—	—	7	6,848,293	33.21%
Keyes	0	0.00%	—	—	0	1,043,465	5.06%
Forbes	0	0.00%	—	—	0	177,685	0.86%
Bauer	0	0.00%	—	—	0	64,344	0.31%

Equalized Statistics — 2000

Candidate	EVX	PVX	ConFBX	ConLBX	PriVX
Bush	272	47,868,653	1,000	—	6,007,726
Gore	266	48,384,658	1,000	—	7,556,211
McCain	—	—	0	—	3,320,481
Bradley	—	—	0	—	2,017,081
Nader	0	2,735,119	—	—	—
Keyes	—	—	0	—	505,937
Forbes	—	—	0	—	86,153
Bauer	—	—	0	—	31,198

Election of 2004

Basics — 2004

Election number — 55
Winner — George W. Bush (R)
Incumbent — George W. Bush (R)
U.S. population — 292,805,298
States — 51
Electoral votes — 538
Popular votes — 122,295,345
Voter turnout — 55.7%

Top Candidates — 2004

George W. Bush (CS 78.71)

John Kerry (CS 73.65)

John Edwards (CS 22.22)

Field — 2004

Candidate	PI	Age	State	Position	N	W	CS
George W. Bush (R)	9.3	58.32	Texas	President	X	X	78.71
John Kerry (D)	6.6	60.89	Mass.	Senator	X	—	73.65
John Edwards (D)	7.8	51.39	N.C.	Senator	—	—	22.22
Howard Dean (D)	6.0	55.96	Vt.	Former governor	—	—	13.32
Wesley Clark (D)	4.2	59.86	Ark.	Former general	—	—	12.00
Joseph Lieberman (D)	7.2	62.69	Conn.	Senator	—	—	11.04
Richard Gephardt (D)	3.9	63.75	Mo.	Representative	—	—	10.23

General Election — 2004

Candidate	EV	EV%	SC	PV	PV%
Bush	286	53.16%	31	62,040,610	50.73%
Kerry	251	46.65%	20	59,028,439	48.27%
Edwards	1	0.19%	0	0	0.00%

Electoral Votes — 2004

Bush (286) — Alabama (9), Alaska (3), Arizona (10), Arkansas (6), Colorado (9), Florida (27), Georgia (15), Idaho (4), Indiana (11), Iowa (7), Kansas (6), Kentucky (8), Louisiana (9), Mississippi (6), Missouri (11), Montana (3), Nebraska (5), Nevada (5), New Mexico (5), North Carolina (15), North Dakota (3), Ohio (20), Oklahoma (7), South Carolina (8), South Dakota (3), Tennessee (11), Texas (34), Utah (5), Virginia (13), West Virginia (5), Wyoming (3)

Kerry (251) — California (55), Connecticut (7), Delaware (3), District of Columbia (3), Hawaii (4), Illinois (21), Maine (4), Maryland (10), Massachusetts (12), Michigan (17), Minnesota (9), New Hampshire (4), New Jersey (15), New York (31), Oregon (7), Pennsylvania (21), Rhode Island (4), Vermont (3), Washington (11), Wisconsin (10)

Edwards (1) — Minnesota (1)

Popular Votes — 2004

State	Total PV	Bush	Kerry	Other
Alabama	1,883,449	1,176,394	693,933	13,122
Alaska	312,598	190,889	111,025	10,684
Arizona	2,012,585	1,104,294	893,524	14,767
Arkansas	1,054,945	572,898	469,953	12,094
California	12,421,852	5,509,826	6,745,485	166,541
Colorado	2,130,330	1,101,255	1,001,732	27,343
Connecticut	1,578,769	693,826	857,488	27,455
Delaware	375,190	171,660	200,152	3,378
District of Columbia	227,586	21,256	202,970	3,360
Florida	7,609,810	3,964,522	3,583,544	61,744
Georgia	3,301,875	1,914,254	1,366,149	21,472
Hawaii	429,013	194,191	231,708	3,114
Idaho	598,447	409,235	181,098	8,114
Illinois	5,274,322	2,345,946	2,891,550	36,826
Indiana	2,468,002	1,479,438	969,011	19,553
Iowa	1,506,908	751,957	741,898	13,053
Kansas	1,187,756	736,456	434,993	16,307
Kentucky	1,795,882	1,069,439	712,733	13,710
Louisiana	1,943,106	1,102,169	820,299	20,638
Maine	740,752	330,201	396,842	13,709
Maryland	2,386,678	1,024,703	1,334,493	27,482
Massachusetts	2,912,388	1,071,109	1,803,800	37,479
Michigan	4,839,252	2,313,746	2,479,183	46,323
Minnesota	2,828,387	1,346,695	1,445,014	36,678
Mississippi	1,152,145	684,981	458,094	9,070
Missouri	2,731,364	1,455,713	1,259,171	16,480
Montana	450,445	266,063	173,710	10,672
Nebraska	778,186	512,814	254,328	11,044
Nevada	829,587	418,690	397,190	13,707
New Hampshire	677,738	331,237	340,511	5,990
New Jersey	3,611,691	1,670,003	1,911,430	30,258
New Mexico	756,304	376,930	370,942	8,432
New York	7,391,036	2,962,567	4,314,280	114,189
North Carolina	3,501,007	1,961,166	1,525,849	13,992
North Dakota	312,833	196,651	111,052	5,130
Ohio	5,627,908	2,859,768	2,741,167	26,973

State	Total PV	Bush	Kerry	Other
Oklahoma	1,463,758	959,792	503,966	—
Oregon	1,836,782	866,831	943,163	26,788
Pennsylvania	5,769,590	2,793,847	2,938,095	37,648
Rhode Island	437,134	169,046	259,760	8,328
South Carolina	1,617,730	937,974	661,699	18,057
South Dakota	388,215	232,584	149,244	6,387
Tennessee	2,437,319	1,384,375	1,036,477	16,467
Texas	7,410,765	4,526,917	2,832,704	51,144
Utah	927,844	663,742	241,199	22,903
Vermont	312,309	121,180	184,067	7,062
Virginia	3,198,367	1,716,959	1,454,742	26,666
Washington	2,859,084	1,304,894	1,510,201	43,989
West Virginia	755,887	423,778	326,541	5,568
Wisconsin	2,997,007	1,478,120	1,489,504	29,383
Wyoming	243,428	167,629	70,776	5,023
Total	122,295,345	62,040,610	59,028,439	1,226,296

Democratic Nomination — 2004

Candidate	ConFB	FB%	ConLB	LB%	PriW	PriV	PriV%
Kerry	4,253	98.40%	—	—	33	9,753,562	61.06%
Edwards	0	0.00%	—	—	1	3,089,104	19.34%
Dean	0	0.00%	—	—	2	883,808	5.53%
Clark	0	0.00%	—	—	1	532,512	3.33%
Lieberman	0	0.00%	—	—	0	277,050	1.73%
Gephardt	0	0.00%	—	—	0	62,036	0.39%

Republican Nomination — 2004

Candidate	ConFB	FB%	ConLB	LB%	PriW	PriV	PriV%
Bush	2,508	99.96%	—	—	27	7,784,653	98.04%

Equalized Statistics — 2004

Candidate	EVX	PVX	ConFBX	ConLBX	PriVX
Bush	286	50,730,148	1,000	—	9,803,940
Kerry	251	48,267,118	984	—	6,105,491
Edwards	1	0	0	—	1,933,703
Dean	—	—	0	—	553,242
Clark	—	—	0	—	333,339
Lieberman	—	—	0	—	173,427
Gephardt	—	—	0	—	38,833

Election of 2008

Basics — 2008

Election number — 56
Winner — Barack Obama (D)
Incumbent — George W. Bush (R)
U.S. population — 304,093,966
States — 51
Electoral votes — 538
Popular votes — 131,313,820
Voter turnout — 57.1%

Top Candidates — 2008

Barack Obama (CS 84.03)

John McCain (CS 68.78)

Hillary Clinton (CS 43.42)

Field — 2008

Candidate	PI	Age	State	Position	N	W	CS
Barack Obama (D)	6.8	47.24	Ill.	Senator	X	X	84.03
John McCain (R)	5.9	72.17	Ariz.	Senator	X	—	68.78
Hillary Clinton (D)	7.0	61.02	N.Y.	Senator	—	—	43.42
Mitt Romney (R)	6.1	61.64	Mass.	Former governor	—	—	23.13
Mike Huckabee (R)	7.3	53.19	Ark.	Former governor	—	—	22.10
Ron Paul (R/TC)	4.8	73.20	Texas	Representative	—	—	13.62
Rudy Giuliani (R)	3.9	64.43	N.Y.	Former mayor	—	—	11.71
John Edwards (D)	8.9	55.39	N.C.	Former senator	—	—	11.63
Fred Thompson (R)	7.2	66.20	Tenn.	Former senator	—	—	10.81
Bill Richardson (D)	5.9	60.96	N.M.	Governor	—	—	10.17

General Election — 2008

Candidate	EV	EV%	SC	PV	PV%
Obama	365	67.84%	29	69,498,516	52.93%
McCain	173	32.16%	22	59,948,323	45.65%
Paul	0	0.00%	0	38,105	0.03%

Electoral Votes — 2008

Obama (365) — California (55), Colorado (9), Connecticut (7), Delaware (3), District of Columbia (3), Florida (27), Hawaii (4), Illinois (21), Indiana (11), Iowa (7), Maine (4), Maryland (10), Massachusetts (12), Michigan (17), Minnesota (10), Nebraska (1), Nevada (5), New Hampshire (4), New Jersey (15), New Mexico (5), New York (31), North Carolina (15), Ohio (20), Oregon (7), Pennsylvania (21), Rhode Island (4), Vermont (3), Virginia (13), Washington (11), Wisconsin (10)

McCain (173) — Alabama (9), Alaska (3), Arizona (10), Arkansas (6), Georgia (15), Idaho (4), Kansas (6), Kentucky (8), Louisiana (9), Mississippi (6), Missouri (11), Montana (3), Nebraska (4), North Dakota (3), Oklahoma (7), South Carolina (8), South Dakota (3), Tennessee (11), Texas (34), Utah (5), West Virginia (5), Wyoming (3)

Popular Votes — 2008

State	Total PV	Obama	McCain	Other
Alabama	2,099,819	813,479	1,266,546	19,794
Alaska	326,197	123,594	193,841	8,762
Arizona	2,293,475	1,034,707	1,230,111	28,657
Arkansas	1,086,617	422,310	638,017	26,290
California	13,561,900	8,274,473	5,011,781	275,646
Colorado	2,401,462	1,288,633	1,073,629	39,200
Connecticut	1,646,797	997,772	629,428	19,597
Delaware	412,412	255,459	152,374	4,579
District of Columbia	265,853	245,800	17,367	2,686
Florida	8,390,744	4,282,074	4,045,624	63,046
Georgia	3,924,486	1,844,123	2,048,759	31,604
Hawaii	453,568	325,871	120,566	7,131
Idaho	655,122	236,440	403,012	15,670
Illinois	5,522,371	3,419,348	2,031,179	71,844
Indiana	2,751,054	1,374,039	1,345,648	31,367
Iowa	1,537,123	828,940	682,379	25,804
Kansas	1,235,872	514,765	699,655	21,452
Kentucky	1,826,620	751,985	1,048,462	26,173
Louisiana	1,960,761	782,989	1,148,275	29,497
Maine	731,163	421,923	295,273	13,967
Maryland	2,631,596	1,629,467	959,862	42,267
Massachusetts	3,080,985	1,904,097	1,108,854	68,034
Michigan	5,001,766	2,872,579	2,048,639	80,548
Minnesota	2,910,369	1,573,354	1,275,409	61,606
Mississippi	1,289,865	554,662	724,597	10,606
Missouri	2,925,205	1,441,911	1,445,814	37,480
Montana	490,302	231,667	242,763	15,872
Nebraska	801,281	333,319	452,979	14,983
Nevada	967,848	533,736	412,827	21,285
New Hampshire	710,970	384,826	316,534	9,610
New Jersey	3,868,237	2,215,422	1,613,207	39,608
New Mexico	830,158	472,422	346,832	10,904
New York	7,640,931	4,804,945	2,752,771	83,215
North Carolina	4,310,789	2,142,651	2,128,474	39,664
North Dakota	316,621	141,278	168,601	6,742
Ohio	5,708,350	2,940,044	2,677,820	90,486
Oklahoma	1,462,661	502,496	960,165	—

State	Total PV	Obama	McCain	Other
Oregon	1,827,864	1,037,291	738,475	52,098
Pennsylvania	6,013,272	3,276,363	2,655,885	81,024
Rhode Island	471,766	296,571	165,391	9,804
South Carolina	1,920,969	862,449	1,034,896	23,624
South Dakota	381,975	170,924	203,054	7,997
Tennessee	2,599,749	1,087,437	1,479,178	33,134
Texas	8,077,795	3,528,633	4,479,328	69,834
Utah	952,370	327,670	596,030	28,670
Vermont	325,046	219,262	98,974	6,810
Virginia	3,723,260	1,959,532	1,725,005	38,723
Washington	3,036,878	1,750,848	1,229,216	56,814
West Virginia	713,451	303,857	397,466	12,128
Wisconsin	2,983,417	1,677,211	1,262,393	43,813
Wyoming	254,658	82,868	164,958	6,832
Total	131,313,820	69,498,516	59,948,323	1,866,981

Democratic Nomination — 2008

Candidate	ConFB	FB%	ConLB	LB%	PriW	PriV	PriV%
Obama	3,189	72.15%	—	—	21	17,423,182	47.28%
Clinton	1,011	22.87%	—	—	19	17,714,951	48.08%
Edwards	0	0.00%	—	—	0	1,000,862	2.72%
Richardson	0	0.00%	—	—	0	104,616	0.28%

Republican Nomination — 2008

Candidate	ConFB	FB%	ConLB	LB%	PriW	PriV	PriV%
McCain	2,341	98.36%	—	—	33	9,776,631	47.02%
Paul	17	0.71%	—	—	0	1,169,863	5.63%
Romney	2	0.08%	—	—	3	4,544,125	21.86%
Huckabee	0	0.00%	—	—	5	4,194,460	20.18%
Giuliani	0	0.00%	—	—	0	591,395	2.84%
Thompson	0	0.00%	—	—	0	282,185	1.36%

Equalized Statistics — 2008

Candidate	EVX	PVX	ConFBX	ConLBX	PriVX
Obama	365	52,925,515	722	—	4,728,367
McCain	173	45,652,714	984	—	4,702,361
Clinton	—	—	229	—	4,807,548
Romney	—	—	1	—	2,185,632
Huckabee	—	—	0	—	2,017,450
Paul	0	29,018	7	—	562,680
Giuliani	—	—	0	—	284,449
Edwards	—	—	0	—	271,618
Thompson	—	—	0	—	135,725
Richardson	—	—	0	—	28,391

Election of 2012

Basics — 2012

Election number — 57
Winner — Barack Obama (D)
Incumbent — Barack Obama (D)
U.S. population — 313,914,040
States — 51
Electoral votes — 538
Popular votes — 129,085,403
Voter turnout — 53.8%

Top Candidates — 2012

Barack Obama (CS 81.59)

Mitt Romney (CS 70.93)

Rick Santorum (CS 22.25)

Field — 2012

Candidate	PI	Age	State	Position	N	W	CS
Barack Obama (D)	8.3	51.24	Ill.	President	X	X	81.59
Mitt Romney (R)	5.9	65.64	Mass.	Former governor	X	—	70.93
Rick Santorum (R)	7.3	54.48	Pa.	Former senator	—	—	22.25
Newt Gingrich (R)	4.3	69.37	Ga.	Former representative	—	—	18.59
Ron Paul (R)	4.6	77.20	Texas	Representative	—	—	18.11
Jon Huntsman (R)	6.7	52.60	Utah	Former governor	—	—	10.27
Rick Perry (R)	7.5	62.66	Texas	Governor	—	—	10.14
Michele Bachmann (R)	4.3	56.57	Minn.	Representative	—	—	10.11

General Election — 2012

Candidate	EV	EV%	SC	PV	PV%
Obama	332	61.71%	27	65,915,796	51.06%
Romney	206	38.29%	24	60,933,500	47.20%

Electoral Votes — 2012

Obama (332) — California (55), Colorado (9), Connecticut (7), Delaware (3), District of Columbia (3), Florida (29), Hawaii (4), Illinois (20), Iowa (6), Maine (4), Maryland (10), Massachusetts (11), Michigan (16), Minnesota (10), Nevada (6), New Hampshire (4), New Jersey (14), New Mexico (5), New York (29), Ohio (18), Oregon (7), Pennsylvania (20), Rhode Island (4), Vermont (3), Virginia (13), Washington (12), Wisconsin (10)

Romney (206) — Alabama (9), Alaska (3), Arizona (11), Arkansas (6), Georgia (16), Idaho (4), Indiana (11), Kansas (6), Kentucky (8), Louisiana (8), Mississippi (6), Missouri (10), Montana (3), Nebraska (5), North Carolina (15), North Dakota (3), Oklahoma (7), South Carolina (9), South Dakota (3), Tennessee (11), Texas (38), Utah (6), West Virginia (5), Wyoming (3)

Popular Votes — 2012

State	Total PV	Obama	Romney	Other
Alabama	2,074,338	795,696	1,255,925	22,717
Alaska	300,495	122,640	164,676	13,179
Arizona	2,299,254	1,025,232	1,233,654	40,368
Arkansas	1,069,468	394,409	647,744	27,315
California	13,038,547	7,854,285	4,839,958	344,304
Colorado	2,569,522	1,323,102	1,185,243	61,177
Connecticut	1,558,960	905,083	634,892	18,985
Delaware	413,921	242,584	165,484	5,853
District of Columbia	293,764	267,070	21,381	5,313
Florida	8,474,179	4,237,756	4,163,447	72,976
Georgia	3,900,050	1,773,827	2,078,688	47,535
Hawaii	434,697	306,658	121,015	7,024
Idaho	652,274	212,787	420,911	18,576
Illinois	5,242,014	3,019,512	2,135,216	87,286
Indiana	2,624,534	1,152,887	1,420,543	51,104
Iowa	1,582,180	822,544	730,617	29,019
Kansas	1,159,971	440,726	692,634	26,611
Kentucky	1,797,212	679,370	1,087,190	30,652
Louisiana	1,994,065	809,141	1,152,262	32,662
Maine	713,180	401,306	292,276	19,598
Maryland	2,707,327	1,677,844	971,869	57,614
Massachusetts	3,167,767	1,921,290	1,188,314	58,163
Michigan	4,730,961	2,564,569	2,115,256	51,136
Minnesota	2,936,561	1,546,167	1,320,225	70,169
Mississippi	1,285,584	562,949	710,746	11,889
Missouri	2,757,323	1,223,796	1,482,440	51,087
Montana	484,048	201,839	267,928	14,281
Nebraska	794,379	302,081	475,064	17,234
Nevada	1,014,918	531,373	463,567	19,978
New Hampshire	710,972	369,561	329,918	11,493
New Jersey	3,640,292	2,125,101	1,477,568	37,623
New Mexico	783,758	415,335	335,788	32,635
New York	7,081,159	4,485,741	2,490,431	104,987
North Carolina	4,505,372	2,178,391	2,270,395	56,586
North Dakota	322,627	124,827	188,163	9,637
Ohio	5,580,840	2,827,710	2,661,433	91,697
Oklahoma	1,334,872	443,547	891,325	—

State	Total PV	Obama	Romney	Other
Oregon	1,789,270	970,488	754,175	64,607
Pennsylvania	5,753,670	2,990,274	2,680,434	82,962
Rhode Island	446,049	279,677	157,204	9,168
South Carolina	1,964,118	865,941	1,071,645	26,532
South Dakota	363,815	145,039	210,610	8,166
Tennessee	2,458,577	960,709	1,462,330	35,538
Texas	7,993,851	3,308,124	4,569,843	115,884
Utah	1,017,440	251,813	740,600	25,027
Vermont	299,290	199,239	92,698	7,353
Virginia	3,854,489	1,971,820	1,822,522	60,147
Washington	3,125,516	1,755,396	1,290,670	79,450
West Virginia	670,438	238,269	417,655	14,514
Wisconsin	3,068,434	1,620,985	1,407,966	39,483
Wyoming	249,061	69,286	170,962	8,813
Total	129,085,403	65,915,796	60,933,500	2,236,107

Democratic Nomination — 2012

Candidate	ConFB	FB%	ConLB	LB%	PriW	PriV	PriV%
Obama	5,425	97.70%	—	—	30	8,415,194	91.40%

Republican Nomination — 2012

Candidate	ConFB	FB%	ConLB	LB%	PriW	PriV	PriV%
Romney	2,061	90.16%	—	—	31	9,841,300	52.43%
Paul	190	8.31%	—	—	0	2,016,389	10.74%
Santorum	9	0.39%	—	—	6	3,805,655	20.28%
Huntsman	1	0.04%	—	—	0	83,131	0.44%
Bachmann	1	0.04%	—	—	0	35,084	0.19%
Gingrich	0	0.00%	—	—	2	2,687,243	14.32%
Perry	0	0.00%	—	—	0	42,245	0.23%

Equalized Statistics — 2012

Candidate	EVX	PVX	ConFBX	ConLBX	PriVX
Obama	332	51,063,710	977	—	9,140,230
Romney	206	47,204,020	902	—	5,243,091
Santorum	—	—	4	—	2,027,516
Gingrich	—	—	0	—	1,431,666
Paul	—	—	83	—	1,074,260
Huntsman	—	—	0	—	44,289
Perry	—	—	0	—	22,507
Bachmann	—	—	0	—	18,691

Election of 2016

Basics — 2016

Election number — 58
Winner — Donald Trump (R)
Incumbent — Barack Obama (D)
U.S. population — 323,071,342
States — 51
Electoral votes — 538
Popular votes — 136,669,276
Voter turnout — 54.8%

Top Candidates — 2016

Donald Trump (CS 78.79)

Hillary Clinton (CS 72.30)

Bernie Sanders (CS 44.15)

Field — 2016

Candidate	PI	Age	State	Position	N	W	CS
Donald Trump (R)	3.1	70.38	N.Y.	Business executive	X	X	78.79
Hillary Clinton (D)	6.6	69.02	N.Y.	Former Cabinet member	X	—	72.30
Bernie Sanders (D)	5.5	75.15	Vt.	Senator	—	—	44.15
Ted Cruz (R)	7.9	45.86	Texas	Senator	—	—	28.72
Gary Johnson (LIB)	3.9	63.83	N.M.	Former governor	—	—	20.52
John Kasich (R)	6.6	64.47	Ohio	Governor	—	—	19.98
Marco Rubio (R)	7.7	45.43	Fla.	Senator	—	—	17.61
Colin Powell (R)	3.2	79.57	N.Y.	Former Cabinet member	—	—	11.84
Ben Carson (R)	4.3	65.12	Fla.	Movement leader	—	—	11.69
Ron Paul (R)	3.8	81.20	Texas	Former representative	—	—	10.62
Faith Spotted Eagle (D)	2.3	68.00	S.D.	Movement leader	—	—	10.62
Jeb Bush (R)	7.1	63.72	Fla.	Former governor	—	—	10.58
Rand Paul (R)	7.8	53.82	Ky.	Senator	—	—	10.13
Chris Christie (R)	6.7	54.15	N.J.	Governor	—	—	10.11
Carly Fiorina (R)	3.9	62.15	Va.	Business executive	—	—	10.07

General Election — 2016

Candidate	EV	EV%	SC	PV	PV%
Trump	304	56.51%	30	62,984,828	46.09%
Clinton	227	42.19%	21	65,853,514	48.19%
Powell	3	0.56%	0	0	0.00%
Kasich	1	0.19%	0	0	0.00%
Ron Paul	1	0.19%	0	0	0.00%
Sanders	1	0.19%	0	0	0.00%
Spotted Eagle	1	0.19%	0	0	0.00%
Johnson	0	0.00%	0	4,489,341	3.29%

Electoral Votes — 2016

Trump (304) — Alabama (9), Alaska (3), Arizona (11), Arkansas (6), Florida (29), Georgia (16), Idaho (4), Indiana (11), Iowa (6), Kansas (6), Kentucky (8), Louisiana (8), Maine (1), Michigan (16), Mississippi (6), Missouri (10), Montana (3), Nebraska (5), North Carolina (15), North Dakota (3), Ohio (18), Oklahoma (7), Pennsylvania (20), South Carolina (9), South Dakota (3), Tennessee (11), Texas (36), Utah (6), West Virginia (5), Wisconsin (10), Wyoming (3)

Clinton (227) — California (55), Colorado (9), Connecticut (7), Delaware (3), District of Columbia (3), Hawaii (3), Illinois (20), Maine (3), Maryland (10), Massachusetts (11), Minnesota (10), Nevada (6), New Hampshire (4), New Jersey (14), New Mexico (5), New York (29), Oregon (7), Rhode Island (4), Vermont (3), Virginia (13), Washington (8)

Powell (3) — Washington (3)
Kasich (1) — Texas (1)
Ron Paul (1) — Texas (1)
Sanders (1) — Hawaii (1)
Spotted Eagle (1) — Washington (1)

Popular Votes — 2016

State	Total PV	Clinton	Trump	Johnson	Other
Alabama	2,123,372	729,547	1,318,255	44,467	31,103
Alaska	318,608	116,454	163,387	18,725	20,042
Arizona	2,573,165	1,161,167	1,252,401	106,327	53,270
Arkansas	1,130,676	380,494	684,872	29,949	35,361
California	14,181,604	8,753,792	4,483,814	478,500	465,498
Colorado	2,780,247	1,338,870	1,202,484	144,121	94,772
Connecticut	1,644,920	897,572	673,215	48,676	25,457
Delaware	443,814	235,603	185,127	14,757	8,327
District of Columbia	311,268	282,830	12,723	4,906	10,809
Florida	9,420,039	4,504,975	4,617,886	207,043	90,135
Georgia	4,114,732	1,877,963	2,089,104	125,306	22,359
Hawaii	428,937	266,891	128,847	15,954	17,245
Idaho	690,255	189,765	409,055	28,331	63,104
Illinois	5,536,424	3,090,729	2,146,015	209,596	90,084
Indiana	2,734,958	1,033,126	1,557,286	133,993	10,553
Iowa	1,566,031	653,669	800,983	59,186	52,193
Kansas	1,184,402	427,005	671,018	55,406	30,973
Kentucky	1,924,149	628,854	1,202,971	53,752	38,572
Louisiana	2,029,032	780,154	1,178,638	37,978	32,262

State	Total PV	Clinton	Trump	Johnson	Other
Maine	747,927	357,735	335,593	38,105	16,494
Maryland	2,781,446	1,677,928	943,169	79,605	80,744
Massachusetts	3,325,046	1,995,196	1,090,893	138,018	100,939
Michigan	4,799,284	2,268,839	2,279,543	172,136	78,766
Minnesota	2,944,813	1,367,716	1,322,951	112,972	141,174
Mississippi	1,209,357	485,131	700,714	14,435	9,077
Missouri	2,808,605	1,071,068	1,594,511	97,359	45,667
Montana	497,147	177,709	279,240	28,037	12,161
Nebraska	844,227	284,494	495,961	38,946	24,826
Nevada	1,125,385	539,260	512,058	37,384	36,683
New Hampshire	744,296	348,526	345,790	30,777	19,203
New Jersey	3,874,046	2,148,278	1,601,933	72,477	51,358
New Mexico	798,319	385,234	319,667	74,541	18,877
New York	7,721,442	4,556,118	2,819,533	176,598	169,193
North Carolina	4,741,564	2,189,316	2,362,631	130,126	59,491
North Dakota	344,360	93,758	216,794	21,434	12,374
Ohio	5,496,487	2,394,164	2,841,005	174,498	86,820
Oklahoma	1,452,992	420,375	949,136	83,481	—
Oregon	2,001,336	1,002,106	782,403	94,231	122,596
Pennsylvania	6,165,478	2,926,441	2,970,733	146,715	121,589
Rhode Island	464,144	252,525	180,543	14,746	16,330
South Carolina	2,103,027	855,373	1,155,389	49,204	43,061
South Dakota	370,093	117,458	227,721	20,850	4,064
Tennessee	2,508,027	870,695	1,522,925	70,397	44,010
Texas	8,969,226	3,877,868	4,685,047	283,492	122,819
Utah	1,131,430	310,676	515,231	39,608	265,915
Vermont	315,067	178,573	95,369	10,078	31,047
Virginia	3,984,631	1,981,473	1,769,443	118,274	115,441
Washington	3,317,019	1,742,718	1,221,747	160,879	191,675
West Virginia	714,423	188,794	489,371	23,004	13,254
Wisconsin	2,976,150	1,382,536	1,405,284	106,674	81,656
Wyoming	255,849	55,973	174,419	13,287	12,170
Total	136,669,276	65,853,514	62,984,828	4,489,341	3,341,593

Democratic Nomination — 2016

Candidate	ConFB	FB%	ConLB	LB%	PriW	PriV	PriV%
Clinton	2,842	59.68%	—	—	29	17,119,048	55.53%
Sanders	1,865	39.16%	—	—	10	13,209,430	42.85%

Republican Nomination — 2016

Candidate	ConFB	FB%	ConLB	LB%	PriW	PriV	PriV%
Trump	1,725	69.78%	—	—	33	13,757,263	45.57%
Cruz	484	19.58%	—	—	4	7,452,008	24.68%
Kasich	125	5.06%	—	—	1	4,197,478	13.90%
Rubio	123	4.98%	—	—	0	3,324,927	11.01%
Carson	7	0.28%	—	—	0	822,022	2.72%
Bush	3	0.12%	—	—	0	280,628	0.93%
Rand Paul	2	0.08%	—	—	0	57,150	0.19%
Christie	0	0.00%	—	—	0	54,216	0.18%
Fiorina	0	0.00%	—	—	0	36,660	0.12%

Equalized Statistics — 2016

Candidate	EVX	PVX	ConFBX	ConLBX	PriVX
Trump	304	46,085,580	698	—	4,556,463
Clinton	227	48,184,578	597	—	5,552,589
Sanders	1	0	392	—	4,284,499
Cruz	—	—	196	—	2,468,136
Johnson	0	3,284,821	—	—	—
Kasich	1	0	51	—	1,390,222
Rubio	—	—	50	—	1,101,230
Powell	3	0	—	—	—
Carson	—	—	3	—	272,257
Ron Paul	1	0	—	—	—
Spotted Eagle	1	0	—	—	—
Bush	—	—	1	—	92,945
Rand Paul	—	—	1	—	18,928
Christie	—	—	0	—	17,957
Fiorina	—	—	0	—	12,142

Election of 2020

Basics — 2020

Election number — 59
Winner — Joseph Biden (D)
Incumbent — Donald Trump (R)
U.S. population — 331,449,281
States — 51
Electoral votes — 538
Popular votes — 158,429,631
Voter turnout — 62.0%

Top Candidates — 2020

Joseph Biden (CS 80.05)

Donald Trump (CS 72.31)

Bernie Sanders (CS 30.55)

Field — 2020

Candidate	PI	Age	State	Position	N	W	CS
Joseph Biden (D)	4.3	77.95	Del.	Former vice president	X	X	80.05
Donald Trump (R)	7.5	74.38	Fla.	President	X	—	72.31
Bernie Sanders (D)	5.1	79.15	Vt.	Senator	—	—	30.55
Elizabeth Warren (D)	5.4	71.36	Mass.	Senator	—	—	14.59
Michael Bloomberg (D)	2.1	78.71	N.Y.	Former mayor	—	—	14.10
Pete Buttigieg (D)	1.8	38.78	Ind.	Former mayor	—	—	11.42
Bill Weld (R)	5.3	75.25	Mass.	Former governor	—	—	11.41
Amy Klobuchar (D)	6.0	60.44	Minn.	Senator	—	—	10.82

General Election — 2020

Candidate	EV	EV%	SC	PV	PV%
Biden	306	56.88%	26	81,283,501	51.31%
Trump	232	43.12%	25	74,223,975	46.85%

Electoral Votes — 2020

Biden (306) — Arizona (11), California (55), Colorado (9), Connecticut (7), Delaware (3), District of Columbia (3), Georgia (16), Hawaii (4), Illinois (20), Maine (3), Maryland (10), Massachusetts (11), Michigan (16), Minnesota (10), Nebraska (1), Nevada (6), New Hampshire (4), New Jersey (14), New Mexico (5), New York (29), Oregon (7), Pennsylvania (20), Rhode Island (4), Vermont (3), Virginia (13), Washington (12), Wisconsin (10)

Trump (232) — Alabama (9), Alaska (3), Arkansas (6), Florida (29), Idaho (4), Indiana (11), Iowa (6), Kansas (6), Kentucky (8), Louisiana (8), Maine (1), Mississippi (6), Missouri (10), Montana (3), Nebraska (4), North Carolina (15), North Dakota (3), Ohio (18), Oklahoma (7), South Carolina (9), South Dakota (3), Tennessee (11), Texas (38), Utah (6), West Virginia (5), Wyoming (3)

Popular Votes — 2020

State	Total PV	Biden	Trump	Other
Alabama	2,323,282	849,624	1,441,170	32,488
Alaska	359,530	153,778	189,951	15,801
Arizona	3,387,326	1,672,143	1,661,686	53,497
Arkansas	1,219,069	423,932	760,647	34,490
California	17,501,380	11,110,639	6,006,518	384,223
Colorado	3,256,980	1,804,352	1,364,607	88,021
Connecticut	1,823,857	1,080,831	714,717	28,309
Delaware	504,346	296,268	200,603	7,475
District of Columbia	344,356	317,323	18,586	8,447
Florida	11,067,456	5,297,045	5,668,731	101,680
Georgia	4,999,960	2,473,633	2,461,854	64,473
Hawaii	574,469	366,130	196,864	11,475
Idaho	867,934	287,021	554,119	26,794
Illinois	6,033,744	3,471,915	2,446,891	114,938
Indiana	3,033,210	1,242,498	1,729,857	60,855
Iowa	1,690,871	759,061	897,672	34,138
Kansas	1,373,986	570,323	771,406	32,257
Kentucky	2,136,768	772,474	1,326,646	37,648
Louisiana	2,148,062	856,034	1,255,776	36,252
Maine	819,461	435,072	360,737	23,652
Maryland	3,037,030	1,985,023	976,414	75,593
Massachusetts	3,631,402	2,382,202	1,167,202	81,998
Michigan	5,539,302	2,804,040	2,649,852	85,410
Minnesota	3,277,171	1,717,077	1,484,065	76,029
Mississippi	1,313,759	539,398	756,764	17,597
Missouri	3,025,962	1,253,014	1,718,736	54,212
Montana	603,674	244,786	343,602	15,286
Nebraska	956,383	374,583	556,846	24,954
Nevada	1,405,376	703,486	669,890	32,000
New Hampshire	806,205	424,937	365,660	15,608
New Jersey	4,549,457	2,608,400	1,883,313	57,744
New Mexico	923,965	501,614	401,894	20,457
New York	8,616,861	5,244,886	3,251,997	119,978
North Carolina	5,524,804	2,684,292	2,758,775	81,737
North Dakota	362,024	115,042	235,751	11,231
Ohio	5,922,202	2,679,165	3,154,834	88,203
Oklahoma	1,560,699	503,890	1,020,280	36,529
Oregon	2,374,321	1,340,383	958,448	75,490
Pennsylvania	6,936,976	3,458,229	3,377,674	101,073
Rhode Island	517,757	307,486	199,922	10,349
South Carolina	2,513,329	1,091,541	1,385,103	36,685
South Dakota	422,609	150,471	261,043	11,095
Tennessee	3,053,851	1,143,711	1,852,475	57,665
Texas	11,315,056	5,259,126	5,890,347	165,583

State	Total PV	Biden	Trump	Other
Utah	1,488,289	560,282	865,140	62,867
Vermont	367,428	242,820	112,704	11,904
Virginia	4,460,524	2,413,568	1,962,430	84,526
Washington	4,087,631	2,369,612	1,584,651	133,368
West Virginia	794,731	235,984	545,382	13,365
Wisconsin	3,298,041	1,630,866	1,610,184	56,991
Wyoming	276,765	73,491	193,559	9,715
Total	158,429,631	81,283,501	74,223,975	2,922,155

Democratic Nomination — 2020

Candidate	ConFB	FB%	ConLB	LB%	PriW	PriV	PriV%
Biden	3,558	74.92%	—	—	41	19,128,039	52.37%
Sanders	1,151	24.24%	—	—	5	9,572,374	26.21%
Warren	0	0.00%	—	—	0	2,795,787	7.65%
Bloomberg	0	0.00%	—	—	0	2,498,317	6.84%
Buttigieg	0	0.00%	—	—	0	863,692	2.36%
Klobuchar	0	0.00%	—	—	0	501,508	1.37%

Republican Nomination — 2020

Candidate	ConFB	FB%	ConLB	LB%	PriW	PriV	PriV%
Trump	2,550	100.00%	—	—	39	18,213,777	94.04%
Weld	0	0.00%	—	—	0	453,946	2.34%

Equalized Statistics — 2020

Candidate	EVX	PVX	ConFBX	ConLBX	PriVX
Biden	306	51,305,744	749	—	5,236,599
Trump	232	46,849,806	1,000	—	9,403,875
Sanders	—	—	242	—	2,620,586
Warren	—	—	0	—	765,390
Bloomberg	—	—	0	—	683,953
Buttigieg	—	—	0	—	236,449
Weld	—	—	0	—	234,375
Klobuchar	—	—	0	—	137,296

3. Candidates

A TOTAL OF 308 CANDIDATES met this book's qualification standards in at least one of the 59 presidential elections between 1789 and 2020. Dozens of these men and women launched multiple campaigns for the White House—42 contenders ran at least three times apiece—though two-thirds of all presidential hopefuls (210 of 308) bowed out after a single attempt.

This chapter contains statistical breakdowns for all 308 candidates, listing all of their qualified runs. (Any of their campaigns that fell short of the standards—such as Joseph Biden's in 1988 and 2008—are not shown here, though they are included in the career totals in Chapter 5.)

Candidates are listed alphabetically, followed by their birth and death years. Here's what you'll find:

Year: Elections in which the candidate met qualification standards.

Party: Political party or parties. See pages 48 and 50 for abbreviations. A hyphen indicates that a candidate ran on both tickets. A slash indicates that he began in the first party and switched to the second.

PI: Potential index.

N: Major-party nominees are designated by an X.

W: General-election winners are designated by an X.

CS: Campaign score.

ROP: Score for return on potential.

Position: The position for which the candidate was best known, usually his current or most recent position.

Age: The candidate's age as of November 1 of the given year, rounded to two decimal places.

State: The state in which the candidate maintained a voting address.

Additional statistics for any candidate can be found by referring back to the appropriate election or elections in the preceding chapter.

John Adams (1735-1826)

Year	Party	PI	N	W	CS	ROP	Position	Age	State
1789	F	4.4	—	—	64.00	145	Former ambassador	54.01	Massachusetts
1792	F	6.4	—	—	67.23	105	Vice president	57.01	Massachusetts
1796	F	5.7	X	X	77.27	136	Vice president	61.01	Massachusetts
1800	F	7.2	X	—	73.21	102	President	65.01	Massachusetts

John Quincy Adams (1767-1848)

Year	Party	PI	N	W	CS	ROP	Position	Age	State
1820	DR	5.0	—	—	17.96	36	Cabinet member	53.31	Massachusetts
1824	DR	5.6	X	X	67.41	120	Cabinet member	57.31	Massachusetts
1828	NR	7.7	X	—	68.27	89	President	61.31	Massachusetts

Samuel Adams (1722-1803)

Year	Party	PI	N	W	CS	ROP	Position	Age	State
1796	DR	3.7	—	—	50.36	136	Governor	74.10	Massachusetts

Lamar Alexander (1940-)

Year	Party	PI	N	W	CS	ROP	Position	Age	State
1996	R	7.8	—	—	11.97	15	Former governor	56.33	Tennessee

Russell Alger (1836-1907)

Year	Party	PI	N	W	CS	ROP	Position	Age	State
1888	R	7.8	—	—	19.58	25	Former governor	52.68	Michigan

William Allen (1803-1879)

Year	Party	PI	N	W	CS	ROP	Position	Age	State
1876	D	6.9	—	—	15.83	23	Former governor	72.87	Ohio

William Boyd Allison (1829-1908)

Year	Party	PI	N	W	CS	ROP	Position	Age	State
1888	R	7.6	—	—	16.95	22	Senator	59.67	Iowa

John Anderson (1922-2017)

Year	Party	PI	N	W	CS	ROP	Position	Age	State
1980	R/NU	4.7	—	—	38.97	83	Representative	58.71	Illinois

James Armstrong (1728-1800)

Year	Party	PI	N	W	CS	ROP	Position	Age	State
1789	F	4.0	—	—	21.42	54	State official	61.00	Georgia

Chester Arthur (1829-1886)

Year	Party	PI	N	W	CS	ROP	Position	Age	State
1884	R	8.8	—	—	37.07	42	President	55.07	New York

John Ashbrook (1928-1982)

Year	Party	PI	N	W	CS	ROP	Position	Age	State
1972	R	4.2	—	—	13.02	31	Representative	44.11	Ohio

Bruce Babbitt (1938-)

Year	Party	PI	N	W	CS	ROP	Position	Age	State
1988	D	6.2	—	—	10.20	16	Former governor	50.35	Arizona

Michele Bachmann (1956-)

Year	Party	PI	N	W	CS	ROP	Position	Age	State
2012	R	4.3	—	—	10.11	24	Representative	56.57	Minnesota

Howard Baker (1925-2014)

Year	Party	PI	N	W	CS	ROP	Position	Age	State
1980	R	7.7	—	—	10.51	14	Senator	54.96	Tennessee

Alben Barkley (1877-1956)

Year	Party	PI	N	W	CS	ROP	Position	Age	State
1952	D	4.2	—	—	12.74	30	Vice president	74.94	Kentucky

Edward Bates (1793-1869)

Year	Party	PI	N	W	CS	ROP	Position	Age	State
1860	R	5.2	—	—	18.22	35	Former representative	67.16	Missouri

Gary Bauer (1946-)

Year	Party	PI	N	W	CS	ROP	Position	Age	State
2000	R	5.1	—	—	10.19	20	Movement leader	54.49	Virginia

Thomas Bayard (1828-1898)

Year	Party	PI	N	W	CS	ROP	Position	Age	State
1876	D	7.1	—	—	13.59	19	Senator	48.01	Delaware
1880	D	7.1	—	—	26.61	37	Senator	52.01	Delaware
1884	D	6.2	—	—	26.53	43	Senator	56.01	Delaware

Birch Bayh (1928-2019)

Year	Party	PI	N	W	CS	ROP	Position	Age	State
1976	D	6.9	—	—	10.32	15	Senator	48.78	Indiana

John Bell (1796-1869)

Year	Party	PI	N	W	CS	ROP	Position	Age	State
1860	CU	4.6	—	—	46.37	101	Former senator	64.70	Tennessee

Allan Benson (1871-1940)

Year	Party	PI	N	W	CS	ROP	Position	Age	State
1916	SOC	2.7	—	—	20.19	75	Journalist	44.99	New York

Lloyd Bentsen (1921-2006)

Year	Party	PI	N	W	CS	ROP	Position	Age	State
1988	D	7.6	—	—	10.62	14	Senator	67.72	Texas

Joseph Biden (1942-)

Year	Party	PI	N	W	CS	ROP	Position	Age	State
2020	D	4.3	X	X	80.05	186	Former vice president	77.95	Delaware

John Bidwell (1819-1900)

Year	Party	PI	N	W	CS	ROP	Position	Age	State
1892	PRO	0.4	—	—	17.19	430	Movement leader	73.24	California

James Birney (1792-1857)

Year	Party	PI	N	W	CS	ROP	Position	Age	State
1844	LTY	2.6	—	—	17.35	67	Movement leader	52.74	Michigan

Joseph Blackburn (1838-1918)

Year	Party	PI	N	W	CS	ROP	Position	Age	State
1896	D	6.2	—	—	17.03	27	Senator	58.08	Kentucky

James Blaine (1830-1893)

Year	Party	PI	N	W	CS	ROP	Position	Age	State
1876	R	5.1	—	—	47.05	92	Representative	46.75	Maine
1880	R	7.3	—	—	40.02	55	Senator	50.75	Maine
1884	R	6.7	X	—	73.26	109	Former senator	54.75	Maine
1888	R	6.3	—	—	13.35	21	Former nominee	58.75	Maine
1892	R	3.7	—	—	26.05	70	Former nominee	62.75	Maine

Richard Bland (1835-1899)

Year	Party	PI	N	W	CS	ROP	Position	Age	State
1896	D	5.5	—	—	30.20	55	Former representative	61.20	Missouri

Michael Bloomberg (1942-)

Year	Party	PI	N	W	CS	ROP	Position	Age	State
2020	D	2.1	—	—	14.10	67	Former mayor	78.71	New York

Horace Boies (1827-1923)

Year	Party	PI	N	W	CS	ROP	Position	Age	State
1892	D	6.3	—	—	19.02	30	Governor	64.90	Iowa
1896	D	6.3	—	—	15.75	25	Former governor	68.90	Iowa

William Borah (1865-1940)

Year	Party	PI	N	W	CS	ROP	Position	Age	State
1936	R	3.3	—	—	20.02	61	Senator	71.34	Idaho

Bill Bradley (1943-)

Year	Party	PI	N	W	CS	ROP	Position	Age	State
2000	D	7.1	—	—	22.10	31	Former senator	57.26	New Jersey

John Breckinridge (1821-1875)

Year	Party	PI	N	W	CS	ROP	Position	Age	State
1860	D/SD	4.7	X	—	60.76	129	Vice president	39.79	Kentucky

Benjamin Bristow (1832-1896)

Year	Party	PI	N	W	CS	ROP	Position	Age	State
1876	R	4.0	—	—	21.90	55	Cabinet member	44.37	Kentucky

Gratz Brown (1826-1885)

Year	Party	PI	N	W	CS	ROP	Position	Age	State
1872	D-LR	7.8	—	—	27.03	35	Governor	46.43	Missouri

Jerry Brown (1938-)

Year	Party	PI	N	W	CS	ROP	Position	Age	State
1976	D	6.2	—	—	21.16	34	Governor	38.57	California
1980	D	6.4	—	—	11.84	19	Governor	42.57	California
1992	D	6.8	—	—	24.83	37	Former governor	54.57	California

William Jennings Bryan (1860-1925)

Year	Party	PI	N	W	CS	ROP	Position	Age	State
1896	D-POP	4.6	X	—	70.98	154	Former representative	36.62	Nebraska
1900	D	5.6	X	—	69.53	124	Former nominee	40.62	Nebraska
1908	D	5.2	X	—	68.65	132	Former nominee	48.62	Nebraska

James Buchanan (1791-1868)

Year	Party	PI	N	W	CS	ROP	Position	Age	State
1848	D	8.2	—	—	25.17	31	Cabinet member	57.52	Pennsylvania
1852	D	7.9	—	—	35.79	45	Former Cabinet member	61.52	Pennsylvania
1856	D	5.1	X	X	79.35	156	Former Cabinet member	65.52	Pennsylvania

Pat Buchanan (1938-)

Year	Party	PI	N	W	CS	ROP	Position	Age	State
1992	R	5.2	—	—	23.85	46	Journalist	54.00	Virginia
1996	R	5.0	—	—	23.11	46	Journalist	58.00	Virginia

Aaron Burr (1756-1836)

Year	Party	PI	N	W	CS	ROP	Position	Age	State
1792	DR	4.7	—	—	19.07	41	Senator	36.73	New York
1796	DR	4.7	—	—	54.24	115	Senator	40.73	New York
1800	DR	4.9	—	—	65.31	133	Former senator	44.73	New York

Theodore Burton (1851-1929)

Year	Party	PI	N	W	CS	ROP	Position	Age	State
1916	R	5.3	—	—	16.00	30	Former senator	64.87	Ohio

George H.W. Bush (1924-2018)

Year	Party	PI	N	W	CS	ROP	Position	Age	State
1980	R	5.2	—	—	24.15	46	Former ambassador	56.39	Texas
1988	R	6.5	X	X	87.86	135	Vice president	64.39	Texas
1992	R	8.2	X	—	66.86	82	President	68.39	Texas

George W. Bush (1946-)

Year	Party	PI	N	W	CS	ROP	Position	Age	State
2000	R	7.9	X	X	77.21	98	Governor	54.32	Texas
2004	R	9.3	X	X	78.71	85	President	58.32	Texas

Jeb Bush (1953-)

Year	Party	PI	N	W	CS	ROP	Position	Age	State
2016	R	7.1	—	—	10.58	15	Former governor	63.72	Florida

Nicholas Murray Butler (1862-1947)

Year	Party	PI	N	W	CS	ROP	Position	Age	State
1920	R	5.9	—	—	14.25	24	College president	58.58	New York

Pete Buttigieg (1982-)

Year	Party	PI	N	W	CS	ROP	Position	Age	State
2020	D	1.8	—	—	11.42	63	Former mayor	38.78	Indiana

Harry Byrd (1887-1966)

Year	Party	PI	N	W	CS	ROP	Position	Age	State
1944	D	5.1	—	—	14.55	29	Senator	57.39	Virginia
1960	D	6.9	—	—	19.25	28	Senator	73.39	Virginia

Simon Cameron (1799-1889)

Year	Party	PI	N	W	CS	ROP	Position	Age	State
1860	R	7.8	—	—	18.62	24	Senator	61.65	Pennsylvania

Joseph Cannon (1836-1926)

Year	Party	PI	N	W	CS	ROP	Position	Age	State
1908	R	5.3	—	—	14.71	28	Representative	72.49	Illinois

Ben Carson (1951-)

Year	Party	PI	N	W	CS	ROP	Position	Age	State
2016	R	4.3	—	—	11.69	27	Movement leader	65.12	Florida

Jimmy Carter (1924-)

Year	Party	PI	N	W	CS	ROP	Position	Age	State
1976	D	7.4	X	X	79.23	107	Former governor	52.08	Georgia
1980	D	9.0	X	—	60.93	68	President	56.08	Georgia

Lewis Cass (1782-1866)

Year	Party	PI	N	W	CS	ROP	Position	Age	State
1844	D	5.1	—	—	34.91	68	Former Cabinet member	62.06	Michigan
1848	D	6.9	X	—	71.66	104	Senator	66.06	Michigan
1852	D	6.9	—	—	42.18	61	Senator	70.06	Michigan

Salmon Chase (1808-1873)

Year	Party	PI	N	W	CS	ROP	Position	Age	State
1860	R	8.7	—	—	18.38	21	Former governor	52.80	Ohio

Shirley Chisholm (1924-2005)

Year	Party	PI	N	W	CS	ROP	Position	Age	State
1972	D	4.5	—	—	12.62	28	Representative	47.92	New York

Chris Christie (1962-)

Year	Party	PI	N	W	CS	ROP	Position	Age	State
2016	R	6.7	—	—	10.11	15	Governor	54.15	New Jersey

Frank Church (1924-1984)

Year	Party	PI	N	W	CS	ROP	Position	Age	State
1976	D	6.5	—	—	13.23	20	Senator	52.27	Idaho

Sanford Church (1815-1880)

Year	Party	PI	N	W	CS	ROP	Position	Age	State
1868	D	5.0	—	—	18.54	37	Former state official	53.54	New York

Champ Clark (1850-1921)

Year	Party	PI	N	W	CS	ROP	Position	Age	State
1912	D	3.7	—	—	42.45	115	Representative	62.65	Missouri

Wesley Clark (1944-)

Year	Party	PI	N	W	CS	ROP	Position	Age	State
2004	D	4.2	—	—	12.00	29	Former general	59.86	Arkansas

Henry Clay (1777-1852)

Year	Party	PI	N	W	CS	ROP	Position	Age	State
1824	DR	3.7	—	—	46.84	127	Representative	47.55	Kentucky
1832	NR	6.4	X	—	62.61	98	Senator	55.55	Kentucky
1840	W	6.7	—	—	42.42	63	Former nominee	63.55	Kentucky
1844	W	5.6	X	—	71.05	127	Former nominee	67.55	Kentucky
1848	W	5.1	—	—	37.63	74	Former nominee	71.55	Kentucky

Grover Cleveland (1837-1908)

Year	Party	PI	N	W	CS	ROP	Position	Age	State
1884	D	7.5	X	X	78.78	105	Governor	47.62	New York
1888	D	9.2	X	—	72.27	79	President	51.62	New York
1892	D	9.1	X	X	80.73	89	Former president	55.62	New York

Bill Clinton (1946-)

Year	Party	PI	N	W	CS	ROP	Position	Age	State
1992	D	6.5	X	X	82.15	126	Governor	46.20	Arkansas
1996	D	8.5	X	X	84.08	99	President	50.20	Arkansas

DeWitt Clinton (1769-1828)

Year	Party	PI	N	W	CS	ROP	Position	Age	State
1812	F-DR	3.7	X	—	71.10	192	Mayor	43.67	New York

George Clinton (1739-1812)

Year	Party	PI	N	W	CS	ROP	Position	Age	State
1789	DR	2.6	—	—	31.09	120	Governor	50.27	New York
1792	DR	3.2	—	—	59.98	187	Governor	53.27	New York
1796	DR	3.0	—	—	33.54	112	Former governor	57.27	New York
1808	DR	4.0	—	—	28.01	70	Vice president	69.27	New York

Hillary Clinton (1947-)

Year	Party	PI	N	W	CS	ROP	Position	Age	State
2008	D	7.0	—	—	43.42	62	Senator	61.02	New York
2016	D	6.6	X	—	72.30	110	Former Cabinet member	69.02	New York

Francis Cockrell (1834-1915)

Year	Party	PI	N	W	CS	ROP	Position	Age	State
1904	D	7.0	—	—	13.35	19	Senator	70.08	Missouri

Roscoe Conkling (1829-1888)

Year	Party	PI	N	W	CS	ROP	Position	Age	State
1876	R	8.2	—	—	20.46	25	Senator	47.01	New York

John Connally (1917-1993)

Year	Party	PI	N	W	CS	ROP	Position	Age	State
1980	R	7.4	—	—	10.38	14	Former governor	63.68	Texas

Calvin Coolidge (1872-1933)

Year	Party	PI	N	W	CS	ROP	Position	Age	State
1924	R	9.1	X	X	85.63	94	President	52.33	Massachusetts

James Cox (1870-1957)

Year	Party	PI	N	W	CS	ROP	Position	Age	State
1920	D	5.9	X	—	64.01	108	Governor	50.59	Ohio
1924	D	7.5	—	—	15.17	20	Former nominee	54.59	Ohio

Jacob Coxey (1854-1951)

Year	Party	PI	N	W	CS	ROP	Position	Age	State
1932	R/FL	2.5	—	—	10.92	44	Mayor	78.54	Ohio

Phil Crane (1930-2014)

Year	Party	PI	N	W	CS	ROP	Position	Age	State
1980	R	4.7	—	—	10.46	22	Representative	49.99	Illinois

Alan Cranston (1914-2000)

Year	Party	PI	N	W	CS	ROP	Position	Age	State
1984	D	7.0	—	—	10.17	15	Senator	70.37	California

William Crawford (1772-1834)

Year	Party	PI	N	W	CS	ROP	Position	Age	State
1824	DR	5.4	—	—	46.97	87	Cabinet member	52.69	Georgia

Ted Cruz (1970-)

Year	Party	PI	N	W	CS	ROP	Position	Age	State
2016	R	7.9	—	—	28.72	36	Senator	45.86	Texas

Albert Cummins (1850-1926)

Year	Party	PI	N	W	CS	ROP	Position	Age	State
1916	R	5.3	—	—	17.15	32	Senator	66.71	Iowa

Charles Curtis (1860-1936)

Year	Party	PI	N	W	CS	ROP	Position	Age	State
1928	R	4.1	—	—	13.53	33	Senator	68.77	Kansas

David Davis (1815-1886)

Year	Party	PI	N	W	CS	ROP	Position	Age	State
1872	D	5.1	—	—	10.97	22	Supreme Court justice	57.65	Illinois

John Davis (1873-1955)

Year	Party	PI	N	W	CS	ROP	Position	Age	State
1920	D	3.7	—	—	12.87	35	Ambassador	47.55	West Virginia
1924	D	4.4	X	—	63.46	144	Former ambassador	51.55	West Virginia

Howard Dean (1948-)

Year	Party	PI	N	W	CS	ROP	Position	Age	State
2004	D	6.0	—	—	13.32	22	Former governor	55.96	Vermont

Eugene Debs (1855-1926)

Year	Party	PI	N	W	CS	ROP	Position	Age	State
1904	SOC	2.9	—	—	19.53	67	Movement leader	48.99	Indiana
1908	SOC	2.9	—	—	19.04	66	Movement leader	52.99	Indiana
1912	SOC	1.5	—	—	29.16	194	Movement leader	56.99	Indiana
1920	SOC	0.1	—	—	20.94	2,094	Movement leader	64.99	Indiana

Chauncey Depew (1834-1928)

Year	Party	PI	N	W	CS	ROP	Position	Age	State
1888	R	4.9	—	—	19.50	40	Business executive	54.52	New York

Thomas Dewey (1902-1971)

Year	Party	PI	N	W	CS	ROP	Position	Age	State
1940	R	4.0	—	—	41.51	104	District attorney	38.61	New York
1944	R	6.3	X	—	64.76	103	Governor	42.61	New York
1948	R	6.6	X	—	69.67	106	Former nominee	46.61	New York

Bob Dole (1923-2021)

Year	Party	PI	N	W	CS	ROP	Position	Age	State
1988	R	7.0	—	—	21.51	31	Senator	65.28	Kansas
1996	R	6.8	X	—	67.01	99	Senator	73.28	Kansas

James Doolittle (1815-1897)

Year	Party	PI	N	W	CS	ROP	Position	Age	State
1868	D	7.9	—	—	13.27	17	Senator	53.83	Wisconsin

Stephen Douglas (1813-1861)

Year	Party	PI	N	W	CS	ROP	Position	Age	State
1852	D	6.9	—	—	15.51	22	Senator	39.52	Illinois
1856	D	7.1	—	—	18.86	27	Senator	43.52	Illinois
1860	D	7.0	X	—	57.06	82	Senator	47.52	Illinois

Michael Dukakis (1933-)

Year	Party	PI	N	W	CS	ROP	Position	Age	State
1988	D	6.7	X	—	65.32	97	Governor	54.99	Massachusetts

Pete du Pont (1935-2021)

Year	Party	PI	N	W	CS	ROP	Position	Age	State
1988	R	6.6	—	—	10.25	16	Former governor	53.78	Delaware

George Edmunds (1828-1919)

Year	Party	PI	N	W	CS	ROP	Position	Age	State
1880	R	7.3	—	—	13.59	19	Senator	52.75	Vermont
1884	R	7.0	—	—	19.02	27	Senator	56.75	Vermont

Edward Edwards (1863-1931)

Year	Party	PI	N	W	CS	ROP	Position	Age	State
1920	D	6.6	—	—	13.28	20	Governor	56.92	New Jersey

John Edwards (1953-)

Year	Party	PI	N	W	CS	ROP	Position	Age	State
2004	D	7.8	—	—	22.22	28	Senator	51.39	North Carolina
2008	D	8.9	—	—	11.63	13	Former senator	55.39	North Carolina

Dwight Eisenhower (1890-1969)

Year	Party	PI	N	W	CS	ROP	Position	Age	State
1952	R	5.6	X	X	89.56	160	General	62.05	New York
1956	R	8.7	X	X	91.03	105	President	66.05	New York

Oliver Ellsworth (1745-1807)

Year	Party	PI	N	W	CS	ROP	Position	Age	State
1796	F	4.8	—	—	43.29	90	Supreme Court justice	51.51	Connecticut

James English (1812-1890)

Year	Party	PI	N	W	CS	ROP	Position	Age	State
1868	D	7.0	—	—	13.99	20	Governor	56.64	Connecticut

Charles Fairbanks (1852-1918)

Year	Party	PI	N	W	CS	ROP	Position	Age	State
1908	R	8.8	—	—	13.27	15	Vice president	56.48	Indiana
1916	R	4.7	—	—	16.32	35	Former vice president	64.48	Indiana

James Farley (1888-1976)

Year	Party	PI	N	W	CS	ROP	Position	Age	State
1940	D	6.3	—	—	13.95	22	Cabinet member	52.42	New York

Stephen Field (1816-1899)

Year	Party	PI	N	W	CS	ROP	Position	Age	State
1880	D	2.3	—	—	17.03	74	Supreme Court justice	63.99	California

Millard Fillmore (1800-1874)

Year	Party	PI	N	W	CS	ROP	Position	Age	State
1852	W	9.1	—	—	45.85	50	President	52.82	New York
1856	AW	7.4	—	—	45.15	61	Former president	56.82	New York

Carly Fiorina (1954-)

Year	Party	PI	N	W	CS	ROP	Position	Age	State
2016	R	3.9	—	—	10.07	26	Business executive	62.15	Virginia

Clinton Fisk (1828-1890)

Year	Party	PI	N	W	CS	ROP	Position	Age	State
1888	PRO	3.8	—	—	17.02	45	Former general	59.90	New Jersey

John Floyd (1783-1837)

Year	Party	PI	N	W	CS	ROP	Position	Age	State
1832	D	4.2	—	—	22.71	54	Governor	49.52	Virginia

Steve Forbes (1947-)

Year	Party	PI	N	W	CS	ROP	Position	Age	State
1996	R	3.6	—	—	16.96	47	Journalist	49.29	New Jersey
2000	R	4.0	—	—	10.52	26	Journalist	53.29	New Jersey

Gerald Ford (1913-2006)

Year	Party	PI	N	W	CS	ROP	Position	Age	State
1976	R	6.6	X	—	72.98	111	President	63.30	Michigan

Henry Ford (1863-1947)

Year	Party	PI	N	W	CS	ROP	Position	Age	State
1916	R	3.8	—	—	13.29	35	Business executive	53.26	Michigan

Joseph France (1873-1939)

Year	Party	PI	N	W	CS	ROP	Position	Age	State
1932	R	5.6	—	—	19.88	36	Former senator	59.06	Maryland

John Fremont (1813-1890)

Year	Party	PI	N	W	CS	ROP	Position	Age	State
1856	R	5.3	X	—	68.16	129	Former senator	43.78	California

James Garfield (1831-1881)

Year	Party	PI	N	W	CS	ROP	Position	Age	State
1880	R	6.6	X	X	79.77	121	Representative	48.95	Ohio

John Nance Garner (1868-1967)

Year	Party	PI	N	W	CS	ROP	Position	Age	State
1932	D	3.3	—	—	16.36	50	Representative	63.94	Texas
1940	D	3.5	—	—	15.20	43	Vice president	71.94	Texas

Walter George (1878-1957)

Year	Party	PI	N	W	CS	ROP	Position	Age	State
1928	D	4.4	—	—	12.87	29	Senator	50.76	Georgia

Richard Gephardt (1941-)

Year	Party	PI	N	W	CS	ROP	Position	Age	State
1988	D	4.0	—	—	13.63	34	Representative	47.75	Missouri
2004	D	3.9	—	—	10.23	26	Representative	63.75	Missouri

Newt Gingrich (1943-)

Year	Party	PI	N	W	CS	ROP	Position	Age	State
2012	R	4.3	—	—	18.59	43	Former representative	69.37	Georgia

Rudy Giuliani (1944-)

Year	Party	PI	N	W	CS	ROP	Position	Age	State
2008	R	3.9	—	—	11.71	30	Former mayor	64.43	New York

John Glenn (1921-2016)

Year	Party	PI	N	W	CS	ROP	Position	Age	State
1984	D	6.8	—	—	12.08	18	Senator	63.29	Ohio

Barry Goldwater (1909-1998)

Year	Party	PI	N	W	CS	ROP	Position	Age	State
1964	R	6.6	X	—	60.59	92	Senator	55.83	Arizona

Al Gore (1948-)

Year	Party	PI	N	W	CS	ROP	Position	Age	State
1988	D	6.8	—	—	18.19	27	Senator	40.59	Tennessee
2000	D	8.8	X	—	74.51	85	Vice president	52.59	Tennessee

Arthur Gorman (1839-1906)

Year	Party	PI	N	W	CS	ROP	Position	Age	State
1892	D	7.4	—	—	13.19	18	Senator	53.64	Maryland

Phil Gramm (1942-)

Year	Party	PI	N	W	CS	ROP	Position	Age	State
1996	R	8.4	—	—	10.30	12	Senator	54.32	Texas

Ulysses Grant (1822-1885)

Year	Party	PI	N	W	CS	ROP	Position	Age	State
1864	R	5.6	—	—	13.35	24	General	42.51	Illinois
1868	R	6.3	X	X	85.63	136	General	46.51	Illinois
1872	R	9.0	X	X	89.28	99	President	50.51	Illinois
1880	R	8.5	—	—	42.34	50	Former president	58.51	Illinois

George Gray (1840-1925)

Year	Party	PI	N	W	CS	ROP	Position	Age	State
1908	D	6.3	—	—	14.71	23	Former senator	68.49	Delaware

Horace Greeley (1811-1872)

Year	Party	PI	N	W	CS	ROP	Position	Age	State
1872	D-LR	4.8	X	—	58.76	122	Journalist	61.74	New York

Dwight Green (1897-1958)

Year	Party	PI	N	W	CS	ROP	Position	Age	State
1948	R	6.5	—	—	13.05	20	Governor	51.81	Illinois

Walter Gresham (1832-1895)

Year	Party	PI	N	W	CS	ROP	Position	Age	State
1888	R	5.7	—	—	20.30	36	Federal judge	56.63	Indiana

James Guthrie (1792-1869)

Year	Party	PI	N	W	CS	ROP	Position	Age	State
1860	D	3.9	—	—	19.34	50	Former Cabinet member	67.91	Kentucky

John Hale (1806-1873)

Year	Party	PI	N	W	CS	ROP	Position	Age	State
1852	FS	5.4	—	—	25.71	48	Senator	46.59	New Hampshire

John Hancock (1737-1793)

Year	Party	PI	N	W	CS	ROP	Position	Age	State
1789	F	4.3	—	—	35.97	84	Governor	52.77	Massachusetts

Winfield Hancock (1824-1886)

Year	Party	PI	N	W	CS	ROP	Position	Age	State
1868	D	6.0	—	—	18.46	31	General	44.71	Pennsylvania
1876	D	6.5	—	—	18.14	28	General	52.71	Pennsylvania
1880	D	5.6	X	—	72.24	129	General	56.71	Pennsylvania

Warren Harding (1865-1923)

Year	Party	PI	N	W	CS	ROP	Position	Age	State
1920	R	6.0	X	X	88.37	147	Senator	55.00	Ohio

Tom Harkin (1939-)

Year	Party	PI	N	W	CS	ROP	Position	Age	State
1992	D	6.9	—	—	10.83	16	Senator	52.95	Iowa

Judson Harmon (1846-1927)

Year	Party	PI	N	W	CS	ROP	Position	Age	State
1912	D	5.6	—	—	20.47	37	Governor	66.74	Ohio

Averell Harriman (1891-1986)

Year	Party	PI	N	W	CS	ROP	Position	Age	State
1952	D	5.8	—	—	15.10	26	Former Cabinet member	60.96	New York
1956	D	7.4	—	—	17.64	24	Governor	64.96	New York

Fred Harris (1930-)

Year	Party	PI	N	W	CS	ROP	Position	Age	State
1976	D	6.9	—	—	10.94	16	Former senator	45.97	Oklahoma

Benjamin Harrison (1833-1901)

Year	Party	PI	N	W	CS	ROP	Position	Age	State
1888	R	7.9	X	X	79.71	101	Former senator	55.20	Indiana
1892	R	8.5	X	—	68.40	80	President	59.20	Indiana

Pat Harrison (1881-1941)

Year	Party	PI	N	W	CS	ROP	Position	Age	State
1924	D	3.4	—	—	12.40	36	Senator	43.17	Mississippi

Robert Harrison (1745-1790)

Year	Party	PI	N	W	CS	ROP	Position	Age	State
1789	F	2.3	—	—	45.73	199	State judge	44.00	Maryland

William Henry Harrison (1773-1841)

Year	Party	PI	N	W	CS	ROP	Position	Age	State
1836	W	4.9	X	—	64.80	132	Former senator	63.73	Ohio
1840	W	8.7	X	X	87.90	101	Former senator	67.73	Ohio

Gary Hart (1936-)

Year	Party	PI	N	W	CS	ROP	Position	Age	State
1984	D	6.3	—	—	37.76	60	Senator	47.93	Colorado
1988	D	6.7	—	—	11.02	16	Former senator	51.93	Colorado

John Hartranft (1830-1889)

Year	Party	PI	N	W	CS	ROP	Position	Age	State
1876	R	7.6	—	—	16.15	21	Governor	45.88	Pennsylvania

Rutherford Hayes (1822-1893)

Year	Party	PI	N	W	CS	ROP	Position	Age	State
1876	R	8.3	X	X	77.12	93	Governor	54.08	Ohio

William Randolph Hearst (1863-1951)

Year	Party	PI	N	W	CS	ROP	Position	Age	State
1904	D	5.5	—	—	24.45	44	Journalist	41.51	New York

Thomas Hendricks (1819-1885)

Year	Party	PI	N	W	CS	ROP	Position	Age	State
1872	D	8.2	—	—	43.62	53	Former senator	53.15	Indiana
1876	D	7.9	—	—	25.17	32	Governor	57.15	Indiana
1880	D	7.4	—	—	15.35	21	Former governor	61.15	Indiana
1884	D	6.4	—	—	14.39	22	Former governor	65.15	Indiana

John Henry (1750-1798)

Year	Party	PI	N	W	CS	ROP	Position	Age	State
1796	DR	4.7	—	—	21.42	46	Senator	46.00	Maryland

David Hill (1843-1910)

Year	Party	PI	N	W	CS	ROP	Position	Age	State
1892	D	8.5	—	—	19.98	24	Senator	49.17	New York

Herbert Hoover (1874-1964)

Year	Party	PI	N	W	CS	ROP	Position	Age	State
1920	R	2.6	—	—	12.56	48	Business executive	46.23	California
1928	R	4.0	X	X	90.41	226	Cabinet member	54.23	California
1932	R	7.3	X	—	61.28	84	President	58.23	California

John Hospers (1918-2011)

Year	Party	PI	N	W	CS	ROP	Position	Age	State
1972	LIB	3.3	—	—	10.62	32	Movement leader	54.40	California

Mike Huckabee (1955-)

Year	Party	PI	N	W	CS	ROP	Position	Age	State
2008	R	7.3	—	—	22.10	30	Former governor	53.19	Arkansas

Charles Evans Hughes (1862-1948)

Year	Party	PI	N	W	CS	ROP	Position	Age	State
1908	R	7.4	—	—	15.43	21	Governor	46.56	New York
1916	R	8.0	X	—	73.55	92	Supreme Court justice	54.56	New York

Cordell Hull (1871-1955)

Year	Party	PI	N	W	CS	ROP	Position	Age	State
1928	D	3.7	—	—	12.75	34	Representative	57.08	Tennessee

Hubert Humphrey (1911-1978)

Year	Party	PI	N	W	CS	ROP	Position	Age	State
1960	D	7.1	—	—	14.46	20	Senator	49.43	Minnesota
1968	D	7.8	X	—	69.19	89	Vice president	57.43	Minnesota
1972	D	6.5	—	—	25.90	40	Former nominee	61.43	Minnesota
1976	D	5.5	—	—	10.29	19	Former nominee	65.43	Minnesota

Robert Hunter (1809-1887)

Year	Party	PI	N	W	CS	ROP	Position	Age	State
1860	D	7.0	—	—	21.10	30	Senator	51.53	Virginia

Samuel Huntington (1731-1796)

Year	Party	PI	N	W	CS	ROP	Position	Age	State
1789	F	4.7	—	—	26.29	56	Governor	58.33	Connecticut

Jon Huntsman (1960-)

Year	Party	PI	N	W	CS	ROP	Position	Age	State
2012	R	6.7	—	—	10.27	15	Former governor	52.60	Utah

James Iredell (1751-1799)

Year	Party	PI	N	W	CS	ROP	Position	Age	State
1796	F	3.6	—	—	23.85	66	Supreme Court justice	45.07	North Carolina

Andrew Jackson (1767-1845)

Year	Party	PI	N	W	CS	ROP	Position	Age	State
1824	DR	5.9	X	—	69.65	118	Senator	57.63	Tennessee
1828	DR	6.9	X	X	84.82	123	Former senator	61.63	Tennessee
1832	D	7.8	X	X	87.20	112	President	65.63	Tennessee

Henry Jackson (1912-1983)

Year	Party	PI	N	W	CS	ROP	Position	Age	State
1972	D	6.3	—	—	15.37	24	Senator	60.42	Washington
1976	D	6.2	—	—	14.30	23	Senator	64.42	Washington

Jesse Jackson (1941-)

Year	Party	PI	N	W	CS	ROP	Position	Age	State
1984	D	3.3	—	—	23.30	71	Movement leader	43.07	Illinois
1988	D	3.6	—	—	33.32	93	Movement leader	47.07	Illinois

Arthur James (1883-1973)

Year	Party	PI	N	W	CS	ROP	Position	Age	State
1940	R	7.1	—	—	14.48	20	Governor	57.30	Pennsylvania

John Jay (1745-1829)

Year	Party	PI	N	W	CS	ROP	Position	Age	State
1789	F	4.1	—	—	51.15	125	Cabinet member	43.89	New York
1796	F	5.1	—	—	28.66	56	Governor	50.89	New York
1800	F	3.3	—	—	18.98	58	Governor	54.89	New York

Thomas Jefferson (1743-1826)

Year	Party	PI	N	W	CS	ROP	Position	Age	State
1792	DR	6.7	—	—	26.68	40	Cabinet member	49.55	Virginia
1796	DR	6.9	X	—	74.00	107	Former Cabinet member	53.55	Virginia
1800	DR	7.6	X	X	77.84	102	Vice president	57.55	Virginia
1804	DR	9.2	X	X	93.05	101	President	61.55	Virginia

Charles Jenkins (1805-1883)

Year	Party	PI	N	W	CS	ROP	Position	Age	State
1872	D	5.1	—	—	11.89	23	Former governor	67.82	Georgia

Andrew Johnson (1808-1875)

Year	Party	PI	N	W	CS	ROP	Position	Age	State
1860	D	6.9	—	—	13.19	19	Senator	51.84	Tennessee
1868	D	7.4	—	—	26.37	36	President	59.84	Tennessee

Gary Johnson (1953-)

Year	Party	PI	N	W	CS	ROP	Position	Age	State
2016	LIB	3.9	—	—	20.52	53	Former governor	63.83	New Mexico

Hiram Johnson (1866-1945)

Year	Party	PI	N	W	CS	ROP	Position	Age	State
1920	R	5.8	—	—	24.20	42	Senator	54.16	California
1924	R	5.4	—	—	16.26	30	Senator	58.16	California

John Johnson (1861-1909)

Year	Party	PI	N	W	CS	ROP	Position	Age	State
1908	D	6.8	—	—	13.67	20	Governor	47.26	Minnesota

Lyndon Johnson (1908-1973)

Year	Party	PI	N	W	CS	ROP	Position	Age	State
1956	D	4.5	—	—	12.89	29	Senator	48.18	Texas
1960	D	8.1	—	—	23.50	29	Senator	52.18	Texas
1964	D	9.3	X	X	93.24	100	President	56.18	Texas
1968	D	8.7	—	—	11.53	13	President	60.18	Texas

Richard Johnson (1780-1850)

Year	Party	PI	N	W	CS	ROP	Position	Age	State
1844	D	5.6	—	—	17.19	31	Former vice president	64.04	Kentucky

Samuel Johnston (1733-1816)

Year	Party	PI	N	W	CS	ROP	Position	Age	State
1796	F	6.5	—	—	21.42	33	Former senator	62.88	North Carolina

Walter Jones (1888-1963)

Year	Party	PI	N	W	CS	ROP	Position	Age	State
1956	D	1.9	—	—	10.62	56	State judge	68.04	Alabama

John Kasich (1952-)

Year	Party	PI	N	W	CS	ROP	Position	Age	State
2016	R	6.6	—	—	19.98	30	Governor	64.47	Ohio

Estes Kefauver (1903-1963)

Year	Party	PI	N	W	CS	ROP	Position	Age	State
1952	D	4.4	—	—	38.77	88	Senator	49.27	Tennessee
1956	D	5.1	—	—	21.72	43	Senator	53.27	Tennessee

Jack Kemp (1935-2009)

Year	Party	PI	N	W	CS	ROP	Position	Age	State
1988	R	5.2	—	—	11.63	22	Representative	53.30	New York

Edward Kennedy (1932-2009)

Year	Party	PI	N	W	CS	ROP	Position	Age	State
1980	D	6.8	—	—	39.18	58	Senator	48.69	Massachusetts

John Kennedy (1917-1963)

Year	Party	PI	N	W	CS	ROP	Position	Age	State
1960	D	6.2	X	X	79.58	128	Senator	43.43	Massachusetts

Robert Kennedy (1925-1968)

Year	Party	PI	N	W	CS	ROP	Position	Age	State
1968	D	6.6	—	—	19.18	29	Senator	42.95	New York

Robert Kerr (1896-1963)

Year	Party	PI	N	W	CS	ROP	Position	Age	State
1952	D	5.3	—	—	12.90	24	Senator	56.14	Oklahoma

Bob Kerrey (1943-)

Year	Party	PI	N	W	CS	ROP	Position	Age	State
1992	D	6.4	—	—	10.95	17	Senator	49.18	Nebraska

John Kerry (1943-)

Year	Party	PI	N	W	CS	ROP	Position	Age	State
2004	D	6.6	X	—	73.65	112	Senator	60.89	Massachusetts

Alan Keyes (1950-)

Year	Party	PI	N	W	CS	ROP	Position	Age	State
1996	R	3.2	—	—	11.81	37	Former ambassador	46.23	Maryland
2000	R	3.7	—	—	13.04	35	Former ambassador	50.23	Maryland

Rufus King (1755-1827)

Year	Party	PI	N	W	CS	ROP	Position	Age	State
1816	F	7.1	X	—	62.07	87	Senator	61.61	New York

Amy Klobuchar (1960-)

Year	Party	PI	N	W	CS	ROP	Position	Age	State
2020	D	6.0	—	—	10.82	18	Senator	60.44	Minnesota

Frank Knox (1874-1944)

Year	Party	PI	N	W	CS	ROP	Position	Age	State
1936	R	3.5	—	—	12.97	37	Journalist	62.83	Illinois

Philander Knox (1853-1921)

Year	Party	PI	N	W	CS	ROP	Position	Age	State
1908	R	8.2	—	—	15.51	19	Senator	55.49	Pennsylvania

Robert La Follette (1855-1925)

Year	Party	PI	N	W	CS	ROP	Position	Age	State
1912	R	6.3	—	—	15.18	24	Senator	57.38	Wisconsin
1916	R	5.2	—	—	12.89	25	Senator	61.38	Wisconsin
1924	R/P	2.2	—	—	46.37	211	Senator	69.38	Wisconsin

Alfred Landon (1887-1987)

Year	Party	PI	N	W	CS	ROP	Position	Age	State
1936	R	4.8	X	—	57.76	120	Governor	49.14	Kansas

Joseph Lane (1801-1881)

Year	Party	PI	N	W	CS	ROP	Position	Age	State
1852	D	3.1	—	—	13.59	44	Territorial delegate	50.88	Oregon

Lyndon LaRouche (1922-2019)

Year	Party	PI	N	W	CS	ROP	Position	Age	State
1996	D	3.6	—	—	13.27	37	Movement leader	74.15	Virginia

Frank Lausche (1895-1990)

Year	Party	PI	N	W	CS	ROP	Position	Age	State
1956	D	5.7	—	—	11.62	20	Governor	60.96	Ohio

William Lemke (1878-1950)

Year	Party	PI	N	W	CS	ROP	Position	Age	State
1936	U	1.8	—	—	16.26	90	Representative	58.22	North Dakota

Joseph Lieberman (1942-)

Year	Party	PI	N	W	CS	ROP	Position	Age	State
2004	D	7.2	—	—	11.04	15	Senator	62.69	Connecticut

Abraham Lincoln (1809-1865)

Year	Party	PI	N	W	CS	ROP	Position	Age	State
1860	R	6.2	X	X	78.38	126	Former representative	51.72	Illinois
1864	R	8.9	X	X	92.17	104	President	55.72	Illinois

Benjamin Lincoln (1733-1810)

Year	Party	PI	N	W	CS	ROP	Position	Age	State
1789	F	4.8	—	—	21.42	45	Former general	56.77	Massachusetts

Henry Cabot Lodge (1902-1985)

Year	Party	PI	N	W	CS	ROP	Position	Age	State
1964	R	4.8	—	—	12.05	25	Former v.p. nominee	62.33	Massachusetts

John Logan (1826-1886)

Year	Party	PI	N	W	CS	ROP	Position	Age	State
1884	R	8.1	—	—	16.15	20	Senator	58.73	Illinois

Frank Lowden (1861-1943)

Year	Party	PI	N	W	CS	ROP	Position	Age	State
1920	R	6.3	—	—	25.31	40	Governor	59.77	Illinois
1928	R	5.7	—	—	20.32	36	Former governor	67.77	Illinois

Richard Lugar (1932-2019)

Year	Party	PI	N	W	CS	ROP	Position	Age	State
1996	R	6.5	—	—	10.51	16	Senator	64.58	Indiana

Douglas MacArthur (1880-1964)

Year	Party	PI	N	W	CS	ROP	Position	Age	State
1944	R	3.9	—	—	15.89	41	General	64.77	Wisconsin

James Madison (1751-1836)

Year	Party	PI	N	W	CS	ROP	Position	Age	State
1808	DR	6.8	X	X	84.36	124	Cabinet member	57.63	Virginia
1812	DR	8.7	X	X	80.17	92	President	61.63	Virginia

Willie Person Mangum (1792-1861)

Year	Party	PI	N	W	CS	ROP	Position	Age	State
1836	W	5.4	—	—	22.34	41	Senator	44.48	North Carolina

William Marcy (1786-1857)

Year	Party	PI	N	W	CS	ROP	Position	Age	State
1852	D	5.9	—	—	17.50	30	Former Cabinet member	65.89	New York

Joseph Martin (1884-1968)

Year	Party	PI	N	W	CS	ROP	Position	Age	State
1940	R	5.1	—	—	12.63	25	Representative	55.99	Massachusetts

Claude Matthews (1845-1898)

Year	Party	PI	N	W	CS	ROP	Position	Age	State
1896	D	7.3	—	—	13.19	18	Governor	50.88	Indiana

William Gibbs McAdoo (1863-1941)

Year	Party	PI	N	W	CS	ROP	Position	Age	State
1920	D	6.3	—	—	27.41	44	Former Cabinet member	57.00	New York
1924	D	3.6	—	—	43.53	121	Former Cabinet member	61.00	California

John McCain (1936-2018)

Year	Party	PI	N	W	CS	ROP	Position	Age	State
2000	R	6.2	—	—	29.92	48	Senator	64.17	Arizona
2008	R	5.9	X	—	68.78	117	Senator	72.17	Arizona

Eugene McCarthy (1916-2005)

Year	Party	PI	N	W	CS	ROP	Position	Age	State
1968	D	6.9	—	—	33.16	48	Senator	52.59	Minnesota

George McClellan (1826-1885)

Year	Party	PI	N	W	CS	ROP	Position	Age	State
1864	D	4.7	X	—	61.66	131	General	37.91	New Jersey

Paul McCloskey (1927-)

Year	Party	PI	N	W	CS	ROP	Position	Age	State
1972	R	4.7	—	—	11.31	24	Representative	45.09	California

Joseph McDonald (1819-1891)

Year	Party	PI	N	W	CS	ROP	Position	Age	State
1884	D	7.3	—	—	15.43	21	Former senator	65.17	Indiana

George McGovern (1922-2012)

Year	Party	PI	N	W	CS	ROP	Position	Age	State
1968	D	6.0	—	—	12.79	21	Senator	46.29	South Dakota
1972	D	6.4	X	—	58.46	91	Senator	50.29	South Dakota
1984	D	6.2	—	—	11.14	18	Former nominee	62.29	South Dakota

William McKinley (1843-1901)

Year	Party	PI	N	W	CS	ROP	Position	Age	State
1892	R	8.2	—	—	26.05	32	Governor	49.76	Ohio
1896	R	8.2	X	X	81.24	99	Former governor	53.76	Ohio
1900	R	8.9	X	X	82.89	93	President	57.76	Ohio

John McLean (1785-1861)

Year	Party	PI	N	W	CS	ROP	Position	Age	State
1856	R	4.2	—	—	15.19	36	Supreme Court justice	71.64	Ohio

John R. McLean (1848-1916)

Year	Party	PI	N	W	CS	ROP	Position	Age	State
1896	D	5.0	—	—	14.63	29	Journalist	48.12	Ohio

Wilbur Mills (1909-1992)

Year	Party	PI	N	W	CS	ROP	Position	Age	State
1972	D	4.3	—	—	10.36	24	Representative	63.44	Arkansas

John Milton (1740-1804)

Year	Party	PI	N	W	CS	ROP	Position	Age	State
1789	F	3.1	—	—	26.29	85	State official	49.00	Georgia

Walter Mondale (1928-2021)

Year	Party	PI	N	W	CS	ROP	Position	Age	State
1984	D	7.8	X	—	58.83	75	Former vice president	56.82	Minnesota

James Monroe (1758-1831)

Year	Party	PI	N	W	CS	ROP	Position	Age	State
1816	DR	7.3	X	X	90.10	123	Cabinet member	58.51	Virginia
1820	DR	8.7	X	X	96.04	110	President	62.51	Virginia

William Morrison (1824-1909)

Year	Party	PI	N	W	CS	ROP	Position	Age	State
1880	D	6.5	—	—	16.71	26	Representative	56.13	Illinois

Levi Morton (1824-1920)

Year	Party	PI	N	W	CS	ROP	Position	Age	State
1896	R	7.8	—	—	15.03	19	Governor	72.46	New York

Oliver Morton (1823-1877)

Year	Party	PI	N	W	CS	ROP	Position	Age	State
1876	R	8.2	—	—	23.09	28	Senator	53.24	Indiana

William Murray (1869-1956)

Year	Party	PI	N	W	CS	ROP	Position	Age	State
1932	D	5.1	—	—	12.73	25	Governor	62.95	Oklahoma

Edmund Muskie (1914-1996)

Year	Party	PI	N	W	CS	ROP	Position	Age	State
1972	D	7.2	—	—	17.06	24	Senator	58.60	Maine

Ralph Nader (1934-)

Year	Party	PI	N	W	CS	ROP	Position	Age	State
2000	GRN	1.3	—	—	18.76	144	Movement leader	66.68	Connecticut

Richard Nixon (1913-1994)

Year	Party	PI	N	W	CS	ROP	Position	Age	State
1960	R	8.0	X	—	72.12	90	Vice president	47.81	California
1964	R	6.7	—	—	11.00	16	Former nominee	51.81	New York
1968	R	6.2	X	X	78.01	126	Former nominee	55.81	New York
1972	R	8.8	X	X	95.25	108	President	59.81	California

George Norris (1861-1944)

Year	Party	PI	N	W	CS	ROP	Position	Age	State
1928	R	4.3	—	—	12.58	29	Senator	67.31	Nebraska

Barack Obama (1961-)

Year	Party	PI	N	W	CS	ROP	Position	Age	State
2008	D	6.8	X	X	84.03	124	Senator	47.24	Illinois
2012	D	8.3	X	X	81.59	98	President	51.24	Illinois

Asa Packer (1805-1879)

Year	Party	PI	N	W	CS	ROP	Position	Age	State
1868	D	6.0	—	—	16.55	28	Former representative	62.84	Pennsylvania

Mitchell Palmer (1872-1936)

Year	Party	PI	N	W	CS	ROP	Position	Age	State
1920	D	4.9	—	—	27.09	55	Cabinet member	48.49	Pennsylvania

Alton Parker (1852-1926)

Year	Party	PI	N	W	CS	ROP	Position	Age	State
1904	D	4.9	X	—	66.33	135	State judge	52.47	New York

Joel Parker (1816-1888)

Year	Party	PI	N	W	CS	ROP	Position	Age	State
1868	D	6.7	—	—	13.27	20	Former governor	51.94	New Jersey

Robert Pattison (1850-1904)

Year	Party	PI	N	W	CS	ROP	Position	Age	State
1896	D	7.2	—	—	18.30	25	Former governor	45.90	Pennsylvania

Rand Paul (1963-)

Year	Party	PI	N	W	CS	ROP	Position	Age	State
2016	R	7.8	—	—	10.13	13	Senator	53.82	Kentucky

Ron Paul (1935-)

Year	Party	PI	N	W	CS	ROP	Position	Age	State
2008	R/TC	4.8	—	—	13.62	28	Representative	73.20	Texas
2012	R	4.6	—	—	18.11	39	Representative	77.20	Texas
2016	R	3.8	—	—	10.62	28	Former representative	81.20	Texas

Henry Payne (1810-1896)

Year	Party	PI	N	W	CS	ROP	Position	Age	State
1880	D	5.6	—	—	18.78	34	Former representative	69.92	Ohio

George Pendleton (1825-1889)

Year	Party	PI	N	W	CS	ROP	Position	Age	State
1868	D	6.7	—	—	36.43	54	Former representative	43.29	Ohio

Ross Perot (1930-2019)

Year	Party	PI	N	W	CS	ROP	Position	Age	State
1992	I	2.9	—	—	43.78	151	Business executive	62.35	Texas
1996	REF	2.6	—	—	36.87	142	Business executive	66.35	Texas

Rick Perry (1950-)

Year	Party	PI	N	W	CS	ROP	Position	Age	State
2012	R	7.5	—	—	10.14	14	Governor	62.66	Texas

Franklin Pierce (1804-1869)

Year	Party	PI	N	W	CS	ROP	Position	Age	State
1852	D	7.0	X	X	89.52	128	Former senator	47.94	New Hampshire
1856	D	8.1	—	—	43.05	53	President	51.94	New Hampshire

Charles Cotesworth Pinckney (1746-1825)

Year	Party	PI	N	W	CS	ROP	Position	Age	State
1796	F	3.9	—	—	18.98	49	Ambassador	50.68	South Carolina
1800	F	4.4	—	—	63.01	143	Former ambassador	54.68	South Carolina
1804	F	5.1	X	—	59.38	116	Former ambassador	58.68	South Carolina
1808	F	3.9	X	—	66.03	169	Former nominee	62.68	South Carolina

Thomas Pinckney (1750-1828)

Year	Party	PI	N	W	CS	ROP	Position	Age	State
1796	F	4.1	—	—	61.70	150	Ambassador	46.02	South Carolina

James Polk (1795-1849)

Year	Party	PI	N	W	CS	ROP	Position	Age	State
1844	D	6.7	X	X	81.33	121	Former governor	49.00	Tennessee

Colin Powell (1937-2021)

Year	Party	PI	N	W	CS	ROP	Position	Age	State
2016	R	3.2	—	—	11.84	37	Former Cabinet member	79.57	New York

Matthew Quay (1833-1904)

Year	Party	PI	N	W	CS	ROP	Position	Age	State
1896	R	7.5	—	—	15.35	20	Senator	63.09	Pennsylvania

Samuel Randall (1828-1890)

Year	Party	PI	N	W	CS	ROP	Position	Age	State
1884	D	6.3	—	—	17.58	28	Representative	56.06	Pennsylvania

Ronald Reagan (1911-2004)

Year	Party	PI	N	W	CS	ROP	Position	Age	State
1968	R	7.3	—	—	28.22	39	Governor	57.73	California
1976	R	6.7	—	—	47.60	71	Former governor	65.73	California
1980	R	5.7	X	X	91.16	160	Former governor	69.73	California
1984	R	8.1	X	X	95.13	117	President	73.73	California

James Reed (1861-1944)

Year	Party	PI	N	W	CS	ROP	Position	Age	State
1928	D	4.8	—	—	16.09	34	Senator	66.98	Missouri

Thomas Reed (1839-1902)

Year	Party	PI	N	W	CS	ROP	Position	Age	State
1896	R	5.2	—	—	17.27	33	Representative	57.04	Maine

James Rhodes (1909-2001)

Year	Party	PI	N	W	CS	ROP	Position	Age	State
1968	R	6.6	—	—	16.17	25	Governor	59.13	Ohio

Bill Richardson (1947-)

Year	Party	PI	N	W	CS	ROP	Position	Age	State
2008	D	5.9	—	—	10.17	17	Governor	60.96	New Mexico

Pat Robertson (1930-2023)

Year	Party	PI	N	W	CS	ROP	Position	Age	State
1988	R	4.5	—	—	15.41	34	Movement leader	58.61	Virginia

Nelson Rockefeller (1908-1979)

Year	Party	PI	N	W	CS	ROP	Position	Age	State
1964	R	7.6	—	—	20.93	28	Governor	56.32	New York
1968	R	7.1	—	—	21.48	30	Governor	60.32	New York

Mitt Romney (1947-)

Year	Party	PI	N	W	CS	ROP	Position	Age	State
2008	R	6.1	—	—	23.13	38	Former governor	61.64	Massachusetts
2012	R	5.9	X	—	70.93	120	Former governor	65.64	Massachusetts

Franklin Roosevelt (1882-1945)

Year	Party	PI	N	W	CS	ROP	Position	Age	State
1932	D	8.3	X	X	91.94	111	Governor	50.75	New York
1936	D	10.0	X	X	95.88	96	President	54.75	New York
1940	D	9.6	X	X	89.94	94	President	58.75	New York
1944	D	9.4	X	X	88.61	94	President	62.75	New York

Theodore Roosevelt (1858-1919)

Year	Party	PI	N	W	CS	ROP	Position	Age	State
1904	R	8.8	X	X	85.72	97	President	46.01	New York
1912	R/P	10.0	—	—	66.37	66	Former president	54.01	New York
1916	R	9.6	—	—	14.78	15	Former president	58.01	New York

Elihu Root (1845-1937)

Year	Party	PI	N	W	CS	ROP	Position	Age	State
1916	R	6.0	—	—	16.23	27	Former senator	71.71	New York

Marco Rubio (1971-)

Year	Party	PI	N	W	CS	ROP	Position	Age	State
2016	R	7.7	—	—	17.61	23	Senator	45.43	Florida

Richard Russell (1897-1971)

Year	Party	PI	N	W	CS	ROP	Position	Age	State
1948	D	4.4	—	—	22.93	52	Senator	51.00	Georgia
1952	D	5.1	—	—	23.13	45	Senator	55.00	Georgia

John Rutledge (1739-1800)

Year	Party	PI	N	W	CS	ROP	Position	Age	State
1789	F	4.5	—	—	45.73	102	Former governor	50.12	South Carolina

Bernie Sanders (1941-)

Year	Party	PI	N	W	CS	ROP	Position	Age	State
2016	D	5.5	—	—	44.15	80	Senator	75.15	Vermont
2020	D	5.1	—	—	30.55	60	Senator	79.15	Vermont

Rick Santorum (1958-)

Year	Party	PI	N	W	CS	ROP	Position	Age	State
2012	R	7.3	—	—	22.25	30	Former senator	54.48	Pennsylvania

Winfield Scott (1786-1866)

Year	Party	PI	N	W	CS	ROP	Position	Age	State
1840	W	5.8	—	—	27.88	48	General	54.39	New Jersey
1848	W	5.0	—	—	27.96	56	General	62.39	New Jersey
1852	W	4.2	X	—	63.01	150	General	66.39	New Jersey

William Scranton (1917-2013)

Year	Party	PI	N	W	CS	ROP	Position	Age	State
1964	R	6.9	—	—	19.42	28	Governor	47.29	Pennsylvania

William Seward (1801-1872)

Year	Party	PI	N	W	CS	ROP	Position	Age	State
1860	R	8.2	—	—	39.70	48	Senator	59.46	New York

Horatio Seymour (1810-1886)

Year	Party	PI	N	W	CS	ROP	Position	Age	State
1864	D	8.0	—	—	14.23	18	Governor	54.42	New York
1868	D	7.5	X	—	67.61	90	Former governor	58.42	New York

Thomas Seymour (1807-1868)

Year	Party	PI	N	W	CS	ROP	Position	Age	State
1864	D	6.8	—	—	23.41	34	Former governor	57.09	Connecticut

John Sherman (1823-1900)

Year	Party	PI	N	W	CS	ROP	Position	Age	State
1880	R	8.1	—	—	19.82	24	Cabinet member	57.48	Ohio
1888	R	7.7	—	—	31.96	42	Senator	65.48	Ohio

Lawrence Sherman (1858-1939)

Year	Party	PI	N	W	CS	ROP	Position	Age	State
1916	R	6.1	—	—	15.63	26	Senator	57.98	Illinois

Sargent Shriver (1915-2011)

Year	Party	PI	N	W	CS	ROP	Position	Age	State
1976	D	4.2	—	—	11.14	27	Former v.p. nominee	60.98	Maryland

Paul Simon (1928-2003)

Year	Party	PI	N	W	CS	ROP	Position	Age	State
1988	D	7.1	—	—	12.66	18	Senator	59.92	Illinois

Alfred Smith (1873-1944)

Year	Party	PI	N	W	CS	ROP	Position	Age	State
1920	D	6.5	—	—	15.99	25	Governor	46.84	New York
1924	D	7.0	—	—	23.54	34	Governor	50.84	New York
1928	D	6.9	X	—	63.06	91	Governor	54.84	New York
1932	D	6.6	—	—	23.23	35	Former nominee	58.84	New York

Faith Spotted Eagle (1948-)

Year	Party	PI	N	W	CS	ROP	Position	Age	State
2016	D	2.3	—	—	10.62	46	Movement leader	68.00	South Dakota

William Sproul (1870-1928)

Year	Party	PI	N	W	CS	ROP	Position	Age	State
1920	R	6.4	—	—	15.09	24	Governor	50.13	Pennsylvania

Harold Stassen (1907-2001)

Year	Party	PI	N	W	CS	ROP	Position	Age	State
1948	R	4.5	—	—	22.01	49	Former governor	41.55	Minnesota
1952	R	3.9	—	—	13.39	34	College president	45.55	Pennsylvania

Adlai Stevenson (1900-1965)

Year	Party	PI	N	W	CS	ROP	Position	Age	State
1952	D	6.7	X	—	63.90	95	Governor	52.74	Illinois
1956	D	7.6	X	—	62.52	82	Former nominee	56.74	Illinois
1960	D	7.2	—	—	12.86	18	Former nominee	60.74	Illinois

Stuart Symington (1901-1988)

Year	Party	PI	N	W	CS	ROP	Position	Age	State
1960	D	6.9	—	—	13.00	19	Senator	59.35	Missouri

Robert Taft (1889-1953)

Year	Party	PI	N	W	CS	ROP	Position	Age	State
1940	R	5.8	—	—	32.24	56	Senator	51.15	Ohio
1948	R	5.6	—	—	22.57	40	Senator	59.15	Ohio
1952	R	4.6	—	—	32.33	70	Senator	63.15	Ohio

William Howard Taft (1857-1930)

Year	Party	PI	N	W	CS	ROP	Position	Age	State
1908	R	6.0	X	X	83.31	139	Cabinet member	51.13	Ohio
1912	R	8.2	X	—	55.09	67	President	55.13	Ohio

Zachary Taylor (1784-1850)

Year	Party	PI	N	W	CS	ROP	Position	Age	State
1848	W	4.1	X	X	78.93	193	General	63.94	Louisiana

Edward Telfair (1735-1807)

Year	Party	PI	N	W	CS	ROP	Position	Age	State
1789	DR	4.8	—	—	21.42	45	Former governor	54.00	Georgia

Norman Thomas (1884-1968)

Year	Party	PI	N	W	CS	ROP	Position	Age	State
1932	SOC	3.0	—	—	17.13	57	Movement leader	47.95	New York

Fred Thompson (1942-2015)

Year	Party	PI	N	W	CS	ROP	Position	Age	State
2008	R	7.2	—	—	10.81	15	Former senator	66.20	Tennessee

Allen Thurman (1813-1895)

Year	Party	PI	N	W	CS	ROP	Position	Age	State
1880	D	7.7	—	—	17.43	23	Senator	66.97	Ohio
1884	D	7.4	—	—	18.54	25	Former senator	70.97	Ohio

Strom Thurmond (1902-2003)

Year	Party	PI	N	W	CS	ROP	Position	Age	State
1948	SRD	2.2	—	—	34.75	158	Governor	45.91	South Carolina

Samuel Tilden (1814-1886)

Year	Party	PI	N	W	CS	ROP	Position	Age	State
1876	D	7.2	X	—	75.14	104	Governor	62.73	New York
1880	D	8.0	—	—	14.07	18	Former nominee	66.73	New York

Harry Truman (1884-1972)

Year	Party	PI	N	W	CS	ROP	Position	Age	State
1948	D	7.6	X	X	79.72	105	President	64.48	Missouri

Donald Trump (1946-)

Year	Party	PI	N	W	CS	ROP	Position	Age	State
2016	R	3.1	X	X	78.79	254	Business executive	70.38	New York
2020	R	7.5	X	—	72.31	96	President	74.38	Florida

Paul Tsongas (1941-1997)

Year	Party	PI	N	W	CS	ROP	Position	Age	State
1992	D	7.0	—	—	21.82	31	Former senator	51.71	Massachusetts

Morris Udall (1922-1998)

Year	Party	PI	N	W	CS	ROP	Position	Age	State
1976	D	4.3	—	—	18.22	42	Representative	54.38	Arizona

Oscar Underwood (1862-1929)

Year	Party	PI	N	W	CS	ROP	Position	Age	State
1912	D	3.0	—	—	16.41	55	Representative	50.49	Alabama
1924	D	4.5	—	—	15.57	35	Senator	62.49	Alabama

Martin Van Buren (1782-1862)

Year	Party	PI	N	W	CS	ROP	Position	Age	State
1836	D	6.8	X	X	80.26	118	Vice president	53.91	New York
1840	D	9.1	X	—	65.49	72	President	57.91	New York
1844	D	8.7	—	—	50.00	57	Former president	61.91	New York
1848	FS	7.1	—	—	42.02	59	Former president	65.91	New York

Arthur Vandenberg (1884-1951)

Year	Party	PI	N	W	CS	ROP	Position	Age	State
1940	R	5.8	—	—	15.17	26	Senator	56.61	Michigan
1948	R	5.1	—	—	13.55	27	Senator	64.61	Michigan

George Wallace (1919-1998)

Year	Party	PI	N	W	CS	ROP	Position	Age	State
1964	D	6.4	—	—	13.23	21	Governor	45.19	Alabama
1968	D/AI	5.4	—	—	45.41	84	Former governor	49.19	Alabama
1972	D	6.5	—	—	26.62	41	Governor	53.19	Alabama
1976	D	5.6	—	—	17.84	32	Governor	57.19	Alabama

Henry Wallace (1888-1965)

Year	Party	PI	N	W	CS	ROP	Position	Age	State
1948	D/P	3.1	—	—	17.65	57	Former vice president	60.07	Iowa

Thomas Walsh (1859-1933)

Year	Party	PI	N	W	CS	ROP	Position	Age	State
1924	D	4.0	—	—	13.17	33	Senator	65.39	Montana
1928	D	3.5	—	—	10.95	31	Senator	69.39	Montana

Earl Warren (1891-1974)

Year	Party	PI	N	W	CS	ROP	Position	Age	State
1948	R	5.7	—	—	19.04	33	Governor	57.62	California
1952	R	6.2	—	—	18.38	30	Governor	61.62	California

Elizabeth Warren (1949-)

Year	Party	PI	N	W	CS	ROP	Position	Age	State
2020	D	5.4	—	—	14.59	27	Senator	71.36	Massachusetts

Elihu Washburne (1816-1887)

Year	Party	PI	N	W	CS	ROP	Position	Age	State
1880	R	4.4	—	—	13.19	30	Former ambassador	64.11	Illinois

George Washington (1732-1799)

Year	Party	PI	N	W	CS	ROP	Position	Age	State
1789	F	5.6	X	X	96.18	172	Former general	57.69	Virginia
1792	F	9.7	X	X	96.18	99	President	60.69	Virginia
1796	F	9.1	—	—	21.42	24	President	64.69	Virginia

James Watson (1864-1948)

Year	Party	PI	N	W	CS	ROP	Position	Age	State
1928	R	5.1	—	—	13.57	27	Senator	64.00	Indiana

James Weaver (1833-1912)

Year	Party	PI	N	W	CS	ROP	Position	Age	State
1880	GBK	4.2	—	—	20.66	49	Representative	47.39	Iowa
1892	POP	4.1	—	—	38.80	95	Former representative	59.39	Iowa

Daniel Webster (1782-1852)

Year	Party	PI	N	W	CS	ROP	Position	Age	State
1836	W	5.0	—	—	26.29	53	Senator	54.79	Massachusetts
1848	W	7.0	—	—	16.31	23	Senator	66.79	Massachusetts
1852	W	6.0	—	—	18.52	31	Cabinet member	70.79	Massachusetts

John Weeks (1860-1926)

Year	Party	PI	N	W	CS	ROP	Position	Age	State
1916	R	6.5	—	—	16.35	25	Senator	56.56	Massachusetts

Bill Weld (1945-)

Year	Party	PI	N	W	CS	ROP	Position	Age	State
2020	R	5.3	—	—	11.41	22	Former governor	75.25	Massachusetts

George White (1872-1953)

Year	Party	PI	N	W	CS	ROP	Position	Age	State
1932	D	6.1	—	—	12.70	21	Governor	60.20	Ohio

Hugh White (1773-1840)

Year	Party	PI	N	W	CS	ROP	Position	Age	State
1836	W	6.3	X	—	54.62	87	Senator	63.01	Tennessee

Wendell Willkie (1892-1944)

Year	Party	PI	N	W	CS	ROP	Position	Age	State
1940	R	4.7	X	—	63.60	135	Business executive	48.70	New York

Woodrow Wilson (1856-1924)

Year	Party	PI	N	W	CS	ROP	Position	Age	State
1912	D	6.6	X	X	86.26	131	Governor	55.84	New Jersey
1916	D	8.6	X	X	78.07	91	President	59.84	New Jersey

William Wirt (1772-1834)

Year	Party	PI	N	W	CS	ROP	Position	Age	State
1832	AM	3.9	—	—	35.63	91	Former Cabinet member	59.98	Maryland

Leonard Wood (1860-1927)

Year	Party	PI	N	W	CS	ROP	Position	Age	State
1920	R	4.3	—	—	31.95	74	General	60.06	New Hampshire

Levi Woodbury (1789-1851)

Year	Party	PI	N	W	CS	ROP	Position	Age	State
1848	D	7.0	—	—	24.61	35	Supreme Court justice	58.86	New Hampshire

Sam Yorty (1909-1998)

Year	Party	PI	N	W	CS	ROP	Position	Age	State
1972	D	4.3	—	—	10.30	24	Mayor	63.08	California

4. States

This chapter is comprised of 51 state-by-state breakdowns of presidential-election results. Why 51? The District of Columbia has been casting electoral votes since 1964, elevating it to the same political level as the 50 actual states.

Here's a guide to the chapter's tables and graphs:

Basics

State party winners: The number of times each party has won a majority or plurality of the state's electoral votes since the state began participating in presidential elections. Flip back to pages 48 and 50 for lists of party abbreviations. If two or more parties shared the lead in a given year, a tie is indicated.

General-election matches: The times that the statewide winner was identical to the national election winner, followed by the number of times the state failed to match the national trend. The matching percentage is in parentheses.

Current party streak (through 2020): The present string of presidential elections (dating backward from 2020) in which a specific party has carried the state. The party abbreviation is followed by the number of elections in the current streak.

Current match streak (through 2020): The present string of elections (dating back from 2020) in which the state has been carried by the winner of the national election, regardless of party.

2020 party indexes: The relative levels of support for the Democratic and Republican nominees in 2020. Baselines are set at 100 points. An index greater than 100 indicates that a candidate did better in the state than in the nation as a whole, while a figure below 100 signifies a substandard performance in the state. Each index is calculated by dividing a candidate's statewide two-party percentage of popular votes by his national two-party percentage, and then multiplying the quotient by 100.

2020 overall results: The percentages of all popular votes within the state that were received by Donald Trump, Joseph Biden, and all other candidates in 2020.

2020 two-party results: The percentages of the state's major-party votes in 2020 received by Trump and Biden. Overall results and two-party results are calculated with different denominators. Overall percentages are based on the votes for all candidates, but two-party percentages are confined to the votes cast for the Republican and Democratic nominees.

Home-state general-election winners: The times when presidential candidates with voting addresses in the state won general elections.

Home-state major-party nominees: The occasions when candidates from the state won major-party nominations.

Home-state qualified candidates: The times when candidates from the state met qualification standards. Campaigns undertaken in different years by the same candidate are counted separately.

Two-Party Results (2008-2020)

This graph depicts statewide splits for Republican and Democratic nominees over the past four presidential elections. Each black bar represents the Republican share of a year's major-party votes, while each gray bar shows the Democratic share. Two-party percentages (as noted above) are based solely on popular votes cast for the major-party nominees. Shares sometimes add to 99.99 or 100.01 percent because of rounding.

Overall Results (1900-2020)

Year: This table covers the span since 1900. If a state did not tabulate popular votes in a given election, it is not listed.

Winner: The candidate who received the most popular votes in the state, with his party in parentheses.

PV%: The popular-vote percentage for the winner. This is an overall percentage, based on the statewide total of votes for all candidates in a given year. (The percentages in this table consequently differ from the two-party figures in the graph above.)

Second: The candidate who received the second-largest number of popular votes in the state.

PV%: The popular-vote percentage for the second-place finisher.

Home-State Candidates

Won: The candidates who maintained voting addresses within the state when they won presidential elections. Winners are listed alphabetically, and the year of each victory is shown in parentheses. (The latter two rules also apply to the next two categories.)

Nominated: The candidates from the state who won major-party nominations.

Qualified: The candidates from the state who met qualification standards.

Additional data for each state can be found in Chapter 2, including the popular votes cast for each candidate in any given election, as well as the distribution of the state's electoral votes.

Alabama

Basics — Alabama

State party winners — D 28, R 15, DR 3, AI 1, ID 1, SD 1, SRD 1
General-election matches — 25-25 (50.00%)
Current party streak (through 2020) — R 11
Current match streak (through 2020) — 0
2020 party indexes — R 131.81, D 70.96
2020 overall results — Trump 62.03%, Biden 36.57%, other 1.40%
2020 two-party results — Trump 62.91%, Biden 37.09%
Home-state general-election winners — 0
Home-state major-party nominees — 0
Home-state qualified candidates — 7

Two-Party Results (2008-2020) — Alabama

2008: John McCain (60.89%)   **Barack Obama (39.11%)**

2012: Mitt Romney (61.22%)   **Barack Obama (38.78%)**

2016: Donald Trump (64.37%)   **Hillary Clinton (35.63%)**

2020: Donald Trump (62.91%)   **Joseph Biden (37.09%)**

Overall Results (1900-2020) — Alabama

Year	Winner	PV%	Second	PV%
1900	William Jennings Bryan (D)	60.05%	William McKinley (R)	34.67%
1904	Alton Parker (D)	73.35%	Theodore Roosevelt (R)	20.66%
1908	William Jennings Bryan (D)	70.75%	William Howard Taft (R)	24.31%
1912	Woodrow Wilson (D)	69.89%	Theodore Roosevelt (P)	19.23%
1916	Woodrow Wilson (D)	75.80%	Charles Evans Hughes (R)	21.97%
1920	James Cox (D)	66.71%	Warren Harding (R)	31.94%
1924	John Davis (D)	67.81%	Calvin Coolidge (R)	27.02%
1928	Alfred Smith (D)	51.33%	Herbert Hoover (R)	48.49%
1932	Franklin Roosevelt (D)	84.76%	Herbert Hoover (R)	14.14%
1936	Franklin Roosevelt (D)	86.38%	Alfred Landon (R)	12.82%
1940	Franklin Roosevelt (D)	85.22%	Wendell Willkie (R)	14.34%
1944	Franklin Roosevelt (D)	81.28%	Thomas Dewey (R)	18.20%
1948	Strom Thurmond (SRD)	79.75%	Thomas Dewey (R)	19.04%
1952	Adlai Stevenson (D)	64.55%	Dwight Eisenhower (R)	35.02%
1956	Adlai Stevenson (D)	56.52%	Dwight Eisenhower (R)	39.39%
1960	John Kennedy (D)	56.83%	Richard Nixon (R)	41.74%
1964	Barry Goldwater (R)	69.45%	Unpledged slate (D)	30.55%

Year	Winner	PV%	Second	PV%
1968	George Wallace (AI)	65.86%	Hubert Humphrey (D)	18.72%
1972	Richard Nixon (R)	72.43%	George McGovern (D)	25.54%
1976	Jimmy Carter (D)	55.73%	Gerald Ford (R)	42.62%
1980	Ronald Reagan (R)	48.75%	Jimmy Carter (D)	47.45%
1984	Ronald Reagan (R)	60.54%	Walter Mondale (D)	38.28%
1988	George H.W. Bush (R)	59.17%	Michael Dukakis (D)	39.86%
1992	George H.W. Bush (R)	47.65%	Bill Clinton (D)	40.88%
1996	Bob Dole (R)	50.12%	Bill Clinton (D)	43.16%
2000	George W. Bush (R)	56.48%	Al Gore (D)	41.57%
2004	George W. Bush (R)	62.46%	John Kerry (D)	36.84%
2008	John McCain (R)	60.32%	Barack Obama (D)	38.74%
2012	Mitt Romney (R)	60.55%	Barack Obama (D)	38.36%
2016	Donald Trump (R)	62.08%	Hillary Clinton (D)	34.36%
2020	Donald Trump (R)	62.03%	Joseph Biden (D)	36.57%

Home-State Candidates — Alabama

Qualified — Walter Jones (1956), Oscar Underwood (1912, 1924), George Wallace (1964, 1968, 1972, 1976)

Alaska

Basics — Alaska

State party winners — R 15, D 1
General-election matches — 9-7 (56.25%)
Current party streak (through 2020) — R 14
Current match streak (through 2020) — 0
2020 party indexes — R 115.78, D 85.59
2020 overall results — Trump 52.83%, Biden 42.77%, other 4.40%
2020 two-party results — Trump 55.26%, Biden 44.74%
Home-state general-election winners — 0
Home-state major-party nominees — 0
Home-state qualified candidates — 0

Two-Party Results (2008-2020) — Alaska

2008: John McCain (61.07%)　　　　　　**Barack Obama (38.94%)**

2012: Mitt Romney (57.32%)　　　　　　**Barack Obama (42.69%)**

2016: Donald Trump (58.39%)　　　　　　**Hillary Clinton (41.61%)**

2020: Donald Trump (55.26%)　　　　　　**Joseph Biden (44.74%)**

Overall Results (1900-2020) — Alaska

Year	Winner	PV%	Second	PV%
1960	Richard Nixon (R)	50.94%	John Kennedy (D)	49.06%
1964	Lyndon Johnson (D)	65.91%	Barry Goldwater (R)	34.09%
1968	Richard Nixon (R)	45.28%	Hubert Humphrey (D)	42.65%
1972	Richard Nixon (R)	58.13%	George McGovern (D)	34.62%
1976	Gerald Ford (R)	57.91%	Jimmy Carter (D)	35.65%
1980	Ronald Reagan (R)	54.35%	Jimmy Carter (D)	26.41%
1984	Ronald Reagan (R)	66.65%	Walter Mondale (D)	29.87%
1988	George H.W. Bush (R)	59.59%	Michael Dukakis (D)	36.27%
1992	George H.W. Bush (R)	39.46%	Bill Clinton (D)	30.29%
1996	Bob Dole (R)	50.80%	Bill Clinton (D)	33.27%
2000	George W. Bush (R)	58.62%	Al Gore (D)	27.67%
2004	George W. Bush (R)	61.07%	John Kerry (D)	35.52%
2008	John McCain (R)	59.43%	Barack Obama (D)	37.89%
2012	Mitt Romney (R)	54.80%	Barack Obama (D)	40.81%
2016	Donald Trump (R)	51.28%	Hillary Clinton (D)	36.55%
2020	Donald Trump (R)	52.83%	Joseph Biden (D)	42.77%

<u>Home-State Candidates — Alaska</u>

(none)

Arizona

Basics — Arizona

State party winners — R 19, D 9
General-election matches — 22-6 (78.57%)
Current party streak (through 2020) — D 1
Current match streak (through 2020) — 2
2020 party indexes — R 104.43, D 95.96
2020 overall results — Biden 49.37%, Trump 49.06%, other 1.58%
2020 two-party results — Biden 50.16%, Trump 49.84%
Home-state general-election winners — 0
Home-state major-party nominees — 2
Home-state qualified candidates — 5

Two-Party Results (2008-2020) — Arizona

2008: John McCain (54.31%)   **Barack Obama (45.69%)**

2012: Mitt Romney (54.61%)   **Barack Obama (45.39%)**

2016: Donald Trump (51.89%)   **Hillary Clinton (48.11%)**

2020: Donald Trump (49.84%)   **Joseph Biden (50.16%)**

Overall Results (1900-2020) — Arizona

Year	Winner	PV%	Second	PV%
1912	Woodrow Wilson (D)	43.59%	Theodore Roosevelt (P)	29.34%
1916	Woodrow Wilson (D)	57.17%	Charles Evans Hughes (R)	35.37%
1920	Warren Harding (R)	55.41%	James Cox (D)	44.23%
1924	Calvin Coolidge (R)	41.26%	John Davis (D)	35.47%
1928	Herbert Hoover (R)	57.57%	Alfred Smith (D)	42.23%
1932	Franklin Roosevelt (D)	67.03%	Herbert Hoover (R)	30.53%
1936	Franklin Roosevelt (D)	69.85%	Alfred Landon (R)	26.93%
1940	Franklin Roosevelt (D)	63.50%	Wendell Willkie (R)	36.01%
1944	Franklin Roosevelt (D)	58.80%	Thomas Dewey (R)	40.90%
1948	Harry Truman (D)	53.79%	Thomas Dewey (R)	43.82%
1952	Dwight Eisenhower (R)	58.35%	Adlai Stevenson (D)	41.65%
1956	Dwight Eisenhower (R)	61.00%	Adlai Stevenson (D)	38.90%
1960	Richard Nixon (R)	55.52%	John Kennedy (D)	44.36%
1964	Barry Goldwater (R)	50.45%	Lyndon Johnson (D)	49.45%
1968	Richard Nixon (R)	54.78%	Hubert Humphrey (D)	35.02%
1972	Richard Nixon (R)	64.67%	George McGovern (D)	31.87%
1976	Gerald Ford (R)	56.37%	Jimmy Carter (D)	39.80%

Year	Winner	PV%	Second	PV%
1980	Ronald Reagan (R)	60.61%	Jimmy Carter (D)	28.25%
1984	Ronald Reagan (R)	66.42%	Walter Mondale (D)	32.54%
1988	George H.W. Bush (R)	59.95%	Michael Dukakis (D)	38.74%
1992	George H.W. Bush (R)	38.47%	Bill Clinton (D)	36.52%
1996	Bill Clinton (D)	46.52%	Bob Dole (R)	44.29%
2000	George W. Bush (R)	51.02%	Al Gore (D)	44.74%
2004	George W. Bush (R)	54.87%	John Kerry (D)	44.40%
2008	John McCain (R)	53.64%	Barack Obama (D)	45.12%
2012	Mitt Romney (R)	53.66%	Barack Obama (D)	44.59%
2016	Donald Trump (R)	48.67%	Hillary Clinton (D)	45.13%
2020	Joseph Biden (D)	49.37%	Donald Trump (R)	49.06%

Home-State Candidates — Arizona

Nominated — Barry Goldwater (1964), John McCain (2008)

Qualified — Bruce Babbitt (1988), Barry Goldwater (1964), John McCain (2000, 2008), Morris Udall (1976)

Arkansas

Basics — Arkansas

State party winners — D 32, R 11, AI 1, SD 1
General-election matches — 26-19 (57.78%)
Current party streak (through 2020) — R 6
Current match streak (through 2020) — 0
2020 party indexes — R 134.53, D 68.47
2020 overall results — Trump 62.40%, Biden 34.78%, other 2.83%
2020 two-party results — Trump 64.21%, Biden 35.79%
Home-state general-election winners — 2
Home-state major-party nominees — 2
Home-state qualified candidates — 5

Two-Party Results (2008-2020) — Arkansas

2008: John McCain (60.17%) | **Barack Obama (39.83%)**

2012: Mitt Romney (62.15%) | **Barack Obama (37.85%)**

2016: Donald Trump (64.29%) | **Hillary Clinton (35.72%)**

2020: Donald Trump (64.21%) | **Joseph Biden (35.79%)**

Overall Results (1900-2020) — Arkansas

Year	Winner	PV%	Second	PV%
1900	William Jennings Bryan (D)	63.49%	William McKinley (R)	35.01%
1904	Alton Parker (D)	55.39%	Theodore Roosevelt (R)	40.20%
1908	William Jennings Bryan (D)	57.31%	William Howard Taft (R)	37.33%
1912	Woodrow Wilson (D)	55.01%	William Howard Taft (R)	20.45%
1916	Woodrow Wilson (D)	66.64%	Charles Evans Hughes (R)	28.01%
1920	James Cox (D)	58.49%	Warren Harding (R)	38.73%
1924	John Davis (D)	61.20%	Calvin Coolidge (R)	29.29%
1928	Alfred Smith (D)	60.28%	Herbert Hoover (R)	39.34%
1932	Franklin Roosevelt (D)	86.27%	Herbert Hoover (R)	12.68%
1936	Franklin Roosevelt (D)	81.80%	Alfred Landon (R)	17.86%
1940	Franklin Roosevelt (D)	78.44%	Wendell Willkie (R)	21.02%
1944	Franklin Roosevelt (D)	69.95%	Thomas Dewey (R)	29.84%
1948	Harry Truman (D)	61.72%	Thomas Dewey (R)	21.02%
1952	Adlai Stevenson (D)	55.90%	Dwight Eisenhower (R)	43.76%
1956	Adlai Stevenson (D)	52.46%	Dwight Eisenhower (R)	45.82%
1960	John Kennedy (D)	50.19%	Richard Nixon (R)	43.06%
1964	Lyndon Johnson (D)	56.06%	Barry Goldwater (R)	43.41%

Year	Winner	PV%	Second	PV%
1968	George Wallace (AI)	38.87%	Richard Nixon (R)	30.77%
1972	Richard Nixon (R)	68.87%	George McGovern (D)	30.69%
1976	Jimmy Carter (D)	64.96%	Gerald Ford (R)	34.90%
1980	Ronald Reagan (R)	48.13%	Jimmy Carter (D)	47.52%
1984	Ronald Reagan (R)	60.47%	Walter Mondale (D)	38.29%
1988	George H.W. Bush (R)	56.37%	Michael Dukakis (D)	42.19%
1992	Bill Clinton (D)	53.21%	George H.W. Bush (R)	35.48%
1996	Bill Clinton (D)	53.74%	Bob Dole (R)	36.80%
2000	George W. Bush (R)	51.31%	Al Gore (D)	45.86%
2004	George W. Bush (R)	54.31%	John Kerry (D)	44.55%
2008	John McCain (R)	58.72%	Barack Obama (D)	38.87%
2012	Mitt Romney (R)	60.57%	Barack Obama (D)	36.88%
2016	Donald Trump (R)	60.57%	Hillary Clinton (D)	33.65%
2020	Donald Trump (R)	62.40%	Joseph Biden (D)	34.78%

Home-State Candidates — Arkansas

Won — Bill Clinton (1992, 1996)

Nominated — Bill Clinton (1992, 1996)

Qualified — Wesley Clark (2004), Bill Clinton (1992, 1996), Mike Huckabee (2008), Wilbur Mills (1972)

California

Basics — California

State party winners — R 23, D 19, P 1
General-election matches — 35-8 (81.40%)
Current party streak (through 2020) — D 8
Current match streak (through 2020) — 1
2020 party indexes — D 124.18, R 73.52
2020 overall results — Biden 63.48%, Trump 34.32%, other 2.20%
2020 two-party results — Biden 64.91%, Trump 35.09%
Home-state general-election winners — 4
Home-state major-party nominees — 7
Home-state qualified candidates — 24

Two-Party Results (2008-2020) — California

2008: John McCain (37.72%)   **Barack Obama (62.28%)**

2012: Mitt Romney (38.13%)   **Barack Obama (61.87%)**

2016: Donald Trump (33.87%)   **Hillary Clinton (66.13%)**

2020: Donald Trump (35.09%)   **Joseph Biden (64.91%)**

Overall Results (1900-2020) — California

Year	Winner	PV%	Second	PV%
1900	William McKinley (R)	54.48%	William Jennings Bryan (D)	41.33%
1904	Theodore Roosevelt (R)	61.86%	Alton Parker (D)	26.92%
1908	William Howard Taft (R)	55.45%	William Jennings Bryan (D)	32.98%
1912	Theodore Roosevelt (P)	41.84%	Woodrow Wilson (D)	41.81%
1916	Woodrow Wilson (D)	46.63%	Charles Evans Hughes (R)	46.29%
1920	Warren Harding (R)	66.24%	James Cox (D)	24.29%
1924	Calvin Coolidge (R)	57.21%	Robert La Follette (P)	33.13%
1928	Herbert Hoover (R)	64.69%	Alfred Smith (D)	34.20%
1932	Franklin Roosevelt (D)	58.41%	Herbert Hoover (R)	37.40%
1936	Franklin Roosevelt (D)	66.95%	Alfred Landon (R)	31.70%
1940	Franklin Roosevelt (D)	57.44%	Wendell Willkie (R)	41.34%
1944	Franklin Roosevelt (D)	56.48%	Thomas Dewey (R)	42.97%
1948	Harry Truman (D)	47.57%	Thomas Dewey (R)	47.13%
1952	Dwight Eisenhower (R)	56.35%	Adlai Stevenson (D)	42.74%
1956	Dwight Eisenhower (R)	55.39%	Adlai Stevenson (D)	44.27%
1960	Richard Nixon (R)	50.10%	John Kennedy (D)	49.55%
1964	Lyndon Johnson (D)	59.11%	Barry Goldwater (R)	40.80%

Year	Winner	PV%	Second	PV%
1968	Richard Nixon (R)	47.82%	Hubert Humphrey (D)	44.74%
1972	Richard Nixon (R)	55.00%	George McGovern (D)	41.54%
1976	Gerald Ford (R)	49.35%	Jimmy Carter (D)	47.57%
1980	Ronald Reagan (R)	52.69%	Jimmy Carter (D)	35.91%
1984	Ronald Reagan (R)	57.52%	Walter Mondale (D)	41.27%
1988	George H.W. Bush (R)	51.13%	Michael Dukakis (D)	47.56%
1992	Bill Clinton (D)	46.01%	George H.W. Bush (R)	32.62%
1996	Bill Clinton (D)	51.10%	Bob Dole (R)	38.21%
2000	Al Gore (D)	53.45%	George W. Bush (R)	41.65%
2004	John Kerry (D)	54.30%	George W. Bush (R)	44.36%
2008	Barack Obama (D)	61.01%	John McCain (R)	36.96%
2012	Barack Obama (D)	60.24%	Mitt Romney (R)	37.12%
2016	Hillary Clinton (D)	61.73%	Donald Trump (R)	31.62%
2020	Joseph Biden (D)	63.48%	Donald Trump (R)	34.32%

Home-State Candidates — California

Won — Herbert Hoover (1928), Richard Nixon (1972), Ronald Reagan (1980, 1984)

Nominated — John Fremont (1856), Herbert Hoover (1928, 1932), Richard Nixon (1960, 1972), Ronald Reagan (1980, 1984)

Qualified — John Bidwell (1892), Jerry Brown (1976, 1980, 1992), Alan Cranston (1984), Stephen Field (1880), John Fremont (1856), Herbert Hoover (1920, 1928, 1932), John Hospers (1972), Hiram Johnson (1920, 1924), William Gibbs McAdoo (1924), Paul McCloskey (1972), Richard Nixon (1960, 1972), Ronald Reagan (1968, 1976, 1980, 1984), Earl Warren (1948, 1952), Sam Yorty (1972)

Colorado

Basics — Colorado
State party winners — R 22, D 14, POP 1
General-election matches — 26-11 (70.27%)
Current party streak (through 2020) — D 4
Current match streak (through 2020) — 1
2020 party indexes — D 108.93, R 90.22
2020 overall results — Biden 55.40%, Trump 41.90%, other 2.70%
2020 two-party results — Biden 56.94%, Trump 43.06%
Home-state general-election winners — 0
Home-state major-party nominees — 0
Home-state qualified candidates — 2

Two-Party Results (2008-2020) — Colorado
2008: John McCain (45.45%)   **Barack Obama (54.55%)**

2012: Mitt Romney (47.25%)   **Barack Obama (52.75%)**

2016: Donald Trump (47.32%)   **Hillary Clinton (52.68%)**

2020: Donald Trump (43.06%)   **Joseph Biden (56.94%)**

Overall Results (1900-2020) — Colorado

Year	Winner	PV%	Second	PV%
1900	William Jennings Bryan (D)	55.55%	William McKinley (R)	41.97%
1904	Theodore Roosevelt (R)	55.26%	Alton Parker (D)	41.08%
1908	William Jennings Bryan (D)	48.00%	William Howard Taft (R)	46.88%
1912	Woodrow Wilson (D)	42.83%	Theodore Roosevelt (P)	26.98%
1916	Woodrow Wilson (D)	60.74%	Charles Evans Hughes (R)	34.75%
1920	Warren Harding (R)	59.32%	James Cox (D)	35.93%
1924	Calvin Coolidge (R)	57.02%	John Davis (D)	21.98%
1928	Herbert Hoover (R)	64.72%	Alfred Smith (D)	33.94%
1932	Franklin Roosevelt (D)	54.81%	Herbert Hoover (R)	41.43%
1936	Franklin Roosevelt (D)	60.37%	Alfred Landon (R)	37.09%
1940	Wendell Willkie (R)	50.92%	Franklin Roosevelt (D)	48.37%
1944	Thomas Dewey (R)	53.21%	Franklin Roosevelt (D)	46.40%
1948	Harry Truman (D)	51.88%	Thomas Dewey (R)	46.53%
1952	Dwight Eisenhower (R)	60.27%	Adlai Stevenson (D)	38.96%
1956	Dwight Eisenhower (R)	60.04%	Adlai Stevenson (D)	39.27%
1960	Richard Nixon (R)	54.64%	John Kennedy (D)	44.91%
1964	Lyndon Johnson (D)	61.27%	Barry Goldwater (R)	38.20%

Year	Winner	PV%	Second	PV%
1968	Richard Nixon (R)	50.46%	Hubert Humphrey (D)	41.32%
1972	Richard Nixon (R)	62.61%	George McGovern (D)	34.59%
1976	Gerald Ford (R)	54.03%	Jimmy Carter (D)	42.56%
1980	Ronald Reagan (R)	55.07%	Jimmy Carter (D)	31.07%
1984	Ronald Reagan (R)	63.44%	Walter Mondale (D)	35.12%
1988	George H.W. Bush (R)	53.06%	Michael Dukakis (D)	45.28%
1992	Bill Clinton (D)	40.13%	George H.W. Bush (R)	35.87%
1996	Bob Dole (R)	45.80%	Bill Clinton (D)	44.43%
2000	George W. Bush (R)	50.75%	Al Gore (D)	42.39%
2004	George W. Bush (R)	51.69%	John Kerry (D)	47.02%
2008	Barack Obama (D)	53.66%	John McCain (R)	44.71%
2012	Barack Obama (D)	51.49%	Mitt Romney (R)	46.13%
2016	Hillary Clinton (D)	48.16%	Donald Trump (R)	43.25%
2020	Joseph Biden (D)	55.40%	Donald Trump (R)	41.90%

Home-State Candidates — Colorado

Qualified — Gary Hart (1984, 1988)

Connecticut

Basics — Connecticut

State party winners — R 23, D 21, F 8, W 3, DR 2, NR 2
General-election matches — 40-19 (67.80%)
Current party streak (through 2020) — D 8
Current match streak (through 2020) — 1
2020 party indexes — D 115.16, R 83.40
2020 overall results — Biden 59.26%, Trump 39.19%, other 1.55%
2020 two-party results — Biden 60.20%, Trump 39.81%
Home-state general-election winners — 0
Home-state major-party nominees — 0
Home-state qualified candidates — 6

Two-Party Results (2008-2020) — Connecticut

2008: John McCain (38.68%)   **Barack Obama (61.32%)**

2012: Mitt Romney (41.23%)   **Barack Obama (58.77%)**

2016: Donald Trump (42.86%)   **Hillary Clinton (57.14%)**

2020: Donald Trump (39.81%)   **Joseph Biden (60.20%)**

Overall Results (1900-2020) — Connecticut

Year	Winner	PV%	Second	PV%
1900	William McKinley (R)	56.92%	William Jennings Bryan (D)	41.07%
1904	Theodore Roosevelt (R)	58.12%	Alton Parker (D)	38.15%
1908	William Howard Taft (R)	59.41%	William Jennings Bryan (D)	35.94%
1912	Woodrow Wilson (D)	39.16%	William Howard Taft (R)	35.88%
1916	Charles Evans Hughes (R)	49.80%	Woodrow Wilson (D)	46.66%
1920	Warren Harding (R)	62.72%	James Cox (D)	33.03%
1924	Calvin Coolidge (R)	61.52%	John Davis (D)	27.52%
1928	Herbert Hoover (R)	53.63%	Alfred Smith (D)	45.58%
1932	Herbert Hoover (R)	48.54%	Franklin Roosevelt (D)	47.40%
1936	Franklin Roosevelt (D)	55.32%	Alfred Landon (R)	40.35%
1940	Franklin Roosevelt (D)	53.44%	Wendell Willkie (R)	46.30%
1944	Franklin Roosevelt (D)	52.30%	Thomas Dewey (R)	46.94%
1948	Thomas Dewey (R)	49.55%	Harry Truman (D)	47.91%
1952	Dwight Eisenhower (R)	55.70%	Adlai Stevenson (D)	43.91%
1956	Dwight Eisenhower (R)	63.72%	Adlai Stevenson (D)	36.26%
1960	John Kennedy (D)	53.73%	Richard Nixon (R)	46.27%
1964	Lyndon Johnson (D)	67.81%	Barry Goldwater (R)	32.09%

Year	Winner	PV%	Second	PV%
1968	Hubert Humphrey (D)	49.48%	Richard Nixon (R)	44.32%
1972	Richard Nixon (R)	58.57%	George McGovern (D)	40.13%
1976	Gerald Ford (R)	52.06%	Jimmy Carter (D)	46.90%
1980	Ronald Reagan (R)	48.16%	Jimmy Carter (D)	38.52%
1984	Ronald Reagan (R)	60.73%	Walter Mondale (D)	38.83%
1988	George H.W. Bush (R)	51.98%	Michael Dukakis (D)	46.88%
1992	Bill Clinton (D)	42.21%	George H.W. Bush (R)	35.78%
1996	Bill Clinton (D)	52.83%	Bob Dole (R)	34.69%
2000	Al Gore (D)	55.91%	George W. Bush (R)	38.44%
2004	John Kerry (D)	54.31%	George W. Bush (R)	43.95%
2008	Barack Obama (D)	60.59%	John McCain (R)	38.22%
2012	Barack Obama (D)	58.06%	Mitt Romney (R)	40.73%
2016	Hillary Clinton (D)	54.57%	Donald Trump (R)	40.93%
2020	Joseph Biden (D)	59.26%	Donald Trump (R)	39.19%

Home-State Candidates — Connecticut

Qualified — Oliver Ellsworth (1796), James English (1868), Samuel Huntington (1789), Joseph Lieberman (2004), Ralph Nader (2000), Thomas Seymour (1864)

Delaware

Basics — Delaware

State party winners — D 24, R 18, F 8, W 4, DR 2, NR 2, SD 1
General-election matches — 37-22 (62.71%)
Current party streak (through 2020) — D 8
Current match streak (through 2020) — 1
2020 party indexes — D 114.07, R 84.59
2020 overall results — Biden 58.74%, Trump 39.78%, other 1.48%
2020 two-party results — Biden 59.63%, Trump 40.37%
Home-state general-election winners — 1
Home-state major-party nominees — 1
Home-state qualified candidates — 6

Two-Party Results (2008-2020) — Delaware

2008: John McCain (37.36%)   **Barack Obama (62.64%)**

2012: Mitt Romney (40.55%)   **Barack Obama (59.45%)**

2016: Donald Trump (44.00%)   **Hillary Clinton (56.00%)**

2020: Donald Trump (40.37%)   **Joseph Biden (59.63%)**

Overall Results (1900-2020) — Delaware

Year	Winner	PV%	Second	PV%
1900	William McKinley (R)	53.67%	William Jennings Bryan (D)	44.90%
1904	Theodore Roosevelt (R)	54.05%	Alton Parker (D)	44.12%
1908	William Howard Taft (R)	52.11%	William Jennings Bryan (D)	45.94%
1912	Woodrow Wilson (D)	46.48%	William Howard Taft (R)	32.86%
1916	Charles Evans Hughes (R)	50.21%	Woodrow Wilson (D)	47.78%
1920	Warren Harding (R)	55.71%	James Cox (D)	42.07%
1924	Calvin Coolidge (R)	57.70%	John Davis (D)	36.80%
1928	Herbert Hoover (R)	65.83%	Alfred Smith (D)	33.80%
1932	Herbert Hoover (R)	50.55%	Franklin Roosevelt (D)	48.11%
1936	Franklin Roosevelt (D)	54.62%	Alfred Landon (R)	42.33%
1940	Franklin Roosevelt (D)	54.70%	Wendell Willkie (R)	45.05%
1944	Franklin Roosevelt (D)	54.38%	Thomas Dewey (R)	45.27%
1948	Thomas Dewey (R)	50.04%	Harry Truman (D)	48.76%
1952	Dwight Eisenhower (R)	51.75%	Adlai Stevenson (D)	47.88%
1956	Dwight Eisenhower (R)	55.09%	Adlai Stevenson (D)	44.62%
1960	John Kennedy (D)	50.64%	Richard Nixon (R)	49.00%
1964	Lyndon Johnson (D)	60.95%	Barry Goldwater (R)	38.78%

Year	Winner	PV%	Second	PV%
1968	Richard Nixon (R)	45.12%	Hubert Humphrey (D)	41.61%
1972	Richard Nixon (R)	59.60%	George McGovern (D)	39.18%
1976	Jimmy Carter (D)	51.98%	Gerald Ford (R)	46.57%
1980	Ronald Reagan (R)	47.16%	Jimmy Carter (D)	44.83%
1984	Ronald Reagan (R)	59.78%	Walter Mondale (D)	39.93%
1988	George H.W. Bush (R)	55.88%	Michael Dukakis (D)	43.48%
1992	Bill Clinton (D)	43.51%	George H.W. Bush (R)	35.31%
1996	Bill Clinton (D)	51.82%	Bob Dole (R)	36.58%
2000	Al Gore (D)	54.96%	George W. Bush (R)	41.90%
2004	John Kerry (D)	53.35%	George W. Bush (R)	45.75%
2008	Barack Obama (D)	61.94%	John McCain (R)	36.95%
2012	Barack Obama (D)	58.61%	Mitt Romney (R)	39.98%
2016	Hillary Clinton (D)	53.09%	Donald Trump (R)	41.71%
2020	Joseph Biden (D)	58.74%	Donald Trump (R)	39.78%

Home-State Candidates — Delaware

Won — Joseph Biden (2020)

Nominated — Joseph Biden (2020)

Qualified — Thomas Bayard (1876, 1880, 1884), Joseph Biden (2020), Pete du Pont (1988), George Gray (1908)

District of Columbia

Basics — District of Columbia

State party winners — D 15
General-election matches — 7-8 (46.67%)
Current party streak (through 2020) — D 15
Current match streak (through 2020) — 1
2020 party indexes — D 180.73, R 11.59
2020 overall results — Biden 92.15%, Trump 5.40%, other 2.45%
2020 two-party results — Biden 94.47%, Trump 5.53%
Home-state general-election winners — 0
Home-state major-party nominees — 0
Home-state qualified candidates — 0

Two-Party Results (2008-2020) — District of Columbia

2008: John McCain (6.60%)   **Barack Obama (93.40%)**

2012: Mitt Romney (7.41%)   **Barack Obama (92.59%)**

2016: Donald Trump (4.31%)   **Hillary Clinton (95.70%)**

2020: Donald Trump (5.53%)   **Joseph Biden (94.47%)**

Overall Results (1900-2020) — District of Columbia

Year	Winner	PV%	Second	PV%
1964	Lyndon Johnson (D)	85.50%	Barry Goldwater (R)	14.50%
1968	Hubert Humphrey (D)	81.82%	Richard Nixon (R)	18.18%
1972	George McGovern (D)	78.10%	Richard Nixon (R)	21.56%
1976	Jimmy Carter (D)	81.63%	Gerald Ford (R)	16.51%
1980	Jimmy Carter (D)	74.82%	Ronald Reagan (R)	13.44%
1984	Walter Mondale (D)	85.39%	Ronald Reagan (R)	13.73%
1988	Michael Dukakis (D)	82.65%	George H.W. Bush (R)	14.30%
1992	Bill Clinton (D)	84.64%	George H.W. Bush (R)	9.10%
1996	Bill Clinton (D)	85.19%	Bob Dole (R)	9.34%
2000	Al Gore (D)	85.16%	George W. Bush (R)	8.95%
2004	John Kerry (D)	89.18%	George W. Bush (R)	9.34%
2008	Barack Obama (D)	92.46%	John McCain (R)	6.53%
2012	Barack Obama (D)	90.91%	Mitt Romney (R)	7.28%
2016	Hillary Clinton (D)	90.86%	Donald Trump (R)	4.09%
2020	Joseph Biden (D)	92.15%	Donald Trump (R)	5.40%

Home-State Candidates — District of Columbia

(none)

Florida

Basics — Florida

State party winners — D 24, R 17, SD 1, W 1
General-election matches — 31-12 (72.09%)
Current party streak (through 2020) — R 2
Current match streak (through 2020) — 0
2020 party indexes — R 108.31, D 92.41
2020 overall results — Trump 51.22%, Biden 47.86%, other 0.92%
2020 two-party results — Trump 51.70%, Biden 48.31%
Home-state general-election winners — 0
Home-state major-party nominees — 1
Home-state qualified candidates — 4

Two-Party Results (2008-2020) — Florida

2008: John McCain (48.58%)   **Barack Obama (51.42%)**

2012: Mitt Romney (49.56%)   **Barack Obama (50.44%)**

2016: Donald Trump (50.62%)   **Hillary Clinton (49.38%)**

2020: Donald Trump (51.70%)   **Joseph Biden (48.31%)**

Overall Results (1900-2020) — Florida

Year	Winner	PV%	Second	PV%
1900	William Jennings Bryan (D)	71.08%	William McKinley (R)	18.76%
1904	Alton Parker (D)	68.82%	Theodore Roosevelt (R)	21.15%
1908	William Jennings Bryan (D)	63.02%	William Howard Taft (R)	21.58%
1912	Woodrow Wilson (D)	70.15%	Eugene Debs (SOC)	9.26%
1916	Woodrow Wilson (D)	69.34%	Charles Evans Hughes (R)	18.10%
1920	James Cox (D)	62.13%	Warren Harding (R)	30.79%
1924	John Davis (D)	56.87%	Calvin Coolidge (R)	28.06%
1928	Herbert Hoover (R)	56.83%	Alfred Smith (D)	40.12%
1932	Franklin Roosevelt (D)	74.49%	Herbert Hoover (R)	24.98%
1936	Franklin Roosevelt (D)	76.08%	Alfred Landon (R)	23.90%
1940	Franklin Roosevelt (D)	73.99%	Wendell Willkie (R)	25.98%
1944	Franklin Roosevelt (D)	70.29%	Thomas Dewey (R)	29.66%
1948	Harry Truman (D)	48.82%	Thomas Dewey (R)	33.63%
1952	Dwight Eisenhower (R)	54.99%	Adlai Stevenson (D)	44.98%
1956	Dwight Eisenhower (R)	57.19%	Adlai Stevenson (D)	42.67%
1960	Richard Nixon (R)	51.52%	John Kennedy (D)	48.49%
1964	Lyndon Johnson (D)	51.15%	Barry Goldwater (R)	48.85%

Year	Winner	PV%	Second	PV%
1968	Richard Nixon (R)	40.53%	Hubert Humphrey (D)	30.94%
1972	Richard Nixon (R)	71.92%	George McGovern (D)	27.80%
1976	Jimmy Carter (D)	51.93%	Gerald Ford (R)	46.64%
1980	Ronald Reagan (R)	55.52%	Jimmy Carter (D)	38.50%
1984	Ronald Reagan (R)	65.32%	Walter Mondale (D)	34.66%
1988	George H.W. Bush (R)	60.87%	Michael Dukakis (D)	38.51%
1992	George H.W. Bush (R)	40.90%	Bill Clinton (D)	39.00%
1996	Bill Clinton (D)	48.02%	Bob Dole (R)	42.32%
2000	George W. Bush (R)	48.85%	Al Gore (D)	48.84%
2004	George W. Bush (R)	52.10%	John Kerry (D)	47.09%
2008	Barack Obama (D)	51.03%	John McCain (R)	48.22%
2012	Barack Obama (D)	50.01%	Mitt Romney (R)	49.13%
2016	Donald Trump (R)	49.02%	Hillary Clinton (D)	47.82%
2020	Donald Trump (R)	51.22%	Joseph Biden (D)	47.86%

Home-State Candidates — Florida

Nominated — Donald Trump (2020)

Qualified — Jeb Bush (2016), Ben Carson (2016), Marco Rubio (2016), Donald Trump (2020)

Georgia

Basics — Georgia

State party winners — D 32, R 10, DR 9, W 3, AI 1, F 1, SD 1, tie 1
General-election matches — 34-24 (58.62%)
Current party streak (through 2020) — D 1
Current match streak (through 2020) — 2
2020 party indexes — R 104.51, D 95.88
2020 overall results — Biden 49.47%, Trump 49.24%, other 1.29%
2020 two-party results — Biden 50.12%, Trump 49.88%
Home-state general-election winners — 1
Home-state major-party nominees — 2
Home-state qualified candidates — 11

Two-Party Results (2008-2020) — Georgia

2008: John McCain (52.63%)   **Barack Obama (47.37%)**

2012: Mitt Romney (53.96%)   **Barack Obama (46.04%)**

2016: Donald Trump (52.66%)   **Hillary Clinton (47.34%)**

2020: Donald Trump (49.88%)   **Joseph Biden (50.12%)**

Overall Results (1900-2020) — Georgia

Year	Winner	PV%	Second	PV%
1900	William Jennings Bryan (D)	66.86%	William McKinley (R)	28.22%
1904	Alton Parker (D)	63.72%	Theodore Roosevelt (R)	18.33%
1908	William Jennings Bryan (D)	54.53%	William Howard Taft (R)	31.40%
1912	Woodrow Wilson (D)	76.63%	Theodore Roosevelt (P)	18.10%
1916	Woodrow Wilson (D)	79.30%	Unpledged slate (P)	13.02%
1920	James Cox (D)	70.95%	Warren Harding (R)	28.74%
1924	John Davis (D)	73.97%	Calvin Coolidge (R)	18.18%
1928	Alfred Smith (D)	55.96%	Herbert Hoover (R)	43.96%
1932	Franklin Roosevelt (D)	91.60%	Herbert Hoover (R)	7.77%
1936	Franklin Roosevelt (D)	87.10%	Alfred Landon (R)	12.60%
1940	Franklin Roosevelt (D)	84.81%	Wendell Willkie (R)	14.87%
1944	Franklin Roosevelt (D)	81.74%	Thomas Dewey (R)	17.22%
1948	Harry Truman (D)	60.80%	Strom Thurmond (SRD)	20.33%
1952	Adlai Stevenson (D)	69.66%	Dwight Eisenhower (R)	30.34%
1956	Adlai Stevenson (D)	66.41%	Dwight Eisenhower (R)	33.27%
1960	John Kennedy (D)	62.54%	Richard Nixon (R)	37.43%
1964	Barry Goldwater (R)	54.12%	Lyndon Johnson (D)	45.87%

Year	Winner	PV%	Second	PV%
1968	George Wallace (AI)	42.84%	Richard Nixon (R)	30.40%
1972	Richard Nixon (R)	75.04%	George McGovern (D)	24.65%
1976	Jimmy Carter (D)	66.74%	Gerald Ford (R)	32.97%
1980	Jimmy Carter (D)	55.79%	Ronald Reagan (R)	40.97%
1984	Ronald Reagan (R)	60.17%	Walter Mondale (D)	39.79%
1988	George H.W. Bush (R)	59.75%	Michael Dukakis (D)	39.50%
1992	Bill Clinton (D)	43.47%	George H.W. Bush (R)	42.88%
1996	Bob Dole (R)	47.01%	Bill Clinton (D)	45.84%
2000	George W. Bush (R)	54.67%	Al Gore (D)	42.99%
2004	George W. Bush (R)	57.98%	John Kerry (D)	41.38%
2008	John McCain (R)	52.21%	Barack Obama (D)	46.99%
2012	Mitt Romney (R)	53.30%	Barack Obama (D)	45.48%
2016	Donald Trump (R)	50.77%	Hillary Clinton (D)	45.64%
2020	Joseph Biden (D)	49.47%	Donald Trump (R)	49.24%

Home-State Candidates — Georgia

Won — Jimmy Carter (1976)

Nominated — Jimmy Carter (1976, 1980)

Qualified — James Armstrong (1789), Jimmy Carter (1976, 1980), William Crawford (1824), Walter George (1928), Newt Gingrich (2012), Charles Jenkins (1872), John Milton (1789), Richard Russell (1948, 1952), Edward Telfair (1789)

Hawaii

Basics — Hawaii

State party winners — D 14, R 2
General-election matches — 10-6 (62.50%)
Current party streak (through 2020) — D 9
Current match streak (through 2020) — 1
2020 party indexes — D 124.42, R 73.26
2020 overall results — Biden 63.73%, Trump 34.27%, other 2.00%
2020 two-party results — Biden 65.03%, Trump 34.97%
Home-state general-election winners — 0
Home-state major-party nominees — 0
Home-state qualified candidates — 0

Two-Party Results (2008-2020) — Hawaii

2008: John McCain (27.01%)   **Barack Obama (72.99%)**

2012: Mitt Romney (28.30%)   **Barack Obama (71.70%)**

2016: Donald Trump (32.56%)   **Hillary Clinton (67.44%)**

2020: Donald Trump (34.97%)   **Joseph Biden (65.03%)**

Overall Results (1900-2020) — Hawaii

Year	Winner	PV%	Second	PV%
1960	John Kennedy (D)	50.03%	Richard Nixon (R)	49.97%
1964	Lyndon Johnson (D)	78.76%	Barry Goldwater (R)	21.24%
1968	Hubert Humphrey (D)	59.83%	Richard Nixon (R)	38.70%
1972	Richard Nixon (R)	62.48%	George McGovern (D)	37.52%
1976	Jimmy Carter (D)	50.59%	Gerald Ford (R)	48.06%
1980	Jimmy Carter (D)	44.80%	Ronald Reagan (R)	42.90%
1984	Ronald Reagan (R)	55.10%	Walter Mondale (D)	43.82%
1988	Michael Dukakis (D)	54.27%	George H.W. Bush (R)	44.75%
1992	Bill Clinton (D)	48.09%	George H.W. Bush (R)	36.70%
1996	Bill Clinton (D)	56.93%	Bob Dole (R)	31.64%
2000	Al Gore (D)	55.79%	George W. Bush (R)	37.46%
2004	John Kerry (D)	54.01%	George W. Bush (R)	45.27%
2008	Barack Obama (D)	71.85%	John McCain (R)	26.58%
2012	Barack Obama (D)	70.55%	Mitt Romney (R)	27.84%
2016	Hillary Clinton (D)	62.22%	Donald Trump (R)	30.04%
2020	Joseph Biden (D)	63.73%	Donald Trump (R)	34.27%

Home-State Candidates — Hawaii

(none)

Idaho

Basics — Idaho

State party winners — R 22, D 10, POP 1
General-election matches — 23-10 (69.70%)
Current party streak (through 2020) — R 14
Current match streak (through 2020) — 0
2020 party indexes — R 138.02, D 65.28
2020 overall results — Trump 63.84%, Biden 33.07%, other 3.09%
2020 two-party results — Trump 65.88%, Biden 34.12%
Home-state general-election winners — 0
Home-state major-party nominees — 0
Home-state qualified candidates — 2

Two-Party Results (2008-2020) — Idaho

2008: John McCain (63.03%)   **Barack Obama (36.98%)**

2012: Mitt Romney (66.42%)   **Barack Obama (33.58%)**

2016: Donald Trump (68.31%)   **Hillary Clinton (31.69%)**

2020: Donald Trump (65.88%)   **Joseph Biden (34.12%)**

Overall Results (1900-2020) — Idaho

Year	Winner	PV%	Second	PV%
1900	William Jennings Bryan (D)	49.79%	William McKinley (R)	47.92%
1904	Theodore Roosevelt (R)	65.84%	Alton Parker (D)	25.46%
1908	William Howard Taft (R)	54.09%	William Jennings Bryan (D)	37.17%
1912	Woodrow Wilson (D)	32.08%	William Howard Taft (R)	31.03%
1916	Woodrow Wilson (D)	52.04%	Charles Evans Hughes (R)	41.13%
1920	Warren Harding (R)	66.03%	James Cox (D)	33.92%
1924	Calvin Coolidge (R)	47.26%	Robert La Follette (P)	36.53%
1928	Herbert Hoover (R)	64.74%	Alfred Smith (D)	34.41%
1932	Franklin Roosevelt (D)	58.70%	Herbert Hoover (R)	38.23%
1936	Franklin Roosevelt (D)	62.96%	Alfred Landon (R)	33.19%
1940	Franklin Roosevelt (D)	54.36%	Wendell Willkie (R)	45.31%
1944	Franklin Roosevelt (D)	51.56%	Thomas Dewey (R)	48.07%
1948	Harry Truman (D)	49.98%	Thomas Dewey (R)	47.26%
1952	Dwight Eisenhower (R)	65.41%	Adlai Stevenson (D)	34.42%
1956	Dwight Eisenhower (R)	61.17%	Adlai Stevenson (D)	38.78%
1960	Richard Nixon (R)	53.79%	John Kennedy (D)	46.22%
1964	Lyndon Johnson (D)	50.92%	Barry Goldwater (R)	49.08%

Year	Winner	PV%	Second	PV%
1968	Richard Nixon (R)	56.79%	Hubert Humphrey (D)	30.66%
1972	Richard Nixon (R)	64.24%	George McGovern (D)	26.04%
1976	Gerald Ford (R)	59.33%	Jimmy Carter (D)	36.78%
1980	Ronald Reagan (R)	66.46%	Jimmy Carter (D)	25.19%
1984	Ronald Reagan (R)	72.37%	Walter Mondale (D)	26.39%
1988	George H.W. Bush (R)	62.08%	Michael Dukakis (D)	36.01%
1992	George H.W. Bush (R)	42.03%	Bill Clinton (D)	28.42%
1996	Bob Dole (R)	52.18%	Bill Clinton (D)	33.65%
2000	George W. Bush (R)	67.17%	Al Gore (D)	27.64%
2004	George W. Bush (R)	68.38%	John Kerry (D)	30.26%
2008	John McCain (R)	61.52%	Barack Obama (D)	36.09%
2012	Mitt Romney (R)	64.53%	Barack Obama (D)	32.62%
2016	Donald Trump (R)	59.26%	Hillary Clinton (D)	27.49%
2020	Donald Trump (R)	63.84%	Joseph Biden (D)	33.07%

Home-State Candidates — Idaho

Qualified — William Borah (1936), Frank Church (1976)

Illinois

Basics — Illinois

State party winners — D 24, R 24, DR 3
General-election matches — 42-9 (82.35%)
Current party streak (through 2020) — D 8
Current match streak (through 2020) — 1
2020 party indexes — D 112.22, R 86.61
2020 overall results — Biden 57.54%, Trump 40.55%, other 1.91%
2020 two-party results — Biden 58.66%, Trump 41.34%
Home-state general-election winners — 6
Home-state major-party nominees — 9
Home-state qualified candidates — 29

Two-Party Results (2008-2020) — Illinois

2008: John McCain (37.27%)   **Barack Obama (62.73%)**

2012: Mitt Romney (41.42%)   **Barack Obama (58.58%)**

2016: Donald Trump (40.98%)   **Hillary Clinton (59.02%)**

2020: Donald Trump (41.34%)   **Joseph Biden (58.66%)**

Overall Results (1900-2020) — Illinois

Year	Winner	PV%	Second	PV%
1900	William McKinley (R)	52.83%	William Jennings Bryan (D)	44.44%
1904	Theodore Roosevelt (R)	58.77%	Alton Parker (D)	30.43%
1908	William Howard Taft (R)	54.53%	William Jennings Bryan (D)	39.02%
1912	Woodrow Wilson (D)	35.34%	Theodore Roosevelt (P)	33.72%
1916	Charles Evans Hughes (R)	52.56%	Woodrow Wilson (D)	43.34%
1920	Warren Harding (R)	67.81%	James Cox (D)	25.51%
1924	Calvin Coolidge (R)	58.84%	John Davis (D)	23.36%
1928	Herbert Hoover (R)	56.93%	Alfred Smith (D)	42.28%
1932	Franklin Roosevelt (D)	55.23%	Herbert Hoover (R)	42.04%
1936	Franklin Roosevelt (D)	57.70%	Alfred Landon (R)	39.69%
1940	Franklin Roosevelt (D)	50.97%	Wendell Willkie (R)	48.54%
1944	Franklin Roosevelt (D)	51.52%	Thomas Dewey (R)	48.05%
1948	Harry Truman (D)	50.07%	Thomas Dewey (R)	49.22%
1952	Dwight Eisenhower (R)	54.84%	Adlai Stevenson (D)	44.94%
1956	Dwight Eisenhower (R)	59.52%	Adlai Stevenson (D)	40.29%
1960	John Kennedy (D)	49.98%	Richard Nixon (R)	49.80%
1964	Lyndon Johnson (D)	59.47%	Barry Goldwater (R)	40.53%

Year	Winner	PV%	Second	PV%
1968	Richard Nixon (R)	47.08%	Hubert Humphrey (D)	44.15%
1972	Richard Nixon (R)	59.03%	George McGovern (D)	40.51%
1976	Gerald Ford (R)	50.10%	Jimmy Carter (D)	48.13%
1980	Ronald Reagan (R)	49.65%	Jimmy Carter (D)	41.72%
1984	Ronald Reagan (R)	56.18%	Walter Mondale (D)	43.30%
1988	George H.W. Bush (R)	50.69%	Michael Dukakis (D)	48.61%
1992	Bill Clinton (D)	48.58%	George H.W. Bush (R)	34.34%
1996	Bill Clinton (D)	54.32%	Bob Dole (R)	36.81%
2000	Al Gore (D)	54.60%	George W. Bush (R)	42.59%
2004	John Kerry (D)	54.82%	George W. Bush (R)	44.48%
2008	Barack Obama (D)	61.92%	John McCain (R)	36.78%
2012	Barack Obama (D)	57.60%	Mitt Romney (R)	40.73%
2016	Hillary Clinton (D)	55.83%	Donald Trump (R)	38.76%
2020	Joseph Biden (D)	57.54%	Donald Trump (R)	40.55%

Home-State Candidates — Illinois

Won — Ulysses Grant (1868, 1872), Abraham Lincoln (1860, 1864), Barack Obama (2008, 2012)

Nominated — Stephen Douglas (1860), Ulysses Grant (1868, 1872), Abraham Lincoln (1860, 1864), Barack Obama (2008, 2012), Adlai Stevenson (1952, 1956)

Qualified — John Anderson (1980), Joseph Cannon (1908), Phil Crane (1980), David Davis (1872), Stephen Douglas (1852, 1856, 1860), Ulysses Grant (1864, 1868, 1872, 1880), Dwight Green (1948), Jesse Jackson (1984, 1988), Frank Knox (1936), Abraham Lincoln (1860, 1864), John Logan (1884), Frank Lowden (1920, 1928), William Morrison (1880), Barack Obama (2008, 2012), Lawrence Sherman (1916), Paul Simon (1988), Adlai Stevenson (1952, 1956, 1960), Elihu Washburne (1880)

Indiana

Basics — Indiana

State party winners — R 33, D 13, DR 4, W 2
General-election matches — 38-14 (73.08%)
Current party streak (through 2020) — R 3
Current match streak (through 2020) — 0
2020 party indexes — R 121.93, D 79.97
2020 overall results — Trump 57.03%, Biden 40.96%, other 2.01%
2020 two-party results — Trump 58.20%, Biden 41.80%
Home-state general-election winners — 1
Home-state major-party nominees — 2
Home-state qualified candidates — 20

Two-Party Results (2008-2020) — Indiana

2008: John McCain (49.48%)   **Barack Obama (50.52%)**

2012: Mitt Romney (55.20%)   **Barack Obama (44.80%)**

2016: Donald Trump (60.12%)   **Hillary Clinton (39.88%)**

2020: Donald Trump (58.20%)   **Joseph Biden (41.80%)**

Overall Results (1900-2020) — Indiana

Year	Winner	PV%	Second	PV%
1900	William McKinley (R)	50.61%	William Jennings Bryan (D)	46.62%
1904	Theodore Roosevelt (R)	53.99%	Alton Parker (D)	40.22%
1908	William Howard Taft (R)	48.40%	William Jennings Bryan (D)	46.91%
1912	Woodrow Wilson (D)	43.07%	Theodore Roosevelt (P)	24.75%
1916	Charles Evans Hughes (R)	47.44%	Woodrow Wilson (D)	46.47%
1920	Warren Harding (R)	55.14%	James Cox (D)	40.49%
1924	Calvin Coolidge (R)	55.25%	John Davis (D)	38.69%
1928	Herbert Hoover (R)	59.68%	Alfred Smith (D)	39.59%
1932	Franklin Roosevelt (D)	54.67%	Herbert Hoover (R)	42.94%
1936	Franklin Roosevelt (D)	56.63%	Alfred Landon (R)	41.89%
1940	Wendell Willkie (R)	50.45%	Franklin Roosevelt (D)	49.03%
1944	Thomas Dewey (R)	52.38%	Franklin Roosevelt (D)	46.73%
1948	Thomas Dewey (R)	49.58%	Harry Truman (D)	48.78%
1952	Dwight Eisenhower (R)	58.12%	Adlai Stevenson (D)	41.00%
1956	Dwight Eisenhower (R)	59.90%	Adlai Stevenson (D)	39.70%
1960	Richard Nixon (R)	55.03%	John Kennedy (D)	44.60%
1964	Lyndon Johnson (D)	55.98%	Barry Goldwater (R)	43.56%

Year	Winner	PV%	Second	PV%
1968	Richard Nixon (R)	50.29%	Hubert Humphrey (D)	37.99%
1972	Richard Nixon (R)	66.11%	George McGovern (D)	33.34%
1976	Gerald Ford (R)	53.32%	Jimmy Carter (D)	45.70%
1980	Ronald Reagan (R)	56.01%	Jimmy Carter (D)	37.65%
1984	Ronald Reagan (R)	61.67%	Walter Mondale (D)	37.68%
1988	George H.W. Bush (R)	59.84%	Michael Dukakis (D)	39.69%
1992	George H.W. Bush (R)	42.91%	Bill Clinton (D)	36.79%
1996	Bob Dole (R)	47.14%	Bill Clinton (D)	41.56%
2000	George W. Bush (R)	56.65%	Al Gore (D)	41.01%
2004	George W. Bush (R)	59.95%	John Kerry (D)	39.26%
2008	Barack Obama (D)	49.95%	John McCain (R)	48.91%
2012	Mitt Romney (R)	54.13%	Barack Obama (D)	43.93%
2016	Donald Trump (R)	56.94%	Hillary Clinton (D)	37.78%
2020	Donald Trump (R)	57.03%	Joseph Biden (D)	40.96%

Home-State Candidates — Indiana

Won — Benjamin Harrison (1888)

Nominated — Benjamin Harrison (1888, 1892)

Qualified — Birch Bayh (1976), Pete Buttigieg (2020), Eugene Debs (1904, 1908, 1912, 1920), Charles Fairbanks (1908, 1916), Walter Gresham (1888), Benjamin Harrison (1888, 1892), Thomas Hendricks (1872, 1876, 1880, 1884), Richard Lugar (1996), Claude Matthews (1896), Joseph McDonald (1884), Oliver Morton (1876), James Watson (1928)

Iowa

Basics — Iowa

State party winners — R 31, D 13
General-election matches — 32-12 (72.73%)
Current party streak (through 2020) — R 2
Current match streak (through 2020) — 0
2020 party indexes — R 113.52, D 87.65
2020 overall results — Trump 53.09%, Biden 44.89%, other 2.02%
2020 two-party results — Trump 54.18%, Biden 45.82%
Home-state general-election winners — 0
Home-state major-party nominees — 0
Home-state qualified candidates — 8

Two-Party Results (2008-2020) — Iowa

2008: John McCain (45.15%)   **Barack Obama (54.85%)**

2012: Mitt Romney (47.04%)   **Barack Obama (52.96%)**

2016: Donald Trump (55.06%)   **Hillary Clinton (44.94%)**

2020: Donald Trump (54.18%)   **Joseph Biden (45.82%)**

Overall Results (1900-2020) — Iowa

Year	Winner	PV%	Second	PV%
1900	William McKinley (R)	58.04%	William Jennings Bryan (D)	39.46%
1904	Theodore Roosevelt (R)	63.39%	Alton Parker (D)	30.71%
1908	William Howard Taft (R)	55.62%	William Jennings Bryan (D)	40.58%
1912	Woodrow Wilson (D)	37.64%	Theodore Roosevelt (P)	32.87%
1916	Charles Evans Hughes (R)	54.06%	Woodrow Wilson (D)	42.74%
1920	Warren Harding (R)	70.92%	James Cox (D)	25.45%
1924	Calvin Coolidge (R)	55.02%	Robert La Follette (P)	28.10%
1928	Herbert Hoover (R)	61.79%	Alfred Smith (D)	37.56%
1932	Franklin Roosevelt (D)	57.69%	Herbert Hoover (R)	39.98%
1936	Franklin Roosevelt (D)	54.41%	Alfred Landon (R)	42.70%
1940	Wendell Willkie (R)	52.03%	Franklin Roosevelt (D)	47.62%
1944	Thomas Dewey (R)	51.99%	Franklin Roosevelt (D)	47.49%
1948	Harry Truman (D)	50.31%	Thomas Dewey (R)	47.58%
1952	Dwight Eisenhower (R)	63.76%	Adlai Stevenson (D)	35.59%
1956	Dwight Eisenhower (R)	59.06%	Adlai Stevenson (D)	40.65%
1960	Richard Nixon (R)	56.71%	John Kennedy (D)	43.22%
1964	Lyndon Johnson (D)	61.88%	Barry Goldwater (R)	37.92%

Year	Winner	PV%	Second	PV%
1968	Richard Nixon (R)	53.01%	Hubert Humphrey (D)	40.82%
1972	Richard Nixon (R)	57.61%	George McGovern (D)	40.48%
1976	Gerald Ford (R)	49.47%	Jimmy Carter (D)	48.46%
1980	Ronald Reagan (R)	51.31%	Jimmy Carter (D)	38.60%
1984	Ronald Reagan (R)	53.27%	Walter Mondale (D)	45.89%
1988	Michael Dukakis (D)	54.71%	George H.W. Bush (R)	44.50%
1992	Bill Clinton (D)	43.29%	George H.W. Bush (R)	37.27%
1996	Bill Clinton (D)	50.26%	Bob Dole (R)	39.92%
2000	Al Gore (D)	48.54%	George W. Bush (R)	48.22%
2004	George W. Bush (R)	49.90%	John Kerry (D)	49.23%
2008	Barack Obama (D)	53.93%	John McCain (R)	44.39%
2012	Barack Obama (D)	51.99%	Mitt Romney (R)	46.18%
2016	Donald Trump (R)	51.15%	Hillary Clinton (D)	41.74%
2020	Donald Trump (R)	53.09%	Joseph Biden (D)	44.89%

Home-State Candidates — Iowa

Qualified — William Boyd Allison (1888), Horace Boies (1892, 1896), Albert Cummins (1916), Tom Harkin (1992), Henry Wallace (1948), James Weaver (1880, 1892)

Kansas

Basics — Kansas

State party winners — R 33, D 6, POP 1
General-election matches — 27-13 (67.50%)
Current party streak (through 2020) — R 14
Current match streak (through 2020) — 0
2020 party indexes — R 120.45, D 81.32
2020 overall results — Trump 56.14%, Biden 41.51%, other 2.35%
2020 two-party results — Trump 57.49%, Biden 42.51%
Home-state general-election winners — 0
Home-state major-party nominees — 2
Home-state qualified candidates — 4

Two-Party Results (2008-2020) — Kansas

2008: John McCain (57.61%)   **Barack Obama (42.39%)**

2012: Mitt Romney (61.11%)   **Barack Obama (38.89%)**

2016: Donald Trump (61.11%)   **Hillary Clinton (38.89%)**

2020: Donald Trump (57.49%)   **Joseph Biden (42.51%)**

Overall Results (1900-2020) — Kansas

Year	Winner	PV%	Second	PV%
1900	William McKinley (R)	52.56%	William Jennings Bryan (D)	45.96%
1904	Theodore Roosevelt (R)	64.87%	Alton Parker (D)	26.19%
1908	William Howard Taft (R)	52.47%	William Jennings Bryan (D)	42.87%
1912	Woodrow Wilson (D)	39.30%	Theodore Roosevelt (P)	32.88%
1916	Woodrow Wilson (D)	49.95%	Charles Evans Hughes (R)	44.09%
1920	Warren Harding (R)	64.76%	James Cox (D)	32.52%
1924	Calvin Coolidge (R)	61.54%	John Davis (D)	23.60%
1928	Herbert Hoover (R)	72.02%	Alfred Smith (D)	27.06%
1932	Franklin Roosevelt (D)	53.56%	Herbert Hoover (R)	44.13%
1936	Franklin Roosevelt (D)	53.67%	Alfred Landon (R)	45.95%
1940	Wendell Willkie (R)	56.86%	Franklin Roosevelt (D)	42.40%
1944	Thomas Dewey (R)	60.25%	Franklin Roosevelt (D)	39.18%
1948	Thomas Dewey (R)	53.63%	Harry Truman (D)	44.61%
1952	Dwight Eisenhower (R)	68.77%	Adlai Stevenson (D)	30.50%
1956	Dwight Eisenhower (R)	65.44%	Adlai Stevenson (D)	34.21%
1960	Richard Nixon (R)	60.45%	John Kennedy (D)	39.11%
1964	Lyndon Johnson (D)	54.09%	Barry Goldwater (R)	45.06%

Year	Winner	PV%	Second	PV%
1968	Richard Nixon (R)	54.85%	Hubert Humphrey (D)	34.72%
1972	Richard Nixon (R)	67.66%	George McGovern (D)	29.50%
1976	Gerald Ford (R)	52.49%	Jimmy Carter (D)	44.94%
1980	Ronald Reagan (R)	57.85%	Jimmy Carter (D)	33.29%
1984	Ronald Reagan (R)	66.27%	Walter Mondale (D)	32.60%
1988	George H.W. Bush (R)	55.79%	Michael Dukakis (D)	42.56%
1992	George H.W. Bush (R)	38.88%	Bill Clinton (D)	33.74%
1996	Bob Dole (R)	54.29%	Bill Clinton (D)	36.09%
2000	George W. Bush (R)	58.04%	Al Gore (D)	37.24%
2004	George W. Bush (R)	62.00%	John Kerry (D)	36.62%
2008	John McCain (R)	56.61%	Barack Obama (D)	41.65%
2012	Mitt Romney (R)	59.71%	Barack Obama (D)	38.00%
2016	Donald Trump (R)	56.66%	Hillary Clinton (D)	36.05%
2020	Donald Trump (R)	56.14%	Joseph Biden (D)	41.51%

Home-State Candidates — Kansas

Nominated — Bob Dole (1996), Alfred Landon (1936)
Qualified — Charles Curtis (1928), Bob Dole (1988, 1996), Alfred Landon (1936)

Kentucky

Basics — Kentucky
State party winners — D 25, R 16, DR 9, W 5, CU 1, NR 1, tie 1
General-election matches — 36-22 (62.07%)
Current party streak (through 2020) — R 6
Current match streak (through 2020) — 0
2020 party indexes — R 132.41, D 70.40
2020 overall results — Trump 62.09%, Biden 36.15%, other 1.76%
2020 two-party results — Trump 63.20%, Biden 36.80%
Home-state general-election winners — 0
Home-state major-party nominees — 3
Home-state qualified candidates — 12

Two-Party Results (2008-2020) — Kentucky
2008: John McCain (58.23%)   **Barack Obama (41.77%)**

2012: Mitt Romney (61.54%)   **Barack Obama (38.46%)**

2016: Donald Trump (65.67%)   **Hillary Clinton (34.33%)**

2020: Donald Trump (63.20%)   **Joseph Biden (36.80%)**

Overall Results (1900-2020) — Kentucky

Year	Winner	PV%	Second	PV%
1900	William Jennings Bryan (D)	50.24%	William McKinley (R)	48.51%
1904	Alton Parker (D)	49.82%	Theodore Roosevelt (R)	47.13%
1908	William Jennings Bryan (D)	49.74%	William Howard Taft (R)	48.03%
1912	Woodrow Wilson (D)	48.40%	William Howard Taft (R)	25.46%
1916	Woodrow Wilson (D)	51.91%	Charles Evans Hughes (R)	46.50%
1920	James Cox (D)	49.69%	Warren Harding (R)	49.26%
1924	Calvin Coolidge (R)	48.89%	John Davis (D)	46.03%
1928	Herbert Hoover (R)	59.34%	Alfred Smith (D)	40.52%
1932	Franklin Roosevelt (D)	59.06%	Herbert Hoover (R)	40.15%
1936	Franklin Roosevelt (D)	58.51%	Alfred Landon (R)	39.92%
1940	Franklin Roosevelt (D)	57.45%	Wendell Willkie (R)	42.30%
1944	Franklin Roosevelt (D)	54.45%	Thomas Dewey (R)	45.22%
1948	Harry Truman (D)	56.74%	Thomas Dewey (R)	41.48%
1952	Adlai Stevenson (D)	49.92%	Dwight Eisenhower (R)	49.84%
1956	Dwight Eisenhower (R)	54.30%	Adlai Stevenson (D)	45.21%
1960	Richard Nixon (R)	53.59%	John Kennedy (D)	46.41%
1964	Lyndon Johnson (D)	64.02%	Barry Goldwater (R)	35.65%

Year	Winner	PV%	Second	PV%
1968	Richard Nixon (R)	43.79%	Hubert Humphrey (D)	37.65%
1972	Richard Nixon (R)	63.37%	George McGovern (D)	34.77%
1976	Jimmy Carter (D)	52.75%	Gerald Ford (R)	45.57%
1980	Ronald Reagan (R)	49.07%	Jimmy Carter (D)	47.61%
1984	Ronald Reagan (R)	60.01%	Walter Mondale (D)	39.40%
1988	George H.W. Bush (R)	55.52%	Michael Dukakis (D)	43.88%
1992	Bill Clinton (D)	44.55%	George H.W. Bush (R)	41.34%
1996	Bill Clinton (D)	45.84%	Bob Dole (R)	44.88%
2000	George W. Bush (R)	56.50%	Al Gore (D)	41.37%
2004	George W. Bush (R)	59.55%	John Kerry (D)	39.69%
2008	John McCain (R)	57.40%	Barack Obama (D)	41.17%
2012	Mitt Romney (R)	60.49%	Barack Obama (D)	37.80%
2016	Donald Trump (R)	62.52%	Hillary Clinton (D)	32.68%
2020	Donald Trump (R)	62.09%	Joseph Biden (D)	36.15%

Home-State Candidates — Kentucky

Nominated — John Breckinridge (1860), Henry Clay (1832, 1844)

Qualified — Alben Barkley (1952), Joseph Blackburn (1896), John Breckinridge (1860), Benjamin Bristow (1876), Henry Clay (1824, 1832, 1840, 1844, 1848), James Guthrie (1860), Richard Johnson (1844), Rand Paul (2016)

Louisiana

Basics — Louisiana

State party winners — D 28, R 13, DR 5, W 2, AI 1, SD 1, SRD 1
General-election matches — 32-19 (62.75%)
Current party streak (through 2020) — R 6
Current match streak (through 2020) — 0
2020 party indexes — R 124.58, D 77.55
2020 overall results — Trump 58.46%, Biden 39.85%, other 1.69%
2020 two-party results — Trump 59.46%, Biden 40.54%
Home-state general-election winners — 1
Home-state major-party nominees — 1
Home-state qualified candidates — 1

Two-Party Results (2008-2020) — Louisiana

2008: John McCain (59.46%)   **Barack Obama (40.54%)**

2012: Mitt Romney (58.75%)   **Barack Obama (41.25%)**

2016: Donald Trump (60.17%)   **Hillary Clinton (39.83%)**

2020: Donald Trump (59.46%)   **Joseph Biden (40.54%)**

Overall Results (1900-2020) — Louisiana

Year	Winner	PV%	Second	PV%
1900	William Jennings Bryan (D)	79.03%	William McKinley (R)	20.96%
1904	Alton Parker (D)	88.50%	Theodore Roosevelt (R)	9.66%
1908	William Jennings Bryan (D)	84.63%	William Howard Taft (R)	11.93%
1912	Woodrow Wilson (D)	76.81%	Theodore Roosevelt (P)	11.71%
1916	Woodrow Wilson (D)	85.91%	Charles Evans Hughes (R)	6.96%
1920	James Cox (D)	69.24%	Warren Harding (R)	30.49%
1924	John Davis (D)	76.44%	Calvin Coolidge (R)	20.23%
1928	Alfred Smith (D)	76.29%	Herbert Hoover (R)	23.70%
1932	Franklin Roosevelt (D)	92.79%	Herbert Hoover (R)	7.01%
1936	Franklin Roosevelt (D)	88.82%	Alfred Landon (R)	11.16%
1940	Franklin Roosevelt (D)	85.88%	Wendell Willkie (R)	14.09%
1944	Franklin Roosevelt (D)	80.59%	Thomas Dewey (R)	19.39%
1948	Strom Thurmond (SRD)	49.07%	Harry Truman (D)	32.75%
1952	Adlai Stevenson (D)	52.92%	Dwight Eisenhower (R)	47.08%
1956	Dwight Eisenhower (R)	53.28%	Adlai Stevenson (D)	39.51%
1960	John Kennedy (D)	50.42%	Richard Nixon (R)	28.59%
1964	Barry Goldwater (R)	56.82%	Lyndon Johnson (D)	43.19%

Year	Winner	PV%	Second	PV%
1968	George Wallace (AI)	48.32%	Hubert Humphrey (D)	28.21%
1972	Richard Nixon (R)	65.32%	George McGovern (D)	28.35%
1976	Jimmy Carter (D)	51.73%	Gerald Ford (R)	45.95%
1980	Ronald Reagan (R)	51.20%	Jimmy Carter (D)	45.75%
1984	Ronald Reagan (R)	60.77%	Walter Mondale (D)	38.18%
1988	George H.W. Bush (R)	54.28%	Michael Dukakis (D)	44.07%
1992	Bill Clinton (D)	45.59%	George H.W. Bush (R)	40.97%
1996	Bill Clinton (D)	52.01%	Bob Dole (R)	39.94%
2000	George W. Bush (R)	52.55%	Al Gore (D)	44.88%
2004	George W. Bush (R)	56.72%	John Kerry (D)	42.22%
2008	John McCain (R)	58.56%	Barack Obama (D)	39.93%
2012	Mitt Romney (R)	57.79%	Barack Obama (D)	40.58%
2016	Donald Trump (R)	58.09%	Hillary Clinton (D)	38.45%
2020	Donald Trump (R)	58.46%	Joseph Biden (D)	39.85%

Home-State Candidates — Louisiana

Won — Zachary Taylor (1848)
Nominated — Zachary Taylor (1848)
Qualified — Zachary Taylor (1848)

Maine

Basics — Maine

State party winners — R 31, D 16, DR 2, NR 1, W 1
General-election matches — 34-17 (66.67%)
Current party streak (through 2020) — D 8
Current match streak (through 2020) — 1
2020 party indexes — D 104.59, R 94.97
2020 overall results — Biden 53.09%, Trump 44.02%, other 2.89%
2020 two-party results — Biden 54.67%, Trump 45.33%
Home-state general-election winners — 0
Home-state major-party nominees — 1
Home-state qualified candidates — 7

Two-Party Results (2008-2020) — Maine

2008: John McCain (41.17%)   **Barack Obama (58.83%)**

2012: Mitt Romney (42.14%)   **Barack Obama (57.86%)**

2016: Donald Trump (48.40%)   **Hillary Clinton (51.60%)**

2020: Donald Trump (45.33%)   **Joseph Biden (54.67%)**

Overall Results (1900-2020) — Maine

Year	Winner	PV%	Second	PV%
1900	William McKinley (R)	61.67%	William Jennings Bryan (D)	35.12%
1904	Theodore Roosevelt (R)	67.10%	Alton Parker (D)	28.79%
1908	William Howard Taft (R)	63.00%	William Jennings Bryan (D)	33.29%
1912	Woodrow Wilson (D)	39.43%	Theodore Roosevelt (P)	37.41%
1916	Charles Evans Hughes (R)	50.99%	Woodrow Wilson (D)	46.98%
1920	Warren Harding (R)	68.92%	James Cox (D)	29.80%
1924	Calvin Coolidge (R)	72.03%	John Davis (D)	21.83%
1928	Herbert Hoover (R)	68.63%	Alfred Smith (D)	30.96%
1932	Herbert Hoover (R)	55.83%	Franklin Roosevelt (D)	43.19%
1936	Alfred Landon (R)	55.49%	Franklin Roosevelt (D)	41.52%
1940	Wendell Willkie (R)	51.10%	Franklin Roosevelt (D)	48.77%
1944	Thomas Dewey (R)	52.44%	Franklin Roosevelt (D)	47.45%
1948	Thomas Dewey (R)	56.74%	Harry Truman (D)	42.27%
1952	Dwight Eisenhower (R)	66.05%	Adlai Stevenson (D)	33.77%
1956	Dwight Eisenhower (R)	70.87%	Adlai Stevenson (D)	29.14%
1960	Richard Nixon (R)	57.05%	John Kennedy (D)	42.95%
1964	Lyndon Johnson (D)	68.84%	Barry Goldwater (R)	31.16%

Year	Winner	PV%	Second	PV%
1968	Hubert Humphrey (D)	55.31%	Richard Nixon (R)	43.07%
1972	Richard Nixon (R)	61.50%	George McGovern (D)	38.51%
1976	Gerald Ford (R)	48.91%	Jimmy Carter (D)	48.07%
1980	Ronald Reagan (R)	45.61%	Jimmy Carter (D)	42.25%
1984	Ronald Reagan (R)	60.83%	Walter Mondale (D)	38.78%
1988	George H.W. Bush (R)	55.34%	Michael Dukakis (D)	43.88%
1992	Bill Clinton (D)	38.77%	Ross Perot (I)	30.44%
1996	Bill Clinton (D)	51.62%	Bob Dole (R)	30.76%
2000	Al Gore (D)	49.09%	George W. Bush (R)	43.97%
2004	John Kerry (D)	53.57%	George W. Bush (R)	44.58%
2008	Barack Obama (D)	57.71%	John McCain (R)	40.38%
2012	Barack Obama (D)	56.27%	Mitt Romney (R)	40.98%
2016	Hillary Clinton (D)	47.83%	Donald Trump (R)	44.87%
2020	Joseph Biden (D)	53.09%	Donald Trump (R)	44.02%

Home-State Candidates — Maine

Nominated — James Blaine (1884)

Qualified — James Blaine (1876, 1880, 1884, 1888, 1892), Edmund Muskie (1972), Thomas Reed (1896)

Maryland

Basics — Maryland

State party winners — D 29, R 12, DR 6, W 4, F 3, NR 2, AW 1, SD 1, tie 1
General-election matches — 39-20 (66.10%)
Current party streak (through 2020) — D 8
Current match streak (through 2020) — 1
2020 party indexes — D 128.24, R 69.08
2020 overall results — Biden 65.36%, Trump 32.15%, other 2.49%
2020 two-party results — Biden 67.03%, Trump 32.97%
Home-state general-election winners — 0
Home-state major-party nominees — 0
Home-state qualified candidates — 8

Two-Party Results (2008-2020) — Maryland

2008: John McCain (37.07%)   **Barack Obama (62.93%)**

2012: Mitt Romney (36.68%)   **Barack Obama (63.32%)**

2016: Donald Trump (35.98%)   **Hillary Clinton (64.02%)**

2020: Donald Trump (32.97%)   **Joseph Biden (67.03%)**

Overall Results (1900-2020) — Maryland

Year	Winner	PV%	Second	PV%
1900	William McKinley (R)	51.50%	William Jennings Bryan (D)	46.23%
1904	Theodore Roosevelt (R)	48.83%	Alton Parker (D)	48.81%
1908	William Howard Taft (R)	48.85%	William Jennings Bryan (D)	48.59%
1912	Woodrow Wilson (D)	48.57%	Theodore Roosevelt (P)	24.91%
1916	Woodrow Wilson (D)	52.80%	Charles Evans Hughes (R)	44.78%
1920	Warren Harding (R)	55.11%	James Cox (D)	42.16%
1924	Calvin Coolidge (R)	45.29%	John Davis (D)	41.29%
1928	Herbert Hoover (R)	57.06%	Alfred Smith (D)	42.33%
1932	Franklin Roosevelt (D)	61.50%	Herbert Hoover (R)	36.04%
1936	Franklin Roosevelt (D)	62.35%	Alfred Landon (R)	37.04%
1940	Franklin Roosevelt (D)	58.26%	Wendell Willkie (R)	40.83%
1944	Franklin Roosevelt (D)	51.85%	Thomas Dewey (R)	48.15%
1948	Thomas Dewey (R)	49.40%	Harry Truman (D)	48.01%
1952	Dwight Eisenhower (R)	55.36%	Adlai Stevenson (D)	43.83%
1956	Dwight Eisenhower (R)	60.00%	Adlai Stevenson (D)	39.94%
1960	John Kennedy (D)	53.61%	Richard Nixon (R)	46.39%
1964	Lyndon Johnson (D)	65.47%	Barry Goldwater (R)	34.53%

Year	Winner	PV%	Second	PV%
1968	Hubert Humphrey (D)	43.59%	Richard Nixon (R)	41.94%
1972	Richard Nixon (R)	61.26%	George McGovern (D)	37.36%
1976	Jimmy Carter (D)	52.76%	Gerald Ford (R)	46.72%
1980	Jimmy Carter (D)	47.14%	Ronald Reagan (R)	44.18%
1984	Ronald Reagan (R)	52.51%	Walter Mondale (D)	47.02%
1988	George H.W. Bush (R)	51.11%	Michael Dukakis (D)	48.20%
1992	Bill Clinton (D)	49.80%	George H.W. Bush (R)	35.62%
1996	Bill Clinton (D)	54.26%	Bob Dole (R)	38.27%
2000	Al Gore (D)	56.57%	George W. Bush (R)	40.18%
2004	John Kerry (D)	55.91%	George W. Bush (R)	42.93%
2008	Barack Obama (D)	61.92%	John McCain (R)	36.48%
2012	Barack Obama (D)	61.97%	Mitt Romney (R)	35.90%
2016	Hillary Clinton (D)	60.33%	Donald Trump (R)	33.91%
2020	Joseph Biden (D)	65.36%	Donald Trump (R)	32.15%

Home-State Candidates — Maryland

Qualified — Joseph France (1932), Arthur Gorman (1892), Robert Harrison (1789), John Henry (1796), Alan Keyes (1996, 2000), Sargent Shriver (1976), William Wirt (1832)

Massachusetts

Basics — Massachusetts

State party winners — D 21, R 21, F 7, W 5, DR 3, NR 2
General-election matches — 39-20 (66.10%)
Current party streak (through 2020) — D 9
Current match streak (through 2020) — 1
2020 party indexes — D 128.40, R 68.90
2020 overall results — Biden 65.60%, Trump 32.14%, other 2.26%
2020 two-party results — Biden 67.12%, Trump 32.88%
Home-state general-election winners — 4
Home-state major-party nominees — 9
Home-state qualified candidates — 26

Two-Party Results (2008-2020) — Massachusetts

2008: John McCain (36.80%)   **Barack Obama (63.20%)**

2012: Mitt Romney (38.21%)   **Barack Obama (61.79%)**

2016: Donald Trump (35.35%)   **Hillary Clinton (64.65%)**

2020: Donald Trump (32.88%)   **Joseph Biden (67.12%)**

Overall Results (1900-2020) — Massachusetts

Year	Winner	PV%	Second	PV%
1900	William McKinley (R)	57.59%	William Jennings Bryan (D)	37.85%
1904	Theodore Roosevelt (R)	57.92%	Alton Parker (D)	37.24%
1908	William Howard Taft (R)	58.21%	William Jennings Bryan (D)	34.04%
1912	Woodrow Wilson (D)	35.53%	William Howard Taft (R)	31.95%
1916	Charles Evans Hughes (R)	50.54%	Woodrow Wilson (D)	46.61%
1920	Warren Harding (R)	68.55%	James Cox (D)	27.84%
1924	Calvin Coolidge (R)	62.26%	John Davis (D)	24.86%
1928	Alfred Smith (D)	50.24%	Herbert Hoover (R)	49.15%
1932	Franklin Roosevelt (D)	50.64%	Herbert Hoover (R)	46.64%
1936	Franklin Roosevelt (D)	51.23%	Alfred Landon (R)	41.76%
1940	Franklin Roosevelt (D)	53.11%	Wendell Willkie (R)	46.36%
1944	Franklin Roosevelt (D)	52.80%	Thomas Dewey (R)	46.99%
1948	Harry Truman (D)	54.66%	Thomas Dewey (R)	43.16%
1952	Dwight Eisenhower (R)	54.22%	Adlai Stevenson (D)	45.46%
1956	Dwight Eisenhower (R)	59.32%	Adlai Stevenson (D)	40.37%
1960	John Kennedy (D)	60.22%	Richard Nixon (R)	39.55%
1964	Lyndon Johnson (D)	76.19%	Barry Goldwater (R)	23.45%

Year	Winner	PV%	Second	PV%
1968	Hubert Humphrey (D)	63.01%	Richard Nixon (R)	32.89%
1972	George McGovern (D)	54.20%	Richard Nixon (R)	45.23%
1976	Jimmy Carter (D)	56.11%	Gerald Ford (R)	40.44%
1980	Ronald Reagan (R)	41.92%	Jimmy Carter (D)	41.77%
1984	Ronald Reagan (R)	51.22%	Walter Mondale (D)	48.43%
1988	Michael Dukakis (D)	53.23%	George H.W. Bush (R)	45.38%
1992	Bill Clinton (D)	47.54%	George H.W. Bush (R)	29.02%
1996	Bill Clinton (D)	61.47%	Bob Dole (R)	28.09%
2000	Al Gore (D)	59.80%	George W. Bush (R)	32.50%
2004	John Kerry (D)	61.94%	George W. Bush (R)	36.78%
2008	Barack Obama (D)	61.80%	John McCain (R)	35.99%
2012	Barack Obama (D)	60.65%	Mitt Romney (R)	37.51%
2016	Hillary Clinton (D)	60.01%	Donald Trump (R)	32.81%
2020	Joseph Biden (D)	65.60%	Donald Trump (R)	32.14%

Home-State Candidates — Massachusetts

Won — John Adams (1796), John Quincy Adams (1824), Calvin Coolidge (1924), John Kennedy (1960)

Nominated — John Adams (1796, 1800), John Quincy Adams (1824, 1828), Calvin Coolidge (1924), Michael Dukakis (1988), John Kennedy (1960), John Kerry (2004), Mitt Romney (2012)

Qualified — John Adams (1789, 1792, 1796, 1800), John Quincy Adams (1820, 1824, 1828), Samuel Adams (1796), Calvin Coolidge (1924), Michael Dukakis (1988), John Hancock (1789), Edward Kennedy (1980), John Kennedy (1960), John Kerry (2004), Benjamin Lincoln (1789), Henry Cabot Lodge (1964), Joseph Martin (1940), Mitt Romney (2008, 2012), Paul Tsongas (1992), Elizabeth Warren (2020), Daniel Webster (1836, 1848, 1852), John Weeks (1916), Bill Weld (2020)

Michigan

Basics — Michigan

State party winners — R 28, D 17, P 1, W 1
General-election matches — 35-12 (74.47%)
Current party streak (through 2020) — D 1
Current match streak (through 2020) — 4
2020 party indexes — R 101.79, D 98.36
2020 overall results — Biden 50.62%, Trump 47.84%, other 1.54%
2020 two-party results — Biden 51.41%, Trump 48.59%
Home-state general-election winners — 0
Home-state major-party nominees — 2
Home-state qualified candidates — 9

Two-Party Results (2008-2020) — Michigan

2008: John McCain (41.63%)   **Barack Obama (58.37%)**

2012: Mitt Romney (45.20%)   **Barack Obama (54.80%)**

2016: Donald Trump (50.12%)   **Hillary Clinton (49.88%)**

2020: Donald Trump (48.59%)   **Joseph Biden (51.41%)**

Overall Results (1900-2020) — Michigan

Year	Winner	PV%	Second	PV%
1900	William McKinley (R)	58.11%	William Jennings Bryan (D)	38.88%
1904	Theodore Roosevelt (R)	69.53%	Alton Parker (D)	25.78%
1908	William Howard Taft (R)	61.94%	William Jennings Bryan (D)	32.45%
1912	Theodore Roosevelt (P)	38.92%	William Howard Taft (R)	27.64%
1916	Charles Evans Hughes (R)	52.24%	Woodrow Wilson (D)	43.90%
1920	Warren Harding (R)	72.76%	James Cox (D)	22.27%
1924	Calvin Coolidge (R)	75.37%	John Davis (D)	13.13%
1928	Herbert Hoover (R)	70.36%	Alfred Smith (D)	28.92%
1932	Franklin Roosevelt (D)	52.36%	Herbert Hoover (R)	44.44%
1936	Franklin Roosevelt (D)	56.33%	Alfred Landon (R)	38.76%
1940	Wendell Willkie (R)	49.85%	Franklin Roosevelt (D)	49.52%
1944	Franklin Roosevelt (D)	50.19%	Thomas Dewey (R)	49.18%
1948	Thomas Dewey (R)	49.23%	Harry Truman (D)	47.57%
1952	Dwight Eisenhower (R)	55.44%	Adlai Stevenson (D)	43.97%
1956	Dwight Eisenhower (R)	55.63%	Adlai Stevenson (D)	44.15%
1960	John Kennedy (D)	50.85%	Richard Nixon (R)	48.84%
1964	Lyndon Johnson (D)	66.71%	Barry Goldwater (R)	33.10%

Year	Winner	PV%	Second	PV%
1968	Hubert Humphrey (D)	48.18%	Richard Nixon (R)	41.46%
1972	Richard Nixon (R)	56.21%	George McGovern (D)	41.82%
1976	Gerald Ford (R)	51.83%	Jimmy Carter (D)	46.44%
1980	Ronald Reagan (R)	48.99%	Jimmy Carter (D)	42.50%
1984	Ronald Reagan (R)	59.23%	Walter Mondale (D)	40.24%
1988	George H.W. Bush (R)	53.57%	Michael Dukakis (D)	45.67%
1992	Bill Clinton (D)	43.77%	George H.W. Bush (R)	36.38%
1996	Bill Clinton (D)	51.70%	Bob Dole (R)	38.49%
2000	Al Gore (D)	51.28%	George W. Bush (R)	46.15%
2004	John Kerry (D)	51.23%	George W. Bush (R)	47.81%
2008	Barack Obama (D)	57.43%	John McCain (R)	40.96%
2012	Barack Obama (D)	54.21%	Mitt Romney (R)	44.71%
2016	Donald Trump (R)	47.50%	Hillary Clinton (D)	47.28%
2020	Joseph Biden (D)	50.62%	Donald Trump (R)	47.84%

Home-State Candidates — Michigan

Nominated — Lewis Cass (1848), Gerald Ford (1976)

Qualified — Russell Alger (1888), James Birney (1844), Lewis Cass (1844, 1848, 1852), Gerald Ford (1976), Henry Ford (1916), Arthur Vandenberg (1940, 1948)

Minnesota

Basics — Minnesota

State party winners — D 20, R 20, P 1
General-election matches — 30-11 (73.17%)
Current party streak (through 2020) — D 12
Current match streak (through 2020) — 1
2020 party indexes — D 102.62, R 97.13
2020 overall results — Biden 52.40%, Trump 45.29%, other 2.32%
2020 two-party results — Biden 53.64%, Trump 46.36%
Home-state general-election winners — 0
Home-state major-party nominees — 2
Home-state qualified candidates — 10

Two-Party Results (2008-2020) — Minnesota

2008: John McCain (44.77%)   **Barack Obama (55.23%)**

2012: Mitt Romney (46.06%)   **Barack Obama (53.94%)**

2016: Donald Trump (49.17%)   **Hillary Clinton (50.83%)**

2020: Donald Trump (46.36%)   **Joseph Biden (53.64%)**

Overall Results (1900-2020) — Minnesota

Year	Winner	PV%	Second	PV%
1900	William McKinley (R)	60.21%	William Jennings Bryan (D)	35.69%
1904	Theodore Roosevelt (R)	73.98%	Alton Parker (D)	18.84%
1908	William Howard Taft (R)	59.11%	William Jennings Bryan (D)	33.02%
1912	Theodore Roosevelt (P)	37.66%	Woodrow Wilson (D)	31.84%
1916	Charles Evans Hughes (R)	46.35%	Woodrow Wilson (D)	46.25%
1920	Warren Harding (R)	70.59%	James Cox (D)	19.43%
1924	Calvin Coolidge (R)	51.18%	Robert La Follette (P)	41.26%
1928	Herbert Hoover (R)	57.78%	Alfred Smith (D)	40.83%
1932	Franklin Roosevelt (D)	59.91%	Herbert Hoover (R)	36.29%
1936	Franklin Roosevelt (D)	61.84%	Alfred Landon (R)	31.02%
1940	Franklin Roosevelt (D)	51.49%	Wendell Willkie (R)	47.66%
1944	Franklin Roosevelt (D)	52.41%	Thomas Dewey (R)	46.86%
1948	Harry Truman (D)	57.17%	Thomas Dewey (R)	39.90%
1952	Dwight Eisenhower (R)	55.33%	Adlai Stevenson (D)	44.11%
1956	Dwight Eisenhower (R)	53.68%	Adlai Stevenson (D)	46.08%
1960	John Kennedy (D)	50.58%	Richard Nixon (R)	49.16%
1964	Lyndon Johnson (D)	63.76%	Barry Goldwater (R)	36.00%

Year	Winner	PV%	Second	PV%
1968	Hubert Humphrey (D)	54.00%	Richard Nixon (R)	41.46%
1972	Richard Nixon (R)	51.58%	George McGovern (D)	46.07%
1976	Jimmy Carter (D)	54.90%	Gerald Ford (R)	42.02%
1980	Jimmy Carter (D)	46.50%	Ronald Reagan (R)	42.56%
1984	Walter Mondale (D)	49.72%	Ronald Reagan (R)	49.54%
1988	Michael Dukakis (D)	52.91%	George H.W. Bush (R)	45.90%
1992	Bill Clinton (D)	43.49%	George H.W. Bush (R)	31.85%
1996	Bill Clinton (D)	51.10%	Bob Dole (R)	34.96%
2000	Al Gore (D)	47.91%	George W. Bush (R)	45.50%
2004	John Kerry (D)	51.09%	George W. Bush (R)	47.61%
2008	Barack Obama (D)	54.06%	John McCain (R)	43.82%
2012	Barack Obama (D)	52.65%	Mitt Romney (R)	44.96%
2016	Hillary Clinton (D)	46.45%	Donald Trump (R)	44.93%
2020	Joseph Biden (D)	52.40%	Donald Trump (R)	45.29%

Home-State Candidates — Minnesota

Nominated — Hubert Humphrey (1968), Walter Mondale (1984)

Qualified — Michele Bachmann (2012), Hubert Humphrey (1960, 1968, 1972, 1976), John Johnson (1908), Amy Klobuchar (2020), Eugene McCarthy (1968), Walter Mondale (1984), Harold Stassen (1948)

Mississippi

Basics — Mississippi

State party winners — D 27, R 14, DR 3, AI 1, ID 1, SD 1, SRD 1, W 1
General-election matches — 25-24 (51.02%)
Current party streak (through 2020) — R 11
Current match streak (through 2020) — 0
2020 party indexes — R 122.32, D 79.62
2020 overall results — Trump 57.60%, Biden 41.06%, other 1.34%
2020 two-party results — Trump 58.39%, Biden 41.62%
Home-state general-election winners — 0
Home-state major-party nominees — 0
Home-state qualified candidates — 1

Two-Party Results (2008-2020) — Mississippi

2008: John McCain (56.64%)   **Barack Obama (43.36%)**

2012: Mitt Romney (55.80%)   **Barack Obama (44.20%)**

2016: Donald Trump (59.09%)   **Hillary Clinton (40.91%)**

2020: Donald Trump (58.39%)   **Joseph Biden (41.62%)**

Overall Results (1900-2020) — Mississippi

Year	Winner	PV%	Second	PV%
1900	William Jennings Bryan (D)	87.56%	William McKinley (R)	9.66%
1904	Alton Parker (D)	91.08%	Theodore Roosevelt (R)	5.59%
1908	William Jennings Bryan (D)	90.11%	William Howard Taft (R)	6.52%
1912	Woodrow Wilson (D)	88.90%	Theodore Roosevelt (P)	5.50%
1916	Woodrow Wilson (D)	92.78%	Charles Evans Hughes (R)	4.91%
1920	James Cox (D)	83.95%	Warren Harding (R)	14.06%
1924	John Davis (D)	89.36%	Calvin Coolidge (R)	7.55%
1928	Alfred Smith (D)	82.17%	Herbert Hoover (R)	17.83%
1932	Franklin Roosevelt (D)	95.98%	Herbert Hoover (R)	3.55%
1936	Franklin Roosevelt (D)	97.03%	Alfred Landon (R)	2.76%
1940	Franklin Roosevelt (D)	95.70%	Wendell Willkie (R)	4.19%
1944	Franklin Roosevelt (D)	93.56%	Thomas Dewey (R)	6.44%
1948	Strom Thurmond (SRD)	87.17%	Harry Truman (D)	10.09%
1952	Adlai Stevenson (D)	60.44%	Dwight Eisenhower (R)	39.56%
1956	Adlai Stevenson (D)	58.22%	Dwight Eisenhower (R)	24.46%
1960	Unpledged slate (D)	38.99%	John Kennedy (D)	36.34%
1964	Barry Goldwater (R)	87.14%	Lyndon Johnson (D)	12.86%

Year	Winner	PV%	Second	PV%
1968	George Wallace (AI)	63.46%	Hubert Humphrey (D)	23.02%
1972	Richard Nixon (R)	78.20%	George McGovern (D)	19.63%
1976	Jimmy Carter (D)	49.56%	Gerald Ford (R)	47.68%
1980	Ronald Reagan (R)	49.42%	Jimmy Carter (D)	48.09%
1984	Ronald Reagan (R)	61.88%	Walter Mondale (D)	37.42%
1988	George H.W. Bush (R)	59.89%	Michael Dukakis (D)	39.07%
1992	George H.W. Bush (R)	49.68%	Bill Clinton (D)	40.77%
1996	Bob Dole (R)	49.21%	Bill Clinton (D)	44.08%
2000	George W. Bush (R)	57.62%	Al Gore (D)	40.70%
2004	George W. Bush (R)	59.45%	John Kerry (D)	39.76%
2008	John McCain (R)	56.18%	Barack Obama (D)	43.00%
2012	Mitt Romney (R)	55.29%	Barack Obama (D)	43.79%
2016	Donald Trump (R)	57.94%	Hillary Clinton (D)	40.12%
2020	Donald Trump (R)	57.60%	Joseph Biden (D)	41.06%

Home-State Candidates — Mississippi

Qualified — Pat Harrison (1924)

Missouri

Basics — Missouri

State party winners — D 29, R 19, DR 3
General-election matches — 37-14 (72.55%)
Current party streak (through 2020) — R 6
Current match streak (through 2020) — 0
2020 party indexes — R 121.17, D 80.67
2020 overall results — Trump 56.80%, Biden 41.41%, other 1.79%
2020 two-party results — Trump 57.84%, Biden 42.16%
Home-state general-election winners — 1
Home-state major-party nominees — 1
Home-state qualified candidates — 10

Two-Party Results (2008-2020) — Missouri

2008: John McCain (50.07%)   **Barack Obama (49.93%)**

2012: Mitt Romney (54.78%)   **Barack Obama (45.22%)**

2016: Donald Trump (59.82%)   **Hillary Clinton (40.18%)**

2020: Donald Trump (57.84%)   **Joseph Biden (42.16%)**

Overall Results (1900-2020) — Missouri

Year	Winner	PV%	Second	PV%
1900	William Jennings Bryan (D)	51.48%	William McKinley (R)	45.94%
1904	Theodore Roosevelt (R)	49.93%	Alton Parker (D)	46.02%
1908	William Howard Taft (R)	48.50%	William Jennings Bryan (D)	48.42%
1912	Woodrow Wilson (D)	47.35%	William Howard Taft (R)	29.75%
1916	Woodrow Wilson (D)	50.59%	Charles Evans Hughes (R)	46.94%
1920	Warren Harding (R)	54.59%	James Cox (D)	43.14%
1924	Calvin Coolidge (R)	49.50%	John Davis (D)	43.89%
1928	Herbert Hoover (R)	55.57%	Alfred Smith (D)	44.15%
1932	Franklin Roosevelt (D)	63.69%	Herbert Hoover (R)	35.08%
1936	Franklin Roosevelt (D)	60.76%	Alfred Landon (R)	38.17%
1940	Franklin Roosevelt (D)	52.27%	Wendell Willkie (R)	47.50%
1944	Franklin Roosevelt (D)	51.37%	Thomas Dewey (R)	48.43%
1948	Harry Truman (D)	58.11%	Thomas Dewey (R)	41.49%
1952	Dwight Eisenhower (R)	50.71%	Adlai Stevenson (D)	49.14%
1956	Adlai Stevenson (D)	50.11%	Dwight Eisenhower (R)	49.89%
1960	John Kennedy (D)	50.26%	Richard Nixon (R)	49.74%
1964	Lyndon Johnson (D)	64.05%	Barry Goldwater (R)	35.95%

Year	Winner	PV%	Second	PV%
1968	Richard Nixon (R)	44.87%	Hubert Humphrey (D)	43.74%
1972	Richard Nixon (R)	62.18%	George McGovern (D)	37.57%
1976	Jimmy Carter (D)	51.11%	Gerald Ford (R)	47.47%
1980	Ronald Reagan (R)	51.16%	Jimmy Carter (D)	44.35%
1984	Ronald Reagan (R)	60.02%	Walter Mondale (D)	39.98%
1988	George H.W. Bush (R)	51.82%	Michael Dukakis (D)	47.84%
1992	Bill Clinton (D)	44.07%	George H.W. Bush (R)	33.92%
1996	Bill Clinton (D)	47.54%	Bob Dole (R)	41.24%
2000	George W. Bush (R)	50.42%	Al Gore (D)	47.08%
2004	George W. Bush (R)	53.30%	John Kerry (D)	46.10%
2008	John McCain (R)	49.43%	Barack Obama (D)	49.29%
2012	Mitt Romney (R)	53.76%	Barack Obama (D)	44.38%
2016	Donald Trump (R)	56.77%	Hillary Clinton (D)	38.14%
2020	Donald Trump (R)	56.80%	Joseph Biden (D)	41.41%

Home-State Candidates — Missouri

Won — Harry Truman (1948)

Nominated — Harry Truman (1948)

Qualified — Edward Bates (1860), Richard Bland (1896), Gratz Brown (1872), Champ Clark (1912), Francis Cockrell (1904), Richard Gephardt (1988, 2004), James Reed (1928), Stuart Symington (1960), Harry Truman (1948)

Montana

Basics — Montana

State party winners — R 22, D 11
General-election matches — 24-9 (72.73%)
Current party streak (through 2020) — R 7
Current match streak (through 2020) — 0
2020 party indexes — R 122.35, D 79.59
2020 overall results — Trump 56.92%, Biden 40.55%, other 2.53%
2020 two-party results — Trump 58.40%, Biden 41.60%
Home-state general-election winners — 0
Home-state major-party nominees — 0
Home-state qualified candidates — 2

Two-Party Results (2008-2020) — Montana

2008: John McCain (51.17%)   **Barack Obama (48.83%)**

2012: Mitt Romney (57.03%)   **Barack Obama (42.97%)**

2016: Donald Trump (61.11%)   **Hillary Clinton (38.89%)**

2020: Donald Trump (58.40%)   **Joseph Biden (41.60%)**

Overall Results (1900-2020) — Montana

Year	Winner	PV%	Second	PV%
1900	William Jennings Bryan (D)	58.43%	William McKinley (R)	39.79%
1904	Theodore Roosevelt (R)	53.48%	Alton Parker (D)	34.32%
1908	William Howard Taft (R)	46.90%	William Jennings Bryan (D)	42.63%
1912	Woodrow Wilson (D)	35.05%	Theodore Roosevelt (P)	28.30%
1916	Woodrow Wilson (D)	56.80%	Charles Evans Hughes (R)	37.60%
1920	Warren Harding (R)	61.13%	James Cox (D)	32.05%
1924	Calvin Coolidge (R)	42.57%	Robert La Follette (P)	37.82%
1928	Herbert Hoover (R)	58.37%	Alfred Smith (D)	40.48%
1932	Franklin Roosevelt (D)	58.80%	Herbert Hoover (R)	36.07%
1936	Franklin Roosevelt (D)	69.28%	Alfred Landon (R)	27.59%
1940	Franklin Roosevelt (D)	58.78%	Wendell Willkie (R)	40.17%
1944	Franklin Roosevelt (D)	54.28%	Thomas Dewey (R)	44.93%
1948	Harry Truman (D)	53.09%	Thomas Dewey (R)	43.15%
1952	Dwight Eisenhower (R)	59.39%	Adlai Stevenson (D)	40.08%
1956	Dwight Eisenhower (R)	57.14%	Adlai Stevenson (D)	42.87%
1960	Richard Nixon (R)	51.10%	John Kennedy (D)	48.60%
1964	Lyndon Johnson (D)	58.95%	Barry Goldwater (R)	40.57%

Year	Winner	PV%	Second	PV%
1968	Richard Nixon (R)	50.60%	Hubert Humphrey (D)	41.59%
1972	Richard Nixon (R)	57.93%	George McGovern (D)	37.85%
1976	Gerald Ford (R)	52.84%	Jimmy Carter (D)	45.40%
1980	Ronald Reagan (R)	56.83%	Jimmy Carter (D)	32.43%
1984	Ronald Reagan (R)	60.47%	Walter Mondale (D)	38.18%
1988	George H.W. Bush (R)	52.07%	Michael Dukakis (D)	46.20%
1992	Bill Clinton (D)	37.63%	George H.W. Bush (R)	35.12%
1996	Bob Dole (R)	44.11%	Bill Clinton (D)	41.23%
2000	George W. Bush (R)	58.44%	Al Gore (D)	33.36%
2004	George W. Bush (R)	59.07%	John Kerry (D)	38.56%
2008	John McCain (R)	49.51%	Barack Obama (D)	47.25%
2012	Mitt Romney (R)	55.35%	Barack Obama (D)	41.70%
2016	Donald Trump (R)	56.17%	Hillary Clinton (D)	35.75%
2020	Donald Trump (R)	56.92%	Joseph Biden (D)	40.55%

Home-State Candidates — Montana

Qualified — Thomas Walsh (1924, 1928)

Nebraska

Basics — Nebraska

State party winners — R 32, D 7
General-election matches — 25-14 (64.10%)
Current party streak (through 2020) — R 14
Current match streak (through 2020) — 0
2020 party indexes — R 125.25, D 76.94
2020 overall results — Trump 58.22%, Biden 39.17%, other 2.61%
2020 two-party results — Trump 59.78%, Biden 40.22%
Home-state general-election winners — 0
Home-state major-party nominees — 3
Home-state qualified candidates — 5

Two-Party Results (2008-2020) — Nebraska

2008: John McCain (57.61%)   **Barack Obama (42.39%)**

2012: Mitt Romney (61.13%)   **Barack Obama (38.87%)**

2016: Donald Trump (63.55%)   **Hillary Clinton (36.45%)**

2020: Donald Trump (59.78%)   **Joseph Biden (40.22%)**

Overall Results (1900-2020) — Nebraska

Year	Winner	PV%	Second	PV%
1900	William McKinley (R)	50.46%	William Jennings Bryan (D)	47.22%
1904	Theodore Roosevelt (R)	61.38%	Alton Parker (D)	23.44%
1908	William Jennings Bryan (D)	49.14%	William Howard Taft (R)	47.60%
1912	Woodrow Wilson (D)	43.69%	Theodore Roosevelt (P)	29.13%
1916	Woodrow Wilson (D)	55.28%	Charles Evans Hughes (R)	40.99%
1920	Warren Harding (R)	64.66%	James Cox (D)	31.25%
1924	Calvin Coolidge (R)	47.24%	John Davis (D)	29.62%
1928	Herbert Hoover (R)	63.19%	Alfred Smith (D)	36.18%
1932	Franklin Roosevelt (D)	62.98%	Herbert Hoover (R)	35.29%
1936	Franklin Roosevelt (D)	57.14%	Alfred Landon (R)	40.74%
1940	Wendell Willkie (R)	57.19%	Franklin Roosevelt (D)	42.81%
1944	Thomas Dewey (R)	58.58%	Franklin Roosevelt (D)	41.42%
1948	Thomas Dewey (R)	54.15%	Harry Truman (D)	45.85%
1952	Dwight Eisenhower (R)	69.15%	Adlai Stevenson (D)	30.85%
1956	Dwight Eisenhower (R)	65.51%	Adlai Stevenson (D)	34.49%
1960	Richard Nixon (R)	62.07%	John Kennedy (D)	37.93%
1964	Lyndon Johnson (D)	52.61%	Barry Goldwater (R)	47.39%

Year	Winner	PV%	Second	PV%
1968	Richard Nixon (R)	59.82%	Hubert Humphrey (D)	31.81%
1972	Richard Nixon (R)	70.50%	George McGovern (D)	29.50%
1976	Gerald Ford (R)	59.19%	Jimmy Carter (D)	38.46%
1980	Ronald Reagan (R)	65.53%	Jimmy Carter (D)	26.04%
1984	Ronald Reagan (R)	70.55%	Walter Mondale (D)	28.81%
1988	George H.W. Bush (R)	60.16%	Michael Dukakis (D)	39.19%
1992	George H.W. Bush (R)	46.60%	Bill Clinton (D)	29.40%
1996	Bob Dole (R)	53.66%	Bill Clinton (D)	34.95%
2000	George W. Bush (R)	62.25%	Al Gore (D)	33.25%
2004	George W. Bush (R)	65.90%	John Kerry (D)	32.68%
2008	John McCain (R)	56.53%	Barack Obama (D)	41.60%
2012	Mitt Romney (R)	59.80%	Barack Obama (D)	38.03%
2016	Donald Trump (R)	58.75%	Hillary Clinton (D)	33.70%
2020	Donald Trump (R)	58.22%	Joseph Biden (D)	39.17%

Home-State Candidates — Nebraska

Nominated — William Jennings Bryan (1896, 1900, 1908)

Qualified — William Jennings Bryan (1896, 1900, 1908), Bob Kerrey (1992), George Norris (1928)

Nevada

Basics — Nevada

State party winners — R 20, D 19, POP 1
General-election matches — 32-8 (80.00%)
Current party streak (through 2020) — D 4
Current match streak (through 2020) — 1
2020 party indexes — R 102.19, D 98.00
2020 overall results — Biden 50.06%, Trump 47.67%, other 2.28%
2020 two-party results — Biden 51.22%, Trump 48.78%
Home-state general-election winners — 0
Home-state major-party nominees — 0
Home-state qualified candidates — 0

Two-Party Results (2008-2020) — Nevada

2008: John McCain (43.61%)   **Barack Obama (56.39%)**

2012: Mitt Romney (46.59%)   **Barack Obama (53.41%)**

2016: Donald Trump (48.71%)   **Hillary Clinton (51.29%)**

2020: Donald Trump (48.78%)   **Joseph Biden (51.22%)**

Overall Results (1900-2020) — Nevada

Year	Winner	PV%	Second	PV%
1900	William Jennings Bryan (D)	62.25%	William McKinley (R)	37.75%
1904	Theodore Roosevelt (R)	56.66%	Alton Parker (D)	32.87%
1908	William Jennings Bryan (D)	45.72%	William Howard Taft (R)	43.93%
1912	Woodrow Wilson (D)	39.70%	Theodore Roosevelt (P)	27.94%
1916	Woodrow Wilson (D)	53.36%	Charles Evans Hughes (R)	36.40%
1920	Warren Harding (R)	56.92%	James Cox (D)	36.23%
1924	Calvin Coolidge (R)	41.76%	Robert La Follette (P)	36.29%
1928	Herbert Hoover (R)	56.54%	Alfred Smith (D)	43.47%
1932	Franklin Roosevelt (D)	69.41%	Herbert Hoover (R)	30.59%
1936	Franklin Roosevelt (D)	72.81%	Alfred Landon (R)	27.19%
1940	Franklin Roosevelt (D)	60.08%	Wendell Willkie (R)	39.92%
1944	Franklin Roosevelt (D)	54.62%	Thomas Dewey (R)	45.38%
1948	Harry Truman (D)	50.37%	Thomas Dewey (R)	47.26%
1952	Dwight Eisenhower (R)	61.45%	Adlai Stevenson (D)	38.56%
1956	Dwight Eisenhower (R)	57.97%	Adlai Stevenson (D)	42.03%
1960	John Kennedy (D)	51.16%	Richard Nixon (R)	48.84%
1964	Lyndon Johnson (D)	58.58%	Barry Goldwater (R)	41.42%

Year	Winner	PV%	Second	PV%
1968	Richard Nixon (R)	47.46%	Hubert Humphrey (D)	39.29%
1972	Richard Nixon (R)	63.68%	George McGovern (D)	36.32%
1976	Gerald Ford (R)	50.17%	Jimmy Carter (D)	45.81%
1980	Ronald Reagan (R)	62.54%	Jimmy Carter (D)	26.89%
1984	Ronald Reagan (R)	65.85%	Walter Mondale (D)	31.97%
1988	George H.W. Bush (R)	58.86%	Michael Dukakis (D)	37.92%
1992	Bill Clinton (D)	37.36%	George H.W. Bush (R)	34.73%
1996	Bill Clinton (D)	43.93%	Bob Dole (R)	42.92%
2000	George W. Bush (R)	49.52%	Al Gore (D)	45.98%
2004	George W. Bush (R)	50.47%	John Kerry (D)	47.88%
2008	Barack Obama (D)	55.15%	John McCain (R)	42.65%
2012	Barack Obama (D)	52.36%	Mitt Romney (R)	45.68%
2016	Hillary Clinton (D)	47.92%	Donald Trump (R)	45.50%
2020	Joseph Biden (D)	50.06%	Donald Trump (R)	47.67%

Home-State Candidates — Nevada

(none)

New Hampshire

Basics — New Hampshire

State party winners — R 29, D 19, F 6, DR 4, NR 1
General-election matches — 44-15 (74.58%)
Current party streak (through 2020) — D 5
Current match streak (through 2020) — 1
2020 party indexes — D 102.83, R 96.90
2020 overall results — Biden 52.71%, Trump 45.36%, other 1.94%
2020 two-party results — Biden 53.75%, Trump 46.25%
Home-state general-election winners — 1
Home-state major-party nominees — 1
Home-state qualified candidates — 5

Two-Party Results (2008-2020) — New Hampshire

2008: John McCain (45.13%)   **Barack Obama (54.87%)**

2012: Mitt Romney (47.17%)   **Barack Obama (52.83%)**

2016: Donald Trump (49.80%)   **Hillary Clinton (50.20%)**

2020: Donald Trump (46.25%)   **Joseph Biden (53.75%)**

Overall Results (1900-2020) — New Hampshire

Year	Winner	PV%	Second	PV%
1900	William McKinley (R)	59.33%	William Jennings Bryan (D)	38.42%
1904	Theodore Roosevelt (R)	60.07%	Alton Parker (D)	37.79%
1908	William Howard Taft (R)	59.32%	William Jennings Bryan (D)	37.56%
1912	Woodrow Wilson (D)	39.48%	William Howard Taft (R)	37.43%
1916	Woodrow Wilson (D)	49.12%	Charles Evans Hughes (R)	49.06%
1920	Warren Harding (R)	59.84%	James Cox (D)	39.39%
1924	Calvin Coolidge (R)	59.83%	John Davis (D)	34.72%
1928	Herbert Hoover (R)	58.65%	Alfred Smith (D)	41.02%
1932	Herbert Hoover (R)	50.42%	Franklin Roosevelt (D)	48.99%
1936	Franklin Roosevelt (D)	49.73%	Alfred Landon (R)	47.98%
1940	Franklin Roosevelt (D)	53.22%	Wendell Willkie (R)	46.78%
1944	Franklin Roosevelt (D)	52.11%	Thomas Dewey (R)	47.87%
1948	Thomas Dewey (R)	52.41%	Harry Truman (D)	46.66%
1952	Dwight Eisenhower (R)	60.92%	Adlai Stevenson (D)	39.08%
1956	Dwight Eisenhower (R)	66.11%	Adlai Stevenson (D)	33.85%
1960	Richard Nixon (R)	53.42%	John Kennedy (D)	46.58%
1964	Lyndon Johnson (D)	63.89%	Barry Goldwater (R)	36.11%

Year	Winner	PV%	Second	PV%
1968	Richard Nixon (R)	52.10%	Hubert Humphrey (D)	43.93%
1972	Richard Nixon (R)	63.98%	George McGovern (D)	34.86%
1976	Gerald Ford (R)	54.75%	Jimmy Carter (D)	43.47%
1980	Ronald Reagan (R)	57.74%	Jimmy Carter (D)	28.35%
1984	Ronald Reagan (R)	68.64%	Walter Mondale (D)	30.95%
1988	George H.W. Bush (R)	62.42%	Michael Dukakis (D)	36.29%
1992	Bill Clinton (D)	38.86%	George H.W. Bush (R)	37.64%
1996	Bill Clinton (D)	49.32%	Bob Dole (R)	39.37%
2000	George W. Bush (R)	48.07%	Al Gore (D)	46.80%
2004	John Kerry (D)	50.24%	George W. Bush (R)	48.87%
2008	Barack Obama (D)	54.13%	John McCain (R)	44.52%
2012	Barack Obama (D)	51.98%	Mitt Romney (R)	46.40%
2016	Hillary Clinton (D)	46.83%	Donald Trump (R)	46.46%
2020	Joseph Biden (D)	52.71%	Donald Trump (R)	45.36%

Home-State Candidates — New Hampshire

Won — Franklin Pierce (1852)

Nominated — Franklin Pierce (1852)

Qualified — John Hale (1852), Franklin Pierce (1852, 1856), Leonard Wood (1920), Levi Woodbury (1848)

New Jersey

Basics — New Jersey

State party winners — D 25, R 19, DR 5, F 5, W 4, NR 1
General-election matches — 42-17 (71.19%)
Current party streak (through 2020) — D 8
Current match streak (through 2020) — 1
2020 party indexes — D 111.10, R 87.85
2020 overall results — Biden 57.33%, Trump 41.40%, other 1.27%
2020 two-party results — Biden 58.07%, Trump 41.93%
Home-state general-election winners — 2
Home-state major-party nominees — 4
Home-state qualified candidates — 13

Two-Party Results (2008-2020) — New Jersey

2008: John McCain (42.14%) **Barack Obama (57.87%)**

2012: Mitt Romney (41.01%) **Barack Obama (58.99%)**

2016: Donald Trump (42.72%) **Hillary Clinton (57.28%)**

2020: Donald Trump (41.93%) **Joseph Biden (58.07%)**

Overall Results (1900-2020) — New Jersey

Year	Winner	PV%	Second	PV%
1900	William McKinley (R)	55.28%	William Jennings Bryan (D)	41.09%
1904	Theodore Roosevelt (R)	56.68%	Alton Parker (D)	38.05%
1908	William Howard Taft (R)	56.80%	William Jennings Bryan (D)	39.08%
1912	Woodrow Wilson (D)	41.19%	Theodore Roosevelt (P)	33.59%
1916	Charles Evans Hughes (R)	54.40%	Woodrow Wilson (D)	42.68%
1920	Warren Harding (R)	67.60%	James Cox (D)	28.43%
1924	Calvin Coolidge (R)	62.16%	John Davis (D)	27.39%
1928	Herbert Hoover (R)	59.77%	Alfred Smith (D)	39.79%
1932	Franklin Roosevelt (D)	49.49%	Herbert Hoover (R)	47.59%
1936	Franklin Roosevelt (D)	59.54%	Alfred Landon (R)	39.57%
1940	Franklin Roosevelt (D)	51.55%	Wendell Willkie (R)	47.93%
1944	Franklin Roosevelt (D)	50.31%	Thomas Dewey (R)	48.95%
1948	Thomas Dewey (R)	50.33%	Harry Truman (D)	45.93%
1952	Dwight Eisenhower (R)	56.80%	Adlai Stevenson (D)	42.01%
1956	Dwight Eisenhower (R)	64.68%	Adlai Stevenson (D)	34.23%
1960	John Kennedy (D)	49.96%	Richard Nixon (R)	49.16%
1964	Lyndon Johnson (D)	65.61%	Barry Goldwater (R)	33.86%

Year	Winner	PV%	Second	PV%
1968	Richard Nixon (R)	46.10%	Hubert Humphrey (D)	43.97%
1972	Richard Nixon (R)	61.57%	George McGovern (D)	36.77%
1976	Gerald Ford (R)	50.08%	Jimmy Carter (D)	47.92%
1980	Ronald Reagan (R)	51.97%	Jimmy Carter (D)	38.56%
1984	Ronald Reagan (R)	60.09%	Walter Mondale (D)	39.20%
1988	George H.W. Bush (R)	56.24%	Michael Dukakis (D)	42.60%
1992	Bill Clinton (D)	42.95%	George H.W. Bush (R)	40.58%
1996	Bill Clinton (D)	53.72%	Bob Dole (R)	35.86%
2000	Al Gore (D)	56.13%	George W. Bush (R)	40.29%
2004	John Kerry (D)	52.92%	George W. Bush (R)	46.24%
2008	Barack Obama (D)	57.27%	John McCain (R)	41.70%
2012	Barack Obama (D)	58.38%	Mitt Romney (R)	40.59%
2016	Hillary Clinton (D)	55.45%	Donald Trump (R)	41.35%
2020	Joseph Biden (D)	57.33%	Donald Trump (R)	41.40%

Home-State Candidates — New Jersey

Won — Woodrow Wilson (1912, 1916)

Nominated — George McClellan (1864), Winfield Scott (1852), Woodrow Wilson (1912, 1916)

Qualified — Bill Bradley (2000), Chris Christie (2016), Edward Edwards (1920), Clinton Fisk (1888), Steve Forbes (1996, 2000), George McClellan (1864), Joel Parker (1868), Winfield Scott (1840, 1848, 1852), Woodrow Wilson (1912, 1916)

New Mexico

Basics — New Mexico

State party winners — D 16, R 12
General-election matches — 25-3 (89.29%)
Current party streak (through 2020) — D 4
Current match streak (through 2020) — 1
2020 party indexes — D 106.21, R 93.20
2020 overall results — Biden 54.29%, Trump 43.50%, other 2.21%
2020 two-party results — Biden 55.52%, Trump 44.48%
Home-state general-election winners — 0
Home-state major-party nominees — 0
Home-state qualified candidates — 2

Two-Party Results (2008-2020) — New Mexico

2008: John McCain (42.34%)   **Barack Obama (57.67%)**

2012: Mitt Romney (44.71%)   **Barack Obama (55.30%)**

2016: Donald Trump (45.35%)   **Hillary Clinton (54.65%)**

2020: Donald Trump (44.48%)   **Joseph Biden (55.52%)**

Overall Results (1900-2020) — New Mexico

Year	Winner	PV%	Second	PV%
1912	Woodrow Wilson (D)	41.87%	William Howard Taft (R)	35.17%
1916	Woodrow Wilson (D)	50.38%	Charles Evans Hughes (R)	46.50%
1920	Warren Harding (R)	54.68%	James Cox (D)	44.27%
1924	Calvin Coolidge (R)	48.52%	John Davis (D)	43.02%
1928	Herbert Hoover (R)	59.04%	Alfred Smith (D)	40.83%
1932	Franklin Roosevelt (D)	62.72%	Herbert Hoover (R)	35.76%
1936	Franklin Roosevelt (D)	62.69%	Alfred Landon (R)	36.50%
1940	Franklin Roosevelt (D)	56.59%	Wendell Willkie (R)	43.28%
1944	Franklin Roosevelt (D)	53.47%	Thomas Dewey (R)	46.44%
1948	Harry Truman (D)	56.38%	Thomas Dewey (R)	42.93%
1952	Dwight Eisenhower (R)	55.39%	Adlai Stevenson (D)	44.28%
1956	Dwight Eisenhower (R)	57.81%	Adlai Stevenson (D)	41.78%
1960	John Kennedy (D)	50.15%	Richard Nixon (R)	49.42%
1964	Lyndon Johnson (D)	59.04%	Barry Goldwater (R)	40.42%
1968	Richard Nixon (R)	51.84%	Hubert Humphrey (D)	39.74%
1972	Richard Nixon (R)	61.00%	George McGovern (D)	36.53%
1976	Gerald Ford (R)	50.53%	Jimmy Carter (D)	48.07%

Year	Winner	PV%	Second	PV%
1980	Ronald Reagan (R)	54.88%	Jimmy Carter (D)	36.73%
1984	Ronald Reagan (R)	59.70%	Walter Mondale (D)	39.23%
1988	George H.W. Bush (R)	51.86%	Michael Dukakis (D)	46.90%
1992	Bill Clinton (D)	45.90%	George H.W. Bush (R)	37.34%
1996	Bill Clinton (D)	49.18%	Bob Dole (R)	41.86%
2000	Al Gore (D)	47.91%	George W. Bush (R)	47.85%
2004	George W. Bush (R)	49.84%	John Kerry (D)	49.05%
2008	Barack Obama (D)	56.91%	John McCain (R)	41.78%
2012	Barack Obama (D)	52.99%	Mitt Romney (R)	42.84%
2016	Hillary Clinton (D)	48.26%	Donald Trump (R)	40.04%
2020	Joseph Biden (D)	54.29%	Donald Trump (R)	43.50%

Home-State Candidates — New Mexico

Qualified — Gary Johnson (2016), Bill Richardson (2008)

New York

Basics — New York
State party winners — D 26, R 20, DR 7, F 2, W 2, tie 1
General-election matches — 47-11 (81.03%)
Current party streak (through 2020) — D 9
Current match streak (through 2020) — 1
2020 party indexes — D 118.09, R 80.19
2020 overall results — Biden 60.87%, Trump 37.74%, other 1.39%
2020 two-party results — Biden 61.73%, Trump 38.27%
Home-state general-election winners — 12
Home-state major-party nominees — 26
Home-state qualified candidates — 76

Two-Party Results (2008-2020) — New York

2008: John McCain (36.42%)   **Barack Obama (63.58%)**

2012: Mitt Romney (35.70%)   **Barack Obama (64.30%)**

2016: Donald Trump (38.23%)   **Hillary Clinton (61.77%)**

2020: Donald Trump (38.27%)   **Joseph Biden (61.73%)**

Overall Results (1900-2020) — New York

Year	Winner	PV%	Second	PV%
1900	William McKinley (R)	53.10%	William Jennings Bryan (D)	43.83%
1904	Theodore Roosevelt (R)	53.13%	Alton Parker (D)	42.28%
1908	William Howard Taft (R)	53.11%	William Jennings Bryan (D)	40.74%
1912	Woodrow Wilson (D)	41.28%	William Howard Taft (R)	28.68%
1916	Charles Evans Hughes (R)	51.53%	Woodrow Wilson (D)	44.51%
1920	Warren Harding (R)	64.56%	James Cox (D)	26.95%
1924	Calvin Coolidge (R)	55.76%	John Davis (D)	29.13%
1928	Herbert Hoover (R)	49.79%	Alfred Smith (D)	47.44%
1932	Franklin Roosevelt (D)	54.07%	Herbert Hoover (R)	41.33%
1936	Franklin Roosevelt (D)	58.85%	Alfred Landon (R)	38.97%
1940	Franklin Roosevelt (D)	51.61%	Wendell Willkie (R)	48.04%
1944	Franklin Roosevelt (D)	52.31%	Thomas Dewey (R)	47.30%
1948	Thomas Dewey (R)	45.99%	Harry Truman (D)	45.01%
1952	Dwight Eisenhower (R)	55.45%	Adlai Stevenson (D)	43.55%
1956	Dwight Eisenhower (R)	61.24%	Adlai Stevenson (D)	38.73%
1960	John Kennedy (D)	52.53%	Richard Nixon (R)	47.27%
1964	Lyndon Johnson (D)	68.56%	Barry Goldwater (R)	31.31%

Year	Winner	PV%	Second	PV%
1968	Hubert Humphrey (D)	49.74%	Richard Nixon (R)	44.29%
1972	Richard Nixon (R)	58.51%	George McGovern (D)	41.18%
1976	Jimmy Carter (D)	51.87%	Gerald Ford (R)	47.46%
1980	Ronald Reagan (R)	46.66%	Jimmy Carter (D)	43.99%
1984	Ronald Reagan (R)	53.84%	Walter Mondale (D)	45.83%
1988	Michael Dukakis (D)	51.62%	George H.W. Bush (R)	47.52%
1992	Bill Clinton (D)	49.73%	George H.W. Bush (R)	33.88%
1996	Bill Clinton (D)	59.47%	Bob Dole (R)	30.61%
2000	Al Gore (D)	60.21%	George W. Bush (R)	35.23%
2004	John Kerry (D)	58.37%	George W. Bush (R)	40.08%
2008	Barack Obama (D)	62.88%	John McCain (R)	36.03%
2012	Barack Obama (D)	63.35%	Mitt Romney (R)	35.17%
2016	Hillary Clinton (D)	59.01%	Donald Trump (R)	36.52%
2020	Joseph Biden (D)	60.87%	Donald Trump (R)	37.74%

Home-State Candidates — New York

Won — Grover Cleveland (1884, 1892), Dwight Eisenhower (1952, 1956), Richard Nixon (1968), Franklin Roosevelt (1932, 1936, 1940, 1944), Theodore Roosevelt (1904), Donald Trump (2016), Martin Van Buren (1836)

Nominated — Grover Cleveland (1884, 1888, 1892), DeWitt Clinton (1812), Hillary Clinton (2016), Thomas Dewey (1944, 1948), Dwight Eisenhower (1952, 1956), Horace Greeley (1872), Charles Evans Hughes (1916), Rufus King (1816), Richard Nixon (1968), Alton Parker (1904), Franklin Roosevelt (1932, 1936, 1940, 1944), Theodore Roosevelt (1904), Horatio Seymour (1868), Alfred Smith (1928), Samuel Tilden (1876), Donald Trump (2016), Martin Van Buren (1836, 1840), Wendell Willkie (1940)

Qualified — Chester Arthur (1884), Allan Benson (1916), Michael Bloomberg (2020), Aaron Burr (1792, 1796, 1800), Nicholas Murray Butler (1920), Shirley Chisholm (1972), Sanford Church (1868), Grover Cleveland (1884, 1888, 1892), DeWitt Clinton (1812), George Clinton (1789, 1792, 1796, 1808), Hillary Clinton (2008, 2016), Roscoe Conkling (1876), Chauncey Depew (1888), Thomas Dewey (1940, 1944, 1948), Dwight Eisenhower (1952, 1956), James Farley (1940), Millard Fillmore (1852, 1856), Rudy Giuliani (2008), Horace Greeley (1872), Averell Harriman (1952, 1956), William Randolph Hearst (1904), David Hill (1892), Charles Evans Hughes (1908, 1916), John Jay (1789, 1796, 1800), Jack Kemp (1988), Robert Kennedy (1968), Rufus King (1816), William Marcy (1852), William Gibbs McAdoo (1920), Levi Morton (1896), Richard Nixon (1964, 1968), Alton Parker (1904), Colin Powell (2016), Nelson Rockefeller (1964, 1968), Franklin Roosevelt (1932, 1936, 1940, 1944), Theodore Roosevelt (1904, 1912, 1916), Elihu Root (1916), William Seward (1860), Horatio Seymour (1864, 1868), Alfred Smith (1920, 1924, 1928, 1932), Norman Thomas (1932), Samuel Tilden (1876, 1880), Donald Trump (2016), Martin Van Buren (1836, 1840, 1844, 1848), Wendell Willkie (1940)

North Carolina

Basics — North Carolina

State party winners — D 28, R 15, DR 9, W 3, SD 1, tie 1
General-election matches — 38-19 (66.67%)
Current party streak (through 2020) — R 3
Current match streak (through 2020) — 0
2020 party indexes — R 106.19, D 94.35
2020 overall results — Trump 49.93%, Biden 48.59%, other 1.48%
2020 two-party results — Trump 50.68%, Biden 49.32%
Home-state general-election winners — 0
Home-state major-party nominees — 0
Home-state qualified candidates — 5

Two-Party Results (2008-2020) — North Carolina

2008: John McCain (49.83%)   **Barack Obama (50.17%)**

2012: Mitt Romney (51.03%)   **Barack Obama (48.97%)**

2016: Donald Trump (51.90%)   **Hillary Clinton (48.10%)**

2020: Donald Trump (50.68%)   **Joseph Biden (49.32%)**

Overall Results (1900-2020) — North Carolina

Year	Winner	PV%	Second	PV%
1900	William Jennings Bryan (D)	53.92%	William McKinley (R)	45.47%
1904	Alton Parker (D)	59.71%	Theodore Roosevelt (R)	39.67%
1908	William Jennings Bryan (D)	54.22%	William Howard Taft (R)	45.49%
1912	Woodrow Wilson (D)	59.24%	Theodore Roosevelt (P)	28.36%
1916	Woodrow Wilson (D)	58.10%	Charles Evans Hughes (R)	41.71%
1920	James Cox (D)	56.69%	Warren Harding (R)	43.22%
1924	John Davis (D)	59.01%	Calvin Coolidge (R)	39.61%
1928	Herbert Hoover (R)	54.94%	Alfred Smith (D)	45.06%
1932	Franklin Roosevelt (D)	69.93%	Herbert Hoover (R)	29.28%
1936	Franklin Roosevelt (D)	73.40%	Alfred Landon (R)	26.60%
1940	Franklin Roosevelt (D)	74.03%	Wendell Willkie (R)	25.97%
1944	Franklin Roosevelt (D)	66.71%	Thomas Dewey (R)	33.29%
1948	Harry Truman (D)	58.02%	Thomas Dewey (R)	32.68%
1952	Adlai Stevenson (D)	53.91%	Dwight Eisenhower (R)	46.09%
1956	Adlai Stevenson (D)	50.66%	Dwight Eisenhower (R)	49.34%
1960	John Kennedy (D)	52.11%	Richard Nixon (R)	47.89%
1964	Lyndon Johnson (D)	56.15%	Barry Goldwater (R)	43.85%

Year	Winner	PV%	Second	PV%
1968	Richard Nixon (R)	39.51%	George Wallace (AI)	31.26%
1972	Richard Nixon (R)	69.46%	George McGovern (D)	28.89%
1976	Jimmy Carter (D)	55.24%	Gerald Ford (R)	44.19%
1980	Ronald Reagan (R)	49.31%	Jimmy Carter (D)	47.18%
1984	Ronald Reagan (R)	61.90%	Walter Mondale (D)	37.89%
1988	George H.W. Bush (R)	57.97%	Michael Dukakis (D)	41.71%
1992	George H.W. Bush (R)	43.44%	Bill Clinton (D)	42.65%
1996	Bob Dole (R)	48.73%	Bill Clinton (D)	44.04%
2000	George W. Bush (R)	56.03%	Al Gore (D)	43.20%
2004	George W. Bush (R)	56.02%	John Kerry (D)	43.58%
2008	Barack Obama (D)	49.70%	John McCain (R)	49.38%
2012	Mitt Romney (R)	50.39%	Barack Obama (D)	48.35%
2016	Donald Trump (R)	49.83%	Hillary Clinton (D)	46.17%
2020	Donald Trump (R)	49.93%	Joseph Biden (D)	48.59%

Home-State Candidates — North Carolina

Qualified — John Edwards (2004, 2008), James Iredell (1796), Samuel Johnston (1796), Willie Person Mangum (1836)

North Dakota

Basics — North Dakota

State party winners — R 27, D 5, tie 1
General-election matches — 23-10 (69.70%)
Current party streak (through 2020) — R 14
Current match streak (through 2020) — 0
2020 party indexes — R 140.80, D 62.74
2020 overall results — Trump 65.12%, Biden 31.78%, other 3.10%
2020 two-party results — Trump 67.21%, Biden 32.80%
Home-state general-election winners — 0
Home-state major-party nominees — 0
Home-state qualified candidates — 1

Two-Party Results (2008-2020) — North Dakota

2008: John McCain (54.41%)　　　　　　　　**Barack Obama (45.59%)**

2012: Mitt Romney (60.12%)　　　　　　　　**Barack Obama (39.88%)**

2016: Donald Trump (69.81%)　　　　　　　　**Hillary Clinton (30.19%)**

2020: Donald Trump (67.21%)　　　　　　　　**Joseph Biden (32.80%)**

Overall Results (1900-2020) — North Dakota

Year	Winner	PV%	Second	PV%
1900	William McKinley (R)	62.13%	William Jennings Bryan (D)	35.52%
1904	Theodore Roosevelt (R)	74.94%	Alton Parker (D)	20.34%
1908	William Howard Taft (R)	61.02%	William Jennings Bryan (D)	34.79%
1912	Woodrow Wilson (D)	34.17%	Theodore Roosevelt (P)	29.75%
1916	Woodrow Wilson (D)	47.84%	Charles Evans Hughes (R)	46.34%
1920	Warren Harding (R)	77.79%	James Cox (D)	18.19%
1924	Calvin Coolidge (R)	47.69%	Robert La Follette (P)	45.17%
1928	Herbert Hoover (R)	54.79%	Alfred Smith (D)	44.47%
1932	Franklin Roosevelt (D)	69.59%	Herbert Hoover (R)	28.00%
1936	Franklin Roosevelt (D)	59.61%	Alfred Landon (R)	26.58%
1940	Wendell Willkie (R)	55.06%	Franklin Roosevelt (D)	44.18%
1944	Thomas Dewey (R)	53.84%	Franklin Roosevelt (D)	45.48%
1948	Thomas Dewey (R)	52.17%	Harry Truman (D)	43.41%
1952	Dwight Eisenhower (R)	70.97%	Adlai Stevenson (D)	28.39%
1956	Dwight Eisenhower (R)	61.72%	Adlai Stevenson (D)	38.09%
1960	Richard Nixon (R)	55.42%	John Kennedy (D)	44.52%
1964	Lyndon Johnson (D)	57.97%	Barry Goldwater (R)	41.88%

Year	Winner	PV%	Second	PV%
1968	Richard Nixon (R)	55.94%	Hubert Humphrey (D)	38.23%
1972	Richard Nixon (R)	62.07%	George McGovern (D)	35.79%
1976	Gerald Ford (R)	51.64%	Jimmy Carter (D)	45.79%
1980	Ronald Reagan (R)	64.23%	Jimmy Carter (D)	26.26%
1984	Ronald Reagan (R)	64.84%	Walter Mondale (D)	33.80%
1988	George H.W. Bush (R)	56.03%	Michael Dukakis (D)	42.97%
1992	George H.W. Bush (R)	44.22%	Bill Clinton (D)	32.18%
1996	Bob Dole (R)	46.94%	Bill Clinton (D)	40.13%
2000	George W. Bush (R)	60.66%	Al Gore (D)	33.06%
2004	George W. Bush (R)	62.86%	John Kerry (D)	35.50%
2008	John McCain (R)	53.25%	Barack Obama (D)	44.62%
2012	Mitt Romney (R)	58.32%	Barack Obama (D)	38.69%
2016	Donald Trump (R)	62.96%	Hillary Clinton (D)	27.23%
2020	Donald Trump (R)	65.12%	Joseph Biden (D)	31.78%

Home-State Candidates — North Dakota

Qualified — William Lemke (1936)

Ohio

Basics — Ohio

State party winners — R 30, D 15, DR 7, W 3
General-election matches — 45-10 (81.82%)
Current party streak (through 2020) — R 2
Current match streak (through 2020) — 0
2020 party indexes — R 113.30, D 87.86
2020 overall results — Trump 53.27%, Biden 45.24%, other 1.49%
2020 two-party results — Trump 54.08%, Biden 45.92%
Home-state general-election winners — 7
Home-state major-party nominees — 10
Home-state qualified candidates — 34

Two-Party Results (2008-2020) — Ohio

2008: John McCain (47.67%)   **Barack Obama (52.33%)**

2012: Mitt Romney (48.49%)   **Barack Obama (51.52%)**

2016: Donald Trump (54.27%)   **Hillary Clinton (45.73%)**

2020: Donald Trump (54.08%)   **Joseph Biden (45.92%)**

Overall Results (1900-2020) — Ohio

Year	Winner	PV%	Second	PV%
1900	William McKinley (R)	52.30%	William Jennings Bryan (D)	45.66%
1904	Theodore Roosevelt (R)	59.75%	Alton Parker (D)	34.32%
1908	William Howard Taft (R)	51.03%	William Jennings Bryan (D)	44.82%
1912	Woodrow Wilson (D)	40.96%	William Howard Taft (R)	26.82%
1916	Woodrow Wilson (D)	51.86%	Charles Evans Hughes (R)	44.18%
1920	Warren Harding (R)	58.47%	James Cox (D)	38.58%
1924	Calvin Coolidge (R)	58.33%	John Davis (D)	23.70%
1928	Herbert Hoover (R)	64.89%	Alfred Smith (D)	34.45%
1932	Franklin Roosevelt (D)	49.88%	Herbert Hoover (R)	47.03%
1936	Franklin Roosevelt (D)	57.99%	Alfred Landon (R)	37.44%
1940	Franklin Roosevelt (D)	52.20%	Wendell Willkie (R)	47.80%
1944	Thomas Dewey (R)	50.18%	Franklin Roosevelt (D)	49.82%
1948	Harry Truman (D)	49.48%	Thomas Dewey (R)	49.24%
1952	Dwight Eisenhower (R)	56.76%	Adlai Stevenson (D)	43.24%
1956	Dwight Eisenhower (R)	61.11%	Adlai Stevenson (D)	38.89%
1960	Richard Nixon (R)	53.28%	John Kennedy (D)	46.72%
1964	Lyndon Johnson (D)	62.94%	Barry Goldwater (R)	37.06%

Year	Winner	PV%	Second	PV%
1968	Richard Nixon (R)	45.23%	Hubert Humphrey (D)	42.95%
1972	Richard Nixon (R)	59.63%	George McGovern (D)	38.07%
1976	Jimmy Carter (D)	48.92%	Gerald Ford (R)	48.65%
1980	Ronald Reagan (R)	51.51%	Jimmy Carter (D)	40.91%
1984	Ronald Reagan (R)	58.90%	Walter Mondale (D)	40.14%
1988	George H.W. Bush (R)	55.00%	Michael Dukakis (D)	44.15%
1992	Bill Clinton (D)	40.18%	George H.W. Bush (R)	38.35%
1996	Bill Clinton (D)	47.38%	Bob Dole (R)	41.02%
2000	George W. Bush (R)	49.97%	Al Gore (D)	46.46%
2004	George W. Bush (R)	50.81%	John Kerry (D)	48.71%
2008	Barack Obama (D)	51.50%	John McCain (R)	46.91%
2012	Barack Obama (D)	50.67%	Mitt Romney (R)	47.69%
2016	Donald Trump (R)	51.69%	Hillary Clinton (D)	43.56%
2020	Donald Trump (R)	53.27%	Joseph Biden (D)	45.24%

Home-State Candidates — Ohio

Won — James Garfield (1880), Warren Harding (1920), William Henry Harrison (1840), Rutherford Hayes (1876), William McKinley (1896, 1900), William Howard Taft (1908)

Nominated — James Cox (1920), James Garfield (1880), Warren Harding (1920), William Henry Harrison (1836, 1840), Rutherford Hayes (1876), William McKinley (1896, 1900), William Howard Taft (1908, 1912)

Qualified — William Allen (1876), John Ashbrook (1972), Theodore Burton (1916), Salmon Chase (1860), James Cox (1920, 1924), Jacob Coxey (1932), James Garfield (1880), John Glenn (1984), Warren Harding (1920), Judson Harmon (1912), William Henry Harrison (1836, 1840), Rutherford Hayes (1876), John Kasich (2016), Frank Lausche (1956), William McKinley (1892, 1896, 1900), John McLean (1856), John R. McLean (1896), Henry Payne (1880), George Pendleton (1868), James Rhodes (1968), John Sherman (1880, 1888), Robert Taft (1940, 1948, 1952), William Howard Taft (1908, 1912), Allen Thurman (1880, 1884), George White (1932)

Oklahoma

Basics — Oklahoma

State party winners — R 19, D 10
General-election matches — 20-9 (68.97%)
Current party streak (through 2020) — R 14
Current match streak (through 2020) — 0
2020 party indexes — R 140.25, D 63.25
2020 overall results — Trump 65.37%, Biden 32.29%, other 2.34%
2020 two-party results — Trump 66.94%, Biden 33.06%
Home-state general-election winners — 0
Home-state major-party nominees — 0
Home-state qualified candidates — 3

Two-Party Results (2008-2020) — Oklahoma

2008: John McCain (65.65%)   **Barack Obama (34.36%)**

2012: Mitt Romney (66.77%)   **Barack Obama (33.23%)**

2016: Donald Trump (69.31%)   **Hillary Clinton (30.70%)**

2020: Donald Trump (66.94%)   **Joseph Biden (33.06%)**

Overall Results (1900-2020) — Oklahoma

Year	Winner	PV%	Second	PV%
1908	William Jennings Bryan (D)	48.13%	William Howard Taft (R)	43.45%
1912	Woodrow Wilson (D)	46.96%	William Howard Taft (R)	35.76%
1916	Woodrow Wilson (D)	50.67%	Charles Evans Hughes (R)	33.26%
1920	Warren Harding (R)	50.21%	James Cox (D)	44.50%
1924	John Davis (D)	48.45%	Calvin Coolidge (R)	42.76%
1928	Herbert Hoover (R)	63.72%	Alfred Smith (D)	35.44%
1932	Franklin Roosevelt (D)	73.30%	Herbert Hoover (R)	26.70%
1936	Franklin Roosevelt (D)	66.83%	Alfred Landon (R)	32.69%
1940	Franklin Roosevelt (D)	57.41%	Wendell Willkie (R)	42.23%
1944	Franklin Roosevelt (D)	55.57%	Thomas Dewey (R)	44.20%
1948	Harry Truman (D)	62.75%	Thomas Dewey (R)	37.25%
1952	Dwight Eisenhower (R)	54.59%	Adlai Stevenson (D)	45.41%
1956	Dwight Eisenhower (R)	55.13%	Adlai Stevenson (D)	44.87%
1960	Richard Nixon (R)	59.02%	John Kennedy (D)	40.98%
1964	Lyndon Johnson (D)	55.75%	Barry Goldwater (R)	44.25%
1968	Richard Nixon (R)	47.68%	Hubert Humphrey (D)	31.99%
1972	Richard Nixon (R)	73.70%	George McGovern (D)	24.00%

Year	Winner	PV%	Second	PV%
1976	Gerald Ford (R)	49.96%	Jimmy Carter (D)	48.75%
1980	Ronald Reagan (R)	60.50%	Jimmy Carter (D)	34.97%
1984	Ronald Reagan (R)	68.61%	Walter Mondale (D)	30.67%
1988	George H.W. Bush (R)	57.93%	Michael Dukakis (D)	41.28%
1992	George H.W. Bush (R)	42.65%	Bill Clinton (D)	34.03%
1996	Bob Dole (R)	48.26%	Bill Clinton (D)	40.45%
2000	George W. Bush (R)	60.31%	Al Gore (D)	38.43%
2004	George W. Bush (R)	65.57%	John Kerry (D)	34.43%
2008	John McCain (R)	65.65%	Barack Obama (D)	34.36%
2012	Mitt Romney (R)	66.77%	Barack Obama (D)	33.23%
2016	Donald Trump (R)	65.32%	Hillary Clinton (D)	28.93%
2020	Donald Trump (R)	65.37%	Joseph Biden (D)	32.29%

Home-State Candidates — Oklahoma

Qualified — Fred Harris (1976), Robert Kerr (1952), William Murray (1932)

Oregon

Basics — Oregon

State party winners — R 25, D 16
General-election matches — 30-11 (73.17%)
Current party streak (through 2020) — D 9
Current match streak (through 2020) — 1
2020 party indexes — D 111.55, R 87.35
2020 overall results — Biden 56.45%, Trump 40.37%, other 3.18%
2020 two-party results — Biden 58.31%, Trump 41.69%
Home-state general-election winners — 0
Home-state major-party nominees — 0
Home-state qualified candidates — 1

Two-Party Results (2008-2020) — Oregon

2008: John McCain (41.59%)   **Barack Obama (58.41%)**

2012: Mitt Romney (43.73%)   **Barack Obama (56.27%)**

2016: Donald Trump (43.84%)   **Hillary Clinton (56.16%)**

2020: Donald Trump (41.69%)   **Joseph Biden (58.31%)**

Overall Results (1900-2020) — Oregon

Year	Winner	PV%	Second	PV%
1900	William McKinley (R)	55.25%	William Jennings Bryan (D)	39.64%
1904	Theodore Roosevelt (R)	67.27%	Alton Parker (D)	19.33%
1908	William Howard Taft (R)	56.50%	William Jennings Bryan (D)	34.19%
1912	Woodrow Wilson (D)	34.34%	Theodore Roosevelt (P)	27.44%
1916	Charles Evans Hughes (R)	48.47%	Woodrow Wilson (D)	45.90%
1920	Warren Harding (R)	60.20%	James Cox (D)	33.55%
1924	Calvin Coolidge (R)	51.01%	Robert La Follette (P)	24.47%
1928	Herbert Hoover (R)	64.18%	Alfred Smith (D)	34.14%
1932	Franklin Roosevelt (D)	58.00%	Herbert Hoover (R)	36.89%
1936	Franklin Roosevelt (D)	64.43%	Alfred Landon (R)	29.64%
1940	Franklin Roosevelt (D)	53.70%	Wendell Willkie (R)	45.62%
1944	Franklin Roosevelt (D)	51.78%	Thomas Dewey (R)	46.94%
1948	Thomas Dewey (R)	49.78%	Harry Truman (D)	46.40%
1952	Dwight Eisenhower (R)	60.54%	Adlai Stevenson (D)	38.93%
1956	Dwight Eisenhower (R)	55.21%	Adlai Stevenson (D)	44.72%
1960	Richard Nixon (R)	52.56%	John Kennedy (D)	47.32%
1964	Lyndon Johnson (D)	63.72%	Barry Goldwater (R)	35.96%

Year	Winner	PV%	Second	PV%
1968	Richard Nixon (R)	49.83%	Hubert Humphrey (D)	43.78%
1972	Richard Nixon (R)	52.45%	George McGovern (D)	42.33%
1976	Gerald Ford (R)	47.78%	Jimmy Carter (D)	47.62%
1980	Ronald Reagan (R)	48.33%	Jimmy Carter (D)	38.67%
1984	Ronald Reagan (R)	55.91%	Walter Mondale (D)	43.74%
1988	Michael Dukakis (D)	51.28%	George H.W. Bush (R)	46.61%
1992	Bill Clinton (D)	42.48%	George H.W. Bush (R)	32.53%
1996	Bill Clinton (D)	47.15%	Bob Dole (R)	39.06%
2000	Al Gore (D)	46.96%	George W. Bush (R)	46.52%
2004	John Kerry (D)	51.35%	George W. Bush (R)	47.19%
2008	Barack Obama (D)	56.75%	John McCain (R)	40.40%
2012	Barack Obama (D)	54.24%	Mitt Romney (R)	42.15%
2016	Hillary Clinton (D)	50.07%	Donald Trump (R)	39.09%
2020	Joseph Biden (D)	56.45%	Donald Trump (R)	40.37%

Home-State Candidates — Oregon

Qualified — Joseph Lane (1852)

Pennsylvania

Basics — Pennsylvania
State party winners — R 26, D 19, DR 9, F 2, W 2, P 1
General-election matches — 48-11 (81.36%)
Current party streak (through 2020) — D 1
Current match streak (through 2020) — 4
2020 party indexes — R 103.52, D 96.78
2020 overall results — Biden 49.85%, Trump 48.69%, other 1.46%
2020 two-party results — Biden 50.59%, Trump 49.41%
Home-state general-election winners — 1
Home-state major-party nominees — 2
Home-state qualified candidates — 19

Two-Party Results (2008-2020) — Pennsylvania

2008: John McCain (44.77%)   **Barack Obama (55.23%)**

2012: Mitt Romney (47.27%)   **Barack Obama (52.73%)**

2016: Donald Trump (50.38%)   **Hillary Clinton (49.62%)**

2020: Donald Trump (49.41%)   **Joseph Biden (50.59%)**

Overall Results (1900-2020) — Pennsylvania

Year	Winner	PV%	Second	PV%
1900	William McKinley (R)	60.75%	William Jennings Bryan (D)	36.16%
1904	Theodore Roosevelt (R)	68.00%	Alton Parker (D)	27.33%
1908	William Howard Taft (R)	58.84%	William Jennings Bryan (D)	35.41%
1912	Theodore Roosevelt (P)	36.54%	Woodrow Wilson (D)	32.49%
1916	Charles Evans Hughes (R)	54.26%	Woodrow Wilson (D)	40.22%
1920	Warren Harding (R)	65.81%	James Cox (D)	27.18%
1924	Calvin Coolidge (R)	65.34%	John Davis (D)	19.08%
1928	Herbert Hoover (R)	65.24%	Alfred Smith (D)	33.89%
1932	Herbert Hoover (R)	50.84%	Franklin Roosevelt (D)	45.33%
1936	Franklin Roosevelt (D)	56.88%	Alfred Landon (R)	40.85%
1940	Franklin Roosevelt (D)	53.23%	Wendell Willkie (R)	46.33%
1944	Franklin Roosevelt (D)	51.14%	Thomas Dewey (R)	48.36%
1948	Thomas Dewey (R)	50.92%	Harry Truman (D)	46.92%
1952	Dwight Eisenhower (R)	52.74%	Adlai Stevenson (D)	46.85%
1956	Dwight Eisenhower (R)	56.49%	Adlai Stevenson (D)	43.30%
1960	John Kennedy (D)	51.06%	Richard Nixon (R)	48.74%
1964	Lyndon Johnson (D)	64.92%	Barry Goldwater (R)	34.70%

Year	Winner	PV%	Second	PV%
1968	Hubert Humphrey (D)	47.59%	Richard Nixon (R)	44.02%
1972	Richard Nixon (R)	59.11%	George McGovern (D)	39.13%
1976	Jimmy Carter (D)	50.40%	Gerald Ford (R)	47.73%
1980	Ronald Reagan (R)	49.59%	Jimmy Carter (D)	42.48%
1984	Ronald Reagan (R)	53.34%	Walter Mondale (D)	45.99%
1988	George H.W. Bush (R)	50.71%	Michael Dukakis (D)	48.39%
1992	Bill Clinton (D)	45.15%	George H.W. Bush (R)	36.13%
1996	Bill Clinton (D)	49.17%	Bob Dole (R)	39.97%
2000	Al Gore (D)	50.60%	George W. Bush (R)	46.43%
2004	John Kerry (D)	50.92%	George W. Bush (R)	48.42%
2008	Barack Obama (D)	54.49%	John McCain (R)	44.17%
2012	Barack Obama (D)	51.97%	Mitt Romney (R)	46.59%
2016	Donald Trump (R)	48.18%	Hillary Clinton (D)	47.47%
2020	Joseph Biden (D)	49.85%	Donald Trump (R)	48.69%

Home-State Candidates — Pennsylvania

Won — James Buchanan (1856)

Nominated — James Buchanan (1856), Winfield Hancock (1880)

Qualified — James Buchanan (1848, 1852, 1856), Simon Cameron (1860), Winfield Hancock (1868, 1876, 1880), John Hartranft (1876), Arthur James (1940), Philander Knox (1908), Asa Packer (1868), Mitchell Palmer (1920), Robert Pattison (1896), Matthew Quay (1896), Samuel Randall (1884), Rick Santorum (2012), William Scranton (1964), William Sproul (1920), Harold Stassen (1952)

Rhode Island

Basics — Rhode Island

State party winners — D 23, R 21, F 5, DR 4, W 3, NR 2
General-election matches — 41-17 (70.69%)
Current party streak (through 2020) — D 9
Current match streak (through 2020) — 1
2020 party indexes — D 115.93, R 82.55
2020 overall results — Biden 59.39%, Trump 38.61%, other 2.00%
2020 two-party results — Biden 60.60%, Trump 39.40%
Home-state general-election winners — 0
Home-state major-party nominees — 0
Home-state qualified candidates — 0

Two-Party Results (2008-2020) — Rhode Island

2008: John McCain (35.80%)   **Barack Obama (64.20%)**

2012: Mitt Romney (35.98%)   **Barack Obama (64.02%)**

2016: Donald Trump (41.69%)   **Hillary Clinton (58.31%)**

2020: Donald Trump (39.40%)   **Joseph Biden (60.60%)**

Overall Results (1900-2020) — Rhode Island

Year	Winner	PV%	Second	PV%
1900	William McKinley (R)	59.74%	William Jennings Bryan (D)	35.04%
1904	Theodore Roosevelt (R)	60.60%	Alton Parker (D)	36.18%
1908	William Howard Taft (R)	60.76%	William Jennings Bryan (D)	34.16%
1912	Woodrow Wilson (D)	39.04%	William Howard Taft (R)	35.57%
1916	Charles Evans Hughes (R)	51.08%	Woodrow Wilson (D)	46.00%
1920	Warren Harding (R)	63.97%	James Cox (D)	32.78%
1924	Calvin Coolidge (R)	59.63%	John Davis (D)	36.46%
1928	Alfred Smith (D)	50.16%	Herbert Hoover (R)	49.55%
1932	Franklin Roosevelt (D)	55.08%	Herbert Hoover (R)	43.31%
1936	Franklin Roosevelt (D)	52.97%	Alfred Landon (R)	40.30%
1940	Franklin Roosevelt (D)	56.73%	Wendell Willkie (R)	43.17%
1944	Franklin Roosevelt (D)	58.59%	Thomas Dewey (R)	41.26%
1948	Harry Truman (D)	57.59%	Thomas Dewey (R)	41.44%
1952	Dwight Eisenhower (R)	50.89%	Adlai Stevenson (D)	49.05%
1956	Dwight Eisenhower (R)	58.26%	Adlai Stevenson (D)	41.74%
1960	John Kennedy (D)	63.63%	Richard Nixon (R)	36.37%
1964	Lyndon Johnson (D)	80.87%	Barry Goldwater (R)	19.13%

Year	Winner	PV%	Second	PV%
1968	Hubert Humphrey (D)	64.03%	Richard Nixon (R)	31.78%
1972	Richard Nixon (R)	53.00%	George McGovern (D)	46.81%
1976	Jimmy Carter (D)	55.36%	Gerald Ford (R)	44.08%
1980	Jimmy Carter (D)	47.67%	Ronald Reagan (R)	37.20%
1984	Ronald Reagan (R)	51.67%	Walter Mondale (D)	48.02%
1988	Michael Dukakis (D)	55.64%	George H.W. Bush (R)	43.93%
1992	Bill Clinton (D)	47.04%	George H.W. Bush (R)	29.02%
1996	Bill Clinton (D)	59.71%	Bob Dole (R)	26.82%
2000	Al Gore (D)	60.99%	George W. Bush (R)	31.91%
2004	John Kerry (D)	59.42%	George W. Bush (R)	38.67%
2008	Barack Obama (D)	62.86%	John McCain (R)	35.06%
2012	Barack Obama (D)	62.70%	Mitt Romney (R)	35.24%
2016	Hillary Clinton (D)	54.41%	Donald Trump (R)	38.90%
2020	Joseph Biden (D)	59.39%	Donald Trump (R)	38.61%

Home-State Candidates — Rhode Island

(none)

South Carolina

Basics — South Carolina

State party winners — D 26, R 17, DR 8, F 2, ID 1, SD 1, SRD 1, W 1, tie 1
General-election matches — 33-25 (56.90%)
Current party streak (through 2020) — R 11
Current match streak (through 2020) — 0
2020 party indexes — R 117.17, D 84.32
2020 overall results — Trump 55.11%, Biden 43.43%, other 1.46%
2020 two-party results — Trump 55.93%, Biden 44.07%
Home-state general-election winners — 0
Home-state major-party nominees — 2
Home-state qualified candidates — 7

Two-Party Results (2008-2020) — South Carolina

2008: John McCain (54.54%)   **Barack Obama (45.46%)**

2012: Mitt Romney (55.31%)   **Barack Obama (44.69%)**

2016: Donald Trump (57.46%)   **Hillary Clinton (42.54%)**

2020: Donald Trump (55.93%)   **Joseph Biden (44.07%)**

Overall Results (1900-2020) — South Carolina

Year	Winner	PV%	Second	PV%
1900	William Jennings Bryan (D)	93.05%	William McKinley (R)	6.95%
1904	Alton Parker (D)	95.40%	Theodore Roosevelt (R)	4.60%
1908	William Jennings Bryan (D)	93.84%	William Howard Taft (R)	5.94%
1912	Woodrow Wilson (D)	95.94%	Theodore Roosevelt (P)	2.57%
1916	Woodrow Wilson (D)	96.71%	Charles Evans Hughes (R)	2.42%
1920	James Cox (D)	96.05%	Warren Harding (R)	3.91%
1924	John Davis (D)	96.56%	Calvin Coolidge (R)	2.21%
1928	Alfred Smith (D)	91.39%	Herbert Hoover (R)	8.54%
1932	Franklin Roosevelt (D)	98.03%	Herbert Hoover (R)	1.90%
1936	Franklin Roosevelt (D)	98.57%	Alfred Landon (R)	1.43%
1940	Franklin Roosevelt (D)	95.63%	Wendell Willkie (R)	4.37%
1944	Franklin Roosevelt (D)	87.64%	Unpledged slate (D)	7.54%
1948	Strom Thurmond (SRD)	71.97%	Harry Truman (D)	24.14%
1952	Adlai Stevenson (D)	50.72%	Unpledged slate (R)	46.41%
1956	Adlai Stevenson (D)	45.37%	Unpledged slate (D)	29.45%
1960	John Kennedy (D)	51.24%	Richard Nixon (R)	48.76%
1964	Barry Goldwater (R)	58.89%	Lyndon Johnson (D)	41.11%

Year	Winner	PV%	Second	PV%
1968	Richard Nixon (R)	38.09%	George Wallace (AI)	32.30%
1972	Richard Nixon (R)	70.78%	George McGovern (D)	27.72%
1976	Jimmy Carter (D)	56.17%	Gerald Ford (R)	43.13%
1980	Ronald Reagan (R)	49.42%	Jimmy Carter (D)	48.14%
1984	Ronald Reagan (R)	63.55%	Walter Mondale (D)	35.57%
1988	George H.W. Bush (R)	61.51%	Michael Dukakis (D)	37.58%
1992	George H.W. Bush (R)	48.02%	Bill Clinton (D)	39.88%
1996	Bob Dole (R)	49.79%	Bill Clinton (D)	43.96%
2000	George W. Bush (R)	56.84%	Al Gore (D)	40.90%
2004	George W. Bush (R)	57.98%	John Kerry (D)	40.90%
2008	John McCain (R)	53.87%	Barack Obama (D)	44.90%
2012	Mitt Romney (R)	54.56%	Barack Obama (D)	44.09%
2016	Donald Trump (R)	54.94%	Hillary Clinton (D)	40.67%
2020	Donald Trump (R)	55.11%	Joseph Biden (D)	43.43%

Home-State Candidates — South Carolina

Nominated — Charles Cotesworth Pinckney (1804, 1808)

Qualified — Charles Cotesworth Pinckney (1796, 1800, 1804, 1808), Thomas Pinckney (1796), John Rutledge (1789), Strom Thurmond (1948)

South Dakota

Basics — South Dakota

State party winners — R 28, D 4, P 1
General-election matches — 19-14 (57.58%)
Current party streak (through 2020) — R 14
Current match streak (through 2020) — 0
2020 party indexes — R 132.90, D 69.95
2020 overall results — Trump 61.77%, Biden 35.61%, other 2.63%
2020 two-party results — Trump 63.44%, Biden 36.57%
Home-state general-election winners — 0
Home-state major-party nominees — 1
Home-state qualified candidates — 4

Two-Party Results (2008-2020) — South Dakota

2008: John McCain (54.30%)   **Barack Obama (45.70%)**

2012: Mitt Romney (59.22%)   **Barack Obama (40.78%)**

2016: Donald Trump (65.97%)   **Hillary Clinton (34.03%)**

2020: Donald Trump (63.44%)   **Joseph Biden (36.57%)**

Overall Results (1900-2020) — South Dakota

Year	Winner	PV%	Second	PV%
1900	William McKinley (R)	56.75%	William Jennings Bryan (D)	41.11%
1904	Theodore Roosevelt (R)	71.09%	Alton Parker (D)	21.67%
1908	William Howard Taft (R)	58.84%	William Jennings Bryan (D)	35.08%
1912	Theodore Roosevelt (P)	50.56%	Woodrow Wilson (D)	42.07%
1916	Charles Evans Hughes (R)	49.80%	Woodrow Wilson (D)	45.91%
1920	Warren Harding (R)	60.74%	James Cox (D)	19.72%
1924	Calvin Coolidge (R)	49.69%	Robert La Follette (P)	36.96%
1928	Herbert Hoover (R)	60.19%	Alfred Smith (D)	39.21%
1932	Franklin Roosevelt (D)	63.62%	Herbert Hoover (R)	34.40%
1936	Franklin Roosevelt (D)	54.02%	Alfred Landon (R)	42.50%
1940	Wendell Willkie (R)	57.41%	Franklin Roosevelt (D)	42.59%
1944	Thomas Dewey (R)	58.33%	Franklin Roosevelt (D)	41.67%
1948	Thomas Dewey (R)	51.84%	Harry Truman (D)	47.04%
1952	Dwight Eisenhower (R)	69.27%	Adlai Stevenson (D)	30.73%
1956	Dwight Eisenhower (R)	58.39%	Adlai Stevenson (D)	41.62%
1960	Richard Nixon (R)	58.21%	John Kennedy (D)	41.79%
1964	Lyndon Johnson (D)	55.61%	Barry Goldwater (R)	44.39%

Year	Winner	PV%	Second	PV%
1968	Richard Nixon (R)	53.27%	Hubert Humphrey (D)	41.96%
1972	Richard Nixon (R)	54.15%	George McGovern (D)	45.52%
1976	Gerald Ford (R)	50.39%	Jimmy Carter (D)	48.91%
1980	Ronald Reagan (R)	60.53%	Jimmy Carter (D)	31.69%
1984	Ronald Reagan (R)	63.00%	Walter Mondale (D)	36.53%
1988	George H.W. Bush (R)	52.85%	Michael Dukakis (D)	46.51%
1992	George H.W. Bush (R)	40.66%	Bill Clinton (D)	37.14%
1996	Bob Dole (R)	46.49%	Bill Clinton (D)	43.03%
2000	George W. Bush (R)	60.30%	Al Gore (D)	37.56%
2004	George W. Bush (R)	59.91%	John Kerry (D)	38.44%
2008	John McCain (R)	53.16%	Barack Obama (D)	44.75%
2012	Mitt Romney (R)	57.89%	Barack Obama (D)	39.87%
2016	Donald Trump (R)	61.53%	Hillary Clinton (D)	31.74%
2020	Donald Trump (R)	61.77%	Joseph Biden (D)	35.61%

Home-State Candidates — South Dakota

Nominated — George McGovern (1972)
Qualified — George McGovern (1968, 1972, 1984), Faith Spotted Eagle (2016)

Tennessee

Basics — Tennessee
State party winners — D 24, R 17, DR 9, W 5, CU 1
General-election matches — 37-19 (66.07%)
Current party streak (through 2020) — R 6
Current match streak (through 2020) — 0
2020 party indexes — R 129.54, D 73.03
2020 overall results — Trump 60.66%, Biden 37.45%, other 1.89%
2020 two-party results — Trump 61.83%, Biden 38.17%
Home-state general-election winners — 3
Home-state major-party nominees — 6
Home-state qualified candidates — 16

Two-Party Results (2008-2020) — Tennessee

2008: John McCain (57.63%)   **Barack Obama (42.37%)**

2012: Mitt Romney (60.35%)   **Barack Obama (39.65%)**

2016: Donald Trump (63.62%)   **Hillary Clinton (36.38%)**

2020: Donald Trump (61.83%)   **Joseph Biden (38.17%)**

Overall Results (1900-2020) — Tennessee

Year	Winner	PV%	Second	PV%
1900	William Jennings Bryan (D)	53.03%	William McKinley (R)	44.95%
1904	Alton Parker (D)	54.23%	Theodore Roosevelt (R)	43.40%
1908	William Jennings Bryan (D)	52.73%	William Howard Taft (R)	45.87%
1912	Woodrow Wilson (D)	52.80%	William Howard Taft (R)	24.00%
1916	Woodrow Wilson (D)	56.31%	Charles Evans Hughes (R)	42.70%
1920	Warren Harding (R)	51.22%	James Cox (D)	48.26%
1924	John Davis (D)	52.93%	Calvin Coolidge (R)	43.46%
1928	Herbert Hoover (R)	55.32%	Alfred Smith (D)	44.49%
1932	Franklin Roosevelt (D)	66.49%	Herbert Hoover (R)	32.48%
1936	Franklin Roosevelt (D)	68.78%	Alfred Landon (R)	30.81%
1940	Franklin Roosevelt (D)	67.25%	Wendell Willkie (R)	32.35%
1944	Franklin Roosevelt (D)	60.45%	Thomas Dewey (R)	39.22%
1948	Harry Truman (D)	49.14%	Thomas Dewey (R)	36.87%
1952	Dwight Eisenhower (R)	49.99%	Adlai Stevenson (D)	49.71%
1956	Dwight Eisenhower (R)	49.21%	Adlai Stevenson (D)	48.60%
1960	Richard Nixon (R)	52.92%	John Kennedy (D)	45.78%
1964	Lyndon Johnson (D)	55.51%	Barry Goldwater (R)	44.49%

Year	Winner	PV%	Second	PV%
1968	Richard Nixon (R)	37.85%	George Wallace (AI)	34.02%
1972	Richard Nixon (R)	67.70%	George McGovern (D)	29.75%
1976	Jimmy Carter (D)	55.94%	Gerald Ford (R)	42.94%
1980	Ronald Reagan (R)	48.70%	Jimmy Carter (D)	48.41%
1984	Ronald Reagan (R)	57.84%	Walter Mondale (D)	41.57%
1988	George H.W. Bush (R)	57.89%	Michael Dukakis (D)	41.55%
1992	Bill Clinton (D)	47.09%	George H.W. Bush (R)	42.43%
1996	Bill Clinton (D)	48.00%	Bob Dole (R)	45.59%
2000	George W. Bush (R)	51.15%	Al Gore (D)	47.29%
2004	George W. Bush (R)	56.80%	John Kerry (D)	42.53%
2008	John McCain (R)	56.90%	Barack Obama (D)	41.83%
2012	Mitt Romney (R)	59.48%	Barack Obama (D)	39.08%
2016	Donald Trump (R)	60.72%	Hillary Clinton (D)	34.72%
2020	Donald Trump (R)	60.66%	Joseph Biden (D)	37.45%

Home-State Candidates — Tennessee

Won — Andrew Jackson (1828, 1832), James Polk (1844)

Nominated — Al Gore (2000), Andrew Jackson (1824, 1828, 1832), James Polk (1844), Hugh White (1836)

Qualified — Lamar Alexander (1996), Howard Baker (1980), John Bell (1860), Al Gore (1988, 2000), Cordell Hull (1928), Andrew Jackson (1824, 1828, 1832), Andrew Johnson (1860, 1868), Estes Kefauver (1952, 1956), James Polk (1844), Fred Thompson (2008), Hugh White (1836)

Texas

Basics — Texas

State party winners — D 26, R 15, SD 1
General-election matches — 24-18 (57.14%)
Current party streak (through 2020) — R 11
Current match streak (through 2020) — 0
2020 party indexes — R 110.69, D 90.24
2020 overall results — Trump 52.06%, Biden 46.48%, other 1.46%
2020 two-party results — Trump 52.83%, Biden 47.17%
Home-state general-election winners — 4
Home-state major-party nominees — 5
Home-state qualified candidates — 21

Two-Party Results (2008-2020) — Texas

2008: John McCain (55.94%)   **Barack Obama (44.06%)**

2012: Mitt Romney (58.01%)   **Barack Obama (41.99%)**

2016: Donald Trump (54.71%)   **Hillary Clinton (45.29%)**

2020: Donald Trump (52.83%)   **Joseph Biden (47.17%)**

Overall Results (1900-2020) — Texas

Year	Winner	PV%	Second	PV%
1900	William Jennings Bryan (D)	63.15%	William McKinley (R)	30.91%
1904	Alton Parker (D)	71.53%	Theodore Roosevelt (R)	21.96%
1908	William Jennings Bryan (D)	73.97%	William Howard Taft (R)	22.40%
1912	Woodrow Wilson (D)	72.74%	William Howard Taft (R)	9.41%
1916	Woodrow Wilson (D)	76.92%	Charles Evans Hughes (R)	17.45%
1920	James Cox (D)	59.23%	Warren Harding (R)	23.59%
1924	John Davis (D)	73.57%	Calvin Coolidge (R)	19.91%
1928	Herbert Hoover (R)	51.77%	Alfred Smith (D)	48.10%
1932	Franklin Roosevelt (D)	88.06%	Herbert Hoover (R)	11.35%
1936	Franklin Roosevelt (D)	87.08%	Alfred Landon (R)	12.32%
1940	Franklin Roosevelt (D)	80.69%	Wendell Willkie (R)	19.13%
1944	Franklin Roosevelt (D)	71.42%	Thomas Dewey (R)	16.64%
1948	Harry Truman (D)	65.44%	Thomas Dewey (R)	24.60%
1952	Dwight Eisenhower (R)	53.13%	Adlai Stevenson (D)	46.69%
1956	Dwight Eisenhower (R)	55.27%	Adlai Stevenson (D)	43.98%
1960	John Kennedy (D)	50.52%	Richard Nixon (R)	48.52%
1964	Lyndon Johnson (D)	63.32%	Barry Goldwater (R)	36.49%

Year	Winner	PV%	Second	PV%
1968	Hubert Humphrey (D)	41.14%	Richard Nixon (R)	39.88%
1972	Richard Nixon (R)	66.23%	George McGovern (D)	33.25%
1976	Jimmy Carter (D)	51.14%	Gerald Ford (R)	47.97%
1980	Ronald Reagan (R)	55.28%	Jimmy Carter (D)	41.42%
1984	Ronald Reagan (R)	63.61%	Walter Mondale (D)	36.11%
1988	George H.W. Bush (R)	55.95%	Michael Dukakis (D)	43.35%
1992	George H.W. Bush (R)	40.56%	Bill Clinton (D)	37.08%
1996	Bob Dole (R)	48.76%	Bill Clinton (D)	43.83%
2000	George W. Bush (R)	59.30%	Al Gore (D)	37.98%
2004	George W. Bush (R)	61.09%	John Kerry (D)	38.22%
2008	John McCain (R)	55.45%	Barack Obama (D)	43.68%
2012	Mitt Romney (R)	57.17%	Barack Obama (D)	41.38%
2016	Donald Trump (R)	52.24%	Hillary Clinton (D)	43.24%
2020	Donald Trump (R)	52.06%	Joseph Biden (D)	46.48%

Home-State Candidates — Texas

Won — George H.W. Bush (1988), George W. Bush (2000, 2004), Lyndon Johnson (1964)

Nominated — George H.W. Bush (1988, 1992), George W. Bush (2000, 2004), Lyndon Johnson (1964)

Qualified — Lloyd Bentsen (1988), George H.W. Bush (1980, 1988, 1992), George W. Bush (2000, 2004), John Connally (1980), Ted Cruz (2016), John Nance Garner (1932, 1940), Phil Gramm (1996), Lyndon Johnson (1956, 1960, 1964, 1968), Ron Paul (2008, 2012, 2016), Ross Perot (1992, 1996), Rick Perry (2012)

Utah

Basics — Utah

State party winners — R 24, D 8
General-election matches — 23-9 (71.88%)
Current party streak (through 2020) — R 14
Current match streak (through 2020) — 0
2020 party indexes — R 127.16, D 75.20
2020 overall results — Trump 58.13%, Biden 37.65%, other 4.22%
2020 two-party results — Trump 60.69%, Biden 39.31%
Home-state general-election winners — 0
Home-state major-party nominees — 0
Home-state qualified candidates — 1

Two-Party Results (2008-2020) — Utah

2008: John McCain (64.53%)   **Barack Obama (35.47%)**

2012: Mitt Romney (74.63%)   **Barack Obama (25.37%)**

2016: Donald Trump (62.38%)   **Hillary Clinton (37.62%)**

2020: Donald Trump (60.69%)   **Joseph Biden (39.31%)**

Overall Results (1900-2020) — Utah

Year	Winner	PV%	Second	PV%
1900	William McKinley (R)	50.60%	William Jennings Bryan (D)	48.30%
1904	Theodore Roosevelt (R)	61.45%	Alton Parker (D)	32.88%
1908	William Howard Taft (R)	56.24%	William Jennings Bryan (D)	39.18%
1912	William Howard Taft (R)	37.42%	Woodrow Wilson (D)	32.58%
1916	Woodrow Wilson (D)	58.78%	Charles Evans Hughes (R)	37.82%
1920	Warren Harding (R)	55.93%	James Cox (D)	38.84%
1924	Calvin Coolidge (R)	49.26%	John Davis (D)	29.94%
1928	Herbert Hoover (R)	53.58%	Alfred Smith (D)	45.86%
1932	Franklin Roosevelt (D)	56.52%	Herbert Hoover (R)	41.05%
1936	Franklin Roosevelt (D)	69.34%	Alfred Landon (R)	29.79%
1940	Franklin Roosevelt (D)	62.25%	Wendell Willkie (R)	37.59%
1944	Franklin Roosevelt (D)	60.44%	Thomas Dewey (R)	39.42%
1948	Harry Truman (D)	53.98%	Thomas Dewey (R)	45.02%
1952	Dwight Eisenhower (R)	58.93%	Adlai Stevenson (D)	41.08%
1956	Dwight Eisenhower (R)	64.56%	Adlai Stevenson (D)	35.44%
1960	Richard Nixon (R)	54.81%	John Kennedy (D)	45.17%
1964	Lyndon Johnson (D)	54.71%	Barry Goldwater (R)	45.29%

Year	Winner	PV%	Second	PV%
1968	Richard Nixon (R)	56.50%	Hubert Humphrey (D)	37.08%
1972	Richard Nixon (R)	67.64%	George McGovern (D)	26.39%
1976	Gerald Ford (R)	62.44%	Jimmy Carter (D)	33.65%
1980	Ronald Reagan (R)	72.77%	Jimmy Carter (D)	20.57%
1984	Ronald Reagan (R)	74.50%	Walter Mondale (D)	24.68%
1988	George H.W. Bush (R)	66.22%	Michael Dukakis (D)	32.05%
1992	George H.W. Bush (R)	43.37%	Ross Perot (I)	27.34%
1996	Bob Dole (R)	54.37%	Bill Clinton (D)	33.30%
2000	George W. Bush (R)	66.83%	Al Gore (D)	26.35%
2004	George W. Bush (R)	71.54%	John Kerry (D)	26.00%
2008	John McCain (R)	62.58%	Barack Obama (D)	34.41%
2012	Mitt Romney (R)	72.79%	Barack Obama (D)	24.75%
2016	Donald Trump (R)	45.54%	Hillary Clinton (D)	27.46%
2020	Donald Trump (R)	58.13%	Joseph Biden (D)	37.65%

Home-State Candidates — Utah

Qualified — Jon Huntsman (2012)

Vermont

Basics — Vermont

State party winners — R 33, D 9, DR 6, W 5, F 3, AM 1, NR 1
General-election matches — 37-21 (63.79%)
Current party streak (through 2020) — D 8
Current match streak (through 2020) — 1
2020 party indexes — D 130.67, R 66.42
2020 overall results — Biden 66.09%, Trump 30.67%, other 3.24%
2020 two-party results — Biden 68.30%, Trump 31.70%
Home-state general-election winners — 0
Home-state major-party nominees — 0
Home-state qualified candidates — 5

Two-Party Results (2008-2020) — Vermont

2008: John McCain (31.10%)   **Barack Obama (68.90%)**

2012: Mitt Romney (31.75%)   **Barack Obama (68.25%)**

2016: Donald Trump (34.81%)   **Hillary Clinton (65.19%)**

2020: Donald Trump (31.70%)   **Joseph Biden (68.30%)**

Overall Results (1900-2020) — Vermont

Year	Winner	PV%	Second	PV%
1900	William McKinley (R)	75.73%	William Jennings Bryan (D)	22.86%
1904	Theodore Roosevelt (R)	77.97%	Alton Parker (D)	18.84%
1908	William Howard Taft (R)	75.08%	William Jennings Bryan (D)	21.82%
1912	William Howard Taft (R)	37.10%	Theodore Roosevelt (P)	35.24%
1916	Charles Evans Hughes (R)	62.43%	Woodrow Wilson (D)	35.22%
1920	Warren Harding (R)	75.82%	James Cox (D)	23.25%
1924	Calvin Coolidge (R)	78.22%	John Davis (D)	15.67%
1928	Herbert Hoover (R)	66.87%	Alfred Smith (D)	32.87%
1932	Herbert Hoover (R)	57.66%	Franklin Roosevelt (D)	41.08%
1936	Alfred Landon (R)	56.39%	Franklin Roosevelt (D)	43.24%
1940	Wendell Willkie (R)	54.78%	Franklin Roosevelt (D)	44.92%
1944	Thomas Dewey (R)	57.06%	Franklin Roosevelt (D)	42.93%
1948	Thomas Dewey (R)	61.54%	Harry Truman (D)	36.92%
1952	Dwight Eisenhower (R)	71.45%	Adlai Stevenson (D)	28.23%
1956	Dwight Eisenhower (R)	72.16%	Adlai Stevenson (D)	27.81%
1960	Richard Nixon (R)	58.65%	John Kennedy (D)	41.35%
1964	Lyndon Johnson (D)	66.30%	Barry Goldwater (R)	33.69%

Year	Winner	PV%	Second	PV%
1968	Richard Nixon (R)	52.75%	Hubert Humphrey (D)	43.53%
1972	Richard Nixon (R)	62.66%	George McGovern (D)	36.47%
1976	Gerald Ford (R)	54.37%	Jimmy Carter (D)	43.12%
1980	Ronald Reagan (R)	44.36%	Jimmy Carter (D)	38.42%
1984	Ronald Reagan (R)	57.92%	Walter Mondale (D)	40.81%
1988	George H.W. Bush (R)	51.10%	Michael Dukakis (D)	47.58%
1992	Bill Clinton (D)	46.11%	George H.W. Bush (R)	30.42%
1996	Bill Clinton (D)	53.35%	Bob Dole (R)	31.09%
2000	Al Gore (D)	50.64%	George W. Bush (R)	40.70%
2004	John Kerry (D)	58.94%	George W. Bush (R)	38.80%
2008	Barack Obama (D)	67.46%	John McCain (R)	30.45%
2012	Barack Obama (D)	66.57%	Mitt Romney (R)	30.97%
2016	Hillary Clinton (D)	56.68%	Donald Trump (R)	30.27%
2020	Joseph Biden (D)	66.09%	Donald Trump (R)	30.67%

Home-State Candidates — Vermont

Qualified — Howard Dean (2004), George Edmunds (1880, 1884), Bernie Sanders (2016, 2020)

Virginia

Basics — Virginia

State party winners — D 30, R 15, DR 9, CU 1, F 1, tie 1
General-election matches — 38-19 (66.67%)
Current party streak (through 2020) — D 4
Current match streak (through 2020) — 1
2020 party indexes — D 105.52, R 93.96
2020 overall results — Biden 54.11%, Trump 44.00%, other 1.89%
2020 two-party results — Biden 55.16%, Trump 44.85%
Home-state general-election winners — 8
Home-state major-party nominees — 9
Home-state qualified candidates — 21

Two-Party Results (2008-2020) — Virginia

2008: John McCain (46.82%)   **Barack Obama (53.18%)**

2012: Mitt Romney (48.03%)   **Barack Obama (51.97%)**

2016: Donald Trump (47.17%)   **Hillary Clinton (52.83%)**

2020: Donald Trump (44.85%)   **Joseph Biden (55.16%)**

Overall Results (1900-2020) — Virginia

Year	Winner	PV%	Second	PV%
1900	William Jennings Bryan (D)	55.29%	William McKinley (R)	43.82%
1904	Alton Parker (D)	61.84%	Theodore Roosevelt (R)	36.95%
1908	William Jennings Bryan (D)	60.52%	William Howard Taft (R)	38.36%
1912	Woodrow Wilson (D)	65.95%	William Howard Taft (R)	17.00%
1916	Woodrow Wilson (D)	66.77%	Charles Evans Hughes (R)	32.05%
1920	James Cox (D)	61.33%	Warren Harding (R)	37.86%
1924	John Davis (D)	62.48%	Calvin Coolidge (R)	32.79%
1928	Herbert Hoover (R)	53.91%	Alfred Smith (D)	45.90%
1932	Franklin Roosevelt (D)	68.46%	Herbert Hoover (R)	30.09%
1936	Franklin Roosevelt (D)	70.23%	Alfred Landon (R)	29.39%
1940	Franklin Roosevelt (D)	68.08%	Wendell Willkie (R)	31.55%
1944	Franklin Roosevelt (D)	62.36%	Thomas Dewey (R)	37.39%
1948	Harry Truman (D)	47.89%	Thomas Dewey (R)	41.04%
1952	Dwight Eisenhower (R)	56.33%	Adlai Stevenson (D)	43.36%
1956	Dwight Eisenhower (R)	55.37%	Adlai Stevenson (D)	38.36%
1960	Richard Nixon (R)	52.44%	John Kennedy (D)	46.97%
1964	Lyndon Johnson (D)	53.54%	Barry Goldwater (R)	46.18%

Year	Winner	PV%	Second	PV%
1968	Richard Nixon (R)	43.36%	Hubert Humphrey (D)	32.49%
1972	Richard Nixon (R)	67.84%	George McGovern (D)	30.12%
1976	Gerald Ford (R)	49.29%	Jimmy Carter (D)	47.96%
1980	Ronald Reagan (R)	53.03%	Jimmy Carter (D)	40.31%
1984	Ronald Reagan (R)	62.29%	Walter Mondale (D)	37.09%
1988	George H.W. Bush (R)	59.74%	Michael Dukakis (D)	39.23%
1992	George H.W. Bush (R)	44.97%	Bill Clinton (D)	40.59%
1996	Bob Dole (R)	47.11%	Bill Clinton (D)	45.15%
2000	George W. Bush (R)	52.47%	Al Gore (D)	44.44%
2004	George W. Bush (R)	53.68%	John Kerry (D)	45.48%
2008	Barack Obama (D)	52.63%	John McCain (R)	46.33%
2012	Barack Obama (D)	51.16%	Mitt Romney (R)	47.28%
2016	Hillary Clinton (D)	49.73%	Donald Trump (R)	44.41%
2020	Joseph Biden (D)	54.11%	Donald Trump (R)	44.00%

Home-State Candidates — Virginia

Won — Thomas Jefferson (1800, 1804), James Madison (1808, 1812), James Monroe (1816, 1820), George Washington (1789, 1792)

Nominated — Thomas Jefferson (1796, 1800, 1804), James Madison (1808, 1812), James Monroe (1816, 1820), George Washington (1789, 1792)

Qualified — Gary Bauer (2000), Pat Buchanan (1992, 1996), Harry Byrd (1944, 1960), Carly Fiorina (2016), John Floyd (1832), Robert Hunter (1860), Thomas Jefferson (1792, 1796, 1800, 1804), Lyndon LaRouche (1996), James Madison (1808, 1812), James Monroe (1816, 1820), Pat Robertson (1988), George Washington (1789, 1792, 1796)

Washington

Basics — Washington

State party winners — D 18, R 14, P 1
General-election matches — 23-10 (69.70%)
Current party streak (through 2020) — D 9
Current match streak (through 2020) — 1
2020 party indexes — D 114.65, R 83.96
2020 overall results — Biden 57.97%, Trump 38.77%, other 3.26%
2020 two-party results — Biden 59.93%, Trump 40.07%
Home-state general-election winners — 0
Home-state major-party nominees — 0
Home-state qualified candidates — 2

Two-Party Results (2008-2020) — Washington

2008: John McCain (41.25%)   **Barack Obama (58.75%)**

2012: Mitt Romney (42.37%)   **Barack Obama (57.63%)**

2016: Donald Trump (41.21%)   **Hillary Clinton (58.79%)**

2020: Donald Trump (40.07%)   **Joseph Biden (59.93%)**

Overall Results (1900-2020) — Washington

Year	Winner	PV%	Second	PV%
1900	William McKinley (R)	53.44%	William Jennings Bryan (D)	41.70%
1904	Theodore Roosevelt (R)	69.96%	Alton Parker (D)	19.36%
1908	William Howard Taft (R)	57.78%	William Jennings Bryan (D)	31.80%
1912	Theodore Roosevelt (P)	35.22%	Woodrow Wilson (D)	26.90%
1916	Woodrow Wilson (D)	48.13%	Charles Evans Hughes (R)	43.89%
1920	Warren Harding (R)	55.96%	James Cox (D)	21.14%
1924	Calvin Coolidge (R)	52.24%	Robert La Follette (P)	35.76%
1928	Herbert Hoover (R)	67.06%	Alfred Smith (D)	31.30%
1932	Franklin Roosevelt (D)	57.46%	Herbert Hoover (R)	33.94%
1936	Franklin Roosevelt (D)	66.38%	Alfred Landon (R)	29.88%
1940	Franklin Roosevelt (D)	58.22%	Wendell Willkie (R)	40.58%
1944	Franklin Roosevelt (D)	56.84%	Thomas Dewey (R)	42.24%
1948	Harry Truman (D)	52.61%	Thomas Dewey (R)	42.68%
1952	Dwight Eisenhower (R)	54.33%	Adlai Stevenson (D)	44.69%
1956	Dwight Eisenhower (R)	53.91%	Adlai Stevenson (D)	45.44%
1960	Richard Nixon (R)	50.68%	John Kennedy (D)	48.27%
1964	Lyndon Johnson (D)	61.97%	Barry Goldwater (R)	37.37%

Year	Winner	PV%	Second	PV%
1968	Hubert Humphrey (D)	47.23%	Richard Nixon (R)	45.12%
1972	Richard Nixon (R)	56.92%	George McGovern (D)	38.64%
1976	Gerald Ford (R)	50.00%	Jimmy Carter (D)	46.11%
1980	Ronald Reagan (R)	49.66%	Jimmy Carter (D)	37.32%
1984	Ronald Reagan (R)	55.82%	Walter Mondale (D)	42.86%
1988	Michael Dukakis (D)	50.05%	George H.W. Bush (R)	48.46%
1992	Bill Clinton (D)	43.40%	George H.W. Bush (R)	31.96%
1996	Bill Clinton (D)	49.84%	Bob Dole (R)	37.30%
2000	Al Gore (D)	50.16%	George W. Bush (R)	44.58%
2004	John Kerry (D)	52.82%	George W. Bush (R)	45.64%
2008	Barack Obama (D)	57.65%	John McCain (R)	40.48%
2012	Barack Obama (D)	56.16%	Mitt Romney (R)	41.30%
2016	Hillary Clinton (D)	52.54%	Donald Trump (R)	36.83%
2020	Joseph Biden (D)	57.97%	Donald Trump (R)	38.77%

Home-State Candidates — Washington

Qualified — Henry Jackson (1972, 1976)

West Virginia

Basics — West Virginia

State party winners — D 20, R 20
General-election matches — 29-11 (72.50%)
Current party streak (through 2020) — R 6
Current match streak (through 2020) — 0
2020 party indexes — R 146.24, D 57.78
2020 overall results — Trump 68.63%, Biden 29.69%, other 1.68%
2020 two-party results — Trump 69.80%, Biden 30.20%
Home-state general-election winners — 0
Home-state major-party nominees — 1
Home-state qualified candidates — 2

Two-Party Results (2008-2020) — West Virginia

2008: John McCain (56.67%)   **Barack Obama (43.33%)**

2012: Mitt Romney (63.67%)   **Barack Obama (36.33%)**

2016: Donald Trump (72.16%)   **Hillary Clinton (27.84%)**

2020: Donald Trump (69.80%)   **Joseph Biden (30.20%)**

Overall Results (1900-2020) — West Virginia

Year	Winner	PV%	Second	PV%
1900	William McKinley (R)	54.27%	William Jennings Bryan (D)	44.75%
1904	Theodore Roosevelt (R)	55.26%	Alton Parker (D)	42.03%
1908	William Howard Taft (R)	53.42%	William Jennings Bryan (D)	43.17%
1912	Woodrow Wilson (D)	42.09%	Theodore Roosevelt (P)	29.44%
1916	Charles Evans Hughes (R)	49.41%	Woodrow Wilson (D)	48.47%
1920	Warren Harding (R)	55.30%	James Cox (D)	43.30%
1924	Calvin Coolidge (R)	49.45%	John Davis (D)	44.07%
1928	Herbert Hoover (R)	58.43%	Alfred Smith (D)	41.04%
1932	Franklin Roosevelt (D)	54.47%	Herbert Hoover (R)	44.47%
1936	Franklin Roosevelt (D)	60.56%	Alfred Landon (R)	39.20%
1940	Franklin Roosevelt (D)	57.10%	Wendell Willkie (R)	42.90%
1944	Franklin Roosevelt (D)	54.89%	Thomas Dewey (R)	45.11%
1948	Harry Truman (D)	57.32%	Thomas Dewey (R)	42.24%
1952	Adlai Stevenson (D)	51.92%	Dwight Eisenhower (R)	48.08%
1956	Dwight Eisenhower (R)	54.08%	Adlai Stevenson (D)	45.92%
1960	John Kennedy (D)	52.73%	Richard Nixon (R)	47.27%
1964	Lyndon Johnson (D)	67.94%	Barry Goldwater (R)	32.06%

Year	Winner	PV%	Second	PV%
1968	Hubert Humphrey (D)	49.60%	Richard Nixon (R)	40.78%
1972	Richard Nixon (R)	63.61%	George McGovern (D)	36.39%
1976	Jimmy Carter (D)	58.05%	Gerald Ford (R)	41.91%
1980	Jimmy Carter (D)	49.81%	Ronald Reagan (R)	45.30%
1984	Ronald Reagan (R)	55.11%	Walter Mondale (D)	44.60%
1988	Michael Dukakis (D)	52.20%	George H.W. Bush (R)	47.46%
1992	Bill Clinton (D)	48.41%	George H.W. Bush (R)	35.39%
1996	Bill Clinton (D)	51.51%	Bob Dole (R)	36.76%
2000	George W. Bush (R)	51.92%	Al Gore (D)	45.59%
2004	George W. Bush (R)	56.06%	John Kerry (D)	43.20%
2008	John McCain (R)	55.71%	Barack Obama (D)	42.59%
2012	Mitt Romney (R)	62.30%	Barack Obama (D)	35.54%
2016	Donald Trump (R)	68.50%	Hillary Clinton (D)	26.43%
2020	Donald Trump (R)	68.63%	Joseph Biden (D)	29.69%

Home-State Candidates — West Virginia

Nominated — John Davis (1924)
Qualified — John Davis (1920, 1924)

Wisconsin

Basics — Wisconsin
State party winners — R 25, D 18, P 1
General-election matches — 34-10 (77.27%)
Current party streak (through 2020) — D 1
Current match streak (through 2020) — 4
2020 party indexes — R 104.09, D 96.27
2020 overall results — Biden 49.45%, Trump 48.82%, other 1.73%
2020 two-party results — Biden 50.32%, Trump 49.68%
Home-state general-election winners — 0
Home-state major-party nominees — 0
Home-state qualified candidates — 5

Two-Party Results (2008-2020) — Wisconsin

2008: John McCain (42.94%)   **Barack Obama (57.06%)**

2012: Mitt Romney (46.48%)   **Barack Obama (53.52%)**

2016: Donald Trump (50.41%)   **Hillary Clinton (49.59%)**

2020: Donald Trump (49.68%)   **Joseph Biden (50.32%)**

Overall Results (1900-2020) — Wisconsin

Year	Winner	PV%	Second	PV%
1900	William McKinley (R)	60.06%	William Jennings Bryan (D)	35.97%
1904	Theodore Roosevelt (R)	63.21%	Alton Parker (D)	28.01%
1908	William Howard Taft (R)	54.52%	William Jennings Bryan (D)	36.67%
1912	Woodrow Wilson (D)	41.06%	William Howard Taft (R)	32.65%
1916	Charles Evans Hughes (R)	49.39%	Woodrow Wilson (D)	42.80%
1920	Warren Harding (R)	71.10%	James Cox (D)	16.17%
1924	Robert La Follette (P)	53.96%	Calvin Coolidge (R)	37.06%
1928	Herbert Hoover (R)	53.52%	Alfred Smith (D)	44.28%
1932	Franklin Roosevelt (D)	63.46%	Herbert Hoover (R)	31.19%
1936	Franklin Roosevelt (D)	63.80%	Alfred Landon (R)	30.26%
1940	Franklin Roosevelt (D)	50.15%	Wendell Willkie (R)	48.32%
1944	Thomas Dewey (R)	50.37%	Franklin Roosevelt (D)	48.57%
1948	Harry Truman (D)	50.70%	Thomas Dewey (R)	46.28%
1952	Dwight Eisenhower (R)	60.95%	Adlai Stevenson (D)	38.71%
1956	Dwight Eisenhower (R)	61.58%	Adlai Stevenson (D)	37.84%
1960	Richard Nixon (R)	51.77%	John Kennedy (D)	48.05%
1964	Lyndon Johnson (D)	62.09%	Barry Goldwater (R)	37.74%

Year	Winner	PV%	Second	PV%
1968	Richard Nixon (R)	47.89%	Hubert Humphrey (D)	44.27%
1972	Richard Nixon (R)	53.40%	George McGovern (D)	43.73%
1976	Jimmy Carter (D)	49.44%	Gerald Ford (R)	47.76%
1980	Ronald Reagan (R)	47.90%	Jimmy Carter (D)	43.18%
1984	Ronald Reagan (R)	54.19%	Walter Mondale (D)	45.02%
1988	Michael Dukakis (D)	51.41%	George H.W. Bush (R)	47.80%
1992	Bill Clinton (D)	41.13%	George H.W. Bush (R)	36.78%
1996	Bill Clinton (D)	48.81%	Bob Dole (R)	38.48%
2000	Al Gore (D)	47.83%	George W. Bush (R)	47.61%
2004	John Kerry (D)	49.70%	George W. Bush (R)	49.32%
2008	Barack Obama (D)	56.22%	John McCain (R)	42.31%
2012	Barack Obama (D)	52.83%	Mitt Romney (R)	45.89%
2016	Donald Trump (R)	47.22%	Hillary Clinton (D)	46.45%
2020	Joseph Biden (D)	49.45%	Donald Trump (R)	48.82%

Home-State Candidates — Wisconsin

Qualified — James Doolittle (1868), Robert La Follette (1912, 1916, 1924), Douglas MacArthur (1944)

Wyoming

Basics — Wyoming
State party winners — R 25, D 8
General-election matches — 23-10 (69.70%)
Current party streak (through 2020) — R 14
Current match streak (through 2020) — 0
2020 party indexes — R 151.85, D 52.65
2020 overall results — Trump 69.94%, Biden 26.55%, other 3.51%
2020 two-party results — Trump 72.48%, Biden 27.52%
Home-state general-election winners — 0
Home-state major-party nominees — 0
Home-state qualified candidates — 0

Two-Party Results (2008-2020) — Wyoming

2008: John McCain (66.56%)   **Barack Obama (33.44%)**

2012: Mitt Romney (71.16%)   **Barack Obama (28.84%)**

2016: Donald Trump (75.71%)   **Hillary Clinton (24.30%)**

2020: Donald Trump (72.48%)   **Joseph Biden (27.52%)**

Overall Results (1900-2020) — Wyoming

Year	Winner	PV%	Second	PV%
1900	William McKinley (R)	58.61%	William Jennings Bryan (D)	41.14%
1904	Theodore Roosevelt (R)	66.93%	Alton Parker (D)	29.17%
1908	William Howard Taft (R)	55.43%	William Jennings Bryan (D)	39.67%
1912	Woodrow Wilson (D)	36.21%	William Howard Taft (R)	34.44%
1916	Woodrow Wilson (D)	54.67%	Charles Evans Hughes (R)	41.80%
1920	Warren Harding (R)	62.38%	James Cox (D)	30.98%
1924	Calvin Coolidge (R)	52.39%	Robert La Follette (P)	31.51%
1928	Herbert Hoover (R)	63.68%	Alfred Smith (D)	35.37%
1932	Franklin Roosevelt (D)	56.07%	Herbert Hoover (R)	40.82%
1936	Franklin Roosevelt (D)	60.58%	Alfred Landon (R)	37.47%
1940	Franklin Roosevelt (D)	52.82%	Wendell Willkie (R)	46.89%
1944	Thomas Dewey (R)	51.23%	Franklin Roosevelt (D)	48.77%
1948	Harry Truman (D)	51.62%	Thomas Dewey (R)	47.27%
1952	Dwight Eisenhower (R)	62.71%	Adlai Stevenson (D)	37.09%
1956	Dwight Eisenhower (R)	60.08%	Adlai Stevenson (D)	39.92%
1960	Richard Nixon (R)	55.02%	John Kennedy (D)	44.99%
1964	Lyndon Johnson (D)	56.56%	Barry Goldwater (R)	43.44%

Year	Winner	PV%	Second	PV%
1968	Richard Nixon (R)	55.76%	Hubert Humphrey (D)	35.51%
1972	Richard Nixon (R)	69.01%	George McGovern (D)	30.47%
1976	Gerald Ford (R)	59.30%	Jimmy Carter (D)	39.81%
1980	Ronald Reagan (R)	62.64%	Jimmy Carter (D)	27.97%
1984	Ronald Reagan (R)	70.51%	Walter Mondale (D)	28.24%
1988	George H.W. Bush (R)	60.53%	Michael Dukakis (D)	38.01%
1992	George H.W. Bush (R)	39.56%	Bill Clinton (D)	33.98%
1996	Bob Dole (R)	49.81%	Bill Clinton (D)	36.84%
2000	George W. Bush (R)	67.76%	Al Gore (D)	27.70%
2004	George W. Bush (R)	68.86%	John Kerry (D)	29.08%
2008	John McCain (R)	64.78%	Barack Obama (D)	32.54%
2012	Mitt Romney (R)	68.64%	Barack Obama (D)	27.82%
2016	Donald Trump (R)	68.17%	Hillary Clinton (D)	21.88%
2020	Donald Trump (R)	69.94%	Joseph Biden (D)	26.55%

Home-State Candidates — Wyoming

(none)

5. Records

THIS CHAPTER IS SIMILAR IN style to a record book for any sport you might choose. Only the sport here is presidential politics.

You'll find 173 lists of extreme accomplishments—the most, the fewest, the largest, the smallest, the oldest, the youngest—all organized under 12 subheadings.

The concepts and statistical categories you'll encounter have been explained throughout this book. But a few points should be emphasized or reiterated:

1. Most lists show the top or bottom 10 performances within a given category. The exceptions are career rankings (which extend to 25 places) and a few general lists (which include every candidate who met the designated criteria).

2. All statistics in this chapter are actual numbers unless otherwise noted. Exceptions are made solely for career rankings, where both actual and equalized totals are listed (and are labeled as such).

3. Career totals encompass all elections in which a candidate received votes, even if he failed to meet qualification standards in one or more of those years.

4. Listings for single-year performances typically begin with a candidate's name, followed in parentheses by his party and the election year. If two parties are linked by a hyphen, the candidate ran simultaneously on both tickets. If they're separated by a slash, the candidate began the year in one party before switching to the second. These are the party abbreviations:

AI: American Independent
AM: Anti-Masonic
AW: American-Whig

CU: Constitutional Union
D: Democratic
DR: Democratic-Republican
F: Federalist
FL: Farmer-Labor
FS: Free Soil
GBK: Greenback
GRN: Green
I: Independent
LIB: Libertarian
LR: Liberal Republican
LTY: Liberty
NR: National Republican
NU: National Unity
P: Progressive
POP: Populist
PRO: Prohibition
R: Republican
REF: Reform
SD: Southern Democratic
SOC: Socialist
SRD: States' Rights Democratic
TC: Taxpayers and Constitution
U: Union
W: Whig

5. Listings for career records (unlike those for single-election records) include only the name of each candidate, not his party or the years in which he ran. You can find that information in the election-by-election statistical profiles in Chapter 2 and the candidate summaries in Chapter 3.

6. Additional explanations are supplied for several rankings on the following pages. Look for notes at the bottom of particular lists.

Qualified Candidates

Most candidates to qualify in an election

1. 1880..15
1. 2016..15
3. 1920..14
4. 1796..13
4. 1988..13
6. 1789..12
6. 1916..12
6. 1972..12
6. 1976..12
10. 1860..11
10. 1876..11
10. 1896..11

Fewest candidates to qualify in an election

1. 1804...2
1. 1812...2
1. 1816...2
1. 1820...2
1. 1828...2
1. 1900...2
7. 1808...3
8. 1824...4
8. 1832...4
8. 1840...4
8. 1944...4

Individuals with five qualified candidacies

James Blaine (R-1876, 1880, 1884, 1888, 1892)
Henry Clay (DR-1824; NR-1832; W-1840, 1844, 1848)

Individuals with four qualified candidacies

John Adams (F-1789, 1792, 1796, 1800)
George Clinton (DR-1789, 1792, 1796, 1808)
Eugene Debs (SOC-1904, 1908, 1912, 1920)
Ulysses Grant (R-1864, 1868, 1872, 1880)
Thomas Hendricks (D-1872, 1876, 1880, 1884)
Hubert Humphrey (D-1960, 1968, 1972, 1976)
Thomas Jefferson (DR-1792, 1796, 1800, 1804)
Lyndon Johnson (D-1956, 1960, 1964, 1968)
Richard Nixon (R-1960, 1964, 1968, 1972)
Charles Cotesworth Pinckney (F-1796, 1800, 1804, 1808)
Ronald Reagan (R-1968, 1976, 1980, 1984)
Franklin Roosevelt (D-1932, 1936, 1940, 1944)
Alfred Smith (D-1920, 1924, 1928, 1932)
Martin Van Buren (D-1836, 1840, 1844; FS-1848)
George Wallace (D-1964; D/AI-1968; D-1972, 1976)

Individuals with three qualified candidacies

John Quincy Adams (DR-1820, 1824; NR-1828)
Thomas Bayard (D-1876, 1880, 1884)
Jerry Brown (D-1976, 1980, 1992)
William Jennings Bryan (D-POP-1896; D-1900, 1908)
James Buchanan (D-1848, 1852, 1856)
Aaron Burr (DR-1792, 1796, 1800)
George H.W. Bush (R-1980, 1988, 1992)
Lewis Cass (D-1844, 1848, 1852)
Grover Cleveland (D-1884, 1888, 1892)
Thomas Dewey (R-1940, 1944, 1948)
Stephen Douglas (D-1852, 1856, 1860)
Winfield Hancock (D-1868, 1876, 1880)
Herbert Hoover (R-1920, 1928, 1932)
Andrew Jackson (DR-1824, 1828; D-1832)
John Jay (F-1789, 1796, 1800)
Robert La Follette (R-1912, 1916; R/P-1924)
George McGovern (D-1968, 1972, 1984)
William McKinley (R-1892, 1896, 1900)
Ron Paul (R/TC-2008; R-2012, 2016)
Theodore Roosevelt (R-1904; R/P-1912; R-1916)
Winfield Scott (W-1840, 1848, 1852)
Adlai Stevenson (D-1952, 1956, 1960)
Robert Taft (R-1940, 1948, 1952)
George Washington (F-1789, 1792, 1796)
Daniel Webster (W-1836, 1848, 1852)

Qualified candidacies for home-state candidates

24. Arizona 5
24. Arkansas 5
24. Nebraska 5
24. New Hampshire 5
24. North Carolina 5
24. Vermont 5
24. Wisconsin 5
31. Florida 4
31. Kansas 4
31. South Dakota 4
34. Oklahoma 3
35. Colorado 2
35. Idaho 2
35. Montana 2
35. New Mexico 2
35. Washington 2
35. West Virginia 2
41. Louisiana 1
41. Mississippi 1
41. North Dakota 1
41. Oregon 1
41. Utah 1

NOTE: A home state is the place where an individual maintains a voting address during his or her presidential candidacy. Individuals with two or more qualified candidacies are counted multiple times above.

States that have never been home to a qualified candidate

Alaska
District of Columbia
Hawaii
Nevada
Rhode Island
Wyoming

Youngest average ages of qualified candidates

1. 1900 (2 candidates) 49.19
2. 1864 (5 candidates) 49.53
3. 1792 (5 candidates) 51.45
4. 1904 (5 candidates) 51.81
5. 1789 (12 candidates) 52.65
5. 1812 (2 candidates) 52.65
7. 1868 (10 candidates) 53.16
7. 1876 (11 candidates) 53.16
9. 1964 (7 candidates) 53.56
10. 1824 (4 candidates) 53.80

NOTE: All ages are as of November 1 of the given year, which also applies to the next three lists.

Oldest average ages of qualified candidates

1. 2020 (8 candidates).. 69.50
2. 1848 (8 candidates).. 64.13
2. 2016 (15 candidates) 64.13
4. 1808 (3 candidates).. 63.19
5. 1928 (10 candidates) 62.11
6. 2008 (10 candidates) 61.54
7. 1828 (2 candidates).. 61.47
8. 2012 (8 candidates).. 61.22
9. 1840 (4 candidates).. 60.89
10. 1804 (2 candidates) 60.12

Youngest qualified candidates

1. William Jennings Bryan (D-POP-1896)... 36.62
2. Aaron Burr (DR-1792) 36.73
3. George McClellan (D-1864)... 37.91
4. Jerry Brown (D-1976) 38.57
5. Thomas Dewey (R-1940) 38.61
6. Pete Buttigieg (D-2020).. 38.78
7. Stephen Douglas (D-1852).. 39.52
8. John Breckinridge (D/SD-1860)... 39.79
9. Al Gore (D-1988) 40.59
10. William Jennings Bryan (D-1900) 40.62

Oldest qualified candidates

1. Ron Paul (R-2016) 81.20
2. Colin Powell (R-2016) 79.57
3. Bernie Sanders (D-2020) 79.15
4. Michael Bloomberg (D-2020).. 78.71
5. Jacob Coxey (R/FL-1932).. 78.54
6. Joseph Biden (D-2020) 77.95
7. Ron Paul (R-2012) 77.20
8. Bill Weld (R-2020).. 75.25
9. Bernie Sanders (D-2016) 75.15
10. Alben Barkley (D-1952) 74.94

Nominations

Major-party nominations for home-state candidates

NOTE: A home state is the place where an individual maintains a voting address during his or her presidential candidacy. Individuals with two or more major-party nominations are counted multiple times above.

Nominees from the smallest states (electoral votes)

NOTE: Home states are ranked by the number of electoral votes they cast in a given election, which also applies to the next list.

Nominees from the largest states (electoral votes)

1. Franklin Roosevelt (D-1932, New York)..47
1. Franklin Roosevelt (D-1936, New York)..47
1. Franklin Roosevelt (D-1940, New York)..47
1. Wendell Willkie (R-1940, New York)..47
1. Thomas Dewey (R-1944, New York)..47
1. Franklin Roosevelt (D-1944, New York)..47
1. Thomas Dewey (R-1948, New York)..47
1. Ronald Reagan (R-1984, California)...47
9. Charles Evans Hughes (R-1916, New York) 45
9. Alfred Smith (D-1928, New York) 45
9. Dwight Eisenhower (R-1952, New York) 45
9. Dwight Eisenhower (R-1956, New York) 45
9. Richard Nixon (R-1972, California) 45
9. Ronald Reagan (R-1980, California)...45

Nominees from the smallest states (share of electoral votes)

1. Joseph Biden (D-2020, Delaware)..0.56%
2. George McGovern (D-1972, South Dakota) 0.74%
3. Barry Goldwater (R-1964, Arizona)..0.93%
4. Bill Clinton (D-1992, Arkansas) 1.12%
4. Bill Clinton (D-1996, Arkansas) 1.12%
4. Bob Dole (R-1996, Kansas)...1.12%
7. John Fremont (R-1856, California)..1.35%
8. James Blaine (R-1884, Maine)..1.50%
9. John Davis (D-1924, West Virginia)...1.51%
10. William Jennings Bryan (D-1908, Nebraska)......................1.66%

NOTE: Home states are ranked by the share of the nation's electoral votes that they cast in a given election, which also applies to the next list.

Nominees from the largest states (share of electoral votes)

1. George Washington (F-1792, Virginia) 15.91%
2. Thomas Jefferson (DR-1796, Virginia)....................................15.22%
2. Thomas Jefferson (DR-1800, Virginia)....................................15.22%
4. George Washington (F-1789, Virginia) 14.49%
5. Martin Van Buren (D-1836, New York).....................................14.29%
5. Martin Van Buren (D-1840, New York).....................................14.29%
7. James Madison (DR-1808, Virginia)...13.71%
8. Thomas Jefferson (DR-1804, Virginia).....................................13.64%
9. DeWitt Clinton (F-DR-1812, New York) 13.36%
9. Rufus King (F-1816, New York) 13.36%

Youngest average ages of major-party nominees

1. 1896...45.19
2. 1960...45.62
3. 1860...46.35
4. 1864...46.82
5. 1900...49.19

6. 1904 .... 49.24
7. 1908 .... 49.87
8. 1884 .... 51.19
9. 1924 .... 51.94
10. 1936 .... 51.95

NOTE: All ages are as of November 1 of the given election year, which also applies to the remaining lists in this section.

Oldest average ages of major-party nominees

1. 2020 .... 76.17
2. 2016 .... 69.70
3. 1984 .... 65.28
4. 1848 .... 65.00
5. 1980 .... 62.91
6. 1840 .... 62.82
7. 1820 .... 62.51
8. 1996 .... 61.74
9. 1828 .... 61.47
10. 1956 .... 61.39

Youngest major-party nominees

1. William Jennings Bryan (D-1896) 36.62
2. George McClellan (D-1864) 37.91
3. John Breckinridge (SD-1860) 39.79
4. William Jennings Bryan (D-1900) 40.62
5. Thomas Dewey (R-1944) 42.61
6. John Kennedy (D-1960) 43.43
7. DeWitt Clinton (F-1812) 43.67
8. John Fremont (R-1856) 43.78
9. Theodore Roosevelt (R-1904) 46.01
10. Bill Clinton (D-1992) 46.20

Oldest major-party nominees

1. Joseph Biden (D-2020) 77.95
2. Donald Trump (R-2020) 74.38
3. Ronald Reagan (R-1984) 73.73
4. Bob Dole (R-1996) 73.28
5. John McCain (R-2008) 72.17
6. Donald Trump (R-2016) 70.38
7. Ronald Reagan (R-1980) 69.73
8. Hillary Clinton (D-2016) 69.02
9. George H.W. Bush (R-1992) 68.39
10. William Henry Harrison (W-1840) 67.73

Largest age gaps between major-party nominees

1. 2008 (John McCain-Barack Obama)..24.93
2. 1996 (Bob Dole-Bill Clinton) 23.08
3. 1992 (George H.W. Bush-Bill Clinton) 22.19
4. 1856 (James Buchanan-John Fremont) 21.75
5. 1944 (Franklin Roosevelt-Thomas Dewey) 20.15
6. 1844 (Henry Clay-James Polk) 18.56
7. 1852 (Winfield Scott-Franklin Pierce) 18.45
8. 1812 (James Madison-DeWitt Clinton) 17.96
9. 1948 (Harry Truman-Thomas Dewey)...17.88
10. 1864 (Abraham Lincoln-George McClellan) 17.81

NOTE: The older nominee is listed first. The age gap is expressed in years. (Ages beyond two decimal points have been used in these calculations, which means a few gaps differ by 0.01 from results that would be obtained by using the published ages for candidates.) This note also applies to the next list.

Smallest age gaps between major-party nominees

1. 1824 (Andrew Jackson-John Quincy Adams)..0.32
1. 1828 (Andrew Jackson-John Quincy Adams)..0.32
3. 1964 (Lyndon Johnson-Barry Goldwater)...0.35
4. 1928 (Alfred Smith-Herbert Hoover) 0.61
5. 1836 (William Henry Harrison-Hugh White) 0.72
5. 1912 (Woodrow Wilson-William Howard Taft) 0.72
7. 1924 (Calvin Coolidge-John Davis) 0.78
8. 2016 (Donald Trump-Hillary Clinton) 1.37
9. 1968 (Hubert Humphrey-Richard Nixon)..1.62
10. 2000 (George W. Bush-Al Gore)..1.73

NOTE: There were three major-party nominees in 1836. The gap between the two oldest nominees is shown.

Primaries

Most primary elections held by one party in a year

1. 2020 Democratic.. 46
2. 2000 Republican 43
3. 1996 Republican 42
4. 2008 Republican 41
5. 1992 Democratic.. 40
5. 2000 Democratic.. 40
5. 2008 Democratic.. 40
8. 2012 Republican 39
8. 2016 Democratic.. 39
8. 2020 Republican 39

NOTE: Lists in this section encompass Democratic and Republican primaries since 1912 in the 50 states and the District of Columbia, but not in Puerto Rico or other territories.

Most votes cast in one party's primaries in a year

1. 2008 Democratic.. 36,848,204
2. 2020 Democratic.. 36,527,602
3. 2016 Democratic.. 30,830,749
4. 2016 Republican 30,192,856
5. 1988 Democratic.. 22,961,936
6. 2008 Republican 20,790,899
7. 2000 Republican 20,624,401
8. 1992 Democratic.. 20,304,046
9. 2020 Republican 19,368,374
10. 2012 Republican 18,770,036

Most primary wins in a career

1. George H.W. Bush 78
2. Donald Trump 72
3. Bill Clinton 65
3. Ronald Reagan 65
5. George W. Bush 63
6. Barack Obama 51
7. Hillary Clinton 48
8. Al Gore 44
9. Joseph Biden 41
10. Jimmy Carter 40
10. Bob Dole 40
10. John McCain 40
13. Richard Nixon 38
14. Franklin Roosevelt 35
15. Mitt Romney 34
16. John Kerry 33
17. Woodrow Wilson 25
18. Michael Dukakis 22

[List continues on next page.]

Most primary wins in a career (cont.)

19. Estes Kefauver 21
20. Dwight Eisenhower 20
21. Gerald Ford 16
21. Gary Hart 16
23. Calvin Coolidge 15
23. Bernie Sanders 15
25. William Gibbs McAdoo 12

Most primary votes (actual) in a career

1. Hillary Clinton 34,833,999
2. Donald Trump 31,971,040
3. Barack Obama 25,838,376
4. Bernie Sanders 22,781,804
5. Ronald Reagan 20,649,375
6. George H.W. Bush 20,417,667
7. Bill Clinton 20,210,305
8. George W. Bush 20,175,228
9. Joseph Biden 19,209,382
10. John McCain 16,624,924
11. Jimmy Carter 15,828,944
12. Mitt Romney 14,385,425
13. Al Gore 14,215,790
14. Richard Nixon 12,231,613
15. Bob Dole 11,131,566
16. Franklin Roosevelt 10,657,404
17. Jesse Jackson 9,968,079
18. Michael Dukakis 9,817,185
19. John Kerry 9,753,562
20. Ted Cruz 7,452,008
21. Dwight Eisenhower 7,127,572
22. Jerry Brown 7,104,404
23. Edward Kennedy 7,004,175
24. Gary Hart 6,892,971
25. Walter Mondale 6,811,214

Most primary votes (equalized) in a career

1. Franklin Roosevelt 28,002,546
2. Ronald Reagan 24,316,454
3. Richard Nixon 21,763,863
4. George H.W. Bush 16,361,420
5. George W. Bush 15,811,666
6. Woodrow Wilson 14,342,461
7. Bill Clinton 14,029,911
8. Donald Trump 13,960,338
9. Barack Obama 13,868,597
10. Dwight Eisenhower 11,321,964
11. Hillary Clinton 10,360,137
12. Estes Kefauver 10,338,199
13. Herbert Hoover 9,220,545
14. Jimmy Carter 9,001,907

15. Al Gore 8,921,303
16. Earl Warren 8,310,060
17. John McCain 8,022,842
18. Bob Dole...7,753,412
19. Mitt Romney 7,428,723
20. William Gibbs McAdoo 7,292,693
21. Thomas Dewey...7,278,548
22. Bernie Sanders 6,905,085
23. Calvin Coolidge..6,869,141
24. Harry Truman...6,518,419
25. John Kerry..6,105,491

Most primary wins in a year

1. Joseph Biden (D-2020) 41
2. Bob Dole (R-1996) 39
2. Al Gore (D-2000) 39
2. Donald Trump (R-2020) 39
5. George H.W. Bush (R-1992) 38
6. George W. Bush (R-2000) 36
7. George H.W. Bush (R-1988) 35
8. Bill Clinton (D-1996)... 34
9. John Kerry (D-2004)... 33
9. John McCain (R-2008) 33
9. Donald Trump (R-2016) 33

Most primary votes in a year

1. Joseph Biden (D-2020) 19,128,039
2. Donald Trump (R-2020) 18,213,777
3. Hillary Clinton (D-2008).. 17,714,951
4. Barack Obama (D-2008) 17,423,182
5. Hillary Clinton (D-2016).. 17,119,048
6. Donald Trump (R-2016) 13,757,263
7. Bernie Sanders (D-2016) 13,209,430
8. George W. Bush (R-2000) 12,390,575
9. Al Gore (D-2000) 11,081,274
10. Bill Clinton (D-1992) 10,503,503

Largest percentages of primary votes in a year

1. Woodrow Wilson (D-1916) 98.78%
2. Ronald Reagan (R-1984)... 98.62%
3. George W. Bush (R-2004) 98.04%
4. Donald Trump (R-2020) 94.04%
5. Franklin Roosevelt (D-1936) 92.92%
6. Barack Obama (D-2012) 91.40%
7. Richard Nixon (R-1960).. 89.85%
8. Bill Clinton (D-1996).. 88.57%
9. Richard Nixon (R-1972).. 86.92%
10. Dwight Eisenhower (R-1956) 85.93%

Fewest primary wins for major-party nominees

1. John Davis (D-1924)..0
1. Wendell Willkie (R-1940) 0
1. Adlai Stevenson (D-1952)...0
1. Hubert Humphrey (D-1968) 0
5. William Howard Taft (R-1912)...1
5. James Cox (D-1920) 1
5. Warren Harding (R-1920) 1
8. Charles Evans Hughes (R-1916)...2
8. Herbert Hoover (R-1932)..2
8. Alfred Landon (R-1936) 2
8. Thomas Dewey (R-1948) 2

Smallest percentages of primary votes for major-party nominees

1. John Davis (D-1924)..0.00%
2. Wendell Willkie (R-1940) 0.66%
3. Adlai Stevenson (D-1952)..1.60%
4. Hubert Humphrey (D-1968) 2.21%
5. Charles Evans Hughes (R-1916)..4.20%
6. Warren Harding (R-1920) 4.54%
7. Thomas Dewey (R-1948) 11.47%
8. Thomas Dewey (R-1944) 11.57%
9. James Cox (D-1920) 15.08%
10. Lyndon Johnson (D-1964).. 17.72%

Most primary wins for someone not nominated

1. Hillary Clinton (D-2008).. 19
2. Gary Hart (D-1984)... 16
3. Estes Kefauver (D-1952) 12
4. Ronald Reagan (R-1976)... 10
4. Edward Kennedy (D-1980) 10
4. Bernie Sanders (D-2016) 10
7. Theodore Roosevelt (R-1912)...9
7. William Gibbs McAdoo (D-1924)...9
7. Estes Kefauver (D-1956) 9
10. Leonard Wood (R-1920)...8

Largest percentages of primary votes for someone not nominated

1. Estes Kefauver (D-1952) 64.32%
2. William Gibbs McAdoo (D-1924).. 59.79%
3. Theodore Roosevelt (R-1912).. 51.51%
4. Thomas Dewey (R-1940) 49.75%
5. Joseph France (R-1932) 48.49%
6. Hillary Clinton (D-2008).. 48.08%
7. Ronald Reagan (R-1976).. 45.87%
8. William Borah (R-1936) 44.41%
9. Bernie Sanders (D-2016) 42.85%
10. Champ Clark (D-1912) 41.60%

Conventions

Most delegates at a major-party convention

1. 2012 Democratic...5,552
2. 2016 Democratic...4,762
3. 2020 Democratic...4,749
4. 2008 Democratic...4,419
5. 2000 Democratic...4,339
6. 2004 Democratic...4,322
7. 1996 Democratic...4,289
8. 1992 Democratic...4,288
9. 1988 Democratic...4,161
10. 1984 Democratic...3,933

NOTE: Lists in this section encompass conventions since 1832 of the Democratic, National Republican, Republican, and Whig parties, but not of minor parties.

Fewest delegates at a major-party convention

1. 1832 National Republican 168
2. 1864 Democratic..226
3. 1840 Democratic..244
4. 1840 Whig 254
5. 1836 Democratic..265
6. 1844 Democratic..266
7. 1844 Whig 275
8. 1848 Whig 280
9. 1832 Democratic..283
10. 1852 Democratic..288

Most first-ballot convention votes (actual) in a career

1. Barack Obama...8,613
2. Bill Clinton 7,649
3. Ronald Reagan 5,424
4. George W. Bush 4,574
5. George H.W. Bush 4,456
6. Jimmy Carter 4,362
7. Al Gore...4,340
8. Donald Trump 4,275
9. John Kerry 4,253
10. Hillary Clinton...3,853
11. Franklin Roosevelt 3,799
12. Joseph Biden 3,558
13. Richard Nixon 3,360
14. Bernie Sanders 3,016
15. Michael Dukakis 2,876
16. Lyndon Johnson...2,807
17. John McCain 2,341
18. Walter Mondale..2,193

[List continues on next page.]

Most first-ballot convention votes (actual) in a career *(cont.)*

19. Dwight Eisenhower 2,168
20. Mitt Romney 2,063
21. Herbert Hoover 1,986
22. William Jennings Bryan 1,964
23. Bob Dole 1,928
24. Hubert Humphrey 1,903
25. George McGovern 1,879

NOTE: Fractional totals have been rounded to the nearest whole number, which also applies to the remaining lists in this section.

Most first-ballot Democratic convention votes (actual) in a career

1. Barack Obama 8,613
2. Bill Clinton 7,649
3. Jimmy Carter 4,362
4. Al Gore 4,340
5. John Kerry 4,253
6. Hillary Clinton 3,853
7. Franklin Roosevelt 3,799
8. Joseph Biden 3,558
9. Bernie Sanders 3,016
10. Michael Dukakis 2,876

Most first-ballot Republican convention votes (actual) in a career

1. Ronald Reagan 5,424
2. George W. Bush 4,574
3. George H.W. Bush 4,456
4. Donald Trump 4,275
5. Richard Nixon 3,360
6. John McCain 2,341
7. Dwight Eisenhower 2,168
8. Mitt Romney 2,063
9. Herbert Hoover 1,986
10. Bob Dole 1,928

Most first-ballot convention votes (equalized) in a career

1. Franklin Roosevelt 3,360
2. Henry Clay 2,746
3. Ronald Reagan 2,582
4. Martin Van Buren 2,549
5. Richard Nixon 2,510
6. Ulysses Grant 2,444
7. Grover Cleveland 2,156
8. William Jennings Bryan 2,036
9. George W. Bush 2,000
10. George H.W. Bush 1,987
11. William McKinley 1,919
12. Bill Clinton 1,783
13. Herbert Hoover 1,768
14. Thomas Dewey 1,754

15. Dwight Eisenhower 1,701
16. Barack Obama 1,699
17. Donald Trump 1,698
18. James Blaine 1,404
19. Jimmy Carter 1,381
20. Lyndon Johnson 1,327
21. Woodrow Wilson 1,296
22. Alfred Smith 1,266
23. William Howard Taft 1,246
24. Abraham Lincoln 1,171
25. Theodore Roosevelt 1,168

Most last-ballot convention votes (actual) in a career

1. Thomas Dewey 1,105
2. Woodrow Wilson 990
3. Charles Evans Hughes 950
4. Franklin Roosevelt 945
5. James Blaine 939
6. John Davis 896
7. Winfield Hancock 763
8. James Cox 701
9. Grover Cleveland 683
10. Wendell Willkie 655
11. William Jennings Bryan 652
12. Warren Harding 645
13. Adlai Stevenson 618
14. Benjamin Harrison 544
15. Samuel Tilden 536
16. James Garfield 399
17. Rutherford Hayes 384
18. Abraham Lincoln 340
19. James Buchanan 329
20. Robert Taft 318
21. Horatio Seymour 317
22. Ulysses Grant 306
23. William Gibbs McAdoo 282
24. Franklin Pierce 279
25. Estes Kefauver 276

NOTE: Last-ballot votes are the votes cast on the deciding ballot of a multi-ballot convention. Single-ballot conventions are not included. This note also applies to the next list.

Most last-ballot convention votes (equalized) in a career

1. James Blaine 1,186
2. James Buchanan 1,114
3. Winfield Hancock 1,034
4. Thomas Dewey 1,011
5. Horatio Seymour 1,000
6. Franklin Pierce 969
7. Charles Evans Hughes 962

[List continues on next page.]

Most last-ballot convention votes (equalized) in a career *(cont.)*

8. Woodrow Wilson...905
9. James Polk...868
10. Grover Cleveland..833
11. Winfield Scott...825
12. Franklin Roosevelt..819
13. John Davis...817
14. Lewis Cass...733
15. Abraham Lincoln...730
16. Samuel Tilden...726
17. William Jennings Bryan..701
18. Warren Harding...655
18. Wendell Willkie...655
20. Benjamin Harrison..654
21. James Cox...640
22. Stephen Douglas...636
23. Zachary Taylor..611
24. William Henry Harrison..583
25. James Garfield..528

Most ballots needed to achieve a nomination

1. John Davis (D-1924)..103
2. Stephen Douglas (D-1860)...59
3. Winfield Scott (W-1852)..53
4. Franklin Pierce (D-1852)...49
5. Woodrow Wilson (D-1912)...46
6. James Cox (D-1920)...44
7. James Garfield (R-1880)...36
8. Horatio Seymour (D-1868)...22
9. James Buchanan (D-1856)..17
10. Warren Harding (R-1920)..10

Unanimous victories at a major-party convention

Andrew Jackson (D-1832)
Martin Van Buren (D-1836)
Martin Van Buren (D-1840)
Henry Clay (W-1844)
*James Buchanan (D-1856)
*Horatio Seymour (D-1868)
Ulysses Grant (R-1868)
Ulysses Grant (R-1872)
Grover Cleveland (D-1888)
William Jennings Bryan (D-1900)
William McKinley (R-1900)
Theodore Roosevelt (R-1904)
Woodrow Wilson (D-1916)
Franklin Roosevelt (D-1936)
*Thomas Dewey (R-1948)
Dwight Eisenhower (R-1956)
Lyndon Johnson (D-1964)
George H.W. Bush (R-1988)

Al Gore (D-2000)
George W. Bush (R-2000)
Donald Trump (R-2020)

NOTE: An asterisk indicates a unanimous victory on the last ballot of a multi-ballot convention; all others were on the first ballot.

Smallest margins of victory at a convention

1. Rutherford Hayes-James Blaine (R-1876)..4.37
2. Gerald Ford-Ronald Reagan (R-1976)..5.18
3. James Garfield-Ulysses Grant (R-1880).. 12.30
4. Winfield Scott-Millard Fillmore (W-1852)... 15.88
5. Hillary Clinton-Bernie Sanders (D-2016) 20.52
6. William Henry Harrison-Henry Clay (W-1840)....................................... 22.84
7. Walter Mondale-Gary Hart (D-1984).. 25.18
8. John Kennedy-Lyndon Johnson (D-1960).. 26.10
9. Adlai Stevenson-Estes Kefauver (D-1952)... 27.81
10. Jimmy Carter-Edward Kennedy (D-1980).. 29.20

NOTE: The nominee is listed first. The margin of victory is expressed in percentage points, showing the difference between percentages for the top two candidates on a convention's decisive ballot. (Percentages beyond two decimal points have been used in these calculations, which means a few margins differ by 0.01 from results that would be obtained by using the published percentages for candidates.)

Smallest first-ballot percentages for leading candidates

1. Winfield Hancock (D-1880) 23.17%
2. William Gibbs McAdoo (D-1920)... 24.31%
3. Richard Bland (D-1896)... 25.27%
4. Charles Evans Hughes (R-1916) 25.68%
5. John Sherman (R-1888) 27.52%
6. Estes Kefauver (D-1952) 27.64%
7. Leonard Wood (R-1920).. 29.22%
8. George Pendleton (D-1868).. 33.12%
9. Thomas Dewey (R-1940) 36.00%
10. William Seward (R-1860)... 37.23%

NOTE: A leading candidate is the individual who receives the most votes of any candidate on a convention's first ballot.

Smallest first-ballot percentages for multi-ballot nominees

1. James Polk (D-1844) 0.00%
1. Franklin Pierce (D-1852) 0.00%
1. Horatio Seymour (D-1868) 0.00%
1. James Garfield (R-1880) 0.00%
5. John Davis (D-1924)..2.82%
6. Warren Harding (R-1920) 6.66%
7. Rutherford Hayes (R-1876) 8.07%
8. Benjamin Harrison (R-1888).. 10.22%
9. Wendell Willkie (R-1940) 10.50%
10. James Cox (D-1920)... 12.25%

Largest first-ballot percentages for someone not nominated

1. Martin Van Buren (D-1844).. 54.89%
2. Ronald Reagan (R-1976)... 47.37%
3. Millard Fillmore (W-1852) 44.93%
4. Franklin Pierce (D-1856) 41.39%
5. Henry Clay (W-1840)... 40.55%
6. Lewis Cass (D-1852) 40.28%
7. Champ Clark (D-1912)... 40.27%
8. Ulysses Grant (R-1880) 40.21%
9. William Gibbs McAdoo (D-1924).. 39.30%
10. Bernie Sanders (D-2016)... 39.16%

Largest gains from first ballot to last ballot

1. Horatio Seymour (D-1868, from 0.00% on FB
    to 100.00% on LB)..100.00
2. Franklin Pierce (D-1852, from 0.00% on FB to 96.88% on LB) 96.88
3. James Polk (D-1844, from 0.00% on FB to 86.84% on LB)................ 86.84
4. John Davis (D-1924, from 2.82% on FB to 76.87% on LB) 74.04
5. Winfield Hancock (D-1880, from 23.17% on FB
    to 95.53% on LB) 72.36
6. Charles Evans Hughes (R-1916, from 25.68% on FB
    to 96.20% on LB) 70.52
7. Woodrow Wilson (D-1912, from 29.62% on FB
    to 90.49% on LB) 60.88
8. Thomas Dewey (R-1948, from 39.67% on FB to 100.00% on LB).... 60.33
9. Warren Harding (R-1920, from 6.66% on FB to 65.52% on LB)........ 58.86
10. William Jennings Bryan (D-1896, from 14.73% on FB
    to 70.11% on LB) 55.38

NOTE: Changes are expressed in percentage points. (Percentages beyond two decimal points have been used in these calculations, which means a few changes differ by 0.01 from results that would be obtained by using the published percentages for candidates.) This note also applies to the next list.

Largest drops from first ballot to last ballot

1. Martin Van Buren (D-1844, from 54.89% on FB to 0.00% on LB)...-54.89
2. Franklin Pierce (D-1856, from 41.39% on FB to 0.00% on LB) ....-41.39
3. Lewis Cass (D-1852, from 40.28% on FB to 0.69% on LB) ....-39.58
4. William Gibbs McAdoo (D-1924, from 39.30% on FB
    to 1.05% on LB)..-38.25
5. Thomas Dewey (R-1940, from 36.00% on FB to 1.10% on LB)........-34.90
6. George Pendleton (D-1868, from 33.12% on FB
    to 0.00% on LB)..-33.12
7. Champ Clark (D-1912, from 40.27% on FB to 7.68% on LB)............-32.59
8. James Buchanan (D-1852, from 32.29% on FB to 0.00% on LB)....-32.29
9. James Blaine (R-1880, from 37.57% on FB to 5.56% on LB).............-32.01
10. Richard Bland (D-1896, from 25.27% on FB to 1.18% on LB) ....-24.09

General Elections

Largest national voter-turnout rates

1. 1876...81.8%
2. 1860...81.2%
3. 1840...80.2%
4. 1880...79.4%
5. 1888...79.3%
5. 1896...79.3%
7. 1844...78.9%
7. 1856...78.9%
9. 1868...78.1%
10. 1884 ....77.5%

Smallest national voter-turnout rates

1. 1824...26.9%
2. 1924...48.9%
3. 1996...49.0%
4. 1920...49.2%
5. 1988...50.3%
5. 2000...50.3%
7. 1948...51.1%
8. 1932...52.6%
9. 1980...52.8%
10. 1984 ....53.3%

Most popular votes cast in a general election

1. 2020..158,429,631
2. 2016..136,669,276
3. 2008..131,313,820
4. 2012..129,085,403
5. 2004..122,295,345
6. 2000..105,405,100
7. 1992..104,425,014
8. 1996..96,277,223
9. 1984..92,652,842
10. 1988 91,594,809

Largest raw gains in popular votes from previous election

1. 2020..21,760,355
2. 2004..16,890,245
3. 1952..12,859,424
4. 1992..12,830,205
5. 2000..9,127,877

[List continues on next page.]

Largest raw gains in popular votes from previous election *(cont.)*

6. 2008..9,018,475
7. 1920..8,233,012
8. 1928..7,702,389
9. 2016..7,583,873
10. 1960 6,811,311

NOTE: This list shows the change in total popular votes between the election four years earlier and the given election, which also applies to the next list.

Largest raw drops in popular votes from previous election

1. 1996...-8,147,791
2. 2012...-2,228,417
3. 1944...-1,840,500
4. 1988...-1,058,033
5. 1864...-654,575
6. 1904...-453,486

NOTE: These are the only six elections where the total of popular votes was smaller than in the previous election.

Largest percentage gains in popular votes from previous election

1. 1828...213.81%
2. 1840...60.41%
3. 1920...44.42%
4. 1868...41.96%
5. 1876...30.00%
6. 1856...28.24%
7. 1928...26.47%
8. 1952...26.41%
9. 1916...23.22%
10. 1836 ....16.20%

NOTE: This list shows the percentage change in total popular votes between the election four years earlier and the given election, which also applies to the next list.

Largest percentage drops in popular votes from previous election

1. 1864...-13.97%
2. 1996...-7.80%
3. 1944...-3.69%
4. 1904...-3.25%
5. 2012...-1.70%
6. 1988...-1.14%

NOTE: These are the only six elections where the total of popular votes was smaller than in the previous election.

General-election victories for a party

1. Republican 24
2. Democratic 22
3. Democratic-Republican 8
4. Federalist 3
5. Whig 2

Longest general-election winning streaks for a party

1. Democratic-Republican (1800-1828) 8
2. Republican (1860-1880) 6
3. Democratic (1932-1948) 5
4. Republican (1896-1908) 4
5. Federalist (1789-1796) 3
5. Republican (1920-1928) 3
5. Republican (1980-1988) 3
8. Democratic (1832-1836) 2
8. Democratic (1852-1856) 2
8. Democratic (1912-1916) 2
8. Republican (1952-1956) 2
8. Democratic (1960-1964) 2
8. Republican (1968-1972) 2
8. Democratic (1992-1996) 2
8. Republican (2000-2004) 2
8. Democratic (2008-2012) 2

Most consecutive elections won by a different party

1. 1836-1852 (D-W-D-W-D) 5
1. 1880-1896 (R-D-R-D-R) 5
3. 1972-1980 (R-D-R) 3
3. 2012-2020 (D-R-D) 3

NOTE: These are the only instances with a different party winning three or more consecutive elections.

Most consecutive elections won by a different candidate

1. 1832-1860 (Andrew Jackson-Abraham Lincoln) 8
2. 1872-1896 (Ulysses Grant-William McKinley) 7
3. 1916-1932 (Woodrow Wilson-Franklin Roosevelt) 5
4. 1900-1912 (William McKinley-Woodrow Wilson) 4
4. 1956-1968 (Dwight Eisenhower-Richard Nixon) 4
6. 1792-1800 (George Washington-Thomas Jefferson) 3
6. 1820-1828 (James Monroe-Andrew Jackson) 3
6. 1944-1952 (Franklin Roosevelt-Dwight Eisenhower) 3
6. 1972-1980 (Richard Nixon-Ronald Reagan) 3
6. 1984-1992 (Ronald Reagan-Bill Clinton) 3
6. 2012-2020 (Barack Obama-Joseph Biden) 3

NOTE: The first and last presidents in each streak are listed.

Individuals on five major-party tickets

Franklin Roosevelt (PRES: D-1932, 1936, 1940, 1944; VPRES: D-1920)

Richard Nixon (PRES: R-1960, 1968, 1972; VPRES: R-1952, 1956)

NOTE: This list shows candidates who were nominated by a major party for president (PRES) or vice president (VPRES). Vice-presidential nominees under the double-ballot system (1789-1800) are based on the parties' stated intentions, even though all electoral votes counted toward the presidency. This note also applies to the next two lists.

Individuals on four major-party tickets

John Adams (PRES: F-1796, 1800; VPRES: F-1789, 1792)

George H.W. Bush (PRES: R-1988, 1992; VPRES: R-1980, 1984)

Individuals on three major-party tickets

Thomas Jefferson (PRES: DR-1796, 1800, 1804)

Charles Cotesworth Pinckney (PRES: F-1804, 1808; VPRES: F-1800)

Rufus King (PRES: F-1816; VPRES: F-1804, 1808)

Andrew Jackson (PRES: DR-1824, 1828, D-1832)

Martin Van Buren (PRES: D-1836, 1840; VPRES: D-1832)

Grover Cleveland (PRES: D-1884, 1888, 1892)

William Jennings Bryan (PRES: D-1896, 1900, 1908)

Walter Mondale (PRES: D-1984; VPRES: D-1976, 1980)

Al Gore (PRES: D-2000; VPRES: D-1992, 1996)

Joseph Biden (PRES: D-2020; VPRES: D-2008, 2012)

NOTE: Jefferson ran for president in 1796, but was elected vice president under the double-ballot system.

Major-party nominees who faced each other in two elections

1796 and 1800 (John Adams and Thomas Jefferson with one win apiece)

1824 and 1828 (John Quincy Adams and Andrew Jackson with one win apiece)

1836 and 1840 (Martin Van Buren and William Henry Harrison with one win apiece)

1888 and 1892 (Benjamin Harrison and Grover Cleveland with one win apiece)

1896 and 1900 (William McKinley with two wins over William Jennings Bryan)

1952 and 1956 (Dwight Eisenhower with two wins over Adlai Stevenson)

General-election wins for home-state candidates

1. New York 12
2. Virginia 8
3. Ohio 7
4. Illinois 6
5. California 4
5. Massachusetts 4
5. Texas 4
8. Tennessee 3
9. Arkansas 2
9. New Jersey 2

11. Delaware 1
11. Georgia 1
11. Indiana 1
11. Louisiana 1
11. Missouri 1
11. New Hampshire 1
11. Pennsylvania 1

NOTE: A home state is the place where an individual maintains a voting address during his or her presidential candidacy. Individuals with two or more general-election wins are counted multiple times above.

Winners from the smallest states (electoral votes)

1. Joseph Biden (D-2020, Delaware)...3
2. Franklin Pierce (D-1852, New Hampshire)...5
3. Zachary Taylor (W-1848, Louisiana) 6
3. Bill Clinton (D-1992, Arkansas) 6
3. Bill Clinton (D-1996, Arkansas) 6
6. George Washington (F-1789, Virginia) 10
7. Andrew Jackson (DR-1828, Tennessee) 11
7. Abraham Lincoln (R-1860, Illinois)..11
9. Jimmy Carter (D-1976, Georgia)..12
10. James Polk (D-1844, Tennessee)..13
10. Herbert Hoover (R-1928, California) 13

NOTE: Home states are ranked by the number of electoral votes they cast in a given election, which also applies to the next list.

Winners from the largest states (electoral votes)

1. Franklin Roosevelt (D-1932, New York)..47
1. Franklin Roosevelt (D-1936, New York)..47
1. Franklin Roosevelt (D-1940, New York)..47
1. Franklin Roosevelt (D-1944, New York)..47
1. Ronald Reagan (R-1984, California)..47
6. Dwight Eisenhower (R-1952, New York) 45
6. Dwight Eisenhower (R-1956, New York) 45
6. Richard Nixon (R-1972, California)..45
6. Ronald Reagan (R-1980, California)...45
10. Richard Nixon (R-1968, New York)...43

Winners from the smallest states (share of electoral votes)

1. Joseph Biden (D-2020, Delaware)...0.56%
2. Bill Clinton (D-1992, Arkansas) 1.12%
2. Bill Clinton (D-1996, Arkansas) 1.12%
4. Franklin Pierce (D-1852, New Hampshire)..1.69%
5. Zachary Taylor (W-1848, Louisiana) 2.07%
6. Jimmy Carter (D-1976, Georgia)...2.23%
7. Herbert Hoover (R-1928, California) 2.45%
8. Woodrow Wilson (D-1912, New Jersey)..2.64%
8. Woodrow Wilson (D-1916, New Jersey)..2.64%
10. Harry Truman (D-1948, Missouri) 2.83%

NOTE: Home states are ranked by the share of the nation's electoral votes that they cast in a given election, which also applies to the next list.

Winners from the largest states (share of electoral votes)

1. George Washington (F-1792, Virginia) 15.91%
2. Thomas Jefferson (DR-1800, Virginia)... 15.22%
3. George Washington (F-1789, Virginia) 14.49%
4. Martin Van Buren (D-1836, New York)... 14.29%
5. James Madison (DR-1808, Virginia).. 13.71%
6. Thomas Jefferson (DR-1804, Virginia).. 13.64%
7. John Adams (F-1796, Massachusetts) 11.59%
8. James Madison (DR-1812, Virginia).. 11.52%
8. James Monroe (DR-1816, Virginia) 11.52%
10. James Monroe (DR-1820, Virginia).. 10.78%

Elections with two major-party nominees from the same state

1860 (Illinois, Abraham Lincoln-Stephen Douglas)
1904 (New York, Theodore Roosevelt-Alton Parker)
1920 (Ohio, Warren Harding-James Cox)
1940 (New York, Franklin Roosevelt-Wendell Willkie)
1944 (New York, Franklin Roosevelt-Thomas Dewey)
2016 (New York, Donald Trump-Hillary Clinton)

NOTE: The national winner is listed first. The first five national winners also carried their home states, but Trump did not.

Youngest general-election winners

1. John Kennedy (D-1960).. 43.43
2. Theodore Roosevelt (R-1904) 46.01
3. Bill Clinton (D-1992).. 46.20
4. Ulysses Grant (R-1868) 46.51
5. Barack Obama (D-2008) 47.24
6. Grover Cleveland (D-1884) 47.62
7. Franklin Pierce (D-1852) 47.94
8. James Garfield (R-1880) 48.95
9. James Polk (D-1844) 48.99
10. Bill Clinton (D-1996) 50.20

NOTE: All ages are as of November 1 of the given election year, which also applies to the next list.

Oldest general-election winners

1. Joseph Biden (D-2020) 77.95
2. Ronald Reagan (R-1984).. 73.73
3. Donald Trump (R-2016) 70.38
4. Ronald Reagan (R-1980).. 69.73
5. William Henry Harrison (W-1840) 67.73
6. Dwight Eisenhower (R-1956).. 66.05
7. Andrew Jackson (D-1832).. 65.63
8. James Buchanan (D-1856)... 65.52
9. Harry Truman (D-1948) 64.48
10. George H.W. Bush (R-1988)... 64.39

States

States carried the most times by Democrats

1. Arkansas 32
1. Georgia 32
3. Virginia 30
4. Maryland 29
4. Missouri 29
6. Alabama 28
6. Louisiana 28
6. North Carolina 28
9. Mississippi 27
10. New York 26
10. South Carolina 26
10. Texas 26

NOTE: *The District of Columbia is counted as a state. If candidates from two or more parties tie for the most electoral votes from a state, no party is given credit for carrying that state. This note applies to all remaining party lists in this section.*

States carried the most times by Republicans

1. Indiana 33
1. Kansas 33
1. Vermont 33
4. Nebraska 32
5. Iowa 31
5. Maine 31
7. Ohio 30
8. New Hampshire 29
9. Michigan 28
9. South Dakota 28

States carried the most times by Federalists

1. Connecticut 8
1. Delaware 8
3. Massachusetts 7
4. New Hampshire 6
5. New Jersey 5
5. Rhode Island 5
7. Maryland 3
7. Vermont 3
9. New York 2
9. Pennsylvania 2
9. South Carolina 2

States carried the most times by Democratic-Republicans

States carried the most times by Whigs

States carried the most times by minor parties

5. Vermont 1
5. Virginia 1
5. Washington 1
5. Wisconsin 1

NOTE: A minor party is any but the seven major parties (Democratic, Republican, Federalist, Democratic-Republican, National Republican, Whig, and Southern Democratic).

Most states carried in a career

1. Franklin Roosevelt 162
2. Richard Nixon 107
3. Ronald Reagan 93
4. Dwight Eisenhower 80
5. Woodrow Wilson 70
6. Bill Clinton 65
7. Grover Cleveland 62
8. George W. Bush 61
9. George H.W. Bush 58
10. William Jennings Bryan 56
10. Barack Obama 56
12. Ulysses Grant 55
12. Donald Trump 55
14. William McKinley 51
15. Herbert Hoover 46
16. Lyndon Johnson 45
17. Andrew Jackson 42
18. Abraham Lincoln 40
18. James Monroe 40
20. Theodore Roosevelt 38
21. Warren Harding 37
21. Benjamin Harrison 37
23. Calvin Coolidge 35
24. Thomas Jefferson 32
25. Jimmy Carter 31
25. William Howard Taft 31

NOTE: The District of Columbia is counted as a state. If two or more candidates tie for the most electoral votes from a state, each candidate is given credit for carrying that state. (This differs from the party rule, which does not give such credit if two or more parties are involved in a tie.) This note applies to all remaining candidate lists in this section.

Largest percentages of states carried in a career

1. George Washington (25 of 25) 100.00%
2. James Monroe (40 of 43) 93.02%
3. Ronald Reagan (93 of 102) 91.18%
4. Lyndon Johnson (45 of 51) 88.24%
5. Franklin Pierce (27 of 31) 87.10%
6. Franklin Roosevelt (162 of 192) 84.38%
7. Dwight Eisenhower (80 of 96) 83.33%
8. Ulysses Grant (55 of 69) 79.71%

[List continues on next page.]

Largest percentages of states carried in a career *(cont.)*

9. Warren Harding (37 of 48) 77.08%
10. Calvin Coolidge (35 of 48) 72.92%
10. Woodrow Wilson (70 of 96) 72.92%
12. Richard Nixon (107 of 152) 70.39%
13. Abraham Lincoln (40 of 58) 68.97%
14. James Madison (23 of 35) 65.71%
15. Bill Clinton (65 of 102) 63.73%
16. James Buchanan (19 of 31) 61.29%
17. George W. Bush (61 of 102) 59.80%
18. Andrew Jackson (42 of 72) 58.33%
18. Harry Truman (28 of 48) 58.33%
20. James Polk (15 of 26) 57.69%
21. George H.W. Bush (58 of 102) 56.86%
22. William McKinley (51 of 90) 56.67%
23. Rutherford Hayes (21 of 38) 55.26%
24. Barack Obama (56 of 102) 54.90%
25. Donald Trump (55 of 102) 53.92%

*NOTE: The number of states carried and the total number of states are
listed in parentheses. Percentages are based only on those years in which a
candidate met the qualification standards for the general election itself.*

Most states carried in an election

1. Richard Nixon (R-1972) 49
1. Ronald Reagan (R-1984) 49
3. Franklin Roosevelt (D-1936) 46
4. Lyndon Johnson (D-1964) 45
5. Ronald Reagan (R-1980) 44
6. Franklin Roosevelt (D-1932) 42
7. Dwight Eisenhower (R-1956) 41
8. Woodrow Wilson (D-1912) 40
8. Herbert Hoover (R-1928) 40
8. George H.W. Bush (R-1988) 40

Largest percentages of states carried in an election

1. George Washington (F-1789) 100.00%
1. George Washington (F-1792) 100.00%
1. James Monroe (DR-1820) 100.00%
4. Richard Nixon (R-1972) 96.08%
4. Ronald Reagan (R-1984) 96.08%
6. Franklin Roosevelt (D-1936) 95.83%
7. Thomas Jefferson (DR-1804) 88.24%
7. Lyndon Johnson (D-1964) 88.24%
9. Abraham Lincoln (R-1864) 88.00%
10. Franklin Roosevelt (D-1932) 87.50%

General-election winners who carried a minority of states

John Quincy Adams (DR-1824, 7 of 24)
John Kennedy (D-1960, 22 of 50)
Jimmy Carter (D-1976, 24 of 51)

General-election winners who did not carry their home states

James Polk (D-1844, Tennessee)
Woodrow Wilson (D-1916, New Jersey)
Richard Nixon (R-1968, New York)
Donald Trump (R-2016, New York)

NOTE: A home state is the place where an individual maintains a voting address during his or her presidential candidacy. This note also applies to the next list.

General-election losers who did not carry their home states

Charles Cotesworth Pinckney (F-1804, South Carolina)
Charles Cotesworth Pinckney (F-1808, South Carolina)
Rufus King (F-1816, New York)
Martin Van Buren (D-1840, New York)
Winfield Scott (W-1852, New Jersey)
John Fremont (R-1856, California)
Stephen Douglas (D-1860, Illinois)
John Breckinridge (SD-1860, Kentucky)
Horace Greeley (D-1872, New York)
Winfield Hancock (D-1880, Pennsylvania)
Grover Cleveland (D-1888, New York)
Benjamin Harrison (R-1892, Indiana)
William Jennings Bryan (D-1900, Nebraska)
Alton Parker (D-1904, New York)
William Howard Taft (R-1912, Ohio)
James Cox (D-1920, Ohio)
John Davis (D-1924, West Virginia)
Alfred Smith (D-1928, New York)
Herbert Hoover (R-1932, California)
Alfred Landon (R-1936, Kansas)
Wendell Willkie (R-1940, New York)
Thomas Dewey (R-1944, New York)
Adlai Stevenson (D-1952, Illinois)
Adlai Stevenson (D-1956, Illinois)
George McGovern (D-1972, South Dakota)
Al Gore (D-2000, Tennessee)
Mitt Romney (R-2012, Massachusetts)

NOTE: This list is restricted to major-party nominees who failed to win the general election.

Longest streaks of being carried by one party

1. Vermont (Republican, 1856-1960) 27
2. Georgia (Democratic, 1868-1960) 24
3. Arkansas (Democratic, 1876-1964) 23
4. Alabama (Democratic, 1876-1944) 18
4. Mississippi (Democratic, 1876-1944) 18
6. Louisiana (Democratic, 1880-1944) 17
6. South Carolina (Democratic, 1880-1944) 17
8. District of Columbia (Democratic, 1964-2020) 15

[List continues on next page.]

Longest streaks of being carried by one party (cont.)

9. Alaska (Republican, 1968-2020) 14
9. Idaho (Republican, 1968-2020) 14
9. Iowa (Republican, 1856-1908) 14
9. Kansas (Republican, 1968-2020) 14
9. Maine (Republican, 1856-1908) 14
9. Massachusettts (Republican, 1856-1908) 14
9. Michigan (Republican, 1856-1908) 14
9. Nebraska (Republican, 1968-2020) 14
9. New Hampshire (Republican, 1856-1908) 14
9. North Dakota (Republican, 1968-2020) 14
9. Ohio (Republican, 1856-1908) 14
9. Oklahoma (Republican, 1968-2020) 14
9. Rhode Island (Republican, 1856-1908) 14
9. South Dakota (Republican, 1968-2020) 14
9. Texas (Democratic, 1872-1924) 14
9. Utah (Republican, 1968-2020) 14
9. Wyoming (Republican, 1968-2020) 14

NOTE: A streak is defined as a consecutive string of elections. Any deviation (voting for a different party, having a tie, or skipping an election because of the Civil War or Reconstruction) breaks the streak. The first and last elections of the streak are listed.

States with best records of matching general-election winners

1. New Mexico (25 matches, 3 misses) 89.29%
2. Illinois (42 matches, 9 misses) 82.35%
3. Ohio (45 matches, 10 misses) 81.82%
4. California (35 matches, 8 misses) 81.40%
5. Pennsylvania (48 matches, 11 misses) 81.36%
6. New York (47 matches, 11 misses) 81.03%
7. Nevada (32 matches, 8 misses) 80.00%
8. Arizona (22 matches, 6 misses) 78.57%
9. Wisconsin (34 matches, 10 misses) 77.27%
10. New Hampshire (44 matches, 15 misses) 74.58%

NOTE: This list shows how frequently a state has been carried by the national winner (a match) or by one of the national losing candidates (a miss). If the national winner ties one of the national losing candidates for the largest number of electoral votes from a given state (as occasionally happened before 1804), the state is still credited with a match. This note also applies to the next list.

States with worst records of matching general-election winners

1. District of Columbia (7 matches, 8 misses) 46.67%
2. Alabama (25 matches, 25 misses) 50.00%
3. Mississippi (25 matches, 24 misses) 51.02%
4. Alaska (9 matches, 7 misses) 56.25%
5. South Carolina (33 matches, 25 misses) 56.90%
6. Texas (24 matches, 18 misses) 57.14%

7. South Dakota (19 matches, 14 misses) 57.58%
8. Arkansas (26 matches, 19 misses) 57.78%
9. Georgia (34 matches, 24 misses) 58.62%
10. Kentucky (36 matches, 22 misses) 62.07%

Longest streaks of matching national winners

1. Nevada (1912-1972) 16
1. New Mexico (1912-1972) 16
3. Idaho (1904-1956) 14
3. Illinois (1920-1972) 14
3. Montana (1904-1956) 14
3. Ohio (1964-2016) 14
3. Pennsylvania (1828-1880) 14
8. Missouri (1904-1952) 13
9. Arizona (1912-1956) 12
9. Delaware (1952-1996) 12
9. Minnesota (1920-1964) 12
9. Missouri (1960-2004) 12
9. North Dakota (1892-1936) 12
9. Ohio (1896-1940) 12

NOTE: A streak is defined as a consecutive string of elections. Any deviation (voting for a national loser, having a tie, or skipping an election because of the Civil War or Reconstruction) breaks the streak. The first and last elections of the streak are listed.

Popular Votes

Popular votes (actual) for all of a party's qualified candidates

1. Republican 1,074,639,173
2. Democratic 1,073,621,450
3. Independent (Perot) 19,741,657
4. American Independent 9,906,473
5. Reform 8,085,402
6. Whig 6,061,853
7. National Unity 5,720,060
8. Progressive (La Follette) 4,827,184
9. Libertarian 4,493,014
10. Progressive (Roosevelt) 4,120,207
11. Socialist 4,113,562
12. Green 2,882,955
13. States' Rights Democratic 1,169,156
14. Progressive (Wallace) 1,157,172
15. Populist 1,029,357
16. Democratic-Republican 995,333
17. National Republican 985,102
18. Union 892,361
19. American-Whig 873,053
20. Southern Democratic 848,019
21. Constitutional Union 590,901
22. Prohibition 520,892
23. Free Soil 446,711
24. Greenback 306,921
25. Anti-Masonic 100,715
26. Liberty 62,103

NOTE: This list is confined to a party's qualified candidates. A party may have received votes in other elections without reaching qualification levels. If a candidate ran on two tickets (such as William Jennings Bryan in 1896), all popular votes have been awarded to the major party. This note also applies to the next list.

Popular votes (equalized) for all of a party's qualified candidates

1. Democratic 2,237,929,882
2. Republican 2,014,105,982
3. Whig 241,205,968
4. Democratic-Republican 152,402,616
5. National Republican 81,051,482
6. Progressive (Roosevelt) 27,389,475
7. American-Whig 21,532,158
8. Socialist 20,616,565
9. Independent (Perot) 18,905,104
10. Southern Democratic 18,098,559
11. Progressive (La Follette) 16,588,762
12. Free Soil 15,033,297
13. American Independent 13,531,238
14. Constitutional Union 12,611,105
15. Populist 8,527,133

16. Reform...8,398,042
17. Anti-Masonic...7,783,393
18. National Unity 6,611,730
19. Prohibition..4,437,820
20. Greenback...3,328,790
21. Libertarian 3,289,547
22. Green 2,735,119
23. States' Rights Democratic..2,401,150
24. Progressive (Wallace)..2,376,538
25. Liberty..2,296,998
26. Union 1,954,917

Most popular votes (actual) in a career

1. Donald Trump...137,208,803
2. Barack Obama...135,414,312
3. Richard Nixon..113,063,548
4. George W. Bush 112,496,612
5. Franklin Roosevelt..103,425,434
6. Ronald Reagan 98,359,228
7. Bill Clinton.. 92,311,683
8. George H.W. Bush.. 87,989,988
9. Joseph Biden.. 81,283,501
10. Jimmy Carter.. 76,314,646
11. Dwight Eisenhower 69,368,417
12. Hillary Clinton.. 65,853,514
13. Mitt Romney 60,933,500
14. John McCain 59,948,323
15. John Kerry... 59,028,439
16. Adlai Stevenson 53,337,744
17. Al Gore 50,999,897
18. Thomas Dewey... 43,984,224
19. Lyndon Johnson 43,129,566
20. Michael Dukakis 41,809,065
21. Bob Dole.. 39,198,755
22. Gerald Ford... 39,147,793
23. Walter Mondale.. 37,577,185
24. Herbert Hoover... 37,193,248
25. John Kennedy.. 34,226,731

Most popular votes (equalized) in a career

1. Franklin Roosevelt..226,275,350
2. Richard Nixon..153,657,272
3. Andrew Jackson 151,554,896
4. Grover Cleveland 143,491,778
5. William Jennings Bryan 134,364,271
6. Dwight Eisenhower 112,257,137
7. Ronald Reagan 109,521,380
8. Ulysses Grant...108,275,674
9. Martin Van Buren 107,755,054
10. Barack Obama 103,989,225

[List continues on next page.]

Most popular votes (equalized) in a career *(cont.)*

11. William McKinley 102,764,828
12. George W. Bush.. 98,598,801
13. Henry Clay 98,498,789
14. Herbert Hoover.. 97,890,056
15. Abraham Lincoln.. 94,916,847
16. Donald Trump 92,935,386
17. Bill Clinton... 92,241,569
18. Jimmy Carter... 91,080,044
19. Woodrow Wilson 91,077,886
20. Thomas Dewey... 91,006,105
21. George H.W. Bush 90,818,989
22. Benjamin Harrison 90,790,591
23. William Henry Harrison 89,515,830
24. Adlai Stevenson 86,331,852
25. Theodore Roosevelt 83,795,844

Most popular votes in an election

1. Joseph Biden (D-2020) 81,283,501
2. Donald Trump (R-2020) 74,223,975
3. Barack Obama (D-2008) 69,498,516
4. Barack Obama (D-2012) 65,915,796
5. Hillary Clinton (D-2016) 65,853,514
6. Donald Trump (R-2016) 62,984,828
7. George W. Bush (R-2004) 62,040,610
8. Mitt Romney (R-2012) 60,933,500
9. John McCain (R-2008) 59,948,323
10. John Kerry (D-2004) 59,028,439
11. Ronald Reagan (R-1984) 54,455,075
12. Al Gore (D-2000) 50,999,897
13. George W. Bush (R-2000) 50,456,002
14. George H.W. Bush (R-1988).. 48,886,106
15. Bill Clinton (D-1996) 47,402,357
16. Richard Nixon (R-1972) 47,169,911
17. Bill Clinton (D-1992) 44,909,326
18. Ronald Reagan (R-1980) 43,904,153
19. Lyndon Johnson (D-1964)... 43,129,566
20. Michael Dukakis (D-1988) 41,809,065
21. Jimmy Carter (D-1976) 40,830,763
22. Bob Dole (R-1996) 39,198,755
23. Gerald Ford (R-1976) 39,147,793
24. George H.W. Bush (R-1992).. 39,103,882
25. Walter Mondale (D-1984) 37,577,185

Largest popular-vote percentages in an election

1. Lyndon Johnson (D-1964) 61.05%
2. Franklin Roosevelt (D-1936) 60.80%
3. Richard Nixon (R-1972) 60.69%
4. Warren Harding (R-1920) 60.34%
5. Ronald Reagan (R-1984).. 58.77%
6. Herbert Hoover (R-1928)... 58.24%

7. Franklin Roosevelt (D-1932) 57.41%
8. Dwight Eisenhower (R-1956) 57.38%
9. Theodore Roosevelt (R-1904) 56.41%
10. Andrew Jackson (DR-1828) 55.97%
11. Ulysses Grant (R-1872) 55.61%
12. Abraham Lincoln (R-1864) 55.09%
13. Dwight Eisenhower (R-1952) 54.88%
14. Franklin Roosevelt (D-1940) 54.69%
15. Andrew Jackson (D-1832) 54.24%
16. Calvin Coolidge (R-1924) 54.04%
17. Franklin Roosevelt (D-1944) 53.39%
18. George H.W. Bush (R-1988) 53.37%
19. Barack Obama (D-2008) 52.93%
20. William Henry Harrison (W-1840) 52.88%
21. Ulysses Grant (R-1868) 52.66%
22. William McKinley (R-1900) 51.67%
23. William Howard Taft (R-1908) 51.58%
24. Joseph Biden (D-2020) 51.31%
25. William McKinley (R-1896) 51.10%

Smallest popular-vote percentages for election winners

1. John Quincy Adams (DR-1824) 30.92%
2. Abraham Lincoln (R-1860) 39.82%
3. Woodrow Wilson (D-1912) 41.84%
4. Bill Clinton (D-1992) 43.01%
5. Richard Nixon (R-1968) 43.42%
6. James Buchanan (D-1856) 45.28%
7. Grover Cleveland (D-1892) 46.01%
8. Donald Trump (R-2016) 46.09%
9. Zachary Taylor (W-1848) 47.28%
10. Benjamin Harrison (R-1888) 47.82%

Smallest popular-vote percentages for major-party nominees

1. Hugh White (W-1836) 9.72%
2. John Breckinridge (SD-1860) 18.10%
3. William Howard Taft (R-1912) 23.18%
4. John Davis (D-1924) 28.82%
5. Stephen Douglas (D-1860) 29.46%
6. John Quincy Adams (DR-1824) 30.92%
7. John Fremont (R-1856) 33.11%
8. James Cox (D-1920) 34.12%
9. Alfred Landon (R-1936) 36.54%
10. William Henry Harrison (W-1836) 36.64%

Largest popular-vote percentages for election losers

1. Samuel Tilden (D-1876) 50.98%
2. Richard Nixon (R-1960) 49.55%
3. Grover Cleveland (D-1888) 48.61%
4. Al Gore (D-2000) 48.39%
5. John Kerry (D-2004) 48.27%
6. James Blaine (R-1884) 48.25%
7. Winfield Hancock (D-1880) 48.21%
8. Hillary Clinton (D-2016) 48.19%
9. Henry Clay (W-1844) 48.08%
10. Gerald Ford (R-1976) 48.00%

Most popular votes for minor-party candidates

1. Ross Perot (I-1992) 19,741,657
2. George Wallace (AI-1968) 9,906,473
3. Ross Perot (REF-1996) 8,085,402
4. John Anderson (NU-1980) 5,720,060
5. Robert La Follette (P-1924) 4,827,184
6. Gary Johnson (LIB-2016) 4,489,341
7. Theodore Roosevelt (P-1912) 4,120,207
8. Ralph Nader (GRN-2000) 2,882,955
9. Strom Thurmond (SRD-1948) 1,169,156
10. Henry Wallace (P-1948) 1,157,172

NOTE: A minor party is any but the seven major parties (Democratic, Republican, Federalist, Democratic-Republican, National Republican, Whig, and Southern Democratic). This note also applies to the next list.

Largest popular-vote percentages for minor-party candidates

1. Theodore Roosevelt (P-1912) 27.39%
2. Millard Fillmore (AW-1856) 21.53%
3. Ross Perot (I-1992) 18.91%
4. Robert La Follette (P-1924) 16.59%
5. George Wallace (AI-1968) 13.53%
6. John Bell (CU-1860) 12.61%
7. Martin Van Buren (FS-1848) 10.12%
8. James Weaver (POP-1892) 8.53%
9. Ross Perot (REF-1996) 8.40%
10. William Wirt (AM-1832) 7.78%

Largest margins in popular votes

1. 1972 (Richard Nixon-George McGovern) 17,999,528
2. 1984 (Ronald Reagan-Walter Mondale) 16,877,890
3. 1964 (Lyndon Johnson-Barry Goldwater) 15,951,378
4. 1936 (Franklin Roosevelt-Alfred Landon) 11,071,183
5. 1956 (Dwight Eisenhower-Adlai Stevenson) 9,567,720

6. 2008 (Barack Obama-John McCain)...9,550,193
7. 1980 (Ronald Reagan-Jimmy Carter)...8,420,270
8. 1996 (Bill Clinton-Bob Dole) 8,203,602
9. 1924 (Calvin Coolidge-John Davis) 7,337,778
10. 1988 (George H.W. Bush-Michael Dukakis)...............................7,077,041

NOTE: The top two candidates are listed in parentheses, with the popular-vote leader coming first. The margin is the difference between the candidates' vote totals. This note also applies to the next two lists.

Smallest margins in popular votes

1. 1880 (James Garfield-Winfield Hancock).. 8,355
2. 1824 (Andrew Jackson-John Quincy Adams).....................................38,149
3. 1844 (James Polk-Henry Clay)..39,490
4. 1884 (Grover Cleveland-James Blaine) 62,670
5. 1888 (Grover Cleveland-Benjamin Harrison)......................................89,293
6. 1960 (John Kennedy-Richard Nixon).. 118,574
7. 1848 (Zachary Taylor-Lewis Cass) 137,933
8. 1828 (Andrew Jackson-John Quincy Adams) 141,656
9. 1840 (William Henry Harrison-Martin Van Buren) 146,536
10. 1836 (Martin Van Buren-William Henry Harrison) 213,360

Smallest margins in popular votes (since 1900)

1. 1960 (John Kennedy-Richard Nixon).. 118,574
2. 1968 (Richard Nixon-Hubert Humphrey).. 510,314
3. 2000 (Al Gore-George W. Bush)... 543,895
4. 1916 (Woodrow Wilson-Charles Evans Hughes) 579,033
5. 1900 (William McKinley-William Jennings Bryan)......................... 861,495
6. 1908 (William Howard Taft-William Jennings Bryan)................. 1,269,724
7. 1976 (Jimmy Carter-Gerald Ford) 1,682,970
8. 1948 (Harry Truman-Thomas Dewey)...2,135,746
9. 1912 (Woodrow Wilson-Theodore Roosevelt) 2,174,120
10. 1904 (Theodore Roosevelt-Alton Parker)...................................2,542,098

Largest margins in popular-vote percentages

1. 1920 (Warren Harding-James Cox)..26.22
2. 1924 (Calvin Coolidge-John Davis) 25.22
3. 1936 (Franklin Roosevelt-Alfred Landon) 24.25
4. 1972 (Richard Nixon-George McGovern)..23.16
5. 1964 (Lyndon Johnson-Barry Goldwater)..22.58
6. 1904 (Theodore Roosevelt-Alton Parker)..18.80
7. 1984 (Ronald Reagan-Walter Mondale) 18.22
8. 1932 (Franklin Roosevelt-Herbert Hoover) 17.76
9. 1928 (Herbert Hoover-Alfred Smith) 17.47
10. 1832 (Andrew Jackson-Henry Clay)..16.82

NOTE: The top two candidates are listed in parentheses, with the popular-vote leader coming first. The margin is expressed in percentage points, showing the difference between the candidates' percentages. (Percentages beyond two decimal points have been used in these calculations, which means a few margins differ by 0.01 from results that would be obtained by using the published percentages for candidates.) This note also applies to the next list.

Smallest margins in popular-vote percentages

1. 1880 (James Garfield-Winfield Hancock)..0.09
2. 1960 (John Kennedy-Richard Nixon)...0.17
3. 2000 (Al Gore-George W. Bush) 0.52
4. 1884 (Grover Cleveland-James Blaine) 0.62
5. 1968 (Richard Nixon-Hubert Humphrey)...0.70
6. 1888 (Grover Cleveland-Benjamin Harrison)..0.78
7. 1844 (James Polk-Henry Clay)..1.46
8. 1976 (Jimmy Carter-Gerald Ford) 2.06
9. 2016 (Hillary Clinton-Donald Trump) 2.10
10. 2004 (George W. Bush-John Kerry) 2.46

Electoral Votes

Electoral votes (actual) for all of a party's candidates

1. Republican 10,590
2. Democratic 10,383
3. Democratic-Republican 1,599
4. Federalist 811
5. Whig 668
6. National Republican..132
7. Progressive (Roosevelt) 88
8. Southern Democratic...72
9. American Independent...46
10. Constitutional Union..39
10. States' Rights Democratic...39
12. Populist...22
13. Progressive (La Follette)...13
14. American-Whig...8
15. Anti-Masonic..7
16. Libertarian 1

NOTE: If a candidate ran on two tickets (such as William Jennings Bryan in 1896), all electoral votes have been awarded to the major party. This note also applies to the next list.

Electoral votes (equalized) for all of a party's candidates

1. Democratic 12,033
2. Republican 12,022
3. Democratic-Republican 4,402
4. Federalist 3,498
5. Whig 1,239
6. National Republican..263
7. Southern Democratic...128
8. Progressive (Roosevelt) 89
9. Constitutional Union..69
10. American Independent...46
11. States' Rights Democratic.......................................40
12. Populist...27
13. American-Whig..15
14. Anti-Masonic...13
14. Progressive (La Follette)...13
16. Libertarian 1

Most electoral votes (actual) in a career

1. Franklin Roosevelt.. 1,876
2. Richard Nixon.. 1,040
3. Ronald Reagan 1,015
4. Dwight Eisenhower 899
5. Bill Clinton..749
6. Woodrow Wilson...712
7. Barack Obama...697

[List continues on next page.]

Most electoral votes (actual) in a career (cont.)

8. Grover Cleveland 664
9. George H.W. Bush 594
10. William McKinley 563
11. George W. Bush 557
12. Donald Trump 536
13. Herbert Hoover 503
14. Ulysses Grant 500
15. Andrew Jackson 496
16. William Jennings Bryan 493
17. Lyndon Johnson 486
18. Theodore Roosevelt 424
19. James Monroe 414
20. Warren Harding 404
21. Abraham Lincoln 392
22. Calvin Coolidge 382
23. Benjamin Harrison 378
24. Jimmy Carter 346
25. William Howard Taft 329

Most electoral votes (equalized) in a career

1. Franklin Roosevelt 1,901
2. John Adams 1,109
3. George Washington 1,084
4. Thomas Jefferson 1,061
5. Richard Nixon 1,040
6. Ronald Reagan 1,015
7. James Monroe 990
8. Andrew Jackson 983
9. Dwight Eisenhower 911
10. Grover Cleveland 855
11. Ulysses Grant 833
12. Abraham Lincoln 810
13. Bill Clinton 749
14. Woodrow Wilson 722
15. Barack Obama 697
16. James Madison 692
17. William McKinley 677
18. George H.W. Bush 594
19. William Jennings Bryan 579
20. William Henry Harrison 562
21. George W. Bush 558
22. Donald Trump 536
23. Herbert Hoover 510
24. Benjamin Harrison 489
25. Lyndon Johnson 486

Most electoral votes in an election

1. Ronald Reagan (R-1984)...525
2. Franklin Roosevelt (D-1936) 523
3. Richard Nixon (R-1972)...520
4. Ronald Reagan (R-1980)..489
5. Lyndon Johnson (D-1964) 486
6. Franklin Roosevelt (D-1932) 472
7. Dwight Eisenhower (R-1956)..457
8. Franklin Roosevelt (D-1940) 449
9. Herbert Hoover (R-1928)..444
10. Dwight Eisenhower (R-1952) 442
11. Woodrow Wilson (D-1912)..435
12. Franklin Roosevelt (D-1944) 432
13. George H.W. Bush (R-1988)..426
14. Warren Harding (R-1920)...404
15. Calvin Coolidge (R-1924) 382
16. Bill Clinton (D-1996) 379
17. Bill Clinton (D-1992) 370
18. Barack Obama (D-2008)..365
19. Theodore Roosevelt (R-1904) 336
20. Barack Obama (D-2012)..332
21. William Howard Taft (R-1908)...321
22. Joseph Biden (D-2020) 306
23. Donald Trump (R-2016)...304
24. Harry Truman (D-1948) 303
24. John Kennedy (D-1960) 303

Largest electoral-vote percentages in an election

1. George Washington (F-1789) 100.00%
1. George Washington (F-1792) 100.00%
3. James Monroe (DR-1820) 99.57%
4. Franklin Roosevelt (D-1936) 98.49%
5. Ronald Reagan (R-1984)...97.58%
6. Richard Nixon (R-1972)..96.65%
7. Thomas Jefferson (DR-1804) 92.05%
8. Abraham Lincoln (R-1864)..90.99%
9. Ronald Reagan (R-1980) 90.89%
10. Lyndon Johnson (D-1964)..90.34%
11. Franklin Roosevelt (D-1932) 88.89%
12. Dwight Eisenhower (R-1956) 86.06%
13. Franklin Pierce (D-1852)..85.81%
14. Franklin Roosevelt (D-1940) 84.56%
15. James Monroe (DR-1816)...84.33%
16. Herbert Hoover (R-1928) 83.62%
17. Dwight Eisenhower (R-1952) 83.24%
18. Ulysses Grant (R-1872)...81.95%
19. Woodrow Wilson (D-1912)..81.92%

[List continues on next page.]

Largest electoral-vote percentages in an election *(cont.)*

20. Franklin Roosevelt (D-1944).. 81.36%
21. William Henry Harrison (W-1840).. 79.59%
22. George H.W. Bush (R-1988)... 79.18%
23. Andrew Jackson (D-1832) 76.57%
24. Warren Harding (R-1920)... 76.08%
25. Ulysses Grant (R-1868)... 72.79%

Smallest electoral-vote percentages for election winners

1. John Quincy Adams (DR-1824).. 32.18%
2. Rutherford Hayes (R-1876) 50.14%
3. George W. Bush (R-2000) 50.47%
4. John Adams (F-1796) 51.45%
5. Woodrow Wilson (D-1916) 52.17%
6. Thomas Jefferson (DR-1800).. 52.90%
7. George W. Bush (R-2004) 53.16%
8. Grover Cleveland (D-1884).. 54.61%
9. Jimmy Carter (D-1976)... 55.20%
10. Richard Nixon (R-1968) 55.95%

Smallest electoral-vote percentages for major-party nominees

1. William Howard Taft (R-1912) 1.51%
1. Alfred Landon (R-1936) 1.51%
3. Walter Mondale (D-1984)..2.42%
4. George McGovern (D-1972)..3.16%
5. Stephen Douglas (D-1860) 3.96%
6. Charles Cotesworth Pinckney (F-1804)..................................7.96%
7. Hugh White (W-1836) 8.84%
8. George McClellan (D-1864)..9.01%
9. Jimmy Carter (D-1980)..9.11%
10. Barry Goldwater (R-1964)...9.67%

NOTE: *This list does not include Horace Greeley, who died between the general election and the day the Electoral College cast its votes in 1872.*

Largest electoral-vote percentages for election losers

1. John Adams (F-1792) 58.33%
2. Aaron Burr (DR-1800) 52.90%
3. Samuel Tilden (D-1876) 49.86%
4. Al Gore (D-2000) 49.53%
5. John Adams (F-1789) 49.28%
5. Thomas Jefferson (DR-1796).. 49.28%
7. Charles Evans Hughes (R-1916).. 47.83%
8. John Adams (F-1800) 47.10%
9. John Kerry (D-2004).. 46.65%
10. Charles Cotesworth Pinckney (F-1800)............................. 46.38%

NOTE: *John Adams (1789 and 1792), Thomas Jefferson (1796), and Aaron Burr (1800), who are all on this list, were elected vice president under the double-ballot system.*

Largest electoral-vote percentages for losers (after 1800)

1. Samuel Tilden (D-1876)...49.86%
2. Al Gore (D-2000) 49.53%
3. Charles Evans Hughes (R-1916)...47.83%
4. John Kerry (D-2004)..46.65%
5. James Blaine (R-1884) 45.39%
6. Gerald Ford (R-1976) 44.61%
7. Lewis Cass (D-1848) 43.79%
8. Donald Trump (R-2020) 43.12%
9. Hillary Clinton (D-2016)..42.19%
10. Winfield Hancock (D-1880)..42.01%

NOTE: This list removes all candidates who ran under the double-ballot system.

Most electoral votes for minor-party candidates

1. Theodore Roosevelt (P-1912)..88
2. George Wallace (AI-1968) 46
3. John Bell (CU-1860)..39
3. Strom Thurmond (SRD-1948)..39
5. James Weaver (POP-1892)..22
6. Robert La Follette (P-1924)..13
7. Millard Fillmore (AW-1856)...8
8. William Wirt (AM-1832)..7
9. John Hospers (LIB-1972) 1

NOTE: These are the only nine candidates who qualified for this list. A minor party is any but the seven major parties (Democratic, Republican, Federalist, Democratic-Republican, National Republican, Whig, and Southern Democratic). This list does not include individuals who received electoral votes as independent candidates even though they hadn't formally entered the race, such as Walter Jones in 1956 and Harry Byrd in 1960. This note also applies to the next list.

Largest electoral-vote percentages for minor-party candidates

1. Theodore Roosevelt (P-1912) 16.57%
2. John Bell (CU-1860)..12.87%
3. George Wallace (AI-1968) 8.55%
4. Strom Thurmond (SRD-1948)..7.35%
5. James Weaver (POP-1892)...4.96%
6. Millard Fillmore (AW-1856)...2.70%
7. William Wirt (AM-1832)...2.45%
7. Robert La Follette (P-1924)...2.45%
9. John Hospers (LIB-1972) 0.19%

Largest margins in electoral votes

1. 1936 (Franklin Roosevelt-Alfred Landon) 515
2. 1984 (Ronald Reagan-Walter Mondale) 512
3. 1972 (Richard Nixon-George McGovern).....................................503
4. 1980 (Ronald Reagan-Jimmy Carter)..440
5. 1964 (Lyndon Johnson-Barry Goldwater)....................................434
6. 1932 (Franklin Roosevelt-Herbert Hoover) 413
7. 1956 (Dwight Eisenhower-Adlai Stevenson) 384
8. 1940 (Franklin Roosevelt-Wendell Willkie) 367
9. 1928 (Herbert Hoover-Alfred Smith) 357
10. 1952 (Dwight Eisenhower-Adlai Stevenson)...............................353

NOTE: The top two candidates are listed in parentheses, with the electoral-vote leader coming first. The margin is the difference between the candidates' vote totals. This note also applies to the next list.

Smallest margins in electoral votes

1. 1800 (Thomas Jefferson-Aaron Burr) 0
2. 1876 (Rutherford Hayes-Samuel Tilden) 1
3. 1796 (John Adams-Thomas Jefferson)..3
4. 2000 (George W. Bush-Al Gore) 5
5. 1824 (Andrew Jackson-John Quincy Adams)................................ 15
6. 1916 (Woodrow Wilson-Charles Evans Hughes) 23
7. 1789 (George Washington-John Adams) 35
7. 2004 (George W. Bush-John Kerry).. 35
9. 1848 (Zachary Taylor-Lewis Cass) 36
10. 1884 (Grover Cleveland-James Blaine)... 37

Largest margins in electoral-vote percentages

1. 1820 (James Monroe-John Quincy Adams)........................... 99.14
2. 1936 (Franklin Roosevelt-Alfred Landon) 96.99
3. 1984 (Ronald Reagan-Walter Mondale) 95.17
4. 1972 (Richard Nixon-George McGovern)............................... 93.49
5. 1804 (Thomas Jefferson-Charles Cotesworth Pinckney) 84.09
6. 1864 (Abraham Lincoln-George McClellan)........................... 81.97
7. 1980 (Ronald Reagan-Jimmy Carter)..................................... 81.78
8. 1964 (Lyndon Johnson-Barry Goldwater)............................... 80.67
9. 1932 (Franklin Roosevelt-Herbert Hoover) 77.78
10. 1956 (Dwight Eisenhower-Adlai Stevenson)........................... 72.32

NOTE: The top two candidates are listed in parentheses, with the electoral-vote leader first. The margin is expressed in percentage points, showing the difference between the candidates' percentages. (Percentages beyond two decimal points have been used in these calculations, which means a few margins differ by 0.01 from results that would be obtained by using the published percentages for candidates.) This note also applies to the next list.

Smallest margins in electoral-vote percentages

1. 1800 (Thomas Jefferson-Aaron Burr) 0.00
2. 1876 (Rutherford Hayes-Samuel Tilden) 0.27
3. 2000 (George W. Bush-Al Gore) 0.93
4. 1796 (John Adams-Thomas Jefferson)..2.17
5. 1916 (Woodrow Wilson-Charles Evans Hughes) 4.33
6. 1824 (Andrew Jackson-John Quincy Adams)............................5.75
7. 2004 (George W. Bush-John Kerry)..6.51
8. 1884 (Grover Cleveland-James Blaine) 9.23
9. 1976 (Jimmy Carter-Gerald Ford) 10.59
10. 1848 (Zachary Taylor-Lewis Cass).. 12.41

Largest rises between a candidate's EV and PV percentages

1. Ronald Reagan (R-1980, 90.89% for EV, 50.75% for PV)................... 40.14
2. Woodrow Wilson (D-1912, 81.92% for EV, 41.84% for PV) 40.08
3. Ronald Reagan (R-1984, 97.58% for EV, 58.77% for PV)................... 38.81
4. Franklin Roosevelt (D-1936, 98.49% for EV, 60.80% for PV) 37.70
5. Richard Nixon (R-1972, 96.65% for EV, 60.69% for PV)..................... 35.96
6. Abraham Lincoln (R-1864, 90.99% for EV, 55.09% for PV) 35.89
7. Franklin Pierce (D-1852, 85.81% for EV, 50.84% for PV) 34.97
8. Franklin Roosevelt (D-1932, 88.89% for EV, 57.41% for PV) 31.48
9. Franklin Roosevelt (D-1940, 84.56% for EV, 54.69% for PV) 29.87
10. Lyndon Johnson (D-1964, 90.34% for EV, 61.05% for PV) 29.28

NOTE: This list covers all elections since 1828. The difference between a candidate's electoral-vote percentage and popular-vote percentage is expressed in percentage points. (Percentages beyond two decimal points have been used in these calculations, which means a few margins differ by 0.01 from results that would be obtained by using the published percentages for candidates.) This note also applies to the next list.

Largest drops between a candidate's EV and PV percentages

1. Walter Mondale (D-1984, 2.42% for EV, 40.56% for PV)...................-38.14
2. George McClellan (D-1864, 9.01% for EV, 44.89% for PV)...............-35.88
3. Alfred Landon (R-1936, 1.51% for EV, 36.54% for PV)......................-35.03
4. George McGovern (D-1972, 3.16% for EV, 37.53% for PV)..............-34.37
5. Jimmy Carter (D-1980, 9.11% for EV, 41.02% for PV) ....-31.91
6. Winfield Scott (W-1852, 14.19% for EV, 43.87% for PV) ....-29.68
7. Wendell Willkie (R-1940, 15.44% for EV, 44.83% for PV) ....-29.39
8. Barry Goldwater (R-1964, 9.67% for EV, 38.47% for PV)..................-28.81
9. Herbert Hoover (R-1932, 11.11% for EV, 39.65% for PV) ....-28.54
10. Adlai Stevenson (D-1956, 13.75% for EV, 41.95% for PV) ....-28.21

Electoral votes for home-state candidates

1. New York 6,359
2. California 2,372
3. Ohio 2,130
4. Illinois 1,764
5. Massachusetts 1,702
6. Texas 1,639
7. Virginia 1,200
8. Tennessee 997
9. New Jersey 775
10. Arkansas 749
11. Nebraska 493
12. Indiana 420
13. Georgia 393
14. Michigan 367
15. Pennsylvania 329
16. Missouri 321
17. Delaware 306
18. Kentucky 263
19. New Hampshire 254
20. Florida 232
21. South Carolina 230
22. Arizona 225
23. Minnesota 204
24. Maine 182
25. Kansas 167
26. Louisiana 163
27. West Virginia 136
28. Alabama 47
29. Iowa 22
30. South Dakota 18
31. North Carolina 17
32. Maryland 15
33. Connecticut 13
33. Wisconsin 13
35. Vermont 1

NOTE: *A home state is the place where an individual maintains a voting address during his or her presidential candidacy. This note also applies to the next list.*

Home-state electoral votes per 100 EV cast by same state

1. New York (6,359 received, 2,125 cast) 299.25
2. Arkansas (749 received, 301 cast) 248.84
3. Nebraska (493 received, 228 cast) 216.23
4. California (2,372 received, 1,126 cast) 210.66
5. Massachusetts (1,702 received, 926 cast) 183.80
6. Ohio (2,130 received, 1,161 cast) 183.46
7. Texas (1,639 received, 898 cast) 182.52
8. Illinois (1,764 received, 1,055 cast) 167.20
9. Tennessee (997 received, 616 cast) 161.85
10. Delaware (306 received, 191 cast) 160.21
11. Arizona (225 received, 163 cast) 138.04

12. Virginia (1,200 received, 921 cast) 130.29
13. New Jersey (775 received, 714 cast) 108.54
14. New Hampshire (254 received, 313 cast) 81.15
15. Indiana (420 received, 644 cast) 65.22
16. Maine (182 received, 306 cast) 59.48
17. Georgia (393 received, 666 cast) 59.01
18. Kansas (167 received, 303 cast) 55.12
19. Michigan (367 received, 690 cast) 53.19
20. West Virginia (136 received, 257 cast) 52.92
21. Minnesota (204 received, 388 cast) 52.58
22. Missouri (321 received, 619 cast) 51.86
23. Florida (232 received, 491 cast) 47.25
24. South Carolina (230 received, 534 cast) 43.07
25. Kentucky (263 received, 634 cast) 41.48
26. Louisiana (163 received, 414 cast) 39.37
27. Pennsylvania (329 received, 1,690 cast) 19.47
28. South Dakota (18 received, 127 cast) 14.17
29. Alabama (47 received, 477 cast) 9.85
30. Iowa (22 received, 415 cast) 5.30
31. Connecticut (13 received, 471 cast) 2.76
32. Wisconsin (13 received, 472 cast) 2.75
33. Maryland (15 received, 561 cast) 2.67
34. North Carolina (17 received, 767 cast) 2.22
35. Vermont (1 received, 262 cast) 0.38
36. Alaska (0 received, 48 cast) 0.00
36. Colorado (0 received, 230 cast) 0.00
36. District of Columbia (0 received, 44 cast) 0.00
36. Hawaii (0 received, 63 cast) 0.00
36. Idaho (0 received, 127 cast) 0.00
36. Mississippi (0 received, 361 cast) 0.00
36. Montana (0 received, 119 cast) 0.00
36. Nevada (0 received, 137 cast) 0.00
36. New Mexico (0 received, 114 cast) 0.00
36. North Dakota (0 received, 121 cast) 0.00
36. Oklahoma (0 received, 249 cast) 0.00
36. Oregon (0 received, 214 cast) 0.00
36. Rhode Island (0 received, 249 cast) 0.00
36. Utah (0 received, 137 cast) 0.00
36. Washington (0 received, 280 cast) 0.00
36. Wyoming (0 received, 99 cast) 0.00

NOTE: This list compares the electoral votes received by home-state candidates with the electoral votes cast by the same state in all general elections. The rate is the number of electoral votes received per 100 electoral votes cast.

Electoral votes (equalized) in a career prior to 40th birthday

1. William Jennings Bryan 212
2. John Breckinridge 128
3. George McClellan 48
4. Aaron Burr...4

NOTE: All ages are as of November 1 of any given year, which applies to all remaining lists in this section. These are the only four candidates to receive electoral votes before turning 40.

Electoral votes (equalized) in a career prior to 45th birthday

1. Aaron Burr 406
2. William Jennings Bryan 399
3. John Kennedy 304
4. DeWitt Clinton 221
5. John Fremont...207
6. John Breckinridge 128
7. Thomas Dewey..100
8. John Jay... 70
9. George McClellan 48
10. Robert Harrison 47

Electoral votes (equalized) in a career prior to 50th birthday

1. William Jennings Bryan 579
2. Franklin Pierce 462
3. Aaron Burr 406
4. Ulysses Grant..392
5. Theodore Roosevelt..380
6. Bill Clinton 370
7. Barack Obama...365
8. James Polk...333
9. James Garfield 312
10. John Kennedy..304

Electoral votes (equalized) in a career prior to 55th birthday

1. Franklin Roosevelt... 1,008
2. Ulysses Grant..833
3. Bill Clinton 749
4. Barack Obama...697
5. William Jennings Bryan 579
6. Grover Cleveland 519
7. Theodore Roosevelt..469
8. Franklin Pierce 462
9. Herbert Hoover 450
10. Warren Harding...409

Electoral votes (equalized) in a career prior to 60th birthday

1. Franklin Roosevelt... 1,463
2. Richard Nixon... 1,040
3. Grover Cleveland 855
4. Ulysses Grant..833
5. Abraham Lincoln 810
6. Bill Clinton 749
7. Woodrow Wilson...722
8. Barack Obama...697
9. William McKinley...677
10. John Adams...579
10. William Jennings Bryan 579

Electoral votes (equalized) in a career prior to 65th birthday

1. Franklin Roosevelt...1,901
2. George Washington..1,084
3. Thomas Jefferson..1,061
4. Richard Nixon..1,040
5. James Monroe 990
6. John Adams...856
7. Grover Cleveland 855
8. Ulysses Grant..833
9. Abraham Lincoln 810
10. Bill Clinton...749

Electoral votes (equalized) in a career after 65th birthday

1. Ronald Reagan 1,015
2. Donald Trump..536
3. Dwight Eisenhower 463
4. William Henry Harrison...428
5. Andrew Jackson...412
6. James Buchanan...316
7. Joseph Biden...306
8. John Adams...253
9. Lewis Cass..236
10. Hillary Clinton..227

Election Flips

Elections that could have been reversed by one flip

1844: Henry Clay over James Polk by flipping New York
1848: Lewis Cass over Zachary Taylor by flipping Pennsylvania
1876: Samuel Tilden over Rutherford Hayes by flipping any of 20 states, with South Carolina having the smallest margin
1880: Winfield Hancock over James Garfield by flipping New York
1884: James Blaine over Grover Cleveland by flipping New York
1888: Grover Cleveland over Benjamin Harrison by flipping New York
1916: Charles Evans Hughes over Woodrow Wilson by flipping any of nine states, with California having the smallest margin
1976: Gerald Ford over Jimmy Carter by flipping New York
2000: Al Gore over George W. Bush by flipping any of 30 states, with Florida having the smallest margin
2004: John Kerry over George W. Bush by flipping any of three states, with Ohio having the smallest margin
2020: Donald Trump over Joseph Biden by flipping California

NOTE: The candidate listed first would have been the national winner if the flip had occurred. A flip is the hypothetical reversal of a state's popular-vote results, achieved by switching a sufficient number of votes from the candidate who carried the state to the runner-up. (The size of a state's flip is the next whole number larger than one-half of its popular-vote margin.) A flip alters the distribution of electoral votes and potentially the outcome of the election. This note applies to all lists in this section.

Elections that could have been reversed by two flips

1828: John Quincy Adams over Andrew Jackson by flipping Pennsylvania and Virginia
1856: John Fremont over James Buchanan by flipping Pennsylvania and either Illinois or Indiana
1896: William Jennings Bryan over William McKinley by flipping New York and any of eight states, with Indiana having the smallest margin, or by flipping Pennsylvania and either Illinois or Ohio
1960: Richard Nixon over John Kennedy by flipping New York and any of 16 states, with Illinois having the smallest margin, or by flipping Pennsylvania and any of three states, with Illinois again having the smallest margin, or by flipping Illinois and Texas
2012: Mitt Romney over Barack Obama by flipping California and any of 14 states, with Florida having the smallest margin
2016: Hillary Clinton over Donald Trump by flipping Florida and Texas

Smallest flips to reverse an election (popular votes)

1. 2000 (Al Gore-George W. Bush) 269
2. 1876 (Samuel Tilden-Rutherford Hayes) 445
3. 1884 (James Blaine-Grover Cleveland)..524
4. 1916 (Charles Evans Hughes-Woodrow Wilson)................................1,711
5. 1844 (Henry Clay-James Polk)..2,554
6. 1848 (Lewis Cass-Zachary Taylor) 3,706
7. 1888 (Grover Cleveland-Benjamin Harrison).........................7,187

8. 1840 (Martin Van Buren-William Henry Harrison)...............................8,182
9. 1880 (Winfield Hancock-James Garfield)..8,420
10. 1976 (Gerald Ford-Jimmy Carter) 15,629

NOTE: These hypothetical flips are based on a specific number of popular votes being switched in specific states to change the national winner in electoral votes. The minimum switch of popular votes necessary to effect a flip is shown above. The candidate listed first would have been the national winner if the flip had occurred. This note also applies to the next three lists.

Smallest flips to reverse an election (share of popular votes)

1. 2000 (Al Gore-George W. Bush) 0.0003%
2. 1884 (James Blaine-Grover Cleveland)..0.0052%
3. 1876 (Samuel Tilden-Rutherford Hayes) 0.0053%
4. 1916 (Charles Evans Hughes-Woodrow Wilson)............................0.0092%
5. 1976 (Gerald Ford-Jimmy Carter)..0.0192%
6. 2020 (Donald Trump-Joseph Biden)...0.0241%
7. 1960 (Richard Nixon-John Kennedy)...0.0265%
8. 2016 (Hillary Clinton-Donald Trump) 0.0284%
9. 2004 (John Kerry-George W. Bush)..0.0480%
10. 1948 (Thomas Dewey-Harry Truman)..0.0602%

NOTE: This list expresses in a different way the minimum number of popular votes to be flipped, presenting it as a percentage of all votes cast nationally.

Largest flips to reverse an election (popular votes)

1. 1972 (George McGovern-Richard Nixon).......................................3,454,319
2. 1984 (Walter Mondale-Ronald Reagan) 2,973,774
3. 1964 (Barry Goldwater-Lyndon Johnson)......................................2,325,630
4. 1936 (Alfred Landon-Franklin Roosevelt) 2,261,822
5. 1956 (Adlai Stevenson-Dwight Eisenhower) 1,229,767
6. 1932 (Herbert Hoover-Franklin Roosevelt) 1,001,890
7. 1952 (Adlai Stevenson-Dwight Eisenhower) 948,205
8. 1980 (Jimmy Carter-Ronald Reagan)..801,579
9. 1924 (John Davis-Calvin Coolidge) 727,135
10. 1996 (Bob Dole-Bill Clinton)..694,191

NOTE: This list shows the minimum switch of popular votes necessary to effect a flip, which also applies to the next list.

Largest flips to reverse an election (share of popular votes)

1. 1936 (Alfred Landon-Franklin Roosevelt) 4.9550%
2. 1972 (George McGovern-Richard Nixon)..4.4447%
3. 1860 (Stephen Douglas-Abraham Lincoln)......................................3.7311%
4. 1964 (Barry Goldwater-Lyndon Johnson)..3.2920%
5. 1984 (Walter Mondale-Ronald Reagan) 3.2096%
6. 1932 (Herbert Hoover-Franklin Roosevelt) 2.5206%
7. 1924 (John Davis-Calvin Coolidge) 2.4988%
8. 1920 (James Cox-Warren Harding)..2.4955%
9. 1912 (Theodore Roosevelt-Woodrow Wilson) 2.1654%
10. 1956 (Adlai Stevenson-Dwight Eisenhower)..................................1.9826%

NOTE: This list expresses in a different way the minimum number of popular votes to be flipped, presenting it as a percentage of all votes cast nationally.

Campaign Scores

Largest cumulative campaign scores in a career

1. Franklin Roosevelt 366.37
2. John Adams 281.71
3. Thomas Jefferson 271.57
4. Ronald Reagan 262.11
5. Henry Clay 260.55
6. Richard Nixon 256.38
7. Andrew Jackson 241.67
8. Martin Van Buren 237.77
9. Grover Cleveland 231.78
10. Ulysses Grant 230.60
11. George Washington 213.78
12. William Jennings Bryan 209.28
13. Charles Cotesworth Pinckney 207.40
14. James Blaine 199.73
15. William McKinley 190.58
16. James Monroe 186.14
17. Dwight Eisenhower 180.63
18. George H.W. Bush 178.87
19. Thomas Dewey 175.94
20. Abraham Lincoln 170.55
21. Theodore Roosevelt 167.11
22. Bill Clinton 166.23
23. Barack Obama 165.62
24. Herbert Hoover 165.32
25. James Madison 164.53

Largest cumulative campaign scores for someone not elected

1. Henry Clay 260.55
2. William Jennings Bryan 209.28
3. Charles Cotesworth Pinckney 207.40
4. James Blaine 199.73
5. Thomas Dewey 175.94
6. George Clinton 152.62
7. Lewis Cass 150.11
8. Adlai Stevenson 139.28
9. Aaron Burr 138.62
10. Alfred Smith 125.83

NOTE: This list is confined to candidates who never won a general election.

Largest cumulative campaign scores for someone not nominated

1. George Clinton 152.62
2. Aaron Burr 138.62
3. George Wallace 103.10
4. Thomas Hendricks 99.17
5. John Jay 98.79

6. Millard Fillmore 91.00
7. Eugene Debs 88.81
8. Robert Taft 87.14
9. Ross Perot 80.65
10. Robert La Follette 77.96

NOTE: This list is confined to candidates who never won a major-party nomination.

Largest campaign scores in a year

1. George Washington (F-1789) 96.18
1. George Washington (F-1792) 96.18
3. James Monroe (DR-1820) 96.04
4. Franklin Roosevelt (D-1936) 95.88
5. Richard Nixon (R-1972) 95.25
6. Ronald Reagan (R-1984) 95.13
7. Lyndon Johnson (D-1964) 93.24
8. Thomas Jefferson (DR-1804) 93.05
9. Abraham Lincoln (R-1864) 92.17
10. Franklin Roosevelt (D-1932) 91.94

Smallest campaign scores for qualified candidates in a year

1. Carly Fiorina (R-2016) 10.07
2. Michele Bachmann (R-2012) 10.11
2. Chris Christie (R-2016) 10.11
4. Rand Paul (R-2016) 10.13
5. Rick Perry (R-2012) 10.14
6. Alan Cranston (D-1984) 10.17
6. Bill Richardson (D-2008) 10.17
8. Gary Bauer (R-2000) 10.19
9. Bruce Babbitt (D-1988) 10.20
10. Richard Gephardt (D-2004) 10.23

Smallest campaign scores for general-election winners

1. John Quincy Adams (DR-1824) 67.41
2. Rutherford Hayes (R-1876) 77.12
3. George W. Bush (R-2000) 77.21
4. John Adams (F-1796) 77.27
5. Thomas Jefferson (DR-1800) 77.84
6. Richard Nixon (R-1968) 78.01
7. Woodrow Wilson (R-1916) 78.07
8. Abraham Lincoln (R-1860) 78.38
9. George W. Bush (R-2004) 78.71
10. Grover Cleveland (D-1884) 78.78

Smallest campaign scores for major-party nominees

1. Hugh White (W-1836) 54.62
2. William Howard Taft (R-1912) 55.09
3. Stephen Douglas (D-1860) 57.06
4. Alfred Landon (R-1936) 57.76
5. George McGovern (D-1972) 58.46
6. Horace Greeley (D-LR-1872) 58.76
7. Walter Mondale (D-1984) 58.83
8. Charles Cotesworth Pinckney (F-1804) 59.38
9. Barry Goldwater (R-1964) 60.59
10. John Breckinridge (SD-1860) 60.76

Largest campaign scores for election losers

1. Samuel Tilden (D-1876) 75.14
2. Al Gore (D-2000) 74.51
3. Thomas Jefferson (DR-1796) 74.00
4. John Kerry (D-2004) 73.65
5. Charles Evans Hughes (R-1916) 73.55
6. James Blaine (R-1884) 73.26
7. John Adams (F-1800) 73.21
8. Gerald Ford (R-1976) 72.98
9. Donald Trump (R-2020) 72.31
10. Hillary Clinton (D-2016) 72.30

Largest margins in campaign scores

1. 1820 (James Monroe-John Quincy Adams) 78.08
2. 1936 (Franklin Roosevelt-Alfred Landon) 38.12
3. 1972 (Richard Nixon-George McGovern) 36.79
4. 1984 (Ronald Reagan-Walter Mondale) 36.30
5. 1804 (Thomas Jefferson-Charles Cotesworth Pinckney) 33.67
6. 1964 (Lyndon Johnson-Barry Goldwater) 32.65
7. 1789 (George Washington-John Adams) 32.18
8. 1932 (Franklin Roosevelt-Herbert Hoover) 30.66
9. 1872 (Ulysses Grant-Horace Greeley) 30.52
10. 1864 (Abraham Lincoln-George McClellan) 30.51

NOTE: *The top two candidates are listed in parentheses, with the campaign-score leader coming first. The margin is the difference between the candidates' campaign scores. This note also applies to the next list.*

Smallest margins in campaign scores

1. 1876 (Rutherford Hayes-Samuel Tilden) 1.98
2. 1824 (Andrew Jackson-John Quincy Adams) 2.24
3. 2000 (George W. Bush-Al Gore) 2.70
4. 1796 (John Adams-Thomas Jefferson) 3.27
5. 1916 (Woodrow Wilson-Charles Evans Hughes) 4.52
6. 1800 (Thomas Jefferson-John Adams) 4.63
7. 2004 (George W. Bush-John Kerry) 5.06
8. 1884 (Grover Cleveland-James Blaine) 5.52
9. 1976 (Jimmy Carter-Gerald Ford) 6.25
10. 2016 (Donald Trump-Hillary Clinton) 6.49

Largest campaign scores for incumbent presidents

1. George Washington (F-1792) 96.18
2. James Monroe (DR-1820) 96.04
3. Franklin Roosevelt (D-1936) 95.88
4. Richard Nixon (R-1972) 95.25
5. Ronald Reagan (R-1984) 95.13
6. Lyndon Johnson (D-1964) 93.24
7. Thomas Jefferson (DR-1804) 93.05
8. Abraham Lincoln (R-1864) 92.17
9. Dwight Eisenhower (R-1956) 91.03
10. Franklin Roosevelt (D-1940) 89.94

NOTE: This list shows the campaign scores for incumbent presidents who ran
for another term. This note also applies to the next list.

Smallest campaign scores for incumbent presidents

1. Theodore Roosevelt (R-1908) 0.24
2. Harry Truman (D-1952) 0.63
3. Calvin Coolidge (R-1928) 1.02
4. Lyndon Johnson (D-1968) 11.53
5. George Washington (F-1796) 21.42
6. Andrew Johnson (D-1868) 26.37
7. Chester Arthur (R-1884) 37.07
8. Franklin Pierce (D-1856) 43.05
9. Millard Fillmore (W-1852) 45.85
10. William Howard Taft (R-1912).. 55.09

NOTE: The first five presidents on this list either did not run for reelection or
dropped out in the early stages of the race. They still received some support in
primaries, at the convention, and/or in the general election, which yielded the
campaign scores shown above.

Largest gains in campaign scores for incumbent presidents

1. Richard Nixon (78.01 in 1968, 95.25 in 1972) 17.24
2. Thomas Jefferson (77.84 in 1800, 93.05 in 1804)............................. 15.21
3. Abraham Lincoln (78.38 in 1860, 92.17 in 1864) 13.79
4. James Monroe (90.10 in 1816, 96.04 in 1820) 5.94
5. Ronald Reagan (91.16 in 1980, 95.13 in 1984) 3.97
6. Franklin Roosevelt (91.94 in 1932, 95.88 in 1936)..............................3.94
7. Ulysses Grant (85.63 in 1868, 89.28 in 1872)......................................3.65
8. Andrew Jackson (84.82 in 1828, 87.20 in 1832)...................................2.38
9. Bill Clinton (82.15 in 1992, 84.08 in 1996)...1.93
10. William McKinley (81.24 in 1896, 82.89 in 1900)...............................1.65

NOTE: This list is confined to candidates who won the presidency and then
sought reelection four years later, showing the difference between their two
campaign scores. This note also applies to the next list.

Largest drops in campaign scores for incumbent presidents

1. Franklin Pierce (89.52 in 1852, 43.05 in 1856) .... -46.47
2. Herbert Hoover (90.41 in 1928, 61.28 in 1932) .... -29.13
3. William Howard Taft (83.31 in 1908, 55.09 in 1912) .... -28.22
4. George H.W. Bush (87.86 in 1988, 66.86 in 1992) .... -21.00
5. Jimmy Carter (79.23 in 1976, 60.93 in 1980) .... -18.30
6. Martin Van Buren (80.26 in 1836, 65.49 in 1840) .... -14.77
7. Benjamin Harrison (79.71 in 1888, 68.40 in 1892) .... -11.31
8. Woodrow Wilson (86.26 in 1912, 78.07 in 1916) .... -8.19
9. Grover Cleveland (78.78 in 1884, 72.27 in 1888) .... -6.51
10. Donald Trump (78.79 in 2016, 72.31 in 2020) .... -6.48

Largest campaign scores for former presidents

1. Grover Cleveland (D-1892) 80.73
2. Theodore Roosevelt (R/P-1912) 66.37
3. Martin Van Buren (D-1844) 50.00
4. Millard Fillmore (AW-1856) 45.15
5. Ulysses Grant (R-1880) 42.34
6. Martin Van Buren (FS-1848) 42.02
7. Theodore Roosevelt (R-1916) 14.78
8. Herbert Hoover (R-1940) 1.03
9. William Howard Taft (R-1916) 0.84
10. Calvin Coolidge (R-1932) 0.24

NOTE: This list is confined to former presidents who sought another term after leaving office. The final four individuals on the list were not formal candidates, yet still received some support in primaries or at the convention, which yielded the campaign scores shown above.

Largest campaign scores for sitting vice presidents

1. George H.W. Bush (R-1988) 87.86
2. Martin Van Buren (D-1836) 80.26
3. Thomas Jefferson (DR-1800) 77.84
4. John Adams (F-1796) 77.27
5. Al Gore (D-2000) 74.51
6. Richard Nixon (R-1960) 72.12
7. Hubert Humphrey (D-1968) 69.19
8. John Adams (F-1792) 67.23
9. John Breckinridge (D/SD-1860) 60.76
10. George Clinton (DR-1808) 28.01

NOTE: The term "sitting" means the individual was serving as vice president while running for president. The same concept applies to the next four lists. The first four individuals on this list are the only incumbent vice presidents to be directly elected to the presidency.

Largest campaign scores for sitting Cabinet members

1. Herbert Hoover (R-1928) 90.41
2. James Monroe (DR-1816) 90.10
3. James Madison (DR-1808) 84.36
4. William Howard Taft (R-1908) 83.31
5. John Quincy Adams (DR-1824) 67.41

6. John Jay (F-1789) 51.15
7. William Crawford (DR-1824)...46.97
8. Mitchell Palmer (D-1920) 27.09
9. Thomas Jefferson (DR-1792)..26.68
10. James Buchanan (D-1848) 25.17

Largest campaign scores for sitting governors

1. Franklin Roosevelt (D-1932) 91.94
2. Woodrow Wilson (D-1912) 86.26
3. Bill Clinton (D-1992)..82.15
4. Grover Cleveland (D-1884)..78.78
5. George W. Bush (R-2000) 77.21
6. Rutherford Hayes (R-1876) 77.12
7. Samuel Tilden (D-1876) 75.14
8. Thomas Dewey (R-1948) 69.67
9. Michael Dukakis (D-1988) 65.32
10. Thomas Dewey (R-1944)..64.76

Largest campaign scores for sitting senators

1. Warren Harding (R-1920) 88.37
2. Barack Obama (D-2008) 84.03
3. John Kennedy (D-1960)...79.58
4. John Kerry (D-2004)..73.65
5. Lewis Cass (D-1848) 71.66
6. Andrew Jackson (DR-1824) 69.65
7. John McCain (R-2008) 68.78
8. Bob Dole (R-1996) 67.01
9. Henry Clay (NR-1832) 62.61
10. Rufus King (F-1816) 62.07

Largest campaign scores for sitting representatives

1. James Garfield (R-1880) 79.77
2. James Blaine (R-1876) 47.05
3. Henry Clay (DR-1824) 46.84
4. Champ Clark (D-1912)...42.45
5. John Anderson (R/NU-1980)..38.97
6. William Randolph Hearst (D-1904) 24.45
7. James Weaver (GBK-1880) 20.66
8. Morris Udall (D-1976) 18.22
9. Ron Paul (R-2012) 18.11
10. Samuel Randall (D-1884)..17.58

Potential Indexes

Largest potential indexes for qualified candidates

1. Theodore Roosevelt (R/P-1912) 10.0
1. Franklin Roosevelt (D-1936) 10.0
3. George Washington (F-1792) 9.7
4. Theodore Roosevelt (R-1916) 9.6
4. Franklin Roosevelt (D-1940) 9.6
6. Franklin Roosevelt (D-1944) 9.4
7. Lyndon Johnson (D-1964) 9.3
7. George W. Bush (R-2004) 9.3
9. Thomas Jefferson (DR-1804) 9.2
9. Grover Cleveland (D-1888) 9.2

Smallest potential indexes for qualified candidates

1. Eugene Debs (SOC-1920) 0.1
2. John Bidwell (PRO-1892) 0.4
3. Ralph Nader (GRN-2000) 1.3
4. Eugene Debs (SOC-1912) 1.5
5. Pete Buttigieg (D-2020) 1.8
5. William Lemke (U-1936) 1.8
7. Walter Jones (D-1956) 1.9
8. Michael Bloomberg (D-2020) 2.1
9. Robert La Follette (R/P-1924) 2.2
9. Strom Thurmond (SRD-1948) 2.2

Largest potential indexes for general-election winners

1. Franklin Roosevelt (D-1936) 10.0
2. George Washington (F-1792) 9.7
3. Franklin Roosevelt (D-1940) 9.6
4. Franklin Roosevelt (D-1944) 9.4
5. Lyndon Johnson (D-1964) 9.3
5. George W. Bush (R-2004) 9.3
7. Thomas Jefferson (DR-1804) 9.2
8. Grover Cleveland (D-1892) 9.1
8. Calvin Coolidge (R-1924) 9.1
10. Ulysses Grant (R-1872) 9.0

Smallest potential indexes for general-election winners

1. Donald Trump (R-2016) 3.1
2. Herbert Hoover (R-1928) 4.0
3. Zachary Taylor (W-1848) 4.1
4. Joseph Biden (D-2020) 4.3
5. James Buchanan (D-1856) 5.1
6. George Washington (F-1789) 5.6
6. John Quincy Adams (DR-1824) 5.6
6. Dwight Eisenhower (R-1952) 5.6
9. John Adams (F-1796) 5.7
9. Ronald Reagan (R-1980) 5.7

Largest potential indexes for general-election losers

1. Grover Cleveland (D-1888) 9.2
2. Martin Van Buren (D-1840) 9.1
3. Jimmy Carter (D-1980) 9.0
4. Al Gore (D-2000) 8.8
5. Benjamin Harrison (R-1892) 8.5
6. William Howard Taft (R-1912) 8.2
6. George H.W. Bush (R-1992) 8.2
8. Charles Evans Hughes (R-1916) 8.0
8. Richard Nixon (R-1960) 8.0
10. Hubert Humphrey (D-1968) 7.8
10. Walter Mondale (D-1984) 7.8

NOTE: This list is confined to major-party nominees who lost general elections.

Smallest potential indexes for major-party nominees

1. Donald Trump (R-2016) 3.1
2. DeWitt Clinton (F-DR-1812) 3.7
3. Charles Cotesworth Pinckney (F-1808) 3.9
4. Winfield Scott (W-1852) 4.2
5. Joseph Biden (D-2020) 4.3
6. John Davis (D-1924) 4.4
7. William Jennings Bryan (D-POP-1896) 4.6
8. John Breckinridge (SD-1860) 4.7
8. George McClellan (D-1864) 4.7
8. Wendell Willkie (R-1940) 4.7

Largest margins in potential indexes

1. 1936 (Franklin Roosevelt-Alfred Landon) 5.2
2. 1812 (James Madison-DeWitt Clinton) 5.0
3. 1940 (Franklin Roosevelt-Wendell Willkie) 4.9
4. 1924 (Calvin Coolidge-John Davis) 4.7
5. 1864 (Abraham Lincoln-George McClellan) 4.2
5. 1872 (Ulysses Grant-Horace Greeley) 4.2
7. 1804 (Thomas Jefferson-Charles Cotesworth Pinckney) 4.1
8. 1904 (Theodore Roosevelt-Alton Parker) 3.9
9. 1820 (James Monroe-John Quincy Adams) 3.7
10. 1896 (William McKinley-William Jennings Bryan) 3.6

NOTE: The margin is the difference between the potential indexes for the two candidates with the largest campaign scores. The candidate with the larger potential index is listed first. This note also applies to the next list.

Smallest margins in potential indexes

Returns on Potential

Largest returns on potential for qualified candidates

1. Eugene Debs (SOC-1920) 2,094
2. John Bidwell (PRO-1892) 430
3. Donald Trump (R-2016) 254
4. Herbert Hoover (R-1928) 226
5. Robert La Follette (R/P-1924) 211
6. Robert Harrison (F-1789) 199
7. Eugene Debs (SOC-1912) 194
8. Zachary Taylor (W-1848) 193
9. DeWitt Clinton (F-DR-1812) 192
10. George Clinton (DR-1792) 187

Smallest returns on potential for qualified candidates

1. Phil Gramm (R-1996) 12
2. Lyndon Johnson (D-1968) 13
2. John Edwards (D-2008) 13
2. Rand Paul (R-2016) 13
5. Howard Baker (R-1980) 14
5. John Connally (R-1980) 14
5. Lloyd Bentsen (D-1988) 14
5. Rick Perry (R-2012) 14
9. Charles Fairbanks (R-1908) 15
9. Theodore Roosevelt (R-1916) 15
9. Birch Bayh (D-1976) 15
9. Alan Cranston (D-1984) 15
9. Lamar Alexander (R-1996) 15
9. Joseph Lieberman (D-2004) 15
9. Fred Thompson (R-2008) 15
9. Jon Huntsman (R-2012) 15
9. Jeb Bush (R-2016) 15
9. Chris Christie (R-2016) 15

Largest returns on potential for general-election winners

1. Donald Trump (R-2016) 254
2. Herbert Hoover (R-1928) 226
3. Zachary Taylor (W-1848) 193
4. Joseph Biden (D-2020) 186
5. George Washington (F-1789) 172
6. Dwight Eisenhower (R-1952) 160
6. Ronald Reagan (R-1980) 160
8. James Buchanan (D-1856) 156
9. Warren Harding (R-1920) 147
10. William Howard Taft (R-1908) 139

Smallest returns on potential for general-election winners

1. George W. Bush (R-2004) 85
2. Grover Cleveland (D-1892) 89
3. Woodrow Wilson (D-1916) 91
4. James Madison (DR-1812) 92
5. Rutherford Hayes (R-1876) 93
5. William McKinley (R-1900) 93
7. Calvin Coolidge (R-1924) 94
7. Franklin Roosevelt (D-1940) 94
7. Franklin Roosevelt (D-1944) 94
10. Franklin Roosevelt (D-1936) 96

Largest returns on potential for general-election losers

1. DeWitt Clinton (F-DR-1812) 192
2. Charles Cotesworth Pinckney (F-1808) 169
3. William Jennings Bryan (D-POP-1896) 154
4. Winfield Scott (W-1852) 150
5. John Davis (D-1924) 144
6. Alton Parker (D-1904) 135
6. Wendell Willkie (R-1940) 135
8. William Henry Harrison (W-1836) 132
8. William Jennings Bryan (D-1908) 132
10. George McClellan (D-1864) 131

NOTE: This list is confined to major-party nominees who lost general elections.

Smallest returns on potential for major-party nominees

1. William Howard Taft (R-1912) 67
2. Jimmy Carter (D-1980) 68
3. Martin Van Buren (D-1840) 72
4. Walter Mondale (D-1984) 75
5. Grover Cleveland (D-1888) 79
6. Benjamin Harrison (R-1892) 80
7. Stephen Douglas (D-1860) 82
7. Adlai Stevenson (D-1956) 82
7. George H.W. Bush (R-1992) 82
10. Herbert Hoover (R-1932) 84

Key Sources

Statistics for presidential elections from 1789 to 2020 were obtained from the following sources.

Bain, Richard, and Judith Parris. *Convention Decisions and Voting Records.* Washington: Brookings Institution, 1973.

Burnham, W. Dean. *Presidential Ballots, 1836-1892.* Baltimore: Johns Hopkins University Press, 1955.

Clerk of the House of Representatives. *Statistics of the Presidential and Congressional Election.* Washington: United States House of Representatives, 1921-2021, quadrennial.

Cook, Rhodes. *United States Presidential Primary Elections, 1968-1996.* Washington: CQ Press, 2000.

Dubin, Michael. *United States Presidential Elections, 1788-1860.* Jefferson, North Carolina: McFarland & Co., 2002.

Federal Election Commission. *Federal Elections: Election Results for the U.S. President, the U.S. Senate, and the U.S. House of Representatives.* Washington: Federal Election Commission, 1985-2022, quadrennial.

Guide to U.S. Elections. Washington: CQ Press, 2005.

McGillivray, Alice, and Richard Scammon. *America at the Polls, 1920-1956.* Washington: Congressional Quarterly, 1994.

McGillivray, Alice, Richard Scammon, and Rhodes Cook. *America at the Polls, 1960-2004.* Washington: CQ Press, 2005.

Petersen, Svend. *A Statistical History of the American Presidential Elections.* New York: Frederick Ungar, 1963.

Presidential Elections, 1789-2008. Washington: CQ Press, 2010.

Robinson, Edgar Eugene. *The Presidential Vote, 1896-1932.* New York: Octagon, 1970.

Runyon, John, Jennefer Verdini, and Sally Runyon. *Source Book of American Presidential Campaign and Election Statistics, 1948-1968*. New York: Frederick Ungar, 1971.

Scammon, Richard. *America at the Polls, 1920-1964*. Pittsburgh: University of Pittsburgh Press, 1965.

Thomas, G. Scott. *Counting the Votes*. Santa Barbara: Praeger, 2015.

_____. *Presidential Election Record Book 2020*. Buffalo: Niawanda, 2019.

_____. *The Pursuit of the White House*. New York: Greenwood, 1987.

United States Census Bureau. *Historical Statistics of the United States, Colonial Times to 1970*. Washington: United States Government Printing Office, 1975.

_____. *Statistical Abstract of the United States, 2012*. Washington: United States Government Printing Office, 2011.

Printed in Great Britain
by Amazon